Pacific Ocean

WEST
COAST
COOK
BOOK

A REPRINT OF THE ORIGINAL BY
THE COOKBOOK COLLECTORS LIBRARY

THIS IS A BOOK of West Coast cuisine — if anything as simple as our cookery can be called a cuisine. It is an informal book about the foods we eat and the foods we cook; we love to do both, and we think we do them rather well. The recipes are the regional ones of the three Pacific states — California, Oregon, and Washington — and they have become ours in three different ways.

The first group are those of the early settlers — recipes that were brought from various other places, and which proved to be so right for the new world that we now think of them as natives. There were those brought to California by the Spaniards and the Mexicans; and they weren't new even then — they'd been favorites in Mexico since the days of Cortez. There were the recipes of the pioneers of the Oregon Territory, which included what is now the state of Washington, recipes brought over the plains and changed to suit the supplies of the new land. Many of these have a Yankee flavor. Then there are those that show their origin to be of other lands — favorite dishes brought by the many people who came to this new country to dig gold, or build railroads, or to seek adventure or security. Of all these, I have admitted only those that have been generally adopted or adapted by us. There are also recipes that have been all but forgotten, but whose frequent inclusion in our early cook books makes them welcome in this one — providing, of course, that they are both feasible and pleasing. Most important of all are the old recipes that have not been forgotten, recipes for which we are world-famous: cioppino, Olympia pan roast, Green Goddess dressing, fried cream. . . .

The second group of recipes are those using, either as the main ingredient or as the outstanding feature, the foods that are typical of the Pacific slope. These foods are not necessarily indigenous ones, as many were brought early to our bountiful land, and have done nicely, thank you. Probably nowhere else in the world is there a region so calculated to delight the cook. Thousands of miles of coastline with its piscine population; tens of thousands of acres lush with fruits, nuts, vegetables, grain; mountains still teeming with game; valleys given over to cattle and poultry. Avocados, artichokes, salmon, wine grapes, oranges, nuts, olives, turkeys, oysters, figs, and dozens of other choice foods are ours. As Henry Fink, an Oregonian and a gourmet, said: "In Oregon, as in Washington and California, the epicure fares particularly well because the luxuries of life are as cheap as the staples, and quite as abundant."

The third group of recipes is, perhaps, the one in which we take the greatest pride, as they are for the dishes that we prepare in a manner that is distinctively our own. These are the recipes that show the versatility of our cooks — not the high-salaried exponents of la haute cuisine, but the cooks, both male and female, who are fascinated by the kitchen and whose greatest pleasure lies in discovering some new way to serve some old familiar food. West Coast cooks improvise. They have ever since, in the early days, they had to use whatever was on hand, or starve. Today they still improvise although they are blessed with plenty, and they frequently do it with remarkable success. That is why we not only believe we should have the finest food in the world, we don't honestly see how we can avoid it.

I want the recipes in this book to be not only of the

West, but the Best of the West, and so have omitted many that are included in other books of our regional cookery. George Washington said it for me: "If, to please the people, we offer what we ourselves disapprove, how can we afterwards defend our work?" If, for instance, a dish composed of tuna fish, canned mushroom soup, and corn flakes is in any danger of becoming a dish of the region, I prefer to ignore it. If by so doing I can give it ever so gentle a nudge toward oblivion, that is good. Likewise I include no recipes whose only virtue lies in their history or their age. In some cases I have noted them, but only when I have tested them and found them excellent do I give the rules for making them. Other recipes, long forgotten, I have included simply because they delight me.

The recipes have come from many sources. Some were evolved from tantalizing and usually vague descriptions by early historians. Many came from early cook books — books which bear considerable resemblance to one another, as the good ladies of that day stole quite shamelessly from one another. As these books were invariably compiled to raise funds for some worthy cause, this larceny probably had a heavenly blessing. These recipes have been adapted for modern use. Some are recipes from old families, which I have been fortunate in obtaining, and some are for dishes now so well known that, out here, we cook them without benefit of rules, and invariably have our own versions. Then there are some fine recipes from famous eating places on the West Coast. My thanks to those who so graciously shared them. So many thanks, too, to the many friends whose interest has kept me at the skillet.

It is with considerable reluctance that I give approximate numbers of persons the recipes will serve. So much depends on appetites, and so much more on the rest of the menu. This is particularly true of many of the foreign recipes — Chinese, for instance. A recipe which might be barely adequate for four not-too-hungry people would suffice for twelve to sixteen if it were one of the several dishes served at a typical Chinese meal.

There is much to say about West Coast food and West Coast cooks — much more than present space and personal knowledge permit. I have noted some facts (and perhaps some fiction) along with the recipes. I hope that they, and the recipes themselves, will make you hungry, and will convince you that the gourmet who lives on the West Coast is a happy one.

HELEN EVANS BROWN

Pasadena, California

Acknowledgments

I WISH to thank the following for permission to reprint material included in this book: Balzer's Bulletin, The Californian, Flair, Glamour, House and Garden, and McCall's.

I wish also to thank Kay Harline for her help with the manuscript and the many friends, restaurants and companies who contributed information and recipes. Most of all I wish to thank my husband, Philip S. Brown, for my invaluable collection of old cook books and for the many hours he has spent on research and typing.

Contents

Helen Brown's
WEST COAST COOK BOOK

Appetizers

IT WOULD BE NICE *if, on the West Coast, we had a perfect name for these savory bits that are served with the preprandial potables. Actually, we make them better than we name them. We call them hors d'oeuvre most often, which of course they're not, or snacks, or kickshaws. We call them appetizers and then proceed to consume them in such quantity that they sate rather than whet the appetite. We could call them bocados, which is Spanish for tidbit or delicacy or morsel, but we don't. But I must call them something, so let it be appetizers.*

❲ Cypress Point Abalone Cubes

Even Californians, those who know the mollusk best, often fail to recognize these tender little gobbets of goodness as their honored abalone. This recipe, though included in the appetizer section, may be used for an entree, too, for it is abalone at its best.

First find your abalone — a whole one please. Remove it from the shell, trim it of all its soft and brown parts, leaving only the whitish muscle. Slice it about ½-inch thick and thump each slice *gently* with a bottle until it has relaxed. Cut into ½-inch cubes and shake them in a paper sack containing flour. Now make a thick batter: beat the yolks of 2 eggs until thick, add ½ cup of beer and ¼ cup of milk (or all milk), a tablespoon of melted butter or oil, a cup of flour, 1½ teaspoons of salt, and a teaspoon of baking powder. Stir just to mix, then fold in the beaten egg whites. Dip floured abalone cubes in this batter and fry, a few at a time, at 375° until lightly browned. Keep warm on a hot plate in the oven, leaving the door open as further cooking would be disastrous. Abalone will be unbelievably tender when prepared this way. The whole trick is to avoid overcooking. Serve the cubes impaled on toothpicks, and have quarters of lemons and water cress as a garnish. If you want a dunking sauce, do keep it simple. A mayonnaise, perhaps, thinned with white wine. If serving the abalone as a main course, it is better to cut it into strips the size of French fried potatoes.

1 abalone	1 tablespoon melted butter
2 eggs	or oil
½ cup beer ⎱ or all milk	1 cup flour
¼ cup milk ⎰	1½ teaspoons salt
1 teaspoon baking powder	

(Epicurean Butter

From the *Berkeley Cook Book* of 1884 is this really nice appetizer. It was advised that it be served with crackers and cheese.

Mix together 4 chopped anchovies, a minced green onion, a tablespoon of minced tarragon (fresh), the yolks of 2 hard-boiled eggs, 2 tablespoons of butter, and a little salt. Work until smooth, or force through a sieve. Roll in little balls and chill.

4 anchovies	2 hard-boiled egg yolks
1 green onion	2 tablespoons butter
1 tablespoon minced tarragon	Salt

(Oregon Cheddar Pennies

This is a cheese shortbread, a recipe that either came down from British Columbia or dated 'way back to an early currency, for the "penny" is half-dollar size. They are good with drinks or soups or salads, and keep nicely for several weeks if tightly covered.

Grate or chop ½ pound of well-aged Cheddar, and cream it with ¼ pound of butter, a cup of flour, ½ teaspoon of salt,

4

and a whisper of cayenne — about as much as you can take up on the end of a toothpick. Get in there with your hands and work it smooth, then chill for an hour or so. Roll ⅓ of an inch thick and cut in rounds 1¼ inches across. (Or form the dough in a roll, wrap in waxed paper and chill, then slice as you would icebox cookies.) These pennies may be varied in a number of ways: savory seeds or nuts on top, chili powder or herbs mixed in — take it from there. Bake them at 350°, and watch carefully, until they are a pale, pale gold. The least little bit of overbaking will spoil the flavor, for over-cooked cheese acquires an unpleasant bitterness.

> ½ *pound Cheddar cheese* 1 *cup flour*
> ¼ *pound butter* ½ *teaspoon salt*
> *Cayenne*

(*Cheese Danieto*

In Novato, California, they make a wonderful little cheese called a Sierra. It is small and round and weighs a quarter of a pound, and is a sort of cross between a Neufchâtel and a Camembert. This recipe, an early one, uses it delightfully.

Rub a bowl with a crushed clove of garlic. Add one Sierra cheese, mash it well, and mix with ¼ cup of minced ripe olives (they come, ready-minced and inexpensive, in small tins) and a teaspoon of paprika. Serve cold, with hot toasted crackers.

> 1 *clove garlic* ¼ *cup minced ripe olives*
> 1 *Sierra cheese* 1 *teaspoon paprika*

(*Jack Snacks*

These are easy and good with cocktails, but somehow I think they are at their best when served with a rather robust red wine — perhaps as an evening refreshment, or while waiting for a roast that's sizzling on the outdoor grill.

Using small metal skewers or long wooden sticks, string on them squares of sourdough bread, pieces of Jack cheese, and rolled fillets of anchovies. Brush with melted butter and broil or bake until toasted and the cheese melted.

❮ Langlois Loaf

This recipe stars the blue-veined cheese of Langlois, Oregon (page 46). It has a dozen variations and hundreds of possibilities, as you will see.

Cream ½ pound of Langlois blue cheese, ½ pound of cream cheese, and ¼ cup of butter. Mix in a tablespoon of finely minced chives or shallots, a tablespoon of brandy, and, if you wish, ¼ cup of minced ripe olives. Form in a roll, cover the outside with chopped toasted or salted almonds, and chill. Serve on a plate garnished with greenery and accompanied with crackers, preferably hot ones. Sometimes this is frozen and served as a first course, or as a salad. Sometimes garlic is used, and sherry, and often grated Parmesan is worked in. There are those who like a touch of Worcestershire, and others swear it must have cayenne. Actually, we roll our own, and quite often into tiny balls rather than this loaf, which requires slicing.

½ pound Langlois blue
    cheese
½ pound cream cheese
¼ cup butter
1 tablespoon minced chives
    or shallots

1 tablespoon brandy
¼ cup minced ripe olives
    (optional)
Chopped almonds

❮ Quesadillas

Little cheese turnovers, these are a favorite with Southern Californians, who learned them from the Mexican settlers. We use tortillas, which are available in most markets, or sometimes buy the masa and make our tortillas of less imposing size. Here we cheat, by rolling the masa like a piecrust and cutting it with a cookie cutter, then pinching the edges to make them look like handmade miniatures. I evolved this system after wasting a good hour trying to get a professional, at a tortilleria, to make diminutive tortillas. She couldn't, or wouldn't. She managed the wanted circumference once or

6

twice, but they were as thick as codfish cakes. Finally we gave up, I suspecting she was not quite bright, and she convinced that I was daft. But for you who have neither masa nor tortillas, this version is not only acceptable, but wonderfully good.

Break an egg into a cup measure and fill it to the top with milk. Mix together 1½ cups each of flour and corn meal, 2 teaspoons of baking powder, and 1½ teaspoons of salt. Work in 2 tablespoons of soft butter and the egg-milk mixture. Knead until smooth, then roll thin on a floured board. Cut in 3-inch circles, put pieces of Monterey Jack (2 × 1 × ½ inches) on one side, dampen the edge, fold over and press firmly together. (When using tortillas, which are already cooked and thus stiffer, you'd better pin the edges with a toothpick. An early cook book says to "sew the edges of the tortilla together," but this seems laborious. Besides, you'd have to take out bastings.) Bake the quesadillas in a hot oven (400°) until lightly browned. Other cheeses may be used, or other fillings. Or large-sized quesadillas may be made and served with fried beans and Balboa salad for a superb dinner.

1 egg	2 teaspoons baking powder
Milk	1½ teaspoons salt
1½ cups flour	2 tablespoons butter
1½ cups corn meal	Monterey Jack Cheese

❰ Rumaki, or Chicken Livers with Water Chestnuts

One of our very best appetizers, this. Chicken livers wrapped in bacon and broiled are tremendously popular, but the added crispness of the water chestnut makes them particularly enticing. The water chestnuts, fortunately for you who have no Chinatown in your area, are available in tins in most fancy grocery stores the country over.

Clean a pound of chicken livers, removing the gall, and cut them in halves. Peel water chestnuts and wash (or use tinned ones), and cut them in 3 horizontal slices. Cut slices of bacon into halves. Now the assembly: put a piece of chicken liver on top of a slice of water chestnut, wrap in a piece of bacon, and fasten securely with two toothpicks. (Maybe you can do a neat job with one pick, or maybe you don't care, but I find that I need two.) Arrange the little bundles on a cake rack, place in a pan, and bake in a hot oven until the bacon is crisp. These reheat quite successfully, but if you plan on that, it's smart to do the initial cooking a little less than usual. No turning is necessary when using this rack method, which should be all right by a busy cook.

> For each 3 chicken livers
> 3 slices bacon
> 2 water chestnuts

(Trader Vic's Fried Chicken Livers

Trader Vic's, in Oakland, California, is one of the most popular restaurants on the West Coast. Specializing in Oriental cuisine and potent rum drinks, Vic serves a chicken liver appetizer that will keep customers blissful for hours while they sip their Pondo punch and wait, not at all impatiently, for a table. A generous host, he shares this recipe:

"Cut chicken livers in strips, dip in the following batter, and fry in deep fat. The batter: 1 egg, 1 tablespoon cornstarch, 1 cup flour, 1½ teaspoons baking powder, 2 teaspoons salt, 1 cup milk, 1 cup water, 3 teaspoons sugar, 1 teaspoon Mai Kai. Beat eggs slightly, add dry ingredients, then liquids, slowly. Beat till smooth." Mai Kai is Trader Vic's name for his seasoning, which contains monosodium glutamate and other ingredients. This batter is sufficient for a couple of pounds of livers, but, as Trader Vic says, you'll probably want them for a cocktail party. The livers, by the way, may be dipped in soy sauce before their batter bath.

2 pounds chicken livers
1 egg
1 tablespoon cornstarch
1 cup flour
1½ teaspoons baking pow-
    der

2 teaspoons salt
1 cup milk
1 cup water
3 teaspoons sugar
1 teaspoon monosodium glu-
    tamate

8

❨ Coquille Clam Jam

Minced clams are a favorite food out here, either the fresh
ones, or those excellent minced razor clams that are canned
so successfully by the Pioneer Company. This spread is a cinch
to make, but that doesn't keep it from being one of the Best
in the West.

Drain an 8-ounce tin of Pacific minced clams and save the
juice. Crush a very small clove of garlic in a mortar with ½
teaspoon of salt, and add to the drained clams, along with
½ pound of cream cheese. A speck of cayenne may be added
also. Mix well, and if too stiff for easy dunking or spreading,
thin with clam juice. (Use what's left of the juice to flavor
chicken bouillon.) Serve this with potato chips or crackers.

1 8-ounce can minced clams	*½ teaspoon salt*
1 small clove garlic	*½ pound cream cheese*
Speck of cayenne	

❨ Empanaditas

Here's one of the many recipes we owe to the early Californians — a little meat pie or turnover, usually served on
feast days. One Señora Espinola, in the early nineteenth century, was famous for hers, which were "well seasoned with
chili" and a larger size, hence called empanadas. For a glass
of cider and two of the little meat pies she asked one *real*, a
coin then worth an eighth of a dollar. Today we make the
empanaditas small, and fill them with meat or fish or game,
well seasoned, but not necessarily with chili. An olive or a
slice of one, either green or ripe, is apt to be found in any
of the fillings.

Make a rich pastry (2 cups flour, 1 teaspoon salt, ⅓ cup
each of butter, lard and water (an egg yolk if you wish). Roll
it thin and cut in 3-inch rounds. Put your filling on one side,
dampen the edges, fold over, and press together with your
fingers or with a fork. The filling is made by grinding cooked
meat or fish — chicken, veal, beef, pork, venison, oysters,

shrimps, or such — moistening it with gravy or wine, and seasoning it with minced onion. (I like this better when browned in butter; or use garlic, and chili or cuminos or oregano or parsley.) Salt, of course, and pepper. Sometimes chili sauce (the Mexican kind) is added, or tomato purée or pimientos. There are dozens of recipes for the fillings, so I think it best to work out your own. Besides, you know best what is in your refrigerator. The empanaditas are baked in a hot oven until brown, and served either hot or cold. I'll take mine hot.

PASTRY

2 cups flour	⅓ cup lard
1 teaspoon salt	⅓ cup water
⅓ cup butter	1 egg yolk (optional)

FILLING

Ground meat or fish	Chili powder, cuminos, oregano, or parsley
Gravy or wine	
Minced onion or garlic	Salt and pepper

NOTE: Empanaditas, in the early days, were sometimes made with a sweet filling and served as dessert.

(Guacamole

Here is our favorite dip, another Mexican contribution. I recently saw it spelled, phonetically, "waca molay," but not, I assure you, in a West Coast publication.

You'll want very ripe avocados for this — never mind the blemishes, they are easily cut out. Mash a large one in a bowl that has been rubbed with garlic, and season it with ¼ teaspoon each of salt and chili powder, and a teaspoon of lemon juice. Add 2 teaspoons of very finely minced onion. Now taste it and add more salt if need be, and a little more chili powder, if that's the way you like it. The fleshy part of ripe tomatoes, cut in dice, may be added, or small pieces of canned green chilis, or sliced ripe olives, or crisp and crumbled bacon. Mix well and put in a bowl, covering the top with a thin layer of mayonnaise — this to keep the mixture from blackening. Just before serving, stir it well, and serve with corn chips, corn crisps (page 30), or tortillas, fried crisp. Guacamole may be served with spears of raw vegetables, too: green peppers, celery, sweet red onions. . . . And it may be used as a dressing for lettuce or tomato salads.

1 *large ripe avocado*	¼ *teaspoon chili powder*
¼ *teaspoon salt*	*(or more)*
(or more)	1 *teaspoon lemon juice*
2 *teaspoons minced onion*	

⟨ *Castellar Tarragon Liver Pâté*

I can go into ecstasies over this recipe, but I won't. I'll just hope that the minute you've finished reading it, you'll rush right out to the kitchen and try it out.

Sauté ½ cup of minced green onion in ¼ cup of butter, with a teaspoon of minced fresh tarragon. (If dried tarragon is used, cut the amount to ½ teaspoon.) Add a pound of chicken livers, each one deprived of its gall and cut in about 6 pieces. Cook until the red juices cease to run. Force through a sieve or food mill, add 2 egg yolks which have been beaten with ¼ cup of cream and ½ teaspoon of salt. Now taste it, adding more salt if needed, and more tarragon if that flavor is not a definite one. Put in a small earthenware casserole, cover with buttered paper, fastened down securely, and bake at 300° for an hour, or until a knife comes clean when thrust into its savory center. (Cut right through the paper!) Serve cold, garnished with branches of fresh tarragon if the season is right. When served with cocktails, or better with champagne or sherry, it should be passed with thin, hot, crisp toast. For a first course, serve it sliced, on leaves of baby lettuce. Enough said.

½ *cup minced green onion*	1 *pound chicken livers*
¼ *cup butter*	2 *egg yolks*
1 *teaspoon minced fresh tar-*	¼ *cup cream*
ragon (or more)	½ *teaspoon salt (or more)*

⟨ Sebastopol Piroshki

The Russians had quite a hand in the early pioneering of the West Coast, and when they sold out their Fort Ross settlement to Captain Sutter, some of them stayed on anyway. The Gold Rush brought more of them, many armed with their favorite recipes.

Their piroshki is very like the Mexican empanadita, a turnover made with a fish or meat filling. The main difference is in the seasoning, and in the folding. Sour cream is apt to be the moistening agent, and the filling usually contains mushrooms or dill or chopped hard-boiled eggs or brains. Also parsley and onion. The piroshki are rolled and cut as are the empanaditas, but the filling is put in the center, and the edges brought together at the top, resulting in a shape that is elliptical rather than semicircular. It takes patience to press the edges together so that they stay that way, but they look so nice it is worth the time. Glaze the tops with beaten egg, and bake to a shiny brown. And lest you think that I am shirking, here is a recipe for one filling. Sauté ¼ cup of minced onion in 2 tablespoons of butter, add a cup of chopped cooked fish (or brains, or meat, or chicken livers, or mushrooms), ¼ teaspoon of dill seed, crushed, 2 hard-boiled eggs, chopped, 2 tablespoons of minced parsley, enough sour cream to moisten, and salt to taste.

PASTRY
See empanaditas (page 9)

FILLING

¼ cup minced onion	2 hard-boiled eggs
2 tablespoons butter	2 tablespoons minced parsley
1 cup chopped cooked fish	Sour cream
¼ teaspoon crushed dill seed	Salt

⟨ Novato Cocktail Pizzas

We don't claim to have invented pizzas on the West Coast, but we are pretty sure we first made them in miniature to serve with cocktails. Anyway, we've hit upon a quick and easy way to make them.

Use frozen cloverleaf rolls, dividing each into its three sections, and rolling them into rounds about the size of a tumbler top. (Or use frozen hot-roll mix, or, if you must start from scratch, make a batch of bread dough. In either case, roll them about 1/4-inch thick and cut in circles.) Arrange the rounds on cookie sheets that have been painted with olive oil. Slice small onions and separate them into rings. (No need to peel them, the skins will slip right off after slicing.) Slice small tomatoes (these peeled) in thick slices, and have at hand anchovy fillets, sliced ripe olives (they come that way, in tins), grated cheese — either mozzarella, Cheddar, or whatever suits your fancy. We don't have to be authentic about these unauthentic pizzas. But back to work. Brush the rounds with olive oil that has been in close contact with a crushed clove of garlic. Arrange on top the sliced tomato (have your bread rounds pretty well covered with it), the rings of onion, the olives, and the anchovies. (These may be omitted, as may the olives; or sardines may be substituted. For that matter almost anything goes — tuna, ham, salami, prosciutto. . . .) The top layer should be cheese. Bake in a hot oven (450°) until nicely browned. And *serve hot,* with large napkins, of paper if you're smart.

Roll dough	*Sliced ripe olives*
Sliced onion	*Anchovy fillets*
Sliced tomato	*Grated cheese*

❨ Sandwich Notes

Sandwiches are pretty much the same the world over, and except for a few West Coast specialties, so are ours. The sandwiches are included with the appetizers for convenience' sake, and lest anyone object too violently, I hasten to point out that sandwiches may be cut into tiny squares, and served with potables.

Abalone Sandwich. Leftover cooked abalone may be used for this sandwich. So may canned abalone. Put it through the meat grinder, combine with mayonnaise, and season very sparingly with curry powder. Diced celery or green pepper is sometimes mixed with the shellfish.

Almond and Bacon Sandwich. Mix ¼ pound of cream cheese with 2 slices of crisp bacon, the bacon fat, 3 tablespoons of chopped almonds, and ¼ teaspoon of curry powder.

Avocado and Bacon Sandwich. A favorite, usually served on toast. Sliced ripe avocado, lettuce, mayonnaise, and crisp bacon — a version of the bacon-tomato sandwich which has become an American standby. Sometimes we use tomato as well as the avocado, making a triple decker, and oftentimes we make tiny open-faced sandwiches or canapés, using rounds of avocado on rounds of bread or toast, and topping with a curl of bacon. Sometimes sliced turkey or chicken is added, making an avocado club sandwich.

Chicken and Oyster Sandwich. Poach oysters in their own liquor until their edges scallop, then drain and mince fine. Add an equal amount of chopped cooked chicken, and bind the two with creamed butter seasoned with salt, pepper, minced parsley, and a few drops of lemon juice. Spread on buttered brown bread, with or without lettuce, and either on full-sized slices of sandwich bread or on dainty little rounds for tea or cocktails.

Cowpuncher's Sandwich. Slice sweet red onions fairly thick (¼ inch). Sprinkle with plenty of oregano and with salt, cover with ice water and vinegar (half-and-half), and let stand overnight. Drain and place between buttered slices of bread, the bread preferably fresh from the oven.

Egg and Ripe Olive Sandwich. Two hard-boiled eggs are mashed with 2 tablespoons each of minced ripe olives, chopped toasted filberts, and mayonnaise. Salt and pepper to taste.

Monte Cristo and Monte Carlo Sandwiches. These have become very popular of late. They originated, I believe, in San

14

Francisco, but now one finds them everywhere. The Monte Cristo is sliced chicken or turkey and sliced cheese, usually Monterey Jack, though it may be Swiss or a Cheddar. The Monte Carlo has tongue instead of chicken. Both sandwiches are made in 3 layers, buttered ones, with the middle buttered on both sides, and are dipped in egg and milk (2 eggs to 1 cup of milk and ¼ teaspoon of salt), then fried to a golden brown in butter. When this type of sandwich, with either of the above fillings, is cut into little 1-inch squares, they are called Monte Benitos, and are served with cocktails.

Monterey Sandwich. Slice Monterey Jack cheese for this, with big pieces of seeded green pepper and thin slices of Italian salami. Very filling, very fine.

Another Jack Cheese Sandwich. This is made with the creamy flavorful cheese mashed with minced ripe olives, and seasoned with oregano and chili powder. (This may also be rolled in balls, for appetizers.)

Oyster Club Sandwich. This may be tampering with a classic recipe, but the results are more than worth it. Fried oysters are sandwiched between toast, with lettuce, mayonnaise, sliced tomatoes, and bacon.

Toasted Mexican Sandwich. Though a taco is a Mexican-type sandwich, the Mexicans serve more conventional ones, too, and their bread is usually far superior to ours. Mash a can of green chili peppers and spread as thick or as thin a layer as you can take on bread. Top with a goodly slice of Monterey Jack cheese, and another slice of buttered bread. Toast until the cheese is melted, or better, dip in egg and milk (1 cup of milk to 2 eggs), and fry. These have the same flavor combination as chiles rellenos, which means they're wonderful.

Green Peppers. We think that our green peppers are unsurpassed. Their flesh is thick, juicy, and tender, with a wonderful crispness and flavor. Big slices of them are often used in sandwiches to add crispness and greenery — a good substitute for lettuce which *will* wilt.

15

([Shrimp Wun Tun

A favorite with Occidentals, fried wun tun (or won ton) is served by the Chinese as one of their main dishes, accompanied by a sweet and sour sauce. We've discovered that they make a wonderful something to serve with drinks, with or without the sauce. (For the sake of a cook's accuracy, Orientals also serve a boiled wun tun, usually in soups. It is very like ravioli — so like it that some call it, quite seriously, "Chinese ravioli.") Wun tun, either boiled or fried, may have a variety of fillings — a popular one is of shrimps. In the large cities on the Coast we almost always have a Chinatown, so we can purchase the wun tun paste ready to use. It comes in neat little packages of six dozen or so squares, and at a remarkably low price. Any that are not used may be frozen for the future.

First make the paste if you can't buy it. It's something of a chore, but worth it. Mix together 3 cups of flour, 2½ teaspoons of salt, 2 eggs, and ¼ cup of warm water, and knead until smooth. Form it into a ball, cover it, and allow to stand for a half hour, then roll it very thin. Now cut the thinly rolled paste into 3½-inch squares, dust them lightly with cornstarch or flour, and stack them until the task is done. The rest is fun: make a filling by grinding together 1 pound of shelled and cleaned raw shrimps, ¼ pound of raw pork, and 4 green onions. Add a tablespoon each of soy sauce and sherry, and a teaspoon of cornstarch, and work together. Put a small spoonful (actually ½ teaspoon is right) on each square, a little off center, and fold diagonally in halves and then again in quarters, doing it casually so that the corners don't jibe. Press each square just above (or is it below?) the filling, and fry them in deep fat (350°) until a good brown. Because of the raw pork in the filling, it really is important to cook them well, but it is perfectly safe when the wun tun are a little browner than the proverbial "golden." Drain the pretty things on paper and serve hot. Wun tun may be made ahead and reheated, but I find the best way is to have them filled and folded, just ready for that last-minute frying.

For those of you who wish to serve a sauce, or to serve

sauce and wun tun at a dinner, I give you this: select 3 red but firm tomatoes and remove the skins by holding them over a gas flame. Cut them into sections like an orange, having about 12 of them (or cut them into uniform dice). Separate from juice and seeds. Now cut 2 fleshy green peppers into the same size and shape, also discarding seeds. Mix 2 tablespoons of cornstarch with ¾ of a cup each of vinegar and sugar, add ¾ of a cup of water or the tomato juice, from which you have strained the seeds. Add ½ teaspoon of salt, and cook this mixture until it is clear, then add the green peppers. As soon as they turn bright green, add the tomatoes and serve with the wun tun. The tomatoes are *not* cooked!

WUN TUN

3 cups flour	*2 eggs*
2½ teaspoons salt	*¼ cup warm water*

FILLING

1 pound raw shrimps	*1 tablespoon soy sauce*
¼ pound raw pork	*1 tablespoon sherry*
4 green onions	*1 teaspoon cornstarch*

SAUCE

3 tomatoes	*¾ cup vinegar*
2 green peppers	*¾ cup sugar*
2 tablespoons cornstarch	*¾ cup water or tomato juice*
½ teaspoon salt	

NOTE: Sweet and sour sauce is made like wun tun sauce, except that the green peppers and tomatoes are omitted.

ℂ *Curried Shrimp Puffs*

The cocktail puff is popular and better than its name implies. It is a noble way of using up egg whites, a commodity that good cooks seem always to have, probably because they thicken their soups and sauces with yolks and make their own mayonnaise.

Chop cooked shrimps and measure ½ to ¾ of a cup of them.

Beat an egg white stiff, add ½ cup of mayonnaise, ½ teaspoon of curry powder (more or less, according to your taste, and to the strength of your curry powder), and ¼ teaspoon of salt. Combine with shrimps, pile on crackers or on toast squares, and slip under the broiler until inflated and brown. Minced clams, smoked oysters, ham, crab, or lobster may be used in this recipe, and the curry may be omitted. When made with clams (1 egg white, 1 can minced clams, drained, ½ cup mayonnaise) and piled into tiny tart shells before browning, they are extra fancy and very, very good.

½ to ¾ cup chopped cooked shrimps	½ cup mayonnaise
	½ teaspoon curry powder
1 egg white	¼ teaspoon salt

❲ More Ideas for Appetizers

Angels on Horseback, or *ostras angeles,* as the Spanish used to call them, will always be popular here. Oysters are wrapped in bacon and broiled until the covering is crisp. Angelenos are the same except that the oyster is first circled with an anchovy fillet, then wrapped in bacon. Shad roe is often used instead of the oysters, as are pitted olives, shrimps, cubes of lobster. And sometimes a filling is *spread* on the bacon, which is then rolled and broiled.

Rolls. Rolls of various kinds are always good. Slices of rare roast beef, or smoked salmon, or prosciutto, or such, are spread with suitable fillings: cream cheese mixed with horseradish or ripe olives; butter savory with herbs; Jack cheese spiked with dill seed; sour cream or mayonnaise mixed with ground nuts; or anything that suits the fancy or is found in the refrigerator. These are rolled tight, like a jelly roll, then cut into inch lengths and speared with toothpicks. Sometimes two meats are used together — say veal and smoked salmon, or turkey and ham — in which case the filling is kept simpler — butter flecked with chives, perhaps, or just plain tarragon mustard.

Vegetables on Ice are seen at many patio parties or barbecues, but they're usually not seen for long. Great bowls or specially made deep trays are filled with cracked ice, and raw vegetables of all kinds are laid upon or stuck into the shimmering bed. Celery hearts or curls, green onions, carrot strips, green pepper sticks, wedges of thick-meated sweet red onions, slices of tender turnips, cherry tomatoes (preferably peeled), celery root, fenucchio, and sometimes, surprisingly, raw potato. Bowls of various "dips" are provided, usually themselves sunk into the ice (or kept hot), and often oysters or clams on the half shell, shrimps, cracked crab, and lobster are chilling with the vegetables, as are olives — black or green. It is a pleasant device, refreshing and not so filling that it will dull the appetite for the meat that is wafting a tantalizing aroma from the barbecue.

Chicken Livers again, and this time with a shrimp, wrapped in bacon and broiled. A surprising but very good combination. Use half a liver and one medium or half a jumbo shrimp. A half slice of bacon will make it around the pair.

Chip Dips, for dunking potato chips. A favorite simple one is mayonnaise with soy sauce or curry sauce, or anchovy paste added. We also like sour cream, spiked with soy sauce and grated ginger, perhaps, or chopped chives, or minced ripe or green olives. We soften cream cheese and add blue cheese, or chopped anchovies, or savory seeds, or actually anything that suits our fancy. We like a sour cream or Louis dressing (page 134) when we have shrimps or fish to dip, and then there's our favorite dip of all — guacamole (page 10).

Aspics

To INCLUDE ASPICS *in the salad section is a tacit admission that they are salads — a shuddery thought for all who eschew the molded "salads" made with sweetened and fruit-flavored gelatin mixes. Aspics do of course fit into the salad category in two ways: one being that they are usually garnished with lettuce or other greenery, the other that a salad dressing of sorts is often served with them. Some of them — those in which meat or fish predominate — can, and often do, constitute the main dish at a summer meal. In the early days of West Coast cookery, aspics were unheard of, except those made by cooking a chicken or some veal or such until it would jell in its own juices. As hotels featuring* haute cuisine *appeared on the scene, so did galantines and aspics, but the early cook books never mention them, and their use of gelatin seemed limited to such dishes as "wine jelly" and blancmange.*

❲ Altivo Avocado Aspic

Soak an envelope (1 tablespoon) of plain gelatin in ¼ cup of cold water, then dissolve in ½ cup of boiling chicken stock. Allow to set until the consistency of egg white, then mix with 1¼ cups of sieved ripe avocado, ½ cup of either sour cream or mayonnaise, ½ teaspoon of salt, and 2 teaspoons of lemon juice, with a speck of cayenne. (If sour cream is used, the seasoning may have to be increased a trifle.) Pour into a small mold and allow to set, then unmold on a bed of greenery.

Serve with mayonnaise or sour cream. Double this for larger servings. SERVES 4.

1 envelope gelatin
¼ cup cold water
½ cup chicken stock
1¼ cups sieved avocado

½ cup sour cream or mayon-
    naise
½ teaspoon salt
2 teaspoons lemon juice
Cayenne

❨ Mushroom and Sour Cream Mousse

This is particularly good when served with baked ham.

Clean a pound of mushrooms, remove stems, reserve about a dozen perfect caps, and chop the rest, along with the stems. Cover the chopped mushrooms with 2 cups of water and ½ teaspoon of salt, and simmer gently for a half hour. (A half teaspoon of M.S.G. may be added.) Strain, pressing all the juices from the mushrooms (a ricer is a good gadget to use here). Now cook the caps, covered, in 3 tablespoons of water for about 5 minutes, or until tender. Add the juices from this to the other mushroom stock. If there are not exactly 2 cups of liquid, add water to make that amount. Soften 2 envelopes of plain gelatin in ⅓ cup of cold water, and dissolve it in the hot mushroom liquor. When partially set, mix in 1½ cups of sour cream, and paint the bottom and sides of a mold with a layer of the mix. When set, dip the mushroom caps in the gelatin and arrange them, round side down, in a pretty pattern in the mold. Chill a few minutes to set, then add remainder of the mushroom-sour cream mixture. (If preferred, these mushroom caps may be sliced and folded into the gelatin.) Unmold on cress, and serve with sour cream dressing which has had plenty of chopped chives added. This, with baked ham, clam pie, corn bread, and, if you wish, Balboa salad, makes a never-to-be-forgotten buffet supper. SERVES 8.

1 pound mushrooms
2 cups and 3 tablespoons
    water (or more)
½ teaspoon salt
1½ cups sour cream

½ teaspoon M.S.G.
    (optional)
2 envelopes gelatin in
    ⅓ cup water

21

(Molded Guacamole

This is a bit more highly seasoned than the plain avocado aspic.

Make guacamole (page 10). For each 2 cups, add a mixture of 1 envelope of gelatin mixed with ⅞ of a cup (1 cup minus 2 tablespoons) of cold water or bouillon, and dissolved over hot water, 4 teaspoons of lemon juice, and salt and pepper to taste. Pour into a fancy mold and, when set, turn out on a lettuce-garnished plate, and surround with peeled cherry tomatoes, or sliced larger ones. Canned green chilies may be mixed with this aspic, but in that case the chili powder is omitted. SERVES 4.

For each 2 cups guacamole

1 envelope gelatin   *4 teaspoons lemon juice*
⅞ cup water or bouillon   *Salt and pepper*

(Tomato Aspic with Dill

Another quick aspic. Soak an envelope of gelatin in ¼ cup of cold water. Heat an 8-ounce can of tomato sauce with a cup of water, and ¼ teaspoon of dill seeds, crushed. Simmer 3 or 4 minutes, add a tablespoon of lemon juice and a teaspoon of sugar. Strain over gelatin, stir until dissolved, and pour into a pint mold. Basil may be used instead of dill, if desired. SERVES 4.

1 envelope gelatin in ¼ cup   *1 cup water*
    water   *¼ teaspoon dill seeds*
1 8-ounce can tomato sauce   *1 tablespoon lemon juice*
    1 teaspoon sugar

NOTE: *Tomato Mousse.* Make the tomato aspic as above, but cut water to ¼ cup and lemon juice to 1 teaspoon. When partially set, fold in ¾ cup of cream, whipped until not quite stiff. This is good as a jellied soup if broken lightly with a fork and served with sour cream and chives.

Aspics

❪ *Wine Aspic for Meat, Poultry, Game, or Fish*

This all-purpose aspic base is varied according to the meat used: with beef use beef stock, with fish, make a stock of fish trimmings, with venison, a venison stock. The other variation is in the wine. White wine with fish and poultry, red with meat and game.

Soak 2 envelopes of plain gelatin in ½ cup of cold water, dissolve in 2¾ cups of the desired stock, boiling, add ½ cup of red or white table wine, and season highly with herbs, salt and pepper, and a tablespoon of lemon juice. Partially chill, then fold in 2 pounds (more or less) of the desired meat or fish, cooked tender and either sliced or cut in good-sized pieces. SERVES 8.

2 envelopes gelatin in	Herbs
½ cup water	Salt and pepper
2¾ cups stock	1 tablespoon lemon juice
½ cup wine	2 pounds meat or fish

Barbecuing and Charcoal Grilling

HERE ON THE WEST COAST *we excel in the art of barbecu-ing. When we speak of barbecuing, we usually mean char-coal grilling, and refer to individual or family-sized pieces of meat or fish. Barbecuing also means, perhaps more ac-curately, a whole animal spitted and cooked over a huge pitful of coals, or cut in hunks, laved in sauce, wrapped, and buried in a pit that is lined with red hot stones. This last is usually done when the affair is a large one, and by large we mean when the guests number in the hundreds. This kind of a party is known as a "barbecue." There is one more meaning of the word that has recently, and re-grettably, been accepted by some: meat or seafood cooked with a barbecue sauce, even if that cooking is done at the kitchen range. In this book, unless otherwise noted, bar-becuing means charcoal grilling, and a barbecue means a fireplace or fire pit, or brazier — anything that can burn charcoal and be topped with a grill.*

Way back when the Dons first came to California, grilled meat was a part of every festive gathering. A huge fire was made, a freshly killed beef hung in the shade of a tree, and vaqueros and their ladies cut off pieces every time that hunger called, and cooked it over the waiting fire. The frazada, which is the meat covering the ribs, was a favor-ite morsel. It was, according to one account, "thrown on the coals and eaten half raw, with salt." Another historian,

24

Barbecuing and Charcoal Grilling

marveling at how happy and content were the Californians, said, more approvingly, "Their fine physique was due probably to the quantity of roast meat eaten, without vegetables." It wasn't only charcoal grilling that was practiced by those Californians of the past, they also had their huge pit barbecues even as today. One was given frequently by an early cattle king, William Dunphy, who had started in the ranch business when the rest of the populace was hunting gold. He found the venture a profitable one, and soon acquired the famous La Posa Ranch in Monterey County, and another hunk of land in Humboldt that "in Europe would have been considered a principality." His parties were fabulous — the feature was the barbecue, where several beeves were pit-roasted and served to the happy multitude. In recent years the barbecue held by Sheriff Biscailuz, of Los Angeles County, was perhaps the most famous one in the world. Sixty thousand people were fed, and the marketing order read like a Paul Bunyan yarn and an exaggerated one at that. Over twelve tons of top-quality beef, hundreds of sacks of Mexican red beans, and fifty pounds of chili powder — that was just part of it. A huge pit was dug — or several of them, to be accurate — and lined with bricks or stones. Fires were built in the pits and allowed to burn hotly for twelve hours or thereabouts, so that there was a deep bed of glowing coals. A piece of sheet iron was put on top and some wet burlap sacks. Now came the meat, cut in twenty-five-pound chunks, painted with sauce, and wrapped in cheesecloth, also sauce-saturated (see barbecue sauces, pages 320–322). More coverings of sacks, and either tin or boards, then a final layer of sand to keep the heat in. The meat was allowed to cook from twelve to fourteen hours, and when it came out it was tender as could be, because Charlie Ellison, an expert, was in charge. This pit-barbecuing takes more than the reading of a recipe or even the writing of it.

25

The pioneers of Washington and Oregon roasted much of their meat and game in the open, over campfires. They also learned pit-roasting from the Indians, who used that cookery technique for their camas roots. The pioneers discovered the system good for their clam roasts, and later found that other fish and fowl did very well that way, too — at least when there were a number of people to be fed.

The proper way to barbecue is a matter of opinion, and there is no one as opinionated as an expert at the barbecue. What to cook is a primary consideration. Steak is first choice but it is expensive, so we have learned to grill cheaper cuts of meat as well as fish and fowl. We find them all very good indeed. Our barbecues vary from elaborate engineered jobs with electrically turned spits, to the simplest pot or Chinese wok filled with glowing charcoal. We rarely agree on exactly how far the meat should be from the fire, largely because each variety must be handled differently. Usually those requiring long slow cooking are grilled at some distance from the coals, while quick-cooking meats and fish are allowed to come close to the fire. Charcoal is the usual fuel, but experimenters have found that oak or the wood from fruit or nut trees or grapevines is superlative, actually adding flavor to the food. (Others add the flavor by tossing dried herbs on the fire after the cooking has begun.) As for bastes, that is the most controversial of all subjects. Those included in this book meet with the approval of all save those who go in for liquid smokes or liquid fire. Equipment is another matter of opinion, but there is one thing essential at every barbecue — a cook who knows what he is about. And I say "he" with reason, for this is a phase of culinary endeavor that has been taken over by the men and most cheerfully relinquished by the ladies.

Recipes for charcoal grilling and for barbecue sauces will be found listed in the Index under "Barbecuing."

Bread

THE BREAD OF THE WEST COAST *was originally as varied as the settlers who made it and the ingredients available. In Southern California the tortilla, made either from parched corn or from flour, was most prevalent. Later, around the mining towns, sourdough bread, or yeast bread was common, though not always good. "Bread like white lead," one diary noted, but at that it was probably better than the bread "like absorbent cotton" that we have today. The Indians in both California and the Territory made bread of many things — acorns, camas root, sometimes even from parched grasshoppers. This parching trick stood the early settlers in good stead. Before the days when they had gristmills, they would parch wheat, which was usually plentiful, in frying pans, and then grind it in a coffee mill. Tedious perhaps, but the bread must have been superlative. In the early days bread-making was just all in the day's work. Mary Walker, an early settler, writes of baking six loaves of bread, as well as making "a kettle of mush, a suet pudding, and a kettle of beef," before she took time out to be delivered of another son. The Indians, always curious, were particularly intrigued with the sight of rising dough, and never could resist poking a dirty and inquiring finger into its mysterious softness. They were usually well thwacked for their boldness. Today we have breads of all kinds and everything with which to make them. Bart wheat, grown in Oregon and Washington, makes an exceptionally fine flour with the oomph of hard wheat and*

27

the delicacy of the soft variety. It is good for all baking purposes.

Many early bread recipes, some made with yeast, some not, have intriguing names — Dough Gods, Invincibles, Wigg Waggs, Jolly Boys, and so forth. Those that seem likely to please modern palates are included here, either in their original form or an adapted version.

⟦ Almond Bread

Beat 1 egg, add 5 tablespoons of brown sugar, a cup of milk, 2 tablespoons of melted butter, 2 cups of flour, 2 teaspoons of baking powder, ½ teaspoon of salt, ½ teaspoon of ground coriander, or a tablespoon of grated orange rind, and ¾ of a cup of toasted almonds, chopped. Let stand in pan about 20 minutes before baking at 350° for 45 minutes to 1 hour. MAKES 1 LOAF.

1 egg
5 tablespoons brown sugar
1 cup milk
2 tablespoons melted butter
2 cups flour
2 teaspoons baking powder
½ teaspoon salt
½ teaspoon ground coriander, or 1 tablespoon grated orange rind
¾ cup toasted almonds

⟦ Nugget Bread

The nuggets are golden bits of apricots and paler pieces of almond.

Cook 1½ cups of dried apricots in water to cover for 5 minutes. Drain, saving juice, and cut apricots into bits with scissors. Add 3 tablespoons of butter, 1½ cups of sugar, ½ cup of the apricot juice, ⅓ cup of milk, ½ teaspoon of soda, 2 teaspoons of baking powder, a teaspoon of salt, 2 cups of flour, and ½ cup of coarsely chopped almonds. (This is quite

28

tart. Sweeten apricots while cooking, if desired.) Bake in a loaf pan for about 1 hour at 350°.

1½ cups dried apricots *½ cup apricot juice*
Water to cover *½ teaspoon soda*
3 tablespoons butter *2 teaspoons baking powder*
1½ cups sugar *1 teaspoon salt*
⅓ cup milk *2 cups flour*
½ cup coarsely chopped almonds

❨ *Buñuelos*

Buñuelo means "fritter," so, as in English, there are many kinds. One is a crisp little rosette, light as a rose petal, that is made on an iron resembling a Swedish timbale iron. Another, also deep-fried, is a puffy bit of nothing, often served with a cinnamon-flavored syrup, or with honey for dessert. This same fritter, without the syrup, makes a spectacular and utterly delicious hot bread, a sort of Mexican popover. An early account says of buñuelos, "They were cakes made of white corn meal, generally, and fried in lard in the manner of doughnuts. Women sent them to friends at Christmas time and often, for a joke, would fill them with cotton wool."

Sift 1½ cups of flour with ¾ of a teaspoon of salt and 1½ teaspoons of baking powder. Work 2 tablespoons of lard into the mixture, make a hole in the middle, and drop in a whole egg. Mix well, and add just enough water to make a stiff dough. Roll very thin and cut in diamonds or squares or whatever shape your slashing knife produces. (Or roll the dough in balls and pat out very thin with the palms of the hands.) Fry in deep fat at 400–425 degrees. The buñuelos will puff up as if inflated, and will crisp that way. Serve hot, and at once, for breakfast or lunch. These are sometimes called sopaipillas.

1½ cups flour *2 tablespoons lard*
¾ teaspoon salt *1 egg*
1½ teaspoons baking powder *Water*

29

❨ Clam Pone

This is a bread to serve at lunchtime, perhaps with shirred eggs and bacon and a tomato salad.

Cook a tablespoon of minced onion in 1 tablespoon of butter until wilted, then stir in 1 cup of flour. Add 1½ teaspoons of baking powder, ¼ teaspoon of salt, ⅓ cup of corn meal, an egg, slightly beaten, ½ cup of ground clams (fresh or canned), and ½ cup of clam juice. Put in a well-buttered shallow baking dish, having the dough ½-inch thick, and brush the top with butter. Bake at 350° for 30 minutes, split and butter while hot, and serve at once. SERVES ABOUT 6.

1 tablespoon minced onion	¼ teaspoon salt
1 tablespoon butter	⅓ cup corn meal
1 cup flour	1 egg
1½ teaspoons baking powder	½ cup ground clams
½ cup clam juice	

❨ Corn Crisps

These little thin corn meal wafers are wonderfully good when served with guacamole (page 10) or other appetizer dips.

Pour 1 cup of boiling water over ⅞ of a cup of corn meal (1 cup minus 2 tablespoons). Add ½ teaspoon of salt, 2½ tablespoons of melted butter. Drop from the tip of a teaspoon onto a buttered cookie sheet, then flatten with a spatula dipped in cold water. Sprinkle, if you wish, with poppy, sesame, or celery seeds, and bake at 350° until brown around the edges.

1 cup boiling water	2½ tablespoons melted butter
⅞ cup corn meal	Poppy, sesame, or celery
½ teaspoon salt	seeds (optional)

❨ Sunday Coffeecake

We have, of course, the most wonderful sweet breads and coffeecakes in the Northwest, where there are so many Scandinavians, and a small Danish town in California, called Solvang, is also famous for them. We use our almonds and walnuts and filberts in our coffeecakes, and our figs, dates, prunes, raisins, and oranges as well. Mostly they are of yeast dough, but this recipe, a quick one, is made with baking powder and our beloved sour cream.

Beat 2 eggs until light, then add a cup of sugar, a cup of sour cream, ½ teaspoon of baking soda, 2 cups of flour, 2 teaspoons of grated orange rind, 2 teaspoons of baking powder, and ½ teaspoon of salt. Spread in a buttered square pan and top with a cup of sour cream. Mix together ¼ cup each of dried bread crumbs, brown sugar, and chopped walnuts, add a teaspoon of grated orange rind, and sprinkle this mixture over the sour cream. Bake at 400° for 40 minutes, or until done, and serve warm with butter. SERVES 6 OR 8.

2 *eggs*	3 *teaspoons grated orange*
1 *cup sugar*	*rind (1 for topping)*
2 *cups sour cream*	2 *teaspoons baking powder*
(1 for topping)	½ *teaspoon salt*
½ *teaspoon baking soda*	¼ *cup dried bread crumbs*
2 *cups flour*	¼ *cup brown sugar*
¼ *cup chopped walnuts*	

(*Dough Gods*

There seems to be quite a bit of confusion as to the exact nature of a dough god. To some they were made from a yeast dough, formed into long rolls and allowed to stand overnight, which was then sliced and fried in deep fat. Others insisted that they were yeast pancakes, and still others — and this version I like best — say they were made from the scraps left over from yeast rolls, the dough being fried in whatever shapes remained, or rerolled and cut into strips before the final cooking in a deep lard-filled skillet. These last were also called "doughboys," the same, some say, for which our foot soldiers were nicknamed.

NOTE: *Invincibles,* another relative, were made by rolling "light" bread dough very thin, cutting in strips, and frying in a "dry" frying pan. They, too, were served with butter.

⟨ Bandon Cranberry Bread

Cape Cod has no corner on the cranberry market; the Oregon coast grows large quantities of the piquant berries. At Bandon they even have an annual Cranberry Festival, where the berries are honored and all the cooks in town vie with one another in the making of cranberry specialties.

Chop a cup of raw cranberries and sprinkle them with 3 tablespoons of sugar. Beat 1 egg, add 2 tablespoons of melted butter, 5 tablespoons of sugar, 2 teaspoons of orange rind, grated, and combine with the cranberries. Now add 1½ cups of flour mixed with 2 teaspoons of baking powder and ½ teaspoon of salt, and ½ cup of milk. Last, stir in ½ cup of chopped walnuts. Pour into a medium-sized greased loaf pan, and bake at 350° for one hour.

1 *cup cranberries*	1½ *cups flour*
½ *cup sugar* (8 *tablespoons*)	2 *teaspoons baking*
1 *egg*	*powder*
2 *tablespoons melted butter*	½ *teaspoon salt*
2 *teaspoons grated orange*	½ *cup milk*
rind	½ *cup chopped walnuts*

NOTE: Cranberries may be substituted for blueberries in any recipe for blueberry muffins.

⟨ Date Bread

Date bread is particularly delicious when made from fresh California dates.

Pour 1 cup of boiling water over a cup of dates that have been pitted and cut in pieces with scissors. Add 3 tablespoons of butter and ½ teaspoon of soda, and allow to cool. Now add ¾ of a cup of brown sugar, 1 beaten egg, ½ teaspoon of salt, 2 teaspoons of baking powder, 2¼ cups of flour, and a cup of coarsely chopped walnuts. Bake in a buttered loaf pan for about an hour at 350°.

1 cup boiling water	½ teaspoon salt
1 cup cut-up dates	2 teaspoons baking
3 tablespoons butter	powder
½ teaspoon soda	2¼ cups flour
¾ cup brown sugar	1 cup coarsely chopped
1 egg	walnuts

⟦ *Lumber Camp Doughnuts*

The lumber camp cooks of the Northwest cook doughnuts every day, and by the hundreds. The lumberjacks can't drink coffee without them. Perhaps because they've had so much practice all these cook-house fryers turn out superb light-as-a-leaf doughnuts. They used their own yeast in the old days, but this recipe is adapted to today's cook — either at home or in the woods.

A cup of evaporated milk is mixed with a cup of hot water, 1 cup of dark brown sugar, a cake of yeast dissolved in ¼ cup of water, ⅔ of a cup of lard (bear lard was used in the early days), 2 teaspoons of salt, and enough flour to make a soft dough, about 4 cups. (Eggs were used when available — 4 of them.) This is allowed to rise, then rolled and cut with a doughnut cutter. It is then allowed to rise again (on a floured board), before frying in deep fat (370°). The camp cooks often pinched off big hunks of the soft dough instead of rolling and cutting it, an idea which should be used more often. These doughnuts are light as a feather, as anyone who has ever eaten them will testify.

1 cup evaporated milk	⅔ cup lard
1 cup water	2 teaspoons salt
1 cup brown sugar	4 cups flour
1 cake yeast in ¼ cup water	(or as needed)

NOTE: The reputation of San Francisco doughnuts, at least those served at the free lunches so popular in the saloons of the '70s, '80s, and '90s, was not so good. One story tells of that famous character, White Hat McCarthy (who always wore a white beaver hat as he drove about the city), who wanted to stop at his favorite saloon for a couple of quick ones, but found that he had lost his horse's headweight. A city ordinance made it illegal to leave a horse unhitched or untethered, so McCarthy weighted his reins with a doughnut from the free lunch counter. Haled into court, he was acquitted by the judge, who solemnly declared that everyone knew there was nothing heavier than a free lunch doughnut.

⟪ Dutch Babies

These are a combination popover and pancake, if you can imagine such a thing. They are tremendously popular in Seattle. This recipe does not come from the restaurant that made them famous, but it is a reasonable facsimile.

This recipe makes 4 babies. Beat 4 eggs with ½ cup of cream, a tablespoon of sherry, 4 teaspoons of flour, and ¼ teaspoon each of salt and baking powder. Set oven at 450°. Have ready as many 6-inch frying pans as you can gather, butter them well. Divide this batter into the pans (or into four parts if you have but one pan), and cook slowly on top of the stove. Turn and finish cooking in the oven for 4 or 5 minutes, or until all puffed up. (Again, if there's but one frying pan, turn into hot buttered individual baking dishes, and finish in the oven.) Dutch babies are usually served with butter, sugar, and lemon juice, or with syrup. I like plain butter.

4 eggs	4 teaspoons flour
½ cup cream	¼ teaspoon salt
1 tablespoon sherry	¼ teaspoon baking powder

⟪ Pioneer Flapjacks

Anyone who has ever cooked without proper facilities will know why flapjacks were so popular with the pioneers — a bonfire and a skillet did the trick. This is an early and particularly good recipe.

Bread

Mix 2 cups of sour milk, 1 cup of corn meal, 2 tablespoons of flour, an egg, if available, 1 teaspoon of soda, and ½ teaspoon of salt. Mix well, adding water if desired, and cook in a skillet. Honey, wild berry jam, or sugar and water syrup were usually served with these.

2 cups sour milk	1 egg
1 cup corn meal	1 teaspoon soda
2 tablespoons flour	½ teaspoon salt
Water if necessary	

NOTE: Paul Bunyan made his flapjacks with buttermilk from his buttermilk well and greased the griddle by having boys, with hams tied to their feet, go skating on it.

❨ Orange Pecan Bread

This is a recipe from the Sunkist Kitchens, and a mighty good one it is, too.

Cut a large thick-skinned orange into quarters, remove white core, and grind, using the fine blade of the food chopper. There should be 1 cup of pulp, skin, and juice. Combine with ⅓ cup of sugar, ½ cup of butter, and 1½ teaspoons of salt, and bring to a boil. Cool to lukewarm, add a crumbled yeast cake, and beat well to blend. Add a beaten egg, ½ cup of chopped pecans, and enough flour (about 2½ cups) to make a stiff dough. Knead on a well-floured board for 5 minutes, adding flour as needed to keep it from sticking to the board. Cover with a cloth or bowl, and let rise in a warm place (80° to 85°) until double in bulk. Now knead again for 1 minute, shape into a loaf, and put into a greased loaf pan, 10 × 5 × 3½ inches. Again cover and let rise until a little more than double. Bake at 375° for about 40 minutes. Cool on a cake rack. MAKES 1 LOAF.

1 large orange	1 yeast cake
½ cup butter	1 egg
⅓ cup sugar	½ cup chopped pecans
1½ teaspoons salt	2½ cups flour (more or less)

(Pan Relleno

This is a recipe from an old Southern California family, and it is delicious, though not really "stuffed bread."

Split a long loaf of French or Italian bread. Make a mixture of ⅔ of a cup of grated Cheddar or Monterey Jack cheese, ⅓ cup of chopped onion, 2 tablespoons of olive oil, 1 tablespoon of vinegar, ¼ teaspoon of oregano, and ¼ cup of chopped olives (green or ripe). Spread between and on top of the split loaf of bread, and bake until thoroughly hot.

1 loaf French or Italian bread	*⅓ cup chopped onion*
	2 tablespoons olive oil
⅔ cup grated Cheddar or Monterey Jack	*1 tablespoon vinegar*
	¼ teaspoon oregano
¼ cup chopped olives	

(Jolly Boys

An old recipe, this, and nicely named.

Soak a yeast cake (the original recipe said "1 cup of yeast"!) in ¼ cup of cold water. Scald a cup of milk, add ¼ cup of butter, a tablespoon of sugar, and a teaspoon of salt. Cool slightly, and add 2 well-beaten eggs and the yeast. Stir in 1 cup of corn meal and 2 cups of flour. Allow to rise until double in bulk, then stir down and allow to rise again. Have a kettle of deep fat heated to 360° and, disturbing the remaining batter as little as possible, fry spoonfuls of it until puffy and golden brown. Keep warm and serve with butter.

1 yeast cake in ¼ cup water	*1 teaspoon salt*
1 cup milk	*2 eggs*
¼ cup butter	*1 cup corn meal*
1 tablespoon sugar	*2 cups flour*

(Wild Blackberry or Blueberry Muffins

Wild blackberries were one of Oregon's early blessings. The pioneers counted on them for many of their treats.

36

Bread

Mix together 1¾ cups of flour, 2 teaspoons of baking powder, ½ teaspoon of salt, ¼ cup of sugar (add 2 tablespoons more sugar if desired sweeter). Combine with 1 beaten egg, a cup of milk, ¼ cup of melted butter, and 2 cups of wild blackberries, dusted with ¼ cup of flour. Bake in greased muffin pans for about 20 minutes at 400°.

2 cups flour (reserve ¼ cup)	1 egg
2 teaspoons baking powder	1 cup milk
½ teaspoon salt	¼ cup melted butter
¼ cup sugar (or more)	2 cups wild blackberries

NOTE: Huckleberry muffins, or any fruit muffins for that matter, are made in the same way, substituting berries or cut-up fruit for the blackberries. If raisins are used, try plumping them in hot sherry wine. Walnuts and grated orange rind are another typical and delightful Californian addition.

(Green Onion Rolls

Of course we eat garlic bread in prodigious quantities, particularly when there's something sizzling on the barbecue, but we like these, too.

Sauté 2 cups of finely chopped green onions in ½ cup of butter until wilted. Season them with salt and pepper, and allow them to cool. Now make your favorite roll dough or, if you're feeling indolent, use a yeast roll mix, and if even that seems like too much work, use a frozen roll dough. Anyway, when the "shaping" time has arrived, roll your dough ¼-inch thick and cut it into circles with a cookie cutter. Put a teaspoonful of onion in the center of each, wet one half of the circle with water, fold over and press the little turnovers together firmly. Allow to rise, and bake as usual.

2 cups finely chopped green onions	Salt and pepper
½ cup butter	Roll dough

NOTE: Another onion roll, the Jewish kind, is also a favorite. Roll the dough in a large circle, spread it with sautéed onion, sprinkle thickly with poppy seeds, and cut the dough in pie-shaped pieces, making 12 wedges. Roll each piece from the wide side to the point, put on buttered pans, and allow to rise before baking. Onion bread is made this way, too, but the whole piece is rolled like a jelly roll and then put into the bread pan to rise. They are *all* good!

(Visalia Ripe Olive Bread

California is forever busy developing new ways with ripe olives. This bread, which is robust and moist, is good for buffet suppers, or as a sandwich with a Cheddar filling.

Beat 2 eggs light, add a tablespoon of sugar, ½ teaspoon of salt, 2 tablespoons of olive oil, and 1½ cups of chopped ripe olives. Stir in 2 cups of flour, 2 teaspoons of baking powder, and ½ cup of milk. Don't beat, just mix. Pour into a bread pan that has been greased with olive oil, let stand for 20 minutes, then bake at 350° for 1 hour, or until done.

2 eggs	1½ cups chopped ripe olives
1 tablespoon sugar	2 cups flour
½ teaspoon salt	2 teaspoons baking powder
2 tablespoons olive oil	½ cup milk

(Philpy

Here is a hot bread that is in danger of being forgotten — a thin rice-and-corn meal arrangement that is very pleasing.

Mix 2 cups of cooked rice with 1 cup of milk, 1 cup of corn meal, 2 beaten eggs, a tablespoon of melted butter, and ½ teaspoon of salt. Beat well and pour into a well-buttered 10-inch piepan. It should be thin. Bake at 375° until nicely browned. Break in pieces and serve with butter.

2 cups cooked rice	2 eggs
1 cup milk	1 tablespoon melted butter
1 cup corn meal	½ teaspoon salt

Bread

❨ Oregon Raised Prune Bread

Scald a cup of milk with 1 tablespoon of butter, 2 tablespoons of sugar, and a teaspoon of salt. Cool and add a cake of yeast that has been dissolved in ¼ cup of lukewarm water. Mix in 3¼ cups of flour. Knead until smooth and allow to rise until double in bulk. Turn onto a floured board, add a cup of steamed prunes, pitted and cut in pieces, and ½ cup of chopped nut meats, if desired. Knead until well mixed, and shape in two loaves. Put in buttered bread pans, allow to rise again, and bake at 400° for about 45 minutes. MAKES 2 LOAVES.

1 cup milk	3¼ cups flour
1 tablespoon butter	1 cup steamed prunes
2 tablespoons sugar	½ cup chopped nuts
1 teaspoon salt	(optional)
1 cake yeast in ¼ cup water	

NOTE: A prune bread made with baking powder, and using prune juice for the liquid, is another favorite.

❨ Walnut Rum Rolls

Shockingly rich, and good enough to supplant dessert, or as the feature at a breakfast party. For the rest of the breakfast have chicken livers and bacon *en brochette*, creamed finnan haddie, scrambled eggs, grilled sausages, grilled tomatoes, and thin hot toast.

Make a rich roll dough with 1 cup of scalded milk, ¼ cup of butter, 2 tablespoons of sugar, 2 teaspoons of salt, 1½ cakes of yeast, 2 beaten eggs, and 3½ cups of flour. Put it in the refrigerator overnight, with or without having allowed a preliminary rising. Next day cream together ¼ pound of butter and ½ pound of brown sugar. Roll the dough fairly thin, and in an oblong shape, and spread with half the butter and sugar mixture, then sprinkle with 3 ounces of chopped walnuts. Now roll as for a jelly roll, trying to keep the edges even. When rolled as tightly as possible, pinch the edges together, making a seal. To the remaining half of the butter and

39

sugar mixture, add 2 tablespoons of Jamaica rum. Spread this mixture on the bottom of a deep round cake pan, and sprinkle with ¼ pound of walnuts, unchopped. Now cut the roll of dough in 1-inch slices and arrange (cut sides up and down and the buns just touching) on the bed of sugar mix. Allow to rise until light, then bake in a hot oven until brown on top. Next turn out on another pan, pouring all the syrup over the top and retrieving any walnuts that may have escaped. Return to the top shelf of the oven until the walnuts and syrup have acquired a beautiful golden glaze.

DOUGH

1 cup milk	2 teaspoons salt
¼ cup butter	1½ cakes yeast
2 tablespoons sugar	2 eggs
3½ cups flour	

FILLING

¼ pound butter	¼ pound walnuts
½ pound brown sugar	(unchopped)
3 ounces chopped walnuts	2 tablespoons Jamaica rum

❪ Fly Away Rolls

That's what an old cook book calls them — and for obvious reasons. The same book starts out with an example of the wit of the day: "Why is hot bread like a caterpillar? Ans.: Because it's the grub that makes the butter fly."

Melt ¼ cup of butter in a cup of milk, add 3 tablespoons of sugar and a teaspoon of salt. Add a yeast cake dissolved in ¼ cup of warm water, 2 beaten egg yolks, and a teaspoon of ground coriander, then the 2 egg whites, beaten stiff. Mix in 3½ cups of flour and chill. (This is the modern method.) Pinch off dough in pieces the size of an apricot, and allow to rise on a lightly floured board. When double in size, scoop up very gently with a spatula, and lower into deep fat at 370°, and fry until brown. The less they are handled, the lighter they'll be. They may be baked, if preferred, in which

40

case allow the pinched-off dough to rise on pans in which it is to be baked.

¼ cup butter	1 yeast cake in ¼ cup water
1 cup milk	2 eggs
3 tablespoons sugar	1 teaspoon ground corian-
1 teaspoon salt	der
3½ cups flour	

⟨ West Coast Roll-ups

These may be made with either a yeast roll dough, a biscuit dough, or with a yeast or biscuit mix, and they may be as varied as the fillings that can be dreamed up.

Roll dough about ¼-inch thick and spread with any of the following mixtures; then roll like a jelly roll, cut in ½-inch slices, arrange on buttered pans. If a yeast dough, allow to rise before baking, otherwise bake at once.

The fillings: sautéed chopped onions; chopped ripe olives mixed with enough sour cream to bind; grated cheese mixed with a little melted butter; sautéed chopped mushrooms mixed with a little cream sauce; chopped dates or figs which have been softened by scalding in hot water; chopped raisins or nuts mixed with brown sugar and butter; chopped apples mixed with butter and sugar; clams, ham, bacon, or almost anything, chopped and mixed with minced parsley or crumbs or butter, and bound with gravy or cream sauce or such.

NOTE: Muffins, using the same variations, are made by putting half the amount of batter in the muffin tins, adding a spoonful of any of the above, or a pitted ripe olive, or a cube of cheese, or a pitted prune (and so on), and covering with the remaining batter, then baking as usual.

⟨ Vancouver Cream Scones

This recipe came down from Canada to Seattle, where it is a favorite.

Mix 2 cups of flour with ½ teaspoon of salt, a tablespoon of baking powder, and 2 tablespoons of sugar. Cut in ¼ cup of butter, then mix in ½ cup of cream and 1 beaten egg. Fold in

¼ cup of seeded raisins that have been cut in pieces with scissors. Roll ¾ inch thick, cut in triangles, brush with egg white, shake granulated sugar on top, and bake at 400° for 10 to 18 minutes, or until brown. Split and serve with butter.

2 cups flour	½ cup cream
½ teaspoon salt	1 egg
1 tablespoon baking powder	¼ cup seeded raisins
2 tablespoons sugar	Egg white
¼ cup butter	Sugar (for top)

(Sourdough Biscuits

An all-time favorite with pioneers and miners, and still beloved by prospectors, sheep herders, or anyone who has ever tasted them. There's something about the flavor of sourdough that never can be equaled or imitated. It's a bit difficult to get started on a sour dough unless the right yeasts are in the air. That's why the old-timers guarded their "starter" as they did their gold hoard. The dough was used for flapjacks, for biscuits, or for bread — in other words, they all but lived on it. There are several approved methods of starting a sour dough. Some used stale bread, some flour and milk, and some flour and water. The last is the surest, as some breads don't "work," and pasteurized milk cannot be used.

Mix 2 cups of flour, 2 cups of warm water, and 1 teaspoon of salt, and let stand in a warm place for 2 to 4 days until sour and bubbly. This is your "souring." For biscuits a little of this was mixed with some "sody" and poured right into the top of a bag of flour, then worked around until it had taken up sufficient flour. Or, to be less primitive, the desired amount of "starter" was put in a dish, flour, shortening (often drippings), and salt and soda added by ear, and all mixed with water or milk to the proper consistency for whatever was to be made. Always some of the sourings were kept, usually smelling to heaven, for wild yeasts are hard to tame. But the worse the smell, the better the dough. Many sourdough ex-

42

perts have never started from scratch — they were originally given some starter by an old-timer, and have never allowed it to give out. One story goes that the original came over with Columbus. At any rate, every sheep herder and prospector in the Northwest knows how to make sourdough, and knows it's the best bread there is.

(*Tortillas*

Tortillas are the staff of life to Mexicans and to Californians with a Mexican heritage. There are two kinds: those made of masa, and those made of flour. The masa tortilla is made by leaching dried corn, removing its skin, and then laboriously grinding the kernels in a *metate,* or stone mortar and pestle arrangement. This is the masa, and the tortillas are made by forming it into little balls and patting it into pancakelike cakes with the palms of the hands. The Mexican women are very adept at this, slapping and patting in rhythm as the tortilla grows thinner and larger. Sometimes they even slap the tortilla on a large thigh if it happens to be bare — to the delight or horror of the onlookers. When the proper size, the tortillas are cooked on a griddle, but not browned. When purchased, they are reheated by laying them on a hot griddle or directly over an electric or gas burner. When they get freckles of brown, they are turned and treated the same way on the other side. Tostados are tortillas fried crisp in hot lard.

Early Californians loved to visit, sometimes staying a month at a time. The tortilla makers would then be hard at it, working day and night. Today most Southern California cities have tortillerias, or tortilla factories, where the staple food is turned out in quantities. Until recently these places were staffed by Mexican women who made them by hand, but lately machines have been used. This is a pity, for the tortillas are not as good, and besides, the fun of watching is gone forever. Some energetic souls buy the masa and pat out tortillas at home, but most of us bow our heads to progress and purchase the inferior machine-made jobs.

❧ Tortillas de Harina (*Flour Tortillas*)

Wheat was one of the early crops around the Missions, so these wheat tortillas were common in early days, and are still preferred to the corn variety by many Californian-Mexicans. More water was needed to grow corn than wheat, so flour tortillas were the true early Californian bread.

Cut ¼ cup of lard into 3 cups of flour. Add 1½ teaspoons of salt, and enough tepid water to make a stiff dough. Knead until smooth, adding water if necessary. Roll into balls the size of a golf ball. Cover and let stand for 15 or 20 minutes, then roll thin, keeping the tortillas round. They should be about the size of a dessert plate. Bake on a hot ungreased griddle, about 1½ minutes on each side. Serve hot, whenever tortillas are indicated.

¼ cup lard	*1½ teaspoons salt*
3 cups flour	*Water as needed*

❧ Waffle Notes

We don't use the old cast-iron waffle irons that the early settlers heated in the open fire, but we make waffles of many kinds.

We add such things as nuts, any kind, grated or chopped; dates, figs, raisins, or prunes, chopped; grated rind of lemon or orange; berries, almost any kind; ground chocolate; crisp bacon; chopped ripe olives; chopped mushrooms; grated cheese; chopped cranberries; and anything else that occurs to us. The waffles are served at breakfast or for dessert, depending upon their content.

Cheese

CHEESE IS MADE *in all three Pacific states, but it is Oregon that turns out the largest quantity. The Oregon coast, from the California line to Clatsop, the northernmost county, is one cheese factory after another. (It's beautiful country as well, so there's not a pleasanter place for a cook's tour.) This country was destined to be a dairyland — even the whales knew it: according to Indian legend (and how they could think them up) these huge animals swam into Tillamook Bay to be milked. The dairy industry started a hundred years ago when a pioneer named Wilson drove a herd of cows into the lush green valley that was Tillamook. With this rich pasturage the cows gave their all, enough for the settlers to have all the milk and butter they could use. Soon there was more than enough, for, as an old-timer said, you can't turn off a cow. The surplus butter was salted — very heavily — and shipped to other communities in firkins made of spruce. It brought a pretty price in the Bonanza Days of San Francisco, but those good times did not last forever. Cheese was the answer. The first batch, made in 1889, was something old Oregonians would rather not talk about. But by 1894 they were turning out such a creditable product that the cheese makers of the area later formed a co-operative. Today Tillamook cheese is so well known throughout the West that it is synonymous with "Cheddar," which type it is. Of course there are other cheeses made on the Oregon coast. The first factory, after crossing the California line, is Pistol*

River, where they make a rich Cheddar that is, even when only a few months old, exceptionally fine. The plant is a tiny one, which is good, as the best things do seem to come in small batches. On up the line we find other fine cheeses. At Sixes (the word was the Chinook way of saying "hi"), at Denmark, at Bandon, Coos Bay, and other places they are turning out fine Cheddars. And at Langlois they started, only a few years ago, another type of cheese that is so startlingly good that it is already famous. Rich as butter, this Langlois cheese has a blue mold somewhat like a Roquefort, but for many palates, far better. Langlois blue-veined cheese, they call it.

Although they started to make cheese in what is now Washington long before they did in Oregon, they didn't go in for it in as big a way. The Hudson's Bay Company's factor, the "White Eagle," appreciated cheese so much that he occasionally broke his own rule and allowed a calf to be butchered for its rennet. (Deer rennet was later used for cheese-making by those who thought it a pity to eat veal when, by waiting a few months, they could have beef.) The many Scandinavian settlers in Washington made the cheeses of their homeland, and some still do. There was also a man named Miggs who became famous for his cheese, which was made in the Swiss manner. Today the cheese factories are more scattered than they are in Oregon, and the cheese makers are not so well organized, but they nevertheless turn out some that is truly excellent.

California has her own cheeses, and mighty good they are, too. Monterey Jack is the most famous. Until the First World War it was little known outside of Monterey County, where it was made, but you can't keep a good cheese down. A rich, creamy white cheese, the high-moisture Jack is semisoft and wholly delicious. It is good eating in hand, with fruit or crackers, or cooked, being particularly famous in chilis rellenos, frijoles con queso, or in a fondue. Teleme is a similar cheese, though the manufacturing process differs slightly, and in shape it's rectangular and not as thick as the Monterey, which is round. (The California Teleme is made from cow's milk, unlike the Rumanian cheese of the same name, which is made with sheep's milk.) When expertly aged, a Teleme acquires a mold on the outside, and the most delectable runny interior imaginable. It is seldom found in this state of perfection, but even a new Teleme is a gourmet's treat. Another California cheese is Sierra, which is made, at least some of it, in Novato. Small and round, weighing only 4 ounces, it is somewhat like a Neufchâtel, somewhat like a Camembert, but with a characteristic and very fine flavor of its own. Another delectable cheese from Novato is the little "Breakfast Cheese," not unlike the Sierra, but a little milder. Serving cheese at breakfast, incidentally, is a pleasant West Coast habit. Cream and cottage cheese are used most often, served with toast and jam — an ingenious way of getting that extra milk into the family diet. Another California cheese-making triumph is the Camembert. In Petaluma a Camembert, the Rouge et Noir brand, has reached perfection. We make other cheese on the West Coast: the fascinating quesa fresca of the Mexicans, and their panela, another fresh cheese drained in a basket so that its weave leaves a print on the cheese. We make Italian cheese, too, ricotta, mozzarella, provolone, and grating cheese. And then there are the tons of cottage and cream cheese that we make, and eat. . . .

Such are the fine cheeses of our West Coast. Is it any wonder that we use it lavishly in our cooking, and that it, either with or without fruit, is our favorite dessert?

Chocolate

THE MEXICANS *on the West Coast still make their favorite beverage, chocolate, just as they did when they first crossed the border in the wake of the Franciscans. A rich and frothy drink, it is mixed with a little hand mill called a molinillo. This is a stick encircled with wooden rings which, when twirled expertly between the palms, does a very efficient job of whipping. They also use chocolate in a way strange to those who think of it only as a sweet. It is an ingredient in the famous Mexican holiday dish, turkey mole (mole de guajolote) and usually in other dishes designated molé poblano. But it wasn't only the Mexicans who liked chocolate; its popularity with the Argonauts started one chocolate business that is still flourishing today. Domingo Ghirardelli arrived in California in 1849, in search, like everyone else, of gold. After a trip or two to the mines, he decided to stick to the business he knew best. He opened a grocery store in San Francisco, with branches in Stockton. In 1852 he began the manufacture of his superlative chocolate, and soon was making it at Hornitos, Melones, and Columbia. The ruins of the Hornitos store are still viewed by visitors to the Mother Lode country, and Ghirardelli's ground chocolate is still made by members of the founder's family. It is a sweetened chocolate used by good West Coast cooks whenever chocolate is indicated, as a beverage, and also in cakes, puddings, icings, and candies. Alfred Ghirardelli, who now heads the chocolate company, says that he remembers, as a small boy, buttering slices of homemade bread and spreading them with the chocolate. I tried it, and I promise that you don't have to be either small or masculine to enjoy it.*

Desserts

SWEETS WERE SCARCE *in the very early days. The Indians, who invariably had a yen for them, had to be satisfied with wild berries, sun-dried for extra concentration of sugar, or with what wild honey they could find. The first Mexicans to come to California had their panocha, a cone of moist brown sugar that had to be used sparingly because of its rarity. Later they dried their fruits, which they called orejones. Anise was almost invariably the flavoring they used, probably because it grew wild everywhere. Chocolate was a great favorite, but it was used as a beverage rather than a flavoring. What few sweets the early Californians did have were usually served after the noon siesta, a pleasant little meal known as* merienda. *At the Missions the big treat for the neophytes was a drink of sweetened water and vinegar that was carried to them when they worked the fields in the heat of the day. The Mission fathers themselves settled for a bit of cake and a spot of brandy. The scarcity of sugar was apparently of some concern to these early Californians. General Vallejo hired one character who claimed he could perform magic — make sugar from beets — but he failed to produce even a low-grade one. The very idea was so amusing that he gained a nickname that he could never shake — "El Azucarero," meaning "sugar maker." Today beet sugar is one of California's great industries, and the product is as good, in every way, as sugar made from cane. In 1843, according to Dr. Maxwell, a prominent physician of San*

Francisco, "The female population of Monterey have never tasted cake, mince pie, or anything of that sort." A very few years later, Dame Shirley, writing from the gold fields, said "no milk, no eggs, no nothing," which, one would think, would have meant "no desserts" as well. But the lady had a genius cook named Ned, who produced "mince pie and pudding made without eggs," and sundry other delicacies. Later she wrote sadly, "Ned, the cook, departed. Yes, Vattal Ned to the valley has gone, in a Marysville kitchen you'll find him." The miners in Marysville had lured him with more gold.

Farther north, in Oregon and what was later to be Washington, there was also a craving for sweets, but there the pioneer women took to the woods for their pie fillings. Pies were made of wild berries — blueberries, blackberries, sometimes salal berries. The crust itself, more often than not, was shortened with bear lard, and the mincemeat made of venison. These busy women also dried wild berries for winter use, and these were said to have been unbelievably delicious. In spite of all the scarcity of dessert makings, the good ladies of that early day managed to put on some remarkable spreads. Fourth of July was a big day in Oregon and was usually celebrated by huge community picnics. One, in the '50s, listed an elaborate selection of pastries — "Pound cake, fruit cake, jelly cake, Sweetwater Mountain cake, peach pie, apple pie, strawberry pie, custard pie," and a dozen more varieties of cakes and pies. Another holiday party, a family Christmas, had "oval mince pies, and huge fruit cakes baked in milk pans." This account tells of the children all helping with the baking. They seeded "big plummy raisins" and were allowed to eat every tenth one. Their plum puddings were "made in the English manner" and hung in bags in the buttery until the great day arrived.

By the '60s and '70s, everyone apparently had sugar if

51

they had the price, for by that time there were plenty of trading vessels stopping at all Western ports. The earliest cook books all had large sections devoted to cakes and pies, and one charming old book, dated San Francisco, 1872, had a chapter headed "Flummery," which had recipes for chocolate soufflé, caramels, éclairs, meringues aux fruits, ice currants, and blanc mange, among others. The recipe for "strawberry whips" began "Pick ripe strawberries; with dainty hands squeeze and mash them. . . ." By the time the end of the century was close, the cook books gave recipes for little but desserts, apparently feeling that anybody could cook but not everybody could bake. Such recipes, for the most part, are pretty much the same as those in all regional books of the period. It is only when they are typical of the West Coast, or have some special Western trick, that they are included here.

❮ Chinese Almond Cakes

These are the almond cakes that so often end a Chinese meal. This version uses butter, for the Occidental palate, but the Chinese more often use lard or peanut oil.

Mix ¼ pound of butter with ¼ cup of confectioners' sugar, a cup of flour, ⅛ teaspoon of baking powder, and ¼ teaspoon of almond extract. Work until smooth, roll into balls the size of a walnut, put on a cookie sheet, top with half a blanched almond — a Chinese one if you can find them — and press each ball into a round cookie with the bottom of a tumbler. Bake at 325° until a straw color. MAKES 1½ DOZEN.

¼ pound butter	⅛ teaspoon baking powder
¼ cup confectioners' sugar	¼ teaspoon almond extract
1 cup flour	Halved almonds

NOTE: For those who must have the authentic Oriental recipe: 2 cups of rice flour, 1½ cups of powdered sugar, ½ cup peanut or sesame oil (cotton or corn oil may be used), 2 slightly beaten eggs. Mix well, adding a drop or two of almond extract, if you wish. Proceed as in above recipe. MAKES 3 DOZEN.

(*Burnt Almond Cream*

California almonds, and brandy too, give this classic crème brûlée a West Coast flavor.

Scald a pint of whipping cream with 6 tablespoons of brown sugar and ⅛ teaspoon of salt. Beat the yolks of 7 eggs and add to the hot cream, along with a tablespoon of California brandy or sherry. Cook in a double boiler over hot water, stirring or whipping constantly. Watch it as it begins to thicken — it should be smooth as a rose petal, thick as medium cream sauce. Have ready ½ cup of well-toasted almonds, chopped fine. When the cream is the proper consistency, mix in the almonds and pour into a fireproof earthenware or glass dish, and put in the refrigerator for at least 12 hours. An hour or two before serving time, put some soft brown sugar in a sieve and sift a thin even layer over the top of the custard. It should be about ¼-inch thick, or a little less. (Don't have hills and hummocks of sugar — if it is bumpy, smooth it gently with the bowl of a spoon.) Now put the dish under a broiler until the sugar melts and just begins to brown. Watch it. This is a crucial moment. Put the dessert back into the refrigerator until serving time. The melted sugar hardens almost at once into a thin, icelike glaze, which has to be cracked with a sharp rap from a spoon. Beneath lies a dream of a custard. If this is not heavenly enough, brandied fruits — usually cherries or dates — may be served with it, or preserved greengage plums or golden apricots. SERVES 6 OR 8.

1 pint whipping cream	1 tablespoon brandy or
6 tablespoons brown sugar	sherry
⅛ teaspoon salt	½ cup toasted almonds
7 egg yolks	Brown sugar to cover

❨ Rolled Almond Wafers

Cream together ½ cup of powdered sugar and ¼ cup of butter, add ¼ cup of milk, ¾ of a cup of flour plus 2 table-spoons (⅞ cup), and ½ teaspoon of almond extract. Put a heaping teaspoonful at a time on well-greased cookie sheets, and flatten them into nice rounds with a spatula dipped in cold water, or the back of a spoon, likewise dipped. Sprinkle each cookie evenly with chopped almonds (½ cup in all). Bake at 350° until the edges brown. Leave cookies in a warm spot and, working quickly, turn each one over and roll it. If they get too cool to roll without cracking, slip them back into the oven for a minute. These keep beautifully if covered tightly, but will get limp otherwise. Really a delightful cookie to serve with ice cream, fruit, or at teatime. MAKES APPROXIMATELY 2 DOZEN.

½ cup powdered sugar	⅞ cup flour
¼ cup butter	½ teaspoon almond extract
¼ cup milk	½ cup chopped almonds

❨ Almond Roca Rum Pie

Almond Roca is a candy specialty of Tacoma, Washington. It is a sort of English toffee, only better. It stars here in a marvelously rich pie.

Beat 4 egg yolks until light. Add ⅓ cup of sugar and ⅛ teaspoon of salt. Mix 2 teaspoons of plain gelatin with 2 tablespoons of water, and melt over hot water. Add to mixture, along with ½ pint of cream, whipped stiff, and 2 tablespoons of Jamaica rum. Cool slightly, and pour into a baked pie shell that measures 8½ inches across (inside measurement). Cover with 3 or 4 ounces of Almond Roca, coarsely chopped. (English toffee may be used.) Allow to stand in the refrigerator for a while to set before serving. SERVES 6 OR 8.

4 egg yolks	2 tablespoons water
⅓ cup sugar	½ pint cream
⅛ teaspoon salt	2 tablespoons Jamaica rum
2 teaspoons gelatin	3–4 ounces Almond Roca

Desserts

⟨ Linda Vista Deep Dish Apple Pie

The pioneers, or so it is said, ate apple pie for breakfast. The Yankee in them, no doubt. Their matutinal pie may have been good, but it couldn't have compared with this contemporary California recipe, which is *exceedingly* good.

Make a rich almond piecrust: 1½ cups of flour, ¼ cup each of butter and lard, ¼ cup of finely grated almonds, ½ teaspoon of salt, and as much water as you'll need to bind it. Roll the crust rather thin, fold it in quarters, and put it in the refrigerator while you make your filling. Peel 4 pounds of tart green apples and cut them in eighths, or thereabouts. Heap them in a baking dish about 2 inches deep and cover with a mixture made by combining ¼ cup of melted butter, a cup of sugar, the grated rind of a small orange and its juice. Mix this into the apples a bit. Again roll the chilled crust not too thin, cut a couple or three holes in it with a thimble-sized cutter (a thimble will do!), and cover the apples. Press pastry against the edges and trim. Bake at 450° for 15 minutes, then reduce heat to 325° and cook until the apples are tender. After the pie is baked, pour three or four tablespoons of rum or California brandy into the holes, using a funnel. Serve this pie warm, with thick cream, unsweetened, please. SERVES 6 OR 8.

PASTRY

1½ cups flour	¼ cup finely grated almonds
¼ cup butter	½ teaspoon salt
¼ cup lard	Water as needed

FILLING

4 pounds apples	Grated rind and juice of
¼ cup melted butter	small orange
1 cup sugar	3–4 tablespoons brandy or rum

❰ McGinties

This recipe pops up in strange places, as, for instance, the Oregon State Guide, where it is assumed that it was named for a pioneer named Mrs. McGinty.

Soak ½ pound of dried apples overnight, then cook in water to cover until soft. Press through a colander. This should yield about 4 cups of apple pulp. Sweeten with ¾ of a cup of brown sugar, add a teaspoon of cinnamon, a tablespoon of butter, and ⅛ teaspoon of salt. Line a baking pan, about 1 inch deep, with pastry, add apple mix, cover with more pastry, moistening the edges and pressing for a good seal. Prick thoroughly with a fork. Bake at 375° until well browned. Cool slightly, cut in squares, and serve with hard sauce or cream. The pioneers sometimes ate well! SERVES 12.

½ pound dried apples   *1 teaspoon cinnamon*
Water   *1 tablespoon butter*
¾ cup brown sugar   *⅛ teaspoon salt*
Pastry

❰ Apple Dessert Notes

Apple Grunt. This was a pioneer recipe with dozens of variations. It was said to be so irresistible that you'd "eat it till you grunt." Sliced apples or apple sauce, thickly covered with cinnamon, sugar, and butter, were topped with thickly rolled biscuit dough which was gashed in several places. It was baked or steamed, and served warm, turned out upside-down on a dish, with unwhipped but heavy cream.

A California Pioneer Apple Pie, 1852, said Mrs. B. C. Whiting in *How We Cook in Los Angeles* (1894), was made with a filling of soda crackers made tart with citric acid, moist with water, and flavored with brown sugar and cinnamon. "The deception was most complete and readily accepted. Apples at this early date were a dollar a pound, and we young people all craved a piece of Mother's apple pie to appease our homesick feelings."

Desserts

❲ Avocado Mousse

Mix 1 cup of sieved ripe avocado with ¼ teaspoon of salt, ¼ cup of sugar, and a teaspoon of lemon juice. Fold in 2 stiffly beaten egg whites and a cup of cream, whipped stiff. Pack in a freezer tray or put in a mold, and place in freezing unit for three hours. SERVES 4 OR 5.

1 cup sieved ripe avocado	*1 teaspoon lemon juice*
¼ teaspoon salt	*2 egg whites*
¼ cup sugar	*1 cup cream*

❲ Berkeley Banana Fritters

Banana fritters are a favorite around San Francisco. Many restaurants specialize in them, and good they are, too.

Split 4 bananas in half, lengthwise, and then across. Soak them in ¼ cup of California brandy mixed with 3 tablespoons of sugar and ½ teaspoon of grated lemon rind. Drain, dip in flour, shake off all surplus, then dip in batter. (Make a batter by beating 2 egg yolks well, adding ¾ cup of milk or water, a tablespoon of the brandy in which the bananas soaked, ½ teaspoon salt, a cup of sifted flour, and a tablespoon of melted butter or olive oil. Mix well, then fold in the stiffly beaten whites of the 2 eggs.) Pan fry in butter, or fry in deep fat at 360° until brown. Serve with brandy sauce or whipped cream. SERVES 4 TO 6.

4 bananas	*½ teaspoon grated lemon rind*
¼ cup brandy	*Flour*
3 tablespoons sugar	*Batter*

NOTE: *Filbert-Banana Fritters* — another, and marvelous version. Cut peeled bananas in quarters, crosswise. Dip in raspberry jam which has been pushed through a sieve, then roll in ground filberts. Now dip in slightly beaten egg and in cracker crumbs. Chill thoroughly and fry in deep fat at 360° until brown. Serve with or without sauce.

❨ Washington State Blackberry Roll

Wild blackberries covered most of Washington, Oregon, and California in the early days, and are still profuse in some of the "country" spots. Padre Crespi often mentioned them, as did many later arrivals. One young Argonaut, arriving in '51 to dig for gold, found it more profitable to pick blackberries and sell them on the streets of Sacramento for "a dollar a cornucopia." Cultivated blackberries may be used for this recipe, though you may be sure the early version called for berries of the woods.

Make a rich shortcake dough — 2 cups of flour, 2 teaspoons of baking powder, ½ teaspoon of salt, 2 tablespoons of sugar, ⅓ cup of butter, ⅓ cup of milk, and 1 beaten egg. Roll ¼-inch thick, spread with soft butter, then blackberries that have been sugared. Roll like a jelly roll, put on a buttered baking sheet, form into a circle, then slash part way through every 2½ inches with a pair of scissors. Bake at 400° for about 30 minutes or until brown. Serve warm with cream. SERVES 6.

2 cups flour	⅓ cup butter
2 teaspoons baking powder	⅓ cup milk
½ teaspoon salt	1 egg
2 tablespoons sugar	Butter to cover
Sugared blackberries	

❨ Bonanza Blintzes

Cheese blintzes are a present-day rage, especially in Los Angeles.

Beat 3 eggs, add a cup of milk or water, a cup of flour, and ½ teaspoon of salt. Mix well. Brush a small frying pan, that has been heated, with oil or melted butter, then add a tablespoon or a little more of batter and tilt the pan in all directions so that the batter will form a thin film over the bottom. Cook on one side only, then turn out on a cloth, cooked side up. When the cakes are all done, put a spoonful of filling on each cake, and fold over the edges, first the top and bottom, then the sides, making an envelopelike package. Seal the edges with a bit of the uncooked batter. Fry the blintzes in butter, or part butter and part bland oil, until brown on both

58

sides. Serve hot with cold sour cream and preserves, preferably cherry. The filling: 1 cup of "farmer's" or "country style" cottage cheese (small curds), 1 whole egg, beaten slightly, a tablespoon of melted butter, ⅛ teaspoon of salt, and 2 teaspoons of sugar. Some people add the grated rind of ½ a lemon and/or ¼ teaspoon of cinnamon. For an entree, and a good one, omit sugar and spices in the filling, and add flaked fish or chopped ripe olives or hard-boiled eggs. Sour cream with these, too, but of course no preserves. SERVES 6.

BATTER

3 eggs	1 cup flour
1 cup milk or water	½ teaspoon salt

FILLING

1 cup cottage cheese	1 tablespoon melted butter
1 egg	⅛ teaspoon salt
2 teaspoons sugar	

(*California Brandy Balls*

You don't have to know how to cook to make these.

Mix 3 cups of vanilla cookie or graham cracker crumbs and 1 cup of chopped walnuts, with 1½ cups of confectioners' sugar, ¼ cup of corn syrup, ¼ cup of cocoa or ground chocolate, 3 tablespoons of melted butter, ⅛ teaspoon of salt, and ¼ cup of California brandy or Jamaica rum — or enough to moisten. Form into walnut-sized balls and roll in confectioners' sugar. Store in a tightly closed container for a week before serving. MAKES 2 OR 3 DOZEN.

  3 cups crumbs (vanilla cookie or graham cracker)
  1 cup chopped walnuts
 1½ cups confectioners' sugar
  ¼ cup corn syrup
  ¼ cup cocoa or ground chocolate
  3 tablespoons melted butter
  ⅛ teaspoon salt
  ¼ cup California brandy or Jamaica rum
    Confectioners' sugar to cover

(All-California Golden Cake

Every old Western cook book had a score of recipes for cake, most of them using nuts. This one uses California raisins, orange peel, and brandy as well, and will keep a month or two if given an occasional drink of brandy while reposing in a tin box that can be covered tightly. Unlike many of the early recipes, it doesn't call for a pound of butter and a dozen eggs.

Cream a cup of sugar with ¼ pound of butter, then beat in 3 eggs. Add a cup of flour, sifted with a teaspoon of baking powder and ½ teaspoon of salt, along with ¼ cup of California brandy, plus 2 cups of white raisins, 2 cups of chopped blanched walnuts or blanched almonds, and 3 tablespoons of chopped candied orange rind. Bake in a greased 9-inch tube pan, in a moderate oven (350°) for about 65 or 70 minutes.

1 cup sugar	*¼ cup brandy*
¼ pound butter	*2 cups white raisins*
3 eggs	*2 cups chopped walnuts or*
1 cup flour	*almonds*
1 teaspoon baking powder	*3 tablespoons chopped can-*
½ teaspoon salt	*died orange rind*

(Chocolate Rum Icing

For éclairs or torten or just plain cakes.

Melt 5 squares of bitter chocolate, add ¼ pound of butter, and beat well. Now stir in 1 pound of confectioners' sugar, ⅛ teaspoon of salt, and 2 jiggers of Jamaica rum. Continue to add confectioners' sugar until the consistency is right for spreading — usually ½ pound more.

5 squares bitter chocolate	*⅛ teaspoon salt*
¼ pound butter	*2 jiggers Jamaica rum*
1 pound confectioners'	*Confectioners' sugar as*
sugar	*needed*

NOTE: Another chocolate icing, this with brandy. Cream ¼ cup of butter with 2 cups of confectioners' sugar and ¼ cup of Ghirardelli's chocolate. Add 1 tablespoon of California brandy, and beat until fluffy.

Desserts

(Kay's Icing

This is the easiest, most wonderful chocolate icing ever spread on a cake. This quantity will cover the top of a 10-inch layer cake; the top and sides of an 8-inch one.

Melt 1 7-ounce package of semisweet chocolate pieces, add a tiny speck of salt, and ½ cup of thick sour cream. Mix well and spread on cake. This consistency will allow fancy swirls that will stay, for this icing neither runs nor hardens. When slightly cooled it may be used with a pastry tube.

1 7-ounce package semisweet   Speck of salt
    chocolate pieces   ½ cup thick sour cream

(Soused Camembert with Almonds

California cheese, California white wine, and California almonds combine to make this superlative dessert.

Soak a whole ripe Camembert overnight in white wine to cover. Drain, scrape off discolored portion (but not all the crust), and mix the cheese with ¼ pound of butter. Work well until perfectly smooth. Now chill for easier handling, and form into the original shape of the cheese. Cover top, bottom, and sides with finely chopped toasted almonds. Chill again, but remove from refrigerator about a half hour before serving. Hot toasted crackers should accompany this dish. SERVES 8 TO 10.

1 whole Camembert cheese
White wine to cover
¼ pound butter
Finely chopped toasted almonds

(Crêpes or Thin Pancakes

If you can't flip a pancake while standing firmly in front of your stove, you'll probably be impressed with the story, told by Sarah Bixby Smith in *Adobe Days*, of a tightrope walker who flipped flapjacks as he teetered over Main Street, in the Los Angeles of the '70s. Today we like a thinner and more delicate

61

version of the time-honored pancake, and we cook them in a more conventional manner.

We use a standard recipe for crêpes and vary them in the following ways:

1. Fill with apricot jam spiked with rum. Roll and serve warm with cold sour cream.

2. Add ¼ cup of *finely* grated nuts to the batter, and serve with any jam.

3. Fill with strawberry butter (page 75) or crushed sweetened strawberries, and serve with sour or whipped cream.

4. Spread with orange marmalade, roll, brush with butter, sprinkle with chopped nuts, and put under a broiler for a few seconds. Serve with rum sauce.

5. Heat rolled pancakes in orange butter: mix ¼ pound of butter with ½ cup of confectioners' sugar, grated rind and juice of an orange, and 2 tablespoons of California brandy. Pour on more brandy, heat, and light just before serving.

6. Mix chopped walnuts with sweetened whipped cream and spread on pancakes. Roll, sprinkle with confectioners' sugar, and serve.

7. Roll a small broiled pork sausage in each pancake, and serve with fried or poached apples — this for breakfast.

8. Spread pancakes with any minced meat, poultry, or seafood, moistened with gravy or cream sauce. Roll, arrange on a baking dish, pour over a thin cream sauce, sprinkle with cheese, and put under the broiler to brown — this for an entree.

9. Cover with sliced strawberries, slightly sweetened, roll, and serve with crisp bacon for breakfast.

(*Cherry City Shortcake*

It's made of cherries, naturally.

Pit the cherries and sugar them to taste, allowing them to stand in a warmish place for a few hours. Make a rich shortcake dough (see Washington State Blackberry Roll, page 58), roll about ⅓-inch thick, and cut in 2 large circles (or press into a piepan). Spread one circle with softened butter and put other circle on top. Bake at 400° until brown. Split, fill with half the sugared cherries (and more butter, if needed), and top with the remaining fruit. Serve with cream cheese that has been beaten until soft and fluffy with cream.

(*Oregon Torte*

This stars two of Oregon's best — cherries and filberts.

Cream a cup of butter with a cup of sugar, add 3 egg yolks, ¼ teaspoon of almond extract, a cup of grated filberts, 1¼ cups of flour, and ¼ teaspoon of salt. Mix well and chill, then roll ½-inch thick. Line a small piepan, bringing the paste up on the sides. Spread with cherry jam, and cover with a lattice made from the remaining paste. Put half a filbert in each square, and bake at 375° until the crust is brown. SERVES 6 TO 8.

1 cup butter	*1 cup grated filberts*
1 cup sugar	*1¼ cups flour*
3 egg yolks	*¼ teaspoon salt*
¼ teaspoon almond extract	*Cherry jam*
	Filbert halves	

(*Cranberry Sherbet*

With Oregon growing cranberries like crazy, we are naturally using them the same way. This sherbet is good served with the meat course, or as a dessert. Try it with roast pork.

Cook 2 cups of cranberries in 1½ cups of water until tender. Rub through a sieve, add a teaspoon of gelatin that has been soaked in 2 tablespoons of cold water, 2 tablespoons of lemon juice, 1¼ cups of sugar, and a cup of orange juice. Pour in a freezing tray, and when partially frozen beat with an egg beater, and fold in two egg whites, beaten stiff. Return to freezing compartment to complete freezing. SERVES 6 TO 8.

2 cups cranberries	*2 tablespoons lemon juice*
1½ cups water	*1¼ cups sugar*
1 teaspoon gelatin	*1 cup orange juice*
2 tablespoons water	*2 egg whites*

❲ Billy Goats

These little date cakes show up in early books from all three Western states, though how and why they got their name is a mystery I have been unable to solve.

Cream ¼ pound of butter with a cup of sugar. Add 2 eggs, beat well, then mix with ½ cup of sour cream, ½ teaspoon of soda, 2 teaspoons of baking powder, 2 cups of flour, a teaspoon of allspice, a cup of chopped walnuts, and a pound of pitted dates, cut in pieces with scissors. Drop by the spoonful on a buttered cookie sheet. Bake at 350° until browned. MAKES 3 DOZEN.

¼ pound butter	2 teaspoons baking powder
1 cup sugar	2 cups flour
2 eggs	1 teaspoon allspice
½ cup sour cream	1 cup chopped walnuts
½ teaspoon soda	1 pound pitted dates

❲ Sour Cream Date Pie

Mix 1 cup of cut-up dates with a beaten egg, 1 cup of sour cream, ¾ of a cup of brown sugar, ½ cup of chopped walnuts, a tablespoon of brandy, ⅛ teaspoon of salt, and ½ teaspoon of nutmeg. Beat until smooth, put in an unbaked pie shell, cover with crisscross strips of pastry, bake at 425° for 10 minutes, then reduce heat to 325°, and cook until the filling is set. This is very rich. SERVES 6 TO 8.

1 cup cut-up dates	½ cup chopped walnuts
1 egg	1 tablespoon brandy
1 cup sour cream	⅛ teaspoon salt
¾ cup brown sugar	½ teaspoon nutmeg

❲ Figs Fresno

Fresh figs are one of our choicest fruits of summer. This dessert is a simple way to use them.

Peel ripe figs and cut them in quarters. Put a spoonful of

Desserts

vanilla ice cream in a sherbet glass, add four or five pieces of fig, sprinkle with rum, and top with whipped cream.

Ripe figs   Rum
Vanilla ice cream   Whipped cream

(Filbert Macaroons

Oregon filberts are becoming as famous as California's almonds and walnuts, and macaroons made from them are delectable.

Put ½ pound of filberts in a medium oven to toast for about 20 minutes, then rub off the brown skins. Grind, using the finest knife, then crush with 1 pound of sugar, using a mortar and pestle or a heavy bowl and a strong wooden spoon. Work in 4 or 5 egg whites, enough to get the mixture soft, but heavy enough to retain its shape when pulled into a peak. Add a pinch of salt, and work and beat some more. Butter a cookie sheet, dust with cornstarch, and shape macaroon mix, using a pastry bag and star tube. Let stand for 10 minutes, then bake at 300° for 30 minutes. MAKES 5 OR 6 DOZEN.

½ pound filberts   4 or 5 egg whites
1 pound sugar   Pinch of salt

(Salem Filbert or Almond Torte

Separate 8 eggs and beat the yolks light with 1 cup of sugar. Add a pound of grated unblanched almonds or filberts. (You'll need a nut grater for this task.) Beat the whites with ¼ teaspoon of cream of tartar, ⅛ teaspoon of salt, ½ teaspoon of almond extract. Fold the whites into the nut mixture. Bake 1 hour at 300°. (Cook in 2 ten-inch layers.) Cool, split each layer, spread with apricot preserves spiked with Jamaica rum to taste. Ice with Kay's icing (page 61). SERVES 8 TO 12.

8 eggs   ⅛ teaspoon salt
1 cup sugar   ½ teaspoon almond extract
1 pound almonds or filberts   Apricot preserves
¼ teaspoon cream of tartar   Jamaica rum
Icing

⟨ Fried Cream

Gourmets who visit San Francisco enthuse about this dessert, which is to be found at a few of the best hotels and restaurants. It's not often served at home, apparently because most cooks don't dare risk it, but it's really very simple to make. It turns up in a San Diego cook book, under the name of "Bonfire Entré." It was called that because the fried cream was cut in sticklike pieces and stacked up on individual plates like miniature and roofless log cabins. A couple of lumps of sugar, brandy-soaked, went into the center of each pile of "logs," and matches graced the side of each plate. The lights were lowered, and everyone lit up. Whoopee!

Scald a pint of heavy cream and add to it 2 teaspoons of Jamaica rum, ⅛ teaspoon of salt, ¼ cup of sugar, a ½-inch stick of cinnamon, and 5 tablespoons of cornstarch moistened in 3 tablespoons of milk. Cook long enough to remove the starch taste, then beat in 3 egg yolks and cook over hot water, whisking continuously, until thick. Remove cinnamon and pour mixture, about ¾ of an inch deep, into a flat dish (an oblong Pyrex dish is perfect) to become cold. Turn out on a board, cut into squares or oblongs, and roll in very finely grated almonds. Now dip in beaten egg, and then in finely crushed salted crackers. Chill again, then fry in deep fat at 390° just long enough to brown the nuts. Pour on heated rum, set afire, and serve flaming. THIS RECIPE SERVES 8.

1 pint heavy cream	5 tablespoons cornstarch
2 teaspoons Jamaica rum	3 tablespoons milk
⅛ teaspoon salt	3 egg yolks
¼ cup sugar	Grated almonds
½-inch stick of cinnamon	Beaten egg
Cracker crumbs	

⟨ Guava Shells with Cream Cheese

Many Californians have guava trees in their gardens, and no wonder. They are beautifully ornamental and provide fruit enough for innumerable glasses of jelly and jars of preserved shells.

Remove the stems and blossom ends from guavas without cutting into the skins. Cut the fruit across the middle, and scoop out the seeds. For every pound of guava shells, make a syrup with 1½ cups of sugar, a tablespoon of lemon juice, and ¾ of a cup of water. Cook the shells very gently in this syrup until they have acquired a glorious soft rosy color and a semitransparency. They should be tender but not cooked long enough for the shells to become mushy. (These may be packed, while hot, in sterilized jars, and sealed for future use.) When the shells are cold, drain them, and fill each cup with softened cream cheese. Arrange on a platter and sprinkle with slivered toasted almonds, then drizzle the syrup over and around them. Serve with a very plain cracker, like a butter thin or an English water biscuit. Californians who are lacking guava trees and patriotism may buy canned guava shells from Cuba.

For each 1 pound guava shells

1½ *cups sugar*   ¾ *cup water*
1 *tablespoon lemon juice*   *Cream cheese*
Toasted almonds

❲ *Ice Cream Notes*

Back in the '70s, in Los Angeles, there was a Mexican named Nicholas Martinez, who was the forerunner of the Good Humor man. Mrs. Sarah Bixby Smith, in *Adobe Days,* says that he went about town with a "freezer on his head, and in his hand a circular tin carrier, with a place for spoons in the middle and holes for six tumblers in which he served his wares." And just as today, "there was a great scurrying for nickels among the children when his cry was heard." As the first ice was brought to Los Angeles in 1868, all the way from the Truckee River, ice cream must have been a real novelty then. Today it is probably our most frequently served dessert.

In Seattle there are several dessert specialties that one doesn't find elsewhere. One, Frango, is a soft, rich ice cream, served at that town's famous department store, Frederick &

Nelson. It is a private recipe, but a close approximation of it is, for the strawberry Frango, to fold sliced and sugared strawberries into very soft rich vanilla ice cream. Another Seattle favorite is fried pies — little fruit turnovers, fried in deep fat, and served with soft ice cream. (They like their ice cream soft in Seattle.) Still another Seattle favorite is a Dutch Baby (page 34).

Lalla Rookh. This was originally a frozen rum punch, and was served, along with Roman punch, at many early California banquets. Now it has become a dessert — easy to prepare, yet one that could well be served at party time. Simply pour Jamaica rum, rather generously, over rich vanilla ice cream.

Gingered ice cream is another exotic dessert that is no trouble to make. Chop preserved ginger, and ladle it, along with some of the syrup, over vanilla ice cream.

Roman punch, which appeared on many of the hotel menus of the '70s, '80s, and '90s, was served usually just after the roast or the game, and was rather like Lalla Rookh. Lemon ice, in sherbet glasses, had Jamaica rum spooned over it just before serving.

❲ *Lemon Cake-Top Pudding*

This recipe came from the Sunkist Kitchens, and who should know lemons better than they.

Cream 1 tablespoon of butter with 2 tablespoons of flour. Add ¾ of a cup of sugar, 2 well-beaten egg yolks, ¼ cup of lemon juice, and a cup of milk. Fold in the stiffly beaten whites of the 2 eggs, and bake in an unbuttered pudding dish or in custard cups set in a pan of water. Set the oven at 360° and cook 35 minutes. This pudding is like cake on top and custard beneath. It may be baked in a pie shell which has been partially cooked (5 minutes). SERVES 4.

1 tablespoon butter	*2 eggs*
2 tablespoons flour	*¼ cup lemon juice*
¾ cup sugar	*1 cup milk*

Desserts

◖ Lemon Butter Tarts

Lemon butter, or lemon cheese, as it was sometimes called, is too good to stay buried in early receipt books. Scorning cornstarch, its thickening comes from eggs, its richness from butter, its flavor from lemon. It may be used as a cake filling, to spread on tea toast, or, as here, as a filling for tarts.

Melt ¼ pound of butter, add the grated rind of 1 and the juice of 3 large lemons, ¼ teaspoon of salt, and 1½ cups of sugar. Cook over hot water with the yolks of 3 eggs and 3 whole eggs beaten together, whisking constantly, until the mixture is shiny and thick. Cool. This may be kept in the refrigerator for days on end. Make small tart shells and fill with the lemon butter, topping with sour cream. Good. THIS FILLING IS ENOUGH FOR 12 TARTS.

¼ pound butter	¼ teaspoon salt
Grated rind of 1 lemon	1½ cups sugar
Juice of 3 lemons	3 egg yolks
3 whole eggs	

◖ Los Angeles Lemon Pie

There's a myth about that lemon pie is California's favorite dessert. True, we eat a lot of them and have numerous recipes for them, some excellent, some not so excellent. This one is extravagant, but worth every egg that goes into it.

Beat the yolks of 8 eggs well, add ¾ of a cup of sugar, the juice of 3 lemons, and a teaspoon of grated rind. Cook until thick. Cool slightly, fold in the stiffly beaten whites of the 8 eggs, and pour into a baked 9-inch pastry shell. Wrap pie tape around the edge of the shell to keep it from becoming too brown. Bake at 350° until the filling has set. Cool and dust the top lightly with powdered sugar, or sprinkle with grated almonds. Or, if you want to get fancy, decorate with halves of blanched almonds and bits of glacéed fruit. SERVES 8.

8 eggs	Juice of 3 lemons
¾ cup sugar	1 teaspoon grated lemon rind

⟮ Fresh Lime Pie

This gets high praise from the male contingent.

Beat 5 egg yolks thick, add ½ cup of lime juice, ⅛ teaspoon of salt, ½ teaspoon of grated rind of lime, and a cup of sugar. Cook until thick, cool, pour in a baked pie shell, top with meringue made from three of the egg whites and six tablespoons of sugar, and bake till brown. SERVES 6 TO 8.

FILLING

5 egg yolks	⅛ teaspoon salt
½ cup lime juice	½ teaspoon grated lime rind
	1 cup sugar

MERINGUE

3 egg whites
6 tablespoons sugar

NOTE: *Marmelada Pie.* This is a slight variation on the fresh lime pie. When the lime juice and egg yolk mixture is thick, add 2 teaspoons of plain gelatin that has been melted in 3 tablespoons of water over hot water. Cool, fold in half the egg whites, beaten stiff, pour into a baked pie shell and allow to set. Spread with a layer of lime marmalade and garnish the top with dollops of sweetened whipped cream. Rich, this.

⟮ Alison's Orange Caramel Custard
(Pudin de Naranjas)

Caramelize ½ cup of sugar in a heavy pan. Pour it into a round Pyrex casserole, or one of similar shape, and tip so that the bottom and sides will be glazed. Cream 2 tablespoons of butter with ¾ of a cup of sugar. Add ¼ cup of flour, mix well, add well-beaten yolks of 6 eggs, and 1¼ cups of orange juice. Fold in 6 stiffly beaten egg whites. Pour into the casserole and bake in a 350° oven, setting the casserole in a pan of hot water. After one hour, turn out onto a serving dish, so that the caramel glaze is on top, like a crème renversée. Serve hot and, if you wish, flaming with brandy or rum. SERVES 6 TO 8.

GLAZE

½ cup sugar

PUDDING

2 tablespoons butter	*¼ cup flour*
¾ cup sugar	*6 eggs*
1¼ cups orange juice	

❰ Baked Orange Custard

Mix 1 cup of thick cream, heated, with 3 slightly beaten eggs, a cup of orange juice, 1½ teaspoons of grated orange rind, ¼ cup of sugar, and ⅛ teaspoon of salt. Pour in custard cups, place in a pan of warm water, and bake at 325° until firm. SERVES 5 OR 6.

1 cup thick cream	*1½ teaspoons grated orange*
3 eggs	*rind*
1 cup orange juice	*¼ cup sugar*
⅛ teaspoon salt	

❰ Almond Stuffed Peaches

This dessert has an Italian air about it.

Peel the skins from 6 or 8 freestone peaches, and cut in halves. Remove pits and enlarge cavities somewhat. Mix 1 cup of ground almonds with ½ cup of butter and ½ cup of sugar, and fill the peaches, putting two halves together and fastening with a toothpick or two. Bake in a moderate oven, basting with sherry or marsala. Serve warm or cold. SERVES 6 OR 8.

6 or 8 peaches	*½ cup butter*
1 cup ground almonds	*½ cup sugar*
Sherry or marsala	

❨ San Dimas Orange Marmalade Soufflé

This is a soufflé that can wait and wait, so cooks adore it. So do guests.

Allow 1 egg for each guest. For 6, beat 6 egg whites stiff, fold in ⅓ cup of sugar and ⅓ cup of bitter marmalade. Grease the top of a double boiler and pour in the pudding. Steam for one hour. If dinner is delayed, don't remove the cover, but let the soufflé stand over the hot water until needed. The rum sauce is made by beating 4 egg yolks with 2 tablespoons of sugar, and adding to 1½ cups of milk. Cook in a double boiler until thick, and flavor to taste with Jamaica rum. SERVES 6.

SOUFFLÉ

6 egg whites	⅓ cup bitter mar-
⅓ cup sugar	malade

RUM SAUCE

4 egg yolks	1½ cups milk
2 tablespoons sugar	Jamaica rum to taste

❨ Pears Pacifica

Comice or D'Anjou pears, for which Oregon is now famous, make an easy and impressive dessert.

Peel ripe Oregon pears, cut in halves and remove cores. Arrange, cut side up, in a baking dish, and in each cavity put 1 teaspoon of lime juice, 1 teaspoon of California honey, and 1 tablespoon of rum. Bake slowly for an hour, basting with a mixture of 1 part each of the 3 ingredients, and 1 of water. Turn pears over towards the end, sprinkle with chopped almonds, and slip under the broiler to brown. Serve warm with cold sour cream.

For each ½ pear

1 teaspoon lime juice	1 tablespoon rum
1 teaspoon honey	Chopped almonds

Desserts

BASTING MIXTURE

1 *part lime juice*	1 *part rum*
1 *part honey*	1 *part water*

NOTE: A combination of orange juice, sugar, and white wine is also a good baste for baked pears.

❨ Placerito Persimmon Pie

Only a persimmon lover could go for this, and they do!

Mix the pulp of very ripe persimmons with an equal part of whipped cream. Season to taste with lemon juice, sugar, and a little salt, and serve in a baked pastry shell.

1 *part ripe persimmon pulp*	*Lemon juice*
1 *part whipped cream*	*Sugar*
Salt	

❨ Persimmon Pudding

This is one of those dishes that can't be "taken or left alone." You either like it or you don't. It is regional, however, and persimmons are very plentiful out here in the fall, and, as everyone knows, to waste is a sin.

Cream ¼ cup of butter with a cup of sugar. Add 2 well-beaten eggs, 1½ cups of the pulp of very ripe persimmons, 2 cups of flour, 2 teaspoons of baking powder, a teaspoon of salt, a teaspoon of coriander, ½ cup of white seedless raisins soaked in ¼ cup of brandy, and a cup of chopped walnuts. Mix well, and bake in buttered custard cups at 350° for about 25 minutes, or until done. Serve with hard sauce. I am not convinced that the pudding wouldn't be just as good without the persimmons. SERVES 6 TO 60.

¼ *cup butter*	2 *teaspoons baking powder*
1 *cup sugar*	1 *teaspoon salt*
2 *eggs*	1 *teaspoon coriander*
1½ *cups persimmon pulp*	½ *cup white seedless raisins*
2 *cups flour*	¼ *cup brandy*
1 *cup chopped walnuts*	

73

(Oriental Seed Cookies

A dainty little cookie that is just right with tea, or with frozen desserts.

Cream together ½ cup of butter and ⅓ cup of sugar. Add an egg, ¾ of a cup of flour, a teaspoon of vanilla, and ⅛ teaspoon of salt. Drop from the tip of a teaspoon onto a well-buttered cookie sheet, then flatten each cookie with a spatula dipped in cold water. Sprinkle quite thickly with sesame seeds, and bake at 350° until browned around the edges. Remove from the pan while still warm. MAKES APPROXIMATELY 2½ DOZEN.

½ cup butter	¾ cup flour
⅓ cup sugar	1 teaspoon vanilla
1 egg	⅛ teaspoon salt
Sesame seeds	

(Brandied Squash Pie

Sugar and squash were featured together in an early Territorial incident. Sacajawea, the Indian girl who was so valuable to Lewis and Clark, met her long-lost brother, Cameahwait, in the Northwest, and as a sign of great love gave him a gift of sugar and squash. He, history says, was impressed with the sugar if not with the squash. Here the two are combined in a dessert impressive enough for the mightiest chieftain. The early settlers, by the way, didn't always have squash or pumpkin for their autumn (Thanksgiving) pies, but they found that the Indians' favorite camas root made a very satisfactory substitute.

Mix together a cup of cooked strained squash or pumpkin, a cup of heavy cream, scalded, a cup of brown sugar, 3 slightly beaten eggs, ¼ cup of brandy, a teaspoon each of cinnamon and nutmeg, ½ teaspoon each of ginger and mace, and ¾ of a teaspoon of salt. Pour into a large piepan lined with rich pastry, and bake at 450° for 10 minutes, then reduce heat to

325° and bake until firm. Serve garnished with whipped or sour cream. MAKES 1 LARGE PIE.

1 cup cooked squash or pumpkin	¼ cup brandy
1 cup heavy cream	1 teaspoon cinnamon
1 cup brown sugar	1 teaspoon nutmeg
3 eggs	½ teaspoon ginger
	½ teaspoon mace
¾ teaspoon salt	

❨ *Strawberries Romanoff*

Anything that the Palace Hotel, in San Francisco, chooses to feature is bound to become popular on the West Coast. This is their recipe.

For each person mix ½ ounce of maraschino, ½ ounce of brandy, and a dash of anisette into a serving of rich vanilla ice cream. (This will soften the ice cream considerably.) Pour this over selected strawberries and serve.

½ ounce maraschino	Dash of anisette
½ ounce brandy	Vanilla ice cream
Strawberries	

NOTE: Another way — put a quart of hulled ripe berries in a glass bowl and sprinkle with sugar. Whip a cup of cream, fold it into ½ pint of vanilla ice cream, flavor with 3 ounces each of rum and cointreau, and pour over the berries.

❨ *Strawberry-Almond Butter*

This must have come to us by way of England, but we have taken it as ours. We serve it with waffles, with crêpes, or just with toast, for breakfast or tea.

Cream ½ pound of butter with a pound of confectioners' sugar, then work in a pound of hulled strawberries that have been forced through a colander. When well mixed, stir in ½ cup of very finely ground almonds, and ⅛ teaspoon of salt.

½ pound butter	½ cup very finely ground almonds
1 pound confectioners' sugar	
1 pound strawberries	⅛ teaspoon salt

❲ Strawberry-Almond Fritters

Washington strawberries, Oregon apricots, and California almonds combine to make this sensational dessert. The berries do not cook, but warm just enough to bring out the full flavor of a sun-bathed berry.

Select very large and perfect strawberries, wash them, then remove hulls and dry thoroughly on paper toweling. Now force a cup of apricot jam through a coarse strainer, chop a cup of toasted almonds fine, and roll salted crackers until you have a cupful. Also beat 2 eggs slightly. Now, working quickly, dip each berry in the jam and then roll in the almonds. When all are thus coated, dip, two at a time, in egg, and then in crumbs. Put in the refrigerator to chill. Just before serving time, heat deep fat to 360° and cook the fritters until they are golden brown. Serve at once, passing powdered sugar for those who wish it.

> *Strawberries*   *1 cup toasted almonds*
> *1 cup apricot jam*   *1 cup cracker crumbs*
> *2 eggs*

NOTE: For a variation on these fabulous fritters, add a tablespoon of rum to the apricot jam.

NOTE: Peach fritters may be done in exactly the same way, using peaches cut in eighths instead of berries.

❲ Walnut and Orange Torte

Beat yolks of 6 eggs light with ¾ of a cup of sugar. Add ¼ cup of grated raw apple, a tablespoon of lemon juice, a tablespoon of California brandy, the grated rind of ½ an orange, ¼ cup of sifted dry bread crumbs, 1½ cups of finely grated walnuts, and ¼ teaspoon of salt. Add the 6 egg whites, stiffly beaten. Pour into a large spring mold which has been buttered and sprinkled with dry crumbs. Bake 30 minutes at 325°, then turn off heat and allow to cool in the oven for 15 minutes

76

longer. Cover with whipped cream or Kay's icing (page 61).
SERVES 8 TO 10.

6 eggs
¾ cup sugar
¼ cup grated raw apple
1 tablespoon lemon juice
1 tablespoon brandy

Grated rind of ½ orange
¼ cup sifted dry bread
    crumbs
1½ cups finely grated walnuts
¼ teaspoon salt

(San Gabriel Wine Gelatin

This is an old-fashioned recipe that should not be forgotten —
it's a light and refreshing finale for any meal.

Soak 2 envelopes (tablespoons) of plain gelatin in ½ cup
of cold water, and dissolve in ¾ of a cup of boiling water. Add
¼ cup of lemon juice, a cup of sugar, a cup of orange juice,
and a cup of sherry or port. Pour in your prettiest mold to set,
and serve with or without cream, or with fresh fruits. Half
wine and half water may be substituted for the orange juice,
if desired. SERVES 8.

2 envelopes gelatin
½ cup cold water
¾ cup boiling water
1 cup sherry or port

¼ cup lemon juice
1 cup sugar
1 cup orange juice

Eggs

EGGS, AT LEAST AFTER the first very hard years of the earliest pioneers, were apparently taken for granted by the cooks of all three Western states. At least, they seemed to use them lavishly. But that was before the Gold Rush: there are scores of yarns about the high prices paid for them in those days of plenty and of want. Hungry miners, their pockets crammed with gold, would gladly have purchased one fresh egg for its weight in that yellow stuff. There is the story of eggs, which three weeks before sold for 30 cents a dozen, skyrocketing to a dollar apiece. There is a story of an even quicker rise — of a grocer unaware of the sudden demand for eggs, who quoted a price of $6.00 to an inquiring customer, meaning a case, and who was stunned when the purchaser assumed that it was for a dozen and bought them happily at that price. The grocer caught on quickly, however, and didn't bat an eye when he told the next person who entered his store that they were $18.00 a dozen, though it must have been a bit of a shock when that gent bought two dozen! There is a story of a schooner load of 15,000 dozen eggs that were sold for 37½ cents a dozen, and of how the original owner quickly bought them all back at $4.50 a dozen when he found they were now selling at that price on the street corners. He carted them to Sacramento and got $6.00 a dozen for them without effort. There is the story of one sharp operator who noted that the Farallones (a group of tiny islands off the Golden Gate) were so thick with birds that the

*rocks of which the islands are composed were often ob-
scured. That where there were birds there were eggs, he
figured rightly, so he started in business. For several years
thereafter as many as 25,000 dozen bird's eggs a season
were sold around San Francisco at from 35 to 50 cents a
dozen. Then things settled down to normal and eggs were
so common that, except in rare instances, they weren't
even mentioned in the cook books except as an ingredient
of cakes or puddings.*

*A Mexican fiesta is a gay affair, and one of its gayest
features is a basket of* cascarones — *eggshells brightly
colored and filled with confetti. These are broken over the
heads of favored ones, and the compliment has to be returned. For weeks before such a party, cooks are careful
in the breaking of their eggs, chipping a small piece from
the ends in order to keep them as perfect as possible. The
shells are washed and dried and painted in bright colors,
then filled with brilliant confetti. Small pieces of colored
paper are glued over the holes. Sometimes the* cascarones
*have faces painted on them and hair made of paper, but
usually they are just adorned with stripes, swirls, or polka
dots. Sometimes, at very fancy parties, sequins are used
instead of confetti, and sometimes the eggs have perfume
or perfumed water in them. Time was, it is said, when gold
dust was used in place of the confetti!*

*Today egg production is a big industry on the West
Coast. Petaluma, on the Redwood Highway above San
Francisco, is known as the "Egg Basket of the World," and
though you may suspect that the title was bestowed by
the Chamber of Commerce, you can't deny that we do
raise chickens there. The air is loud with proud cacklings,
and white with feathers.*

⟨ Eggs Astoria

Smoked salmon is one of the specialties up Oregon way, and has been ever since the Indians showed us how to do it. Although used mostly as an appetizer, or with the smörgåsbord, it should also have a definite place on both the breakfast and the lunch table. This dish is remarkably simple.

A piece of buttered toast is covered with a slice of smoked salmon, topped with a poached egg, and the whole masked with a cream sauce lightly perfumed with anchovy. (2 tablespoons of flour, 2 of butter, 1⅓ cups of rich milk, 1 teaspoon of anchovy paste.) Asparagus is just right with this when it is served as a lunch dish.

⟨ Chinese Egg Rolls

This is one of those delectable dishes that appear at Chinese banquets. (We also like them cut in sections and served with before-dinner drinks.) The outside of the rolls is like a very thin pancake, though they are thrice cooked, and crisp.

Make a batter by beating a large egg, adding 1 cup of lukewarm water, ¼ cup of cornstarch, 1 cup plus 2 tablespoons of flour, ½ teaspoon of salt and ½ teaspoon each of almond extract and sugar. Beat smooth. Heat a 6- or 7-inch frying pan, grease lightly with oil and pour in about 2 tablespoons (or a little more) of batter, tipping and tilting the pan so that a thin layer will form over the bottom. Do this quickly. Cook lightly on one side, turn, and cook on the other. Continue until the batter, except for a spoonful or two, is used. THIS WILL MAKE 10 OR 12 THIN CAKES.

For the filling mix together 1 cup of finely chopped cooked chicken (or flaked canned tuna fish), ½ cup each of chopped bean sprouts, water chestnuts and bamboo shoots, ¼ cup each of minced green onions and minced green pepper, 1 tablespoon minced green (fresh) ginger, ¼ cup of ground almonds, 2 teaspoons of soy sauce, 1 teaspoon of sugar, and ½ teaspoon of almond extract. Now form a thumb-sized roll of the filling on one edge of a cake, and roll it up, tucking in the edges as you go. Seal with a little of the batter that has been saved. Cook in 2 inches of oil (360°) until very pale amber. Drain. This can all be done in the afternoon (or the morning!). Just before serving, reheat oil to 370° and cook rolls until nicely brown and tenderly crisp. Put rolls on serving dish, then cut each into four pieces, taking care not to disarrange. THIS IS SUFFICIENT FOR A MAIN DISH FOR 6, BUT AS A PART OF A CHINESE MEAL OR FOR APPETIZERS, IT WILL SUFFICE FOR 15 PERSONS.

BATTER

1 large egg
1 cup lukewarm water
¼ cup cornstarch
1 cup plus 2 tablespoons flour

½ teaspoon salt
½ teaspoon almond extract
½ teaspoon sugar

FILLING

1 cup chopped cooked chicken or
1 cup flaked tuna fish
½ cup chopped bean sprouts
½ cup chopped water chestnuts
½ cup chopped bamboo shoots

¼ cup minced green onions
¼ cup minced green pepper
1 tablespoon minced green ginger
¼ cup ground almonds
2 teaspoons soy sauce
1 teaspoon sugar
½ teaspoon almond extract

⟮ *Eggs Foo Yung*

This is a Chinese recipe that has had such an enthusiastic reception by the entire West Coast that we have almost forgotten its Oriental ancestry, though it is typical of the wonderful things that the Chinese do with food. We serve it for breakfast or as the main dish at lunch, and we also serve it as one of the dishes at a Chinese meal. There are many variations of this fine food, so I will give a basic recipe and a few of the different versions.

81

Combine ½ cup of chopped water chestnuts, ¼ cup of sliced green onions, ½ cup of chopped bamboo shoots, ½ cup of bean sprouts, and ½ cup of cut cooked shrimps. Cook these ingredients together for 2 minutes in 2 tablespoons of peanut oil (or other bland oil). Cool. Beat 6 eggs slightly, just enough to mix, season with salt or soy sauce, add the other ingredients, and drop by the ladleful (approximately ½ cup) onto a hot griddle or frying pan which has a good layer of hot oil. Turn as soon as they brown on one side and cook on the other. When the little egg cakes are a delicate brown on both sides, serve with a sauce made as follows: heat a cup of chicken stock, add a tablespoon of soy sauce and/or ½ teaspoon of M.S.G., and thicken with 4 teaspoons of cornstarch mixed with 2 tablespoons of cold water. Cook until transparent. Some cooks prefer to make foo yung all in one mass, like an omelet, and some add a little flour to keep the egg from being quite so runny. It is also good practice to use raw shrimps, cooking them first in the oil before adding the vegetables. SERVES 6 TO 8.

½ cup chopped water chestnuts	½ cup bean sprouts
¼ cup sliced green onions	½ cup cut cooked shrimps
½ cup chopped bamboo shoots	2 tablespoons peanut oil
	6 eggs
	Salt or soy sauce

SAUCE

1 cup chicken stock	4 teaspoons cornstarch
1 tablespoon soy sauce and/or	2 tablespoons cold water
½ teaspoon M.S.G.	

NOTE: It is not necessary to cook the vegetables first if the canned kind are used. The onions and the fresh bean sprouts will cook sufficiently with the eggs — at least for my taste.

NOTE: Nor is it necessary to use both bamboo shoots *and* water chestnuts. Actually the dish can be made without either. Sliced celery is often used for the crispness needed, as is green pepper. Mushrooms are also a frequent ingredient. An Occidental version could have celery, onions, mushrooms, green pepper, and a meat or fish of your choice.

NOTE: Lobster, chicken, crab, canned abalone, tongue, ham, pork, or almost any cooked meat or seafood may be used in an egg foo yung, and the other ingredients may be as variable as the contents of an Irish stew. That's one of the beauties of this celestial dish.

(Frittata

This is an Italian type of omelet that is popular here. Like a foo yung, it has innumerable variations, the only really required ingredients being the eggs and the olive oil — the latter for that flavor that cannot be acquired in any other way. This recipe is full of "or's" so that it is a fine way to use up small amounts of vegetables.

Heat 3 tablespoons of olive oil in a skillet, with or without a crushed clove of garlic. Add whatever vegetables are desired — sliced artichoke hearts or bottoms, sliced zucchini, perhaps spinach or string beans. (About 2 cups of any one, or a mixture of any or all.) Add a cup of diced tomato, too, and chopped or sliced onion if you wish, and/or sliced mushrooms. Add seasonings — salt and pepper, and perhaps oregano or basil. Cook and cover until the vegetables are just tender, then cool. Beat 8 eggs slightly, season them, and pour over the vegetables which are still in the skillet, allowing the egg to run down through to the bottom. Cook for a minute on top of the stove, then put in a 350° oven and cook until the eggs are set. Turn out on a hot platter and cut in wedge-shaped pieces. The frittata may be sprinkled with grated cheese before being put in the oven. SERVES 8.

3 tablespoons olive oil
1 clove garlic (optional)
2 cups vegetables
1 cup diced tomatoes
Onion and/or mushrooms (optional)
Salt and pepper
Oregano or basil (optional)
8 eggs

❲ Huevos con Queso

Which means, simply, eggs with cheese.

Arrange a thin slice of Monterey Jack cheese in each individual baking dish, and cover with 2 crisp slices of bacon. Break an egg on top of the bacon, sprinkle with minced chives or minced green onions and salt, and pour 2 tablespoons of hot cream over each egg. Bake at 350° until the eggs are set. (A variation: just add tiny cubes of diced cheese to scrambled eggs when cooking — about ⅓ cup to 6 eggs.)

FOR ONE SERVING

1 thin slice Monterey Jack cheese	Minced chives
2 slices bacon	Salt
1 egg	2 tablespoons cream

❲ Huevos Rancheros

"Eggs rancher's style," this means, and as each rancher had a different notion of how to cook an egg, there are innumerable ways of doing them. The Mexicans themselves, who ought to know, fry the eggs and pour the sauce over them, but this adaptation is a popular one with the rest of us:

Slice a large onion and a large green pepper, and crush a small clove of garlic. Cook them together with 3 tablespoons of olive oil or lard for about 3 minutes. Add a tablespoon of flour and a No. 2½ can of tomatoes. Blend well, then season to your taste with salt, pepper, and chili powder. (Cumin and oregano may be used, too.) Cook for about 5 minutes longer, remove garlic if you can find it, then pour into a shallow baking dish — one of Mexican earthenware seems to add to the flavor! The rest of the cooking is done in the oven. If you plan to serve the dish shortly, break whole eggs into the ruddy savory sauce (this amount of sauce is enough for 8 to 12 eggs), then slip a teaspoon under each egg, making a little depression so that the egg will slip down into the sauce. Put pitted ripe olives or cubes of Monterey Jack cheese, or both, into the interstices between the eggs, sprinkle with salt, and put into a 350° oven until the eggs are set. Serve with refried beans

Eggs

(page 365) and tortillas. The sauce may be made way ahead of serving time, but, if this is done, be sure to reheat it before adding the eggs. SERVES 8.

1 large onion
1 large green pep-
  per
1 clove garlic
3 tablespoons olive oil or
  lard
1 tablespoon flour

1 No. 2½ can tomatoes
Salt, pepper, chili pow-
  der
8–12 eggs
Pitted ripe olives and/or
  cubed Monterey Jack
  cheese

NOTE: *Tomatoes Kirkpatrick* is another dish made with tomatoes and eggs. Chef Arbogast, long in charge of the Palace Hotel kitchens, created it for Colonel Kirkpatrick, the hotel manager, who was said to breakfast on it almost daily. Made with ripe tomatoes, cooked until thick, it had egg yolks added for extra body.

❲ Olive Eggs

Crush a clove of garlic and heat in 2 tablespoons of olive oil. Discard garlic and add a 4½-ounce can of chopped ripe olives and ½ cup each of white wine and cream to the pan. Break 6 eggs into the mixture and cover, cooking slowly until the eggs are set. Lift each egg carefully onto a piece of toast or a toasted English muffin, and spoon the remaining sauce around the eggs. The olives should be sufficiently salty to make additional seasoning unnecessary. SERVES 6.

1 clove garlic
2 tablespoons olive oil
1 (4½ oz.) can minced ripe
  olives

½ cup white wine
½ cup cream
6 eggs

❲ Artichoke Omelet

There are two ways to make this omelet, each starting with the plain French omelet. The variation lies in the way the filling is prepared. In either case the artichokes are boiled

85

(page 357). For the first way the bottoms (or fonds) are cut into tiny dice and ½ cup of them added to a cup of cream sauce which has been seasoned lightly with dill. This is heated and used as the omelet filling. For the second way — assuming that the hearts are to play another gastronomical role — the pulp is scraped from the leaves until there is a cupful. This is seasoned with a teaspoon of lemon juice, some salt and pepper, and is then heated gently and thinned with cream until of the desired consistency. It is used as a sauce.

(California Omelet

This is really one of our best original egg dishes, one that is bound to become a world classic.

Peel 2 ripe but firm tomatoes, gently press out the juices and seeds, and cut the flesh into dice. Also peel and dice a firm but ripe avocado of medium size. Cut the meat from a dozen large ripe olives, or halve the same number of pitted ones. Heat a small clove of garlic, crushed, in 2 tablespoons of olive oil. Remove the garlic, add the olives and ½ cup of heavy cream, allow to heat, and meanwhile make a six-egg French-type omelet. Using your third hand, add the tomatoes and avocados to the cream just as the omelet is nearing completion. As soon as the vegetables are heated (no cooking, please!), pour part of the mixture on the omelet, which is just ready for folding, turn onto a hot platter, and pour the rest of the mixture around the gorgeous creation. Bacon curls, with this, and corn bread sticks. Happy breakfast! SERVES 3 OR 4.

> 2 ripe tomatoes   1 clove garlic
> 1 medium-sized avocado   2 tablespoons olive oil
> 12 ripe olives   ½ cup heavy cream
>   1 6-egg omelet

(Mexican Omelet

This recipe has had as many liberties taken with it as has that for Spanish omelet, so one more won't do any harm. I know quite well that Mexicans do a laborious lot of peeling and scraping of chili peppers, but I know quite as well that the rest of us won't bother. This recipe uses green chili sauce, instead.

Cook a large chopped onion in 3 tablespoons of lard, along with a crushed clove of garlic. Add a can, more or less, of green chili "salsa" (or sauce), and 2 cups of canned tomatoes. Season the sauce with salt, and pour a little on an omelet before folding — the rest around it on the platter. SERVES 3 OR 4.

1 large onion	2 cups canned tomatoes
3 tablespoons lard	Salt
1 clove garlic	1 6-egg omelet
1 can green chili salsa (or less)	

NOTE: The salsa is a Mexican sauce that comes canned and is available in Mexican markets as well as most grocery stores, at least in Southern California. Ortega Brand is a good one, and has the extra charm of bearing a name famed in California history. Add it gradually if you've never used it, for it's *hot*.

❨ *Pisto Omelet*

This is from an early Oregon cook book.

"Mince cold chicken or turkey with an equal amount of ham or tongue. Add chopped onion and a little sweet marjoram and cayenne pepper. Have enough well-beaten eggs to make an omelet. Stir very hard. Drop into hot lard, making small cakes." (Use 1 cup each of chicken or turkey and ham or tongue, for 8 or 10 stiffly beaten eggs. This is almost a fritter, and should be cooked in hot shortening about an inch deep. SERVES 8.)

1 cup minced cold chicken or turkey	Chopped onion
	Marjoram
1 cup minced cold ham or tongue	Cayenne
	8–10 eggs

(California Oyster Omelet

It was the Palace Hotel that really put the Californian oysters on the world map. It was here that Chef Arbogast served the omelet made from the tiny greenish coppery oysters that were the "natives" of the Bay area. The dish was so elegant, the flavor so unforgettable, that visitors carried its fame home with them, and newcomers rushed to the Palace to savor its charms. It was a specialty of the Ladies' Grill, but don't think that the gentlemen didn't bellow for it, too. The Californian oyster is a thing of the past, but Olympias make a worthy substitute.

Heat a cup of Olympia oysters in ¾ of a cup of rich thick cream sauce until they plump. (When I say cream sauce I mean made with cream.) The juices exuded from the oysters will thin the sauce to the proper consistency. Season with salt and pepper and a spot of sherry. Make a four-egg omelet of the French type, and pour half this mixture on before folding and turning onto a hot platter. Pour the remaining oysters around the omelet, and serve with green peas and a glass of Folle Blanche. Fly away rolls (page 40) with this. SERVES 2.

1 cup Olympia oysters	Salt and pepper
¾ cup rich cream sauce	1 tablespoon sherry
4 eggs	

CREAM SAUCE

2 tablespoons butter
2 tablespoons flour
¾ cup cream

(Browned Scrambled Eggs with Avocado

Cook ¼ cup of butter until it is nut brown, add 6 eggs, lightly beaten, a little salt and pepper, and ¼ cup of cream. Mix. Turn the heat very low, and as the eggs set at the bottom draw a spoon all the way across the bottom of the pan, so that there will be long "curds" of egg. Cook only until just set, with the mixture still having a shiny appearance. Serve on toast that has been topped with sliced ripe avocado, and garnish with crisp bacon. SERVES 4.

> ¼ cup butter   Salt and pepper
> 6 eggs   ¼ cup cream
> Sliced avocado

(*Tarragon Eggs with Lobster*

This is a lovely luncheon dish. Make creamed lobster by melting 2 tablespoons of butter, adding 2 tablespoons of flour, cooking 2 or 3 minutes, then pouring on 1½ cups of cream and cooking until thickened. Now add a cup of cooked lobster cut in dice, salt and pepper to taste, 2 tablespoons of sherry, and ½ teaspoon of tarragon seasoning powder. (This is marketed under the Spice Islands label, and is a combination of tarragon and monosodium glutamate. If unavailable, the tarragon flavor may be introduced by adding ½ teaspoon of fresh, or ¼ teaspoon of dry leaves to the sherry.) Divide this mixture, while hot, among 6 or 8 individual dishes, break an egg on top of each, put a good dollop of tarragon butter on each egg, and bake in a 350° oven until the eggs are set. The tarragon butter is made by creaming ½ cup of butter with 1 tablespoon of minced fresh tarragon. SERVES 6 OR 8.

> 2 tablespoons butter   Salt and pepper
> 2 tablespoons flour   2 tablespoons sherry
> 1½ cups cream   ½ teaspoon tarragon season-
> 1 cup diced cooked lobster   ing powder
> 6–8 eggs

TARRAGON BUTTER

> ½ cup butter
> 1 tablespoon minced fresh tarragon

Entrees

THIS SECTION *includes dishes which, for some reason or another, don't seem to belong under other chapter headings: chiefly dishes with cereals or legumes as the base. Curries, because they are invariably served with rice, are given here. So are sauces for the various Italian pastes.*

⟨ *Alvarado Bacon and Cheese Pie*

This is a Californian interpretation of Quiche Lorraine, and its variants are many. Mushrooms may be used instead of the ripe olives, ham instead of the bacon. Onions or green olives can pinch-hit for the shallots, and the cheese can be omitted. It may be made in miniature and served with cocktails, or in tart size for individual service. However it's done, it is delectable.

Make a rich pastry and line a 9-inch piepan with it, fluting the edges prettily. Brush the bottom with a little beaten egg. Bake at 450° until the crust is set, but remove it before it has begun to brown. Cook 12 slices of bacon until crisp (do this in the oven while the crust is cooking), drain, and crumble over the bottom of the pie shell. Cover with a cup of sliced ripe olives, and on top of them sprinkle a cup of grated Swiss or dry Monterey cheese. Scald a cup of heavy cream, add 2 slightly beaten eggs, ½ teaspoon of salt, and a grinding or two of pepper. Pour over the pie and bake at 350° until the mixture has set, like a custard. Serve hot or cold. This, with slightly

90

chilled vin rosé and a light salad, makes a heavenly lunch.
MAKES 1 LARGE PIE — SERVES 8.

12 slices bacon	2 eggs
1 cup sliced ripe olives	½ teaspoon salt
1 cup grated Swiss cheese	Pepper
1 cup heavy cream	Rich pastry

(*Cassoulet Carpinteria*

Inspired by the French, this dish may be made with white or
lima beans. It's a good casserole for a crowd, particularly when
the budget is poorly. There's nothing poor about the dish,
though. The wine, the pork, and the garlic unite in making
these as good beans as you've ever tasted.

Soak 2 pounds of dried white or lima beans overnight in
water to cover. Next day simmer with an herb bouquet and a
clove of garlic until almost tender. Fry 2 pounds of pork
sausage (either bulk or link) until brown, with 2 cups of
chopped onion and a finely minced clove of garlic. Use any
well-cooked meat — about two pounds of it: lamb or mutton
or beef, duck or rabbit or pork, ham or goose, or a mixture of
two or three. Arrange a layer of drained and salted beans in
a large casserole, then a layer of the cooked meat, cut in pieces
or sliced, then more beans, and then sausage. And so on to
the top. Now mix 3 cups of white wine with 1 cup of tomato
purée, and pour over the casserole. Top with a cup of dried
crumbs mixed with a cup of minced parsley and ½ cup of
butter in which a crushed clove of garlic has previously re-
posed. Bake at 350° until the beans are tender. SERVES 12 TO 18,
DEPENDING ON THE REST OF THE MENU.

2 pounds dried white or lima beans	2 pounds cooked meat
1 herb bouquet	3 cups white wine
3 cloves garlic	1 cup tomato purée
2 pounds pork sausage	1 cup dried crumbs
2 cups chopped onion	1 cup minced parsley
	½ cup butter

Salt

❲ Chili con Carne

By chili con carne, on the West Coast, we usually mean chili con carne *with beans,* though occasionally they are omitted. Chili beans, on the other hand, omits the meat. This is robust fare, and a favorite with men. Because the recipe is available in most cook books it is not included here.

NOTE: *Quick chili con carne* is made by browning hamburg and onion in shortening, seasoning with salt and chili powder, and adding canned kidney beans.

NOTE: A *size* is a hamburger covered with chili beans, which for some strange reason was once quite popular in California.

NOTE: *Turkey chili con carne* (actually chili con guajolote, I suppose) is a popular way of using the end of a holiday bird, and chili con carne made with venison is good, too.

❲ Chiles Rellenos

This means, of course, stuffed chili peppers, so they actually can be, and are, stuffed with anything. However, probably because it's everybody's favorite, chiles rellenos generally means cheese-stuffed peppers, or chiles rellenos con queso. These were popular in the early days, too, as is proved by the number of recipes for them in old cook books, though some of the good ladies were a bit confused by the Spanish. "Chili Renos," one recipe is called, and another "Chiles Reinos," and still another "Chilli Relleuve" — phonetic designations of the same dish, or inability to decipher someone's handwriting. Our residents not long from Mexico always use the fresh green chili peppers, but others use the canned ones because they are easier. For areas where neither is available, it is possible to use canned pimientos or bell peppers, though the flavor is not the same.

Peel green chilies and remove all seeds. (An easy way to do this is to hold over a gas flame until blistered or to cut off the tip and plunge the chilies into hot deep fat for a minute — any drippings will do — then take from the fat and cover with a thick folded cloth or paper, to cool and steam for a few minutes. The skins will then scrape off easily.) Split to remove seeds and cut out core. Cut Monterey Jack cheese in pieces about $2 \times \frac{1}{2} \times 1$ inches, and wrap with strips of the chili, or stuff the whole peppers with the cheese. For the batter — enough for 6 to 8 chilies: beat 4 egg yolks very stiff, add $\frac{1}{2}$ teaspoon of salt and $\frac{1}{4}$ cup of flour, then fold in 4 egg whites, beaten stiff. Now dip your chili-wrapped cheese in this batter, one piece at a time, and taking it up in a large spoon or ladle slide it into a skillet containing 2 inches of hot oil. Turn at once, then cook until the bottom is brown, and turn again to brown the top. (This makes it easier to keep the chilies from turning turtle.) When all are cooked and drained on paper, reheat them in Mexican sauce; this may be done hours after the initial cooking. Serve with refried beans and tortillas, with a Mexican salad, for a delicious meal. SERVES 6 OR 8.

6–8 green chili peppers	*4 eggs*
About ½ pound Monterey	*½ teaspoon salt*
Jack cheese	*¼ cup flour*
Mexican sauce	

NOTE: If the seeds are not completely removed, chilies will be too hot for Northern palates, and even the Mexicans will call them *muy bravo*.

NOTE: Mexican sandwich has very much the same flavor as chiles rellenos. Serve them with Mexican sauce for an interesting entree.

⟨ *Curry*

On the West Coast, when we say "curry" we mean as *we* like it, and that's in innumerable ways. Whether or not it's "genuine" makes little difference, as we know there are as many recipes for curry as there are for pies. The way we like least, we confess, is the way of our earliest cooks. The recipes they toted across the plains were pretty grim affairs — leftover meat "hotted" in curry-flavored gravy. We did better later. Recipes

came to us from seafaring men who had touched the shores
of the East Indies and India, as well as ours, and from Kanakas
who came to search for gold and remained to work for it. These
Kanakas, natives of Owyhee (for so we spelled Hawaii), always included coconut in their curry dishes, and they still do.
(The Islands were nearer to us than was New England, and
we had a flourishing trade with them. Thus it is not at all surprising to find old West Coast cook books mentioning fresh
coconut and pineapple as casually as apples.) Early recipes
for curry included such dubious ones as "curried pigs' feet,"
and "curried cabbage," though today we curry almost everything. Our favorites are chicken, lamb, and shrimp.

❮ West Coast Meat Curry

This is more of a procedure than it is a recipe, for we have far
too many ways with curry to go into them all. (For a number
of excellent curry recipes, I suggest *Far Eastern Cookery*, by
Elinor Burt.) This curry, a little hot, a little sweet, a little tart,
and a little salt, can be made hotter, sweeter, tarter, or saltier
by increasing the obvious ingredients. It can also be made with
just about anything. Chicken or lamb are usually first choice,
but beef, rabbit, mutton, liver, kidneys, veal, or any meat may
be used — and of course there are also fish curries (page 96)
and those of eggs.

Have a 4½-pound chicken or rabbit disjointed and cut in
serving pieces, or cut 3 pounds of any meat in fairly large
pieces. Dust plentifully with seasoned flour and brown in
⅓ cup of shortening. Remove to a pot, and in the skillet cook
2 cups of chopped onions and/or 2 finely minced cloves of
garlic, and a large apple, peeled and chopped. When the
vegetables are wilted, add them to the meat, along with the
juice of ½ lemon and a tablespoon of curry powder. (More
or less: there are curry powders *and* curry powders, and
these are fresh *and* stale, strong *and* weak. Your palate will
have to be your judge.) Add salt and pepper, and water, or
part water and part canned tomatoes, to cover, place lid on

94

pot, and simmer until done. Correct seasoning and, if necessary, bind the sauce with kneaded butter and flour. The *hot*
can be increased with more curry or with cayenne or tabasco;
the *sweet* (which here came from the onion) with sugar or
fruit jelly, or with raisins or chutney; the *tart* with more
lemon; and the *salt* in the obvious manner, or by the inclusion
of Bombay duck among the condiments. And still there are
variations. Some — in fact all who do it in the Hawaiian manner — use coconut milk or cream for part of the liquid. Some
add a ripe banana; some green peppers or celery or both. The
curry is always served with rice and with an assortment of
condiments. These condiments are as various as the recipes
for curry. A chutney is all but a must, and we sometimes have
two or three of them. Chopped nuts — almonds or peanuts or
cashews — are usual, and either sliced or grated coconut, or
toasted coconut chips. Fried onions or just raw ones, chopped,
crisp crumbled bacon, Bombay duck or, as a substitute, toasted
salt codfish crumbled, minced green peppers, chopped hard-
boiled egg, grated orange rind, raisins, sautéed or dried shrimps,
baked bananas, sometimes even sautéed cubes of pineapple
or halves of apricots. You see it's quite a mixture of the Hawaiian and the Indian, and the result is all ours. SERVES 6 OR 8.

1 4½-pound chicken or rabbit or 3 pounds meat	2 cloves garlic
	1 large apple
	Juice of ½ lemon
⅓ cup shortening	1 tablespoon curry powder
2 cups chopped onion	(or more)
	Salt and pepper

Water, or water and canned tomatoes, as needed

NOTE: *Fried Bananas,* or *Galloria,* as an old cook book called
them, are good with curry. Slice lengthwise and fry in olive
oil or butter.

NOTE: Wine is wasted with curry. Better serve beer, or cider,
or just plain water. For this reason I never can see why some
curry recipes *call* for wine as an ingredient. The chance of the
flavor of the wine coming through is infinitesimal.

95

⟮ West Coast Fish Curry

Here is a basic recipe for fish curry; with it we serve rice and the same condiments as for the meat curry.

Have 3 pounds of any firm white fish boned and skinned. Cover the trimmings with 3 cups of water and simmer slowly for 30 minutes. Strain and save liquid. Cut the fish in serving-sized pieces and dust lightly with seasoned flour, then brown in 2 tablespoons of butter. In another pan sauté ½ cup of chopped onion in 4 tablespoons of butter, along with a crushed clove of garlic and ½ cup of chopped apple. Remove garlic when the vegetables have wilted, and stir in 2 teaspoons of curry powder (more or less — depending on your curry powder and your taste). Also add 2 tablespoons of flour, the fish stock, 2 tablespoons of lemon juice, and salt and pepper to taste. Pour this over the fish, and cook very gently until the fish has lost its transparent look. This should be but a matter of minutes. SERVES 6 TO 8.

3 pounds fish	½ cup chopped apple
3 cups water	2 teaspoons curry powder
6 tablespoons butter	(more or less)
½ cup chopped onion	2 tablespoons flour
1 clove garlic	2 tablespoons lemon juice
Salt and pepper	

NOTE: *Curried Shellfish.* Make like meat curry, substituting cleaned shrimps, lobster or crab meat for the meat, and using fish stock. The lobster may be left in its shell, but cut in sections, in the Chinese manner.

NOTE: *Quick Curried Shrimps.* A chafing dish curry is made by cooking 1 pound of cleaned shrimps in ¼ cup of butter with a clove of garlic, then adding a tablespoon of butter, and curry and lemon juice to taste, 2 tablespoons of flour, and 1½ cups of chicken stock or tomato juice.

(*Blue Fox Gnocchi*

The Blue Fox Restaurant in San Francisco is one of the most popular Italian restaurants in California. This is their recipe for gnocchi, given exactly as the proprietors, Mario Mondin and Piero Fassio, wrote it for this book. Try it and you'll know why to eat at the Blue Fox is to eat supremely well.

"Every Thursday the small familylike Roman restaurants instead of serving ravioli or spaghetti serve gnocchi as the paste course. In fact all of Northern Italy considers this dish as a festive paste course to be served at family gatherings. Most people believe that this paste should only be served with butter and parmeggian cheese, but some like it served just as raviolis are, with a good meat gravy and cheese.

"Boil potatoes until cooked, skin them, put through a ricer on a large baking board, add butter, egg yolks and flour a little at a time, knead lightly as for making bread until mixture is pliable (secret is not to work dough too much). Flour board again, take a small piece of the dough at a time and roll into a sticklike effect; then cut in pieces the size of a half thumb, indent each piece with your finger to make a small indentation. Put each piece (or gnocchi) on a towel which has been floured so they will not stick together. When a large pot of salted water comes to boil put in gnocchi a few at a time; as soon as gnocchi come to the top (about 10 minutes) drain — lay on large platter with butter and parmeggian cheese." SERVES ABOUT 12.

4½ pounds large baking potatoes   *2 egg yolks*
   1 pound flour   *1 cube butter (¼ pound)*

NOTE: Another gnocchi, made with farina (1 cup to 4 cups water and 1 teaspoon of salt), is done by adding 1 cup of grated cheese to the hot mush, then pouring into a flat pan to harden. It is then cut in squares, arranged overlapping on a baking dish, painted lavishly with melted butter, sprinkled with grated cheese, and browned in the oven.

❰ Enchiladas

Everyone who likes Mexican food rates enchiladas high on the list. Their savory sauce and delectable filling are perfect foils for the corn flavor of the tortilla.

The sauce must be made first, and it is, incidentally, useful for other purposes. Sauté ½ cup of minced onion in 2 tablespoons of olive oil, along with a crushed clove of garlic. Remove garlic and discard, add 2 teaspoons of chili powder, a cup of tomato purée, and ½ cup of stock. Season with salt and cumin. Fry tortillas in plenty of fat, but not until crisp, dip quickly in the hot sauce, put a spoonful of chopped onion and grated Monterey Jack cheese (mixed in equal parts) on each tortilla, roll or fold them and pour a little more sauce on top, then sprinkle with more cheese, and heat in the oven. Serve garnished with lettuce and radishes. (For notes on Mexican food, see page 179.)

½ cup minced onion	1 cup tomato purée
1 clove garlic	½ cup stock
2 tablespoons olive oil	Salt and cumin
	Tortillas
2 teaspoons chili powder	Chopped onion
Grated Monterey Jack cheese	

NOTE: Sometimes the filling has chopped olives added to it, sometimes fried chorizo (page 265), or chopped cooked meat is used. Actually the variations are as great as a Mexican imagination. Tacos and enchiladas are sometimes confused, even by Mexicans.

❰ Tacos

A taco, the Mexican idea of a sandwich, is a rolled tortilla filled with meat — chicken, lamb, pork, beef, or mutton. It is a taste that has been acquired by most Far Westerners and, judging from the number of *touristas* munching them in Los Angeles's famed Mexican lane — Olvera Street — one quickly acquired by Easterners as well.

Dice chicken, lamb, pork, or other meat and mix with the sauce used with enchiladas (page 98), or any chili-flavored sauce. Spread mixture on tortillas, and roll or fold, fastening with toothpicks. Fry the filled tortillas until crisp, and eat as is, or pour more of the sauce over them. Garnish with lettuce, avocado, radishes, and ripe olives and serve with beans. Often the lettuce is rolled in the tortilla with the filling.

NOTE: *Another taco* is made by spreading the tortilla with diced avocado, minced onion, and sometimes fried beans, and folding and frying as above. Still another has chopped egg, chorizo, and onion as a filling; another beans and cheese, with or without chorizo.

⟨ *Tamales*

Tamales, or so the story goes, saved Cortez and his men from starvation. The Aztecs, finally realizing that the Spaniard was not a god, decided to treat him like an enemy and withhold food. But love stepped into the picture — love in the form of a beautiful Aztec maiden who, supposedly irate, had the handsome Spaniard pelted with tamales. . . . This is probably the best known of the Mexican dishes, and the one most generally available, either in cans or frozen. On the West Coast tamales are also usually found fresh, in meat and delicatessen shops. Back in the San Francisco of the '70s, there was a tamale man who peddled them on the streets, for even then few householders bothered to make their own. It is a tedious job, particularly if starting from scratch. Scratch, for tamales, means making masa (page 43).

The masa is spread on fresh, or dried and soaked, corn husks (available in Mexican grocery stores); on this is placed a spoonful of pork, beef, chicken, cheese, or whatever filling is desired, moistened with Mexican chili sauce, and a couple of ripe olives. (Pitted ripe olives are best as anyone who has bitten into the other kind will testify.) Sometimes a couple of raisins are added, then the husk is rolled around the filling. Another couple of husks spread with masa are rolled around this, the ends are tied securely, and the tamale is steamed for about an hour, and served hot in the husks. The tamales of the early Californians were big fat affairs. Today tiny ones, called cocktail tamales, are often made — for obvious occasions.

NOTE: Corn meal mush may be used instead of the masa, but it won't taste like the real thing. Furthermore, if corn husks are hard to get, a phony tamale may be made using parchment paper, but perhaps it had better be given another name. A Mexican might catch up with you and your "tamale." Some use cabbage leaves which have been wilted in hot water and the thick stems cut out.

NOTE: Sometimes sweet tamales are made by mixing sugar and candied fruits with the corn dough, or with a filling of sweetened rice. These are often flavored with anise, a favorite spice for Mexican desserts.

NOTE: Corn tamales are made without the masa, by mixing green corn with meat, ripe olives, and onions, well seasoned and wrapped in the corn husks. These are seldom served today, but are well worth reviving.

(Tamale Pie

Tamale pie is disowned by many Mexicans, though there are recipes for it in some of their cook books. There are, in fact, recipes for it in far too many cook books, so those who like it — and many apparently do — should have no trouble in learning how to make it.

(Tostados

A tostado may mean, simply, a tortilla fried crisp, or it may mean this easy-to-fix dish that is a great favorite with all. Like a taco, the tortilla is crisp, but it is not rolled or folded.

Fry tortillas crisp in plenty of lard or oil. (Do this in a skillet with an inch or so of shortening, or do it in a deep-fry kettle.) Drain them on paper toweling. Put fried beans (page 365) on each tortilla, sprinkle with chorizo, or Mexican sausage (page 265) which has been fried and chopped (or use chopped cooked pork mixed with a little sauce or gravy), and with grated cheese, then with plenty of finely cut lettuce. Pour over a Spanish type of tomato sauce, or make a sauce by adding 2 tablespoons of chopped green chilies and 2 tablespoons of minced sautéed onions to 1 cup of tomato purée, and seasoning with oregano and salt.

(Polenta

Italian, but common enough in our part of the world to pass as our very own.

Make a corn meal mush with 2 cups of corn meal cooked in 6 cups of water with a teaspoon of salt. Cook in a double boiler for an hour, then spread half of it on a platter, cover with a half-recipe of sauce (use the spaghetti sauce, page 104, or the lasagna sauce, page 106), and top with the remainder of the corn meal mush and the rest of the sauce. Sprinkle with chopped ripe olives and grated cheese and serve. SERVES ABOUT 12.

2 cups corn meal	1 recipe spaghetti or lasagna sauce
6 cups water	Chopped ripe olives
1 teaspoon salt	Grated cheese

NOTE: Sometimes polenta has butter and cheese stirred into it while hot, and is eaten as is, without sauce.

(Fried Rice with Pork

Fried rice is a dish that, though Chinese, is more apt to be eaten by Occidentals than by the Orientals. That is because, to the Chinese, their steamed rice is the very foundation of their meal, the base for the many lovely dishes of meat and vegetables and fish that they serve with it. However, this dish is always to be had at Chinese restaurants, and many cooks have taken to serving it at home. It's a honey of a way to use leftover bits of meat or fish, and, of course, of leftover rice. This basic recipe can be varied in dozens of ways, and it's so utterly delectable that it should be included in every cook's repertoire.

Cook 4 cups of cooked rice in ¼ cup of oil for about 5 minutes, stirring constantly. Now add a cup of shredded cooked pork, 2 tablespoons of finely shredded green onion, and ¼ cup of sliced mushrooms. Cook a couple of minutes, then stir in 2 eggs that have been beaten together with a tablespoon of soy sauce. Cook and stir a little longer, until the egg has set, and serve sprinkled with more shredded green onion. Shrimps are good with this, or green pepper, ham, chicken livers, or crab. In other words, almost anything. SERVES 10.

4 cups cooked rice	¼ cup sliced mushrooms
¼ cup oil	2 eggs
1 cup shredded cooked pork	1 tablespoon soy sauce
2 tablespoons shredded green onions	

NOTE: A common variation of this basic recipe is to cook two slightly beaten eggs like a pancake, cut them in strips, and add to the rice. In this case the eggs are omitted in the above method.

(Chinese Ginger Rice

This is another of those Chinese dishes that can be made with leftover beef, pork, or chicken. As it is mixed at the table it has, like crêpes suzette or cheese fondue, all eyes upon it.

Heat 4 tablespoons of peanut or sesame oil in a heavy pan, then add a cup of shredded meat and 2 tablespoons of tiny slivers of red ginger. (This is a pickled ginger available in Chinese stores.) Cook and stir for about 2 minutes, then add 3 cups of very dry cooked rice and a tablespoon of soy sauce. Stir until the rice is hot, then put in a bowl, sprinkle the top rather thoroughly with minced green onion, and place a soft poached egg on top. Just before serving, mix the egg thoroughly into the rice. The Chinese use chopsticks for mixing,

102

which is a bit more spectacular than fork and spoon. SERVES
ABOUT 8.

4 tablespoons oil	3 cups cooked rice
1 cup shredded leftover meat	1 tablespoon soy sauce
2 tablespoons slivered red ginger	Minced green onions
	1 egg

NOTE: If red ginger is not available, use the green (page 242).

([*Risotto*

Another Italian dish that has been definitely welcomed to our
table, and so is also ours.

Cook ½ cup of chopped onion in ¼ cup of olive oil until
lightly browned, then add a cup of washed and well-drained
rice, and cook slowly, stirring, for about 5 minutes. Add 2
cups of chicken stock and ¼ teaspoon of saffron which has
been soaked in ½ cup of stock for 10 minutes and strained
(or use pulverized saffron). Cook covered for about ¾ of an
hour or until the rice is done, adding more stock as needed.
Towards the end of the cooking, add ¼ cup of grated Parmesan and ½ cup (or more) of chopped cooked chicken
giblets and/or livers. SERVES 6.

½ cup chopped onion	¼ teaspoon saffron
¼ cup olive oil	¼ cup grated Parmesan
1 cup rice	½ cup chopped chicken giblets and/or livers
2 cups chicken stock (or more)	

NOTE: Mushrooms may be added to this, and so, of course,
may our beloved ripe olives.

NOTE: Mexican and Spanish rice are really one and the same,
except that the Spanish are pretty apt to include saffron,
while the Mexicans prefer their own oregano or chili powder.
Recipes for Spanish rice are easy to come by.

❨ Wild Rice with Chicken Livers

Cook ½ pound of washed wild rice. Sauté 6 chopped shallots in ¼ cup of butter, add ½ pound of cut chicken livers, and as soon as they stop bleeding add ¼ cup of heavy cream, and salt and pepper. Combine with rice and reheat in casserole. SERVES 6.

½ pound wild rice	½ pound chicken livers
6 shallots	¼ cup heavy cream
¼ pound butter	Salt and pepper

❨ Wild Rice Notes

Wild Rice Hunter's Style. For each ½ pound of wild rice, steamed, allow ½ cup of toasted bread crumbs and ⅓ cup of melted butter. Mix crumbs with butter and, just before serving, mix with the seasoned wild rice. This is wonderful!

Larkspur Wild Rice. Mix ½ pound of steamed wild rice with ½ cup of slivered almonds that have been browned in ¼ cup of butter. Add more butter if necessary, and salt and pepper to taste.

Wild Rice with Mushrooms. Sliced mushrooms are sautéed in butter and mixed with the wild rice, with salt and pepper for seasoning. Sometimes sautéed onions are added, too.

Wild Rice with Cream. Leftover wild rice is reheated in the double boiler with a little heavy cream. Also, but rarely, wild rice is dressed with seasoned sour cream instead of butter.

❨ Spaghetti Sauce

This sauce, made with plenty of meat, is the most usual one in this part of the world. It differs from the Italian version only in that it is often flavored with the favorite herb of the Mexicans, oregano, and occasionally even with their favorite spice — chili!

Cook ½ cup each of chopped green pepper and chopped onion, along with 2 cloves of garlic, in ⅓ cup of olive oil (or part olive oil and part butter). Add a pound of ground or chopped beef, and (this is optional) from 2 to 4 tablespoons of chopped ham and/or salami, or some sausage meat. Brown the meat lightly, then pour on a cup of canned tomatoes, a can of tomato paste, ½ cup of red table wine (also optional), ½ cup of water, a teaspoon of oregano or basil or rosemary (or a mixture of the three), and salt and pepper (or chili powder) to taste. Dried mushrooms that have been soaked in warm water and cut in strips may be added, as may fresh ones — about ½ cup sliced. Cover this and simmer ever so gently for an hour or four — the long slow cooking will improve the sauce. (Also, like stews and curries and many soups, the spaghetti sauce always tastes better when reheated the next day.) Water may be added during the cooking if necessary, but the sauce should be quite thick. Correct seasoning before serving. THIS IS ENOUGH TO SERVE 6 WITH A POUND OF SPAGHETTI.

½ cup chopped green pepper	1 cup canned tomatoes
½ cup chopped onion	1 can tomato paste
2 cloves garlic	½ cup red wine (optional)
⅓ cup olive oil	½ cup water (or more)
1 pound ground beef	1 teaspoon oregano (or basil or rosemary)
2–4 tablespoons chopped ham and/or salami (optional)	Salt
	Pepper (or chili powder)
	1 pound spaghetti

◖ *Chicken Liver Spaghetti Sauce*

This is said to have been a favorite with Caruso, who invariably ordered it when in San Francisco. The rich flavor of the chicken livers combined with the olive oil and wine is heavenly, it's true.

Cook 2 crushed cloves of garlic in 2 tablespoons each of olive oil and butter, until soft. Remove and discard garlic, and to the pan add ¼ cup of minced green onions and a cup of cut raw chicken livers. Cook lightly for 4 minutes or so, then add a cup of fresh or canned tomatoes, ½ cup of sliced mushrooms, ½ cup of white table wine, salt, pepper, and a little rosemary. Simmer slowly for 20 minutes, correct seasoning, and serve with spaghetti that has been dressed with melted butter. Pass grated Parmesan. SERVES 4 TO 6.

2 cloves garlic	1 cup tomatoes
2 tablespoons olive oil	½ cup sliced mushrooms
2 tablespoons butter	½ cup white wine
¼ cup minced green onions	Salt and pepper
1 cup cut chicken livers	Rosemary

NOTE: Pine nuts, browned in olive oil, may be added to this dish for a wonderful variation.

(Lasagna Lagunita

Lasagna, baked with a very rich sauce, is much liked by patrons of our Italian restaurants. It is said that in the days of the Gold Rush, almost every mining town had an Italian restaurant, specializing in spaghetti and ravioli. Lasagna is apparently a more recent specialty — at least there is no evidence that it was ever served in those early days.

Make a rich tomato sauce by cooking 3 crushed cloves of garlic and a minced green pepper in ¼ cup of olive oil until lightly browned. Discard garlic, and to the pan add a can (6 ounces) of tomato paste, a can (No. 2½) of tomatoes, a cup of water, ¾ of a cup of red table wine, a teaspoon of sweet basil, ½ teaspoon of oregano, a teaspoon or more of salt (taste it!) and some fresh ground pepper. Simmer all together for at least 2 hours. Use half of the sauce in the made dish and a half to serve with it.

Now boil ½ pound of lasagna (the wide ribbonlike paste available in any Italian market) until tender but *not* mushy. Also dice ½ pound of mozzarella (a moist Italian cheese), and, if you wish it, mash a pound of ricotta cheese (Italian fresh milk cheese, a bit like cottage cheese) with 2 tablespoons of

106

water. Also slice ½ pound of Italian "hot" sausage, and brown it lightly. Now paint a casserole generously with olive oil, and arrange in layers, sauce, lasagna, mozzarella, dotted here and there with spoonfuls of ricotta (optional) and pieces of sausage, then repeat until all the ingredients are used (except for half the sauce). Top with grated Parmesan. Bake 20 minutes at 350°, or until the top is brown. Cut in wedges like a pie, or in squares, and serve with the extra sauce, and with more grated Parmesan, if desired. This dish is really rich, so should be served with little else save a light salad and some fruit. SERVES 4 TO 6.

SAUCE

3 *cloves garlic*	¾ *cup red wine*
1 *green pepper*	1 *teaspoon sweet basil*
¼ *cup olive oil*	½ *teaspoon oregano*
1 *6-ounce can tomato paste*	1 *teaspoon salt (or more)*
1 *No. 2½ can tomatoes*	*Pepper*
1 *cup water*	

CASSEROLE

½ *pound lasagna*	½ *pound Italian sausage*
1 *pound ricotta cheese* ⎫	
2 *tablespoons water* ⎬ *(optional)*	*Grated Parmesan cheese*
½ *pound mozzarella cheese* ⎭	

NOTE: Cottage cheese may be substituted for the ricotta.

❰ *Spaghetti Notes*

Spaghetti al Burro. This is the simplest and one of the best sauces for spaghetti. Mix ½ cup of finely minced parsley with ¼ pound of butter, and mix into a pound of boiled spaghetti. Pass grated Parmesan. This may be varied by adding a little grated lemon rind, or chopped green olives, or sautéed chopped almonds.

Spaghetti al Pesto. You'll need mortar, pestle, and fresh basil for this. Pound a clove of garlic and ½ cup of sweet basil leaves in a mortar, adding ¼ cup of olive oil. When all is mixed into a smooth paste, add ¼ cup of melted butter, and dress a pound of cooked spaghetti with it. Pass the cheese, please.

Spaghetti Olio e Aglio. Another simple favorite — if you like garlic, that is. Crush 4 cloves of garlic and cook them in ¼ cup of olive oil for 3 minutes. Discard garlic, add ¼ cup of butter, and ¼ cup of finely minced parsley. Heat and pour over a pound of cooked spaghetti. Mix well and serve with grated cheese.

Spaghetti with Anchovies. Chop a tin (2 ounces) of anchovies and cook them in ¼ cup of olive oil for 2 or 3 minutes. Mix with cooked spaghetti. A little tomato sauce may be added, if you wish, and so may chopped ripe olives.

(*Sukiyaki*

Japanese food has never attained the popularity that has Chinese, but there are many of their dishes that we like tremendously. The chief one, perhaps, is sukiyaki, which, if you care, is pronounced "skiyaki." The sukiyaki is prepared at the table on a charming little stove or brazier, that burns charcoal. (It is also well adapted to the chafing dish.) Sukiyaki is made with beef and vegetables, usually mushrooms, onions, bamboo shoots, and Chinese cabbage or celery, as well as soy bean cake. Perhaps half its charm is the ceremony of preparing it.

Cut 1½ pounds of round steak in thin slices or shreds, and cook it lightly in 3 tablespoons of oil or beef fat for 4 or 5 minutes. Add a bunch of green onions, cut in shreds, and including some of the green part, and ¼ cup of soy sauce (or more, if you wish), ½ cup of water or stock, and a teaspoon of sugar. Cook 3 minutes, then add ½ cup each of sliced mushrooms and bamboo shoots or celery, cut in shreds. Keep the vegetables more or less in separate piles. Cook for 3 minutes

more, then add soy bean cake (if desired) cut in cubes. Cook
only until all is hot, and serve with rice. Sometimes spinach
or Chinese cabbage is used. SERVES 6.

1½ pounds round steak	*1 teaspoon sugar*
3 tablespoons oil	*½ cup sliced mushrooms*
1 bunch green onions	*½ cup shredded bamboo*
¼ cup soy sauce (or more)	*shoots or celery*
½ cup water or stock	*Soy bean cake (optional)*

NOTE: If shellfish is used instead of beef, the dish is called
hamanabe; when made with chicken, it's torinabe.

NOTE: The setup for a sukiyaki party is very charming. The
charcoal brazier is in the middle of a very low table, with the
ingredients for the dish all assembled near it. There is also,
either on the table or on the floor, a wooden tub, with a cover,
which is filled with rice, and from which the rice bowls are
refilled. And at each place there is a soup bowl, a rice bowl,
small dishes for soy (shoyu, to the Japanese), and a teacup.
Also chopsticks and a shallow bowl for the sukiyaki. The
Japanese are also apt to serve hot sake with their sukiyaki.
This is a wine, tasting rather like sherry, and it is served from
the loveliest little porcelain bottle imaginable. The sake cups
match the bottle, and are not much larger than a thimble.

NOTE: The Japanese do not cook all the sukiyaki at once, but
about one third to one half at a time, so that further helpings
will be freshly cooked. They also often serve a raw egg,
barely beaten, in which they dip the hot meat and vegetables.

First Courses

OUR WESTERN CUSTOM *of serving salads as first courses would place this category with the salads, if that were the way we always did it. But it isn't. We often start our meals with antipasto, or hors d'oeuvre, in the Continental manner, and even more often we begin them with fish or fruit or such — not necessarily in the form of a cocktail. This chapter includes such appetizers and savory dishes as are eaten at table, before soup, and are, unless hot, usually at the places when we sit down. Other appetizers, those that are eaten with the preprandial drinks, are in the chapter on appetizers. Because, however, some of these first courses are essentially salads, or even appetizers, they are so listed in the index.*

⟨ Artichokes Santa Anita

Allow 1 artichoke bottom for each serving. Fill with pâté de foie gras or Sell's liver pâté, and garnish each bottom with three crab legs. Serve with a dressing made by thinning mayonnaise with cream, and garnish with wedges of lemon or lime. A rich food, actually so hearty that it makes a good main dish for lunch.

⟨ Aptos Artichoke Cocktail

Dress diced cooked bottoms of artichokes (page 361) with a sauce made by combining ½ cup of mayonnaise, ¼ cup of cream, 2 tablespoons of lemon juice, and salt and pepper to taste. Serve in cocktail glasses with a bit of pimiento or a

slice of olive as a garnish. This is very rich, delectably so, so
keep the portions small.

Diced cooked artichoke	*¼ cup cream*
bottoms	*2 tablespoons lemon juice*
½ cup mayonnaise	*Salt and pepper*

(*Armada Avocado Cocktail*

This is a honey. Dice 2 peeled tomatoes, discarding seeds.
Dice a ripe avocado. Combine gently. Grind ½ teaspoon of
dill seeds in a mortar, add a tablespoon of very finely minced
shallot, 2 tablespoons of lemon juice, 4 tablespoons of olive
oil, and salt and pepper to taste. Pour over combined vegetables, and serve chilled in cocktail glasses. The flavors of the
dill, the avocado, and the tomato blend here in the happiest
of fashions. SERVES 4 TO 6.

2 tomatoes	*2 tablespoons lemon*
1 avocado	*juice*
½ teaspoon dill seeds	*4 tablespoons olive oil*
1 tablespoon finely minced	*Salt and pepper*
shallot	

NOTE: A variation on this is to use a cup of diced mushrooms
that have been cooked in oil and cooled, in place of the tomatoes. Or in place of the avocado, for that matter, though the
dish would have to be rechristened.

(*Avocado San Andreas*

Avocados are a favored first course on the West Coast. Some
like them filled with caviar, some with crab or lobster salad,
and some just plain with a wedge of lemon. But a new and
popular way is this.

Serve ripe avocados on the half shell and accompany each
serving with a whole lime, cut in half for easy squeezing. And
with this pass a decanter of light rum. Each guest will squeeze
the lime and pour the rum in the amounts he thinks most
judicious.

111

([Del Mar Crab Cocktail

I can, and do, get quite noisy about the delicate flavor of shellfish being drowned in tomato catsup hotted up with horseradish and Worcestershire sauce, and served forth as a "cocktail." That is why I welcome this cocktail with particular pleasure.

Arrange big, meaty pieces of freshly cooked and cracked crab in cocktail glasses, and squeeze a little lemon juice over each. Sauce with this mixture: ½ cup each of heavy cream and mayonnaise, ¼ cup of white wine, a tablespoon of lemon juice, 2 tablespoons of minced green pepper, and salt and pepper to taste.

SAUCE

½ cup heavy cream	1 tablespoon lemon juice
½ cup mayonnaise	2 tablespoons minced green pepper
¼ cup white wine	Salt and pepper

([Crab and Avocado Cocktail

This can be so good, and so horrid!

To have it good, use freshly cooked crab, cut in as large pieces as possible. Combine with an equal amount of diced ripe (but firm) avocado, and half the amount of finely diced celery. The sauce should be mayonnaise thinned with lemon juice, or heavy cream and lemon juice combined.

| 1 part cooked cut crab | ½ part diced celery |
| 1 part diced ripe avocado | Mayonnaise thinned with lemon juice |

([California Fruit Cocktail

We do not serve fruit cocktails, as some suppose, at every meal, though it must be confessed that they do appear at an amazing number of "group" luncheons and so-called "banquets." When they are made this way, of fresh fruits in season, no one objects in the least.

First Courses

Combine: sections from grapefruit and oranges, seeds and white inner skin carefully removed, diced pears, diced pineapple, and strawberries, halved. Marinate in one cup of Maraschino, or in sherry or white wine. (In the latter case, a very little sugar may be needed.) Serve cold. One orange, ½ grapefruit, 1 pear, ⅙ pineapple and 12 strawberries WILL SERVE 6 OR MORE.

NOTE: Of course there is no rule about which fruits to use. Any fruit, any berry, any melon may be used in combination with any other, and the marinade may be fruit juice or almost any liquor or fruit brandy. Just remember to handle the fruit carefully so that it won't be mashed to extinction.

❴ Garbanzo Hors d'Oeuvre

Garbanzos, or chick peas, are hearty, so this should be served as an hors d'oeuvre at lunch, along with lighter things such as sliced tomatoes, or as a part of an antipasto. It also makes a very good salad, when a hearty one is indicated — such as at the barbecue.

Use canned garbanzos, or cook the dried ones in stock or water until tender. (The water in which ham, tongue, or corned beef was cooked is a good thought here.) Drain, and for each 2 cups, mix in 3 tablespoons of minced green onions, 3 tablespoons of minced green pepper, 3 tablespoons of red wine vinegar, 6 tablespoons of olive oil or salad oil, and salt and pepper to taste. Minced green chilies may be added to this, as may a little ground cumin. When serving as a salad, surround with crisp leaves of romaine. SERVES 12.

For each 2 cups cooked garbanzos

3 tablespoons minced green onion

3 tablespoons minced green pepper

3 tablespoons red wine vinegar

6 tablespoons olive or salad oil

Salt and pepper

Minced green chilies (optional)

Ground cumin (optional)

113

(Marinated Herring with Sour Cream

So many West Coast restaurants feature this Old World favorite that it would have to be included in a symposium on West Coast eating habits, even if it didn't show up in several of our oldest cook books.

Use fillets of herring or the salt ones. If the latter are used, soak them 24 hours in a mixture of milk and water, then drain them, skin, split, and remove backbones, head, and tail. For 3 herring heat ½ cup of white wine vinegar and a cup of white wine, ¼ cup of sugar, a clove of garlic, and a teaspoon of whole pickling spice. Bring to a boil, remove garlic, cool, and pour over the filleted herring, which have been cut in 1-inch pieces. Allow to stand, covered, for 2 or 3 days. Serve with a generous dollop of sour cream on each portion, garnished with fresh dill or chives, if desired. A thinly sliced onion is often marinated with the fish.

For each 3 herring

½ *cup white wine*	1 *clove garlic*
vinegar	1 *teaspoon whole pickling*
1 *cup white wine*	*spice*
¼ *cup sugar*	1 *sliced onion* (*optional*)

(Becky's Chopped Liver

This is a Jewish dish that is wonderful as a first course if the rest of the meal is to be light. The directions, which may sound ridiculous, have to be followed exactly, or the dish will be a flop. Made this way it is as good as they come.

Bake a 2-pound piece of calf's or baby beef liver at 350° until it is done, but still pink and juicy (150° on your meat thermometer). *Do not season.* Remove the skin and any veins, and chop the liver or, better yet, dice it very fine with a sharp knife. (Do not grind.) Be sure to save all the juices. In the meantime, cook a cup of chopped yellow onion in 3 tablespoons of chicken fat and mix with the liver. Chill. Just before serving mix in ⅓ cup more of rendered chicken fat. Serve nested on lettuce in individual dishes, and give each

114

guest a dish of salt and a warning that they'll really need it. It is a fact that if the salt is added during the cooking or chilling, the liver will have a bitter flavor. This way it rivals the best of pâté de maison. SERVES 8.

> *2 pounds calf's liver*
> *1 cup chopped yellow onion*
> *½ cup chicken fat*

ℂ *Stuffed Mushrooms San Juan*

This is a hot first course, or an appetizer if the mushrooms are arranged singly on small rounds of toast.

Dip oysters in a rich cream sauce flavored with sherry or Madeira. Put each oyster in a mushroom cap that has been cooked, sprinkle with cheese, and put under the broiler until brown. Serve 3 or 4 on a piece of buttered toast on which a little of the sauce has been poured. Garnish with a sprig of fresh tarragon, if available.

ℂ *Stuffed Mushrooms Tarragon*

Clean a pound of mushrooms of uniform size and remove stems. Chop the stems and cook them in 2 tablespoons of butter, with 2 tablespoons of chopped shallots for 4 or 5 minutes. Add a tablespoon each of minced fresh tarragon and parsley, ½ cup of toast crumbs, an egg, and 2 tablespoons of California brandy. Salt and pepper to taste. Cook the mushroom caps in 2 tablespoons of butter, stuff them with this mixture, and broil until brown. Serve hot on a bed of cress, and accompanied by a wedge of lemon. Or, if preferred, serve on a slice of fried tomato, or on toast. SERVES 6.

1 pound mushrooms
4 tablespoons butter
2 tablespoons chopped shallots
1 tablespoon minced fresh tarragon
1 tablespoon minced fresh parsley
½ cup toast crumbs
1 egg
2 tablespoons brandy
Salt and pepper

(Walla Walla Mushroom Cocktail

Serve this just once and you'll be stuck with it. It's one of those superlative dishes that no one will let you forget.

Clean a pound of medium-sized mushrooms by dipping them individually in acidulated water (1 cup water, 2 tablespoons lemon juice), and brushing with a pastry brush. Do not peel them, but remove the stems (save for soup!) and cut the caps into quarters. Sauté them, along with 3 tablespoons of grated onion, in 3 tablespoons of vegetable oil. (Not olive oil this time, it's too strong in flavor.) Cook the mushrooms very gently and not too long — about 5 minutes. Remove from the fire, sprinkle lightly with salt, and pour over them a jigger of brandy and a tablespoon of lemon juice. Let chill for several hours, turning once or twice to assure an even marinade. Before serving, mix lightly with sour cream and garnish with a sprinkle of chives or parsley, or such, for color. SERVES 6.

1 pound mushrooms	*1 jigger brandy*
3 tablespoons grated onion	*1 tablespoon lemon juice*
3 tablespoons vegetable oil	*Salt*
Sour cream	

(Scallop Cocktail

Scallops don't like too much heat — unless they are cooked very gently, and at a very low temperature, they get quite tough about it. Wipe a pound of them and cook them in ¼ cup of white wine and 2 tablespoons of oil, stirring every second and keeping the heat *very* low. *Don't* cook until they shrivel, but only until they have whitened on the outside. This won't take more than 2 or 3 minutes. Cool the scallops and serve with a sauce made with 2 tablespoons of lemon juice and the juices in which they were cooked, lightly seasoned with salt. And if I haven't sold you on that idea, a rich cocktail sauce may be used — 1 part of mayonnaise, 1 part of tomato purée, and 1 part of cream, seasoned with sweet basil. SERVES 6.

1 pound scallops	*2 tablespoons oil*
¼ cup white wine	*2 tablespoons lemon juice*
	Salt

116

First Courses

(Oranges with Rosemary

Sliced oranges make a surprisingly good first course, particularly on a hot summer day. Good for breakfast, too.

Peel them deeply, so that no white remains and the juices run. Slice them thick and arrange 2 or 3 slices on individual dishes. Make sure that there are no seeds or core remaining. Dress lightly with French dressing, and sprinkle with minced fresh rosemary or basil. (If the fresh herb is not at hand, use vinegar so flavored.) Chill well before serving garnished with greenery, or with a flower. In Southern California an orange leaf or two, or an orange blossom is used, and no one thinks it's *too too* cute. Sherry may be used as a marinade instead of the French dressing.

(Bremerton Salmon Rolls

Cook fresh asparagus tips until they are just tender and still bright green. (If medium-sized, this should not take more than 5 minutes after boiling water has been poured on and again comes to a boil.) Drain, cover with French dressing, and chill. Select large thin slices of smoked salmon, arrange 3 or 4 pieces of asparagus on each piece, and roll them in the salmon, allowing the tips to show. Arrange on individual plates with a garnish of cress, a couple of ripe olives, and a wedge of lemon. Pass the pepper mill and a cruet of olive oil. You can imagine how good this is!

(Shad Roe Carquinez

Clean fresh shad roe, or use canned or frozen. (Other roe may be used, too.) Sauté gently in ¼ cup of butter. Chill. Allow ⅓ to ½ roe for each serving, and arrange each on a nest of lettuce on individual plates. Mask completely with a sauce made by combining ½ cup of sour cream with ½ cup of mayonnaise and ½ cup of mashed avocado. This is seasoned lightly with lemon juice. Now sprinkle with finely minced crisp bacon and garnish the plates with wedges of

avocado. This is a delightful dish. MAKES SAUCE FOR 1 POUND
OF ROE.

1 pound shad roe	½ cup mayonnaise
¼ cup butter	½ cup mashed avocado
½ cup sour cream	Lemon juice
Crisp bacon	

◖ Garlic Shrimp Curry (Cold)

Cook a pound of green shrimps, clean, and split if large,
otherwise leave whole. Crush a clove of garlic in a mortar
with a teaspoon of coarse salt, add a cup of mayonnaise, a
teaspoon of curry powder, a teaspoon of lemon juice, and a
tablespoon of tomato purée. Mix with shrimps. Serve nested
in lettuce as a first course, or, if you prefer, as a shrimp cocktail. It also makes a very fine salad, particularly at a buffet
when served with a roast turkey, sweetbreads with mushrooms
in cream, and rice croquettes. SERVES 4 TO 6.

1 pound shrimps	1 cup mayonnaise
1 clove garlic	1 teaspoon curry powder
1 teaspoon salt	1 teaspoon lemon juice
1 tablespoon tomato purée	

◖ More Ideas for First Courses

Artichoke Bottoms with Minced Clams. Mix a 7-ounce can
of drained minced clams with ¼ cup of very finely diced
celery and a little mayonnaise. Fill artichoke bottoms and garnish with sliced stuffed olives.

Melon with Prosciutto. This delicious first course we learned
from our Italian residents. We use honeydew, honeyballs,
Persian, or muskmelon (commonly miscalled cantaloupe), and
cut them in wedges. Then we wrap them in thinner-than-thin
prosciutto and serve them with quarters of lime or lemon.

Eggplant Caviar, so called, I suppose, because it looks like
caviar if the imagination is sufficiently stretched, is very good.
Baked eggplant is mashed with sautéed green pepper and
onion, chopped drained tomato, garlic olive oil, salt and pepper. It is served cold with pumpernickel bread.

118

Fish and Shellfish

MUCH OF THE WEALTH *of the West Coast has come from our waters, but it was many years before that potential gold mine was given much notice. The Indians did depend on fish for a good part of their food, as did the pioneers, and there were early attempts in the Northwest to preserve and market the plentiful salmon. But not the early Californians — they were meat eaters, and they had the meat to eat. They didn't even see any sport in fishing. Colton, in his* Three Years in California, *said that, though Monterey bay was full of fish, none came to table. "Could they [the Californians] go to sea on their horses," he wrote, "and fish from their saddles, they would often be seen dashing through the surf." Times have changed. Monterey is a fishing port — such a well-known one that a type of fishing boat is called a Monterey. Today fishing is a huge industry from San Diego to Seattle. The tuna, sardine, and salmon industries are all Big Business, and scores of other fish and shellfish are caught and marketed. We have learned that fish is not a food to be eaten only when nothing else is available, but is, when properly prepared, food as good as it comes.*

We have also, on the West Coast, many fresh-water fish. Rainbow, as well as many other trout, bass, catfish, crappies, and such. They are cooked in very much the same manner throughout the country. When and if we have our own native touch in the preparation, I have given the recipe (see Index), as I do when the fish are typical of the

119

West Coast, as sturgeon or steelhead trout. Terrapin and sea turtle are not found here, though farther south in Baja California the latter are sometimes captured. The "ellachick," a native fresh-water tortoise named by the Nisquallis, used to be fairly plentiful, but their delicious flavor took care of that. Now one seldom hears of them. Back in the lavish days of San Francisco, terrapin appeared at most of the banquets and even at private parties. One famous caterer, Harkness by name, supplied the oysters and terrapin to all the first families, according to Amelia Neville, in her entertaining book Fantastic City.

❪ Abalone

Abalone may not be shipped from California; it's a law, designed to keep these delectable shellfish from going the way of the great auk. We weren't always so smart. In fact, until rather recently we didn't even know that they were good eating. As late as 1914, gourmet Clarence Edwords wrote, in that delightful little book *Bohemian San Francisco,* "abalones are a univalve that has been much in vogue among the Chinese, but has seldom found place on the tables of restaurants owing to the difficulty of preparing them, as they are tough and insipid under ordinary circumstances. . . . The Hoffman restaurant is now making a specialty of abalones, but it takes sentiment to say that one really finds anything extra good in them." Tsk, tsk. The Chinese, with no sentiment whatsoever, but with well-educated palates, not only feasted on them here, they dried them and shipped them home in such quantities that by the time we *did* learn to cook them, they were close to being nonexistent.

Today most of our fresh abalones come from around Monterey. This stanza from the poem by George Sterling hints that they must have been even more plentiful there in his day.

> Some folks boast of quail on toast
> Because they think it's tony,
> But my tom cat gets nice and fat
> On hunks of abalone.

120

Fish and Shellfish

(Abalone Steaks

This is the most usual way of preparing abalone, but it is done with such varying degrees of skill that the results are sometimes perfect, sometimes deplorable. It's all in the timing, so don't let anything distract you if you're playing chef.

Slice abalone about ⅓-inch thick, or purchase steaks already cut, allowing 1 or 2 to a serving. (These are usually already "tenderized." If not, they may need a few gentle thumps with a bottle or wooden mallet.) Some cooks slash the edges a bit; they say it prevents curling. Dip the slices in an egg beaten with a tablespoon of water, then in very fine bread crumbs, and pan-fry in butter. Here is where the skill comes in: cook them quickly, but not violently, for a very short time — some say not more than 2 minutes on a side. I say not more than 1 minute on a side, or even ½ minute. (A minute is longer than you think!) The trick is to let them become the color of a light topaz on one side, turn, color the other side the same way, and serve at once with quartered lemon.

(Paul's Stuffed Abalone

Paul's Duck Press, in Los Angeles, is fast becoming a gourmet's rendezvous. Although Paul specializes in cooking wild ducks for those who are handier with a gun than with a skillet, he does fine things with shellfish, too. His was among the first restaurants to serve Alaska King Crab (pages 131, 132), and he knows his abalone.

Slice the meat of a lobster tail and sauté it lightly in butter, along with cleaned green shrimps and shelled crab legs. Cook an abalone steak even more lightly than usual, brush it with a rich, well-seasoned cream sauce flavored with sherry. Dip pieces of the shellfish in the same sauce and place on the abalone, then roll it and fasten with a toothpick. Brush with more of the cream sauce and slip under the broiler to brown lightly. Allow 1 to a serving.

⟨ Abalone and Pork

This recipe uses canned abalone which has been deprived of its juice for a very good reason: the Chinese abalone soup on page 330.

Fry a pork chop lightly and cut it, and a canned abalone, in strips. Cut raw green pepper and celery the same, and heat all this together in a sauce made with a cup of chicken or pork stock (there's a use for pork bones!), a tablespoon of whiskey (I said *whiskey*), and a tablespoon of cornstarch moistened in 2 tablespoons of water. Cook until clear. Serve with rice, eggs foo yung, and Chinese peas with water chestnuts, and no one will deny that you know your Oriental cooking. SERVES 6.

1 pork chop	1 cup chicken or pork stock
1 canned abalone	1 tablespoon whiskey
Green pepper	1 tablespoon cornstarch
Celery	2 tablespoons water

⟨ New Albion Abalone Fritters

This recipe is from *The Landmarks Club Cook Book*, a book sold in 1903 to raise money for the preservation of California landmarks. Many well known Angeleños contributed their pet recipes, among them Charles F. Lummis, who did a fascinating chapter on Spanish-American cookery. This recipe, by the way, is the earliest one I have been able to find for abalone. I have revised it slightly.

Trim 2 small abalones, or 1 large one, and put through the food chopper. Add 2 beaten eggs, a cup of milk, 1½ cups of flour, 1½ teaspoons of baking powder, and the same amount of salt. Drop by small spoonfuls into deep fat at 375° until lightly brown. (Very small fritters may be served on toothpicks, for hors d'oeuvre.) Serve with lemon. SERVES 6.

1 or 2 abalones	1½ cups flour
2 eggs	1½ teaspoons baking powder
1 cup milk	1½ teaspoons salt

Fish and Shellfish

❬ Baked Albacore

Albacore is a tuna, the one with the whitest meat of them all. In 1926, for some inexplicable reason, the albacore left California waters and stayed away for 12 years. But the call of the West Coast was too strong for them, because they returned not only to the Southland, but to Oregon and Washington where they had never lived before. The albacore is a game fish as well as a commercial one, so we often — though not often enough — have the fun of cooking it.

Cover a 4-pound piece of albacore with 2 cups of white wine, and marinate for several hours in the refrigerator. (The wine, if it covers the fish, will keep it from perfuming the other foods, a good thing to know.) Put the fish in a casserole, along with the wine, ½ teaspoon of salt and a couple of grindings of pepper. Add a cup of chopped onion and an herb bouquet. Put thin — very thin — slices of lemon on top of the fish and bake at 400°, basting occasionally. When tender, the meat will flake easily when poked with a fork. Before serving, pour off the liquid (or use a glass baster and draw it off) and thicken it with a roux of 3 tablespoons each of flour and butter. Correct seasoning, return to the baking dish with the fish and vegetables, and sprinkle the top of the fish with ¼ cup of minced parsley. String beans are good with this, and baked stuffed potatoes topped with cheese. SERVES 8.

4 pounds albacore	1 herb bouquet
2 cups white wine	Thin lemon slices
½ teaspoon salt	3 tablespoons flour
Pepper	3 tablespoons butter
1 cup chopped onion	¼ cup minced parsley

NOTE: Another way is to squeeze the juice of a couple of lemons inside the fish, then bake, saucing simply with butter and lemon juice.

❬ Barracuda Anacapa

The barracuda's mean expression belies its tender and delicious flesh. We purchase it, we catch it, and we love it. This recipe has a Mexican flavor about it.

123

Put 6 pounds of barracuda (whole or in a piece) in a baking dish and rub with 2 teaspoons of salt that has been ground with a small clove of garlic and mixed with a teaspoon of chili powder and ½ teaspoon of oregano. Top with ½ cup each of minced onion and green pepper. Then pour a No. 2½ can of tomatoes over all. Bake at 425°, basting with the tomato juice in the bottom of the pan. A little water or wine may be added for extra juice. This should take about an hour — test it with a fork to be sure. Correct the seasoning, and serve with a casserole of dried limas. Barracuda is also wonderful broiled or barbecued. SERVES APPROXIMATELY 8 TO 12.

6 pounds barracuda	½ cup minced onion
2 teaspoons salt	½ cup minced green pepper
1 small clove garlic	1 No. 2½ can tomatoes
1 teaspoon chili powder	Water or wine if necessary
½ teaspoon oregano	

⟨ Clams

We have more than 35 kinds of clams on our coast, from the succulent little butter clam to the preposterous geoduck. Some claim that the clam saved Oregon, or at least saved the lives of many pioneers who would otherwise have starved. There's probably quite a lot of truth in that one, for the Oregonians, it was said, ate so many clams that the tides rose and fell in their bellies.

The *Razor Clam* is found up and down the coast, but the farther north it lives, the larger it grows — can't take the heat. It is tremendously popular, and is prepared in every way that has ever been dreamed up by a cook.

The *Pismo Clam* was named after the beach in California where it grew most abundantly. Now, because of the fervency of epicurean clam diggers, the clams are strictly protected, so it is impossible to buy a Pismo clam at Pismo Beach — a native one, that is. Pismo clams may still be dug from their home waters, but the bag limit is small, and the minimum size

124

of clams taken is large. The clam is a good-sized one with a round hard white shell that looks as if it had had a thin coat of yellow shellac applied to its outer surface.

The *Mud Clam,* also known as a soft-shell clam, is not a native, but it is here to stay. The clam is most prevalent in Northern California, but it is found farther north. It has a delicate oval shell about six inches in length, and delightfully flavored flesh. It is only the white flesh that is eaten. The necks are split, cleaned, and skinned, and the black portions of the meat are discarded.

The *Gaper* or *Horse Clam* is the largest except for the geoduck, and is found all up and down the coast. They have to be skinned before eating, but the flavor is excellent — best, perhaps, for bisques, chowders, Newburgs, and hashes.

The *Empire Clam* is another big one, often weighing two or three pounds, sometimes more. It is found on the Oregon coast, particularly around Coos Bay. The necks of this clam are skinned and split, then lightly pounded and fried in the same manner as the necks of the mud clam. The tough part of the body is usually discarded and the remainder crumbed and fried.

The *Butter Clam,* also known as the Washington or money-shell clam, was once the staple diet of the Puget Sound Indians. They, cockles, and jackknife clams are still common. They may be used in any of the recipes given here.

⟨ Geoduck

The geoduck, called "gooeyduck" by those who dig them, and "gweduc" by Mr. Webster, is a clam so enormous that it must have been a favorite of the Brobdingnagians, who lived, according to Swift, where the Olympic Peninsula is actually situated. And probably Paul Bunyan, carelessly dragging his pickax behind him as he gouged out the Hood Canal, swallowed the huge creatures as easily as we down Olympia oysters. Geoduck means "dig deep" in Nisqualli, and how right the Indians were! When one spots the clam's huge siphon protruding from the sand and mud, the only thing to do is to sneak up on it, and then get in and dig — deep. The clams, once they sense danger, are incredibly quick, but on warm days, as they indolently sun themselves, they look like easy game. Their necks, thus relaxed, are such a grotesque sight that ladies of an earlier day stayed at a discreet distance when their men went hunting them. The sight of the reclining geoduck, it was hinted, was not quite nice.

Prepare geoducks by scalding them with hot water, so that they will open up, then skin them and discard the stomach. Grind the neck, using it for a chowder of the Boston variety, with diced salt pork, onions, potatoes, and milk, but add a West Coast touch with some white table wine and chopped parsley. The body itself is cut into steaks, which should be given a gentle thwack with a bottle, then egged and crumbed, and lightly fried in butter until a lovely gold.

⟨ Grilled Mud Clams

Unbelievably good, these clams with the lowly name, but only if they are cooked lightly. Like other mollusks, they toughen when overcooked, so handle them gently and a wonderful tenderness will be your reward.

Clean them by removing all the black portions, and split the necks, washing out the sand that's sure to be there. Use them in any clam recipe, but best, I think, cleaned, dipped in melted butter, then in fine seasoned cracker crumbs, and grilled over charcoal or in the broiler.

⟨ Clam Hash

A favorite up Seattle way, it is said to have been originated by Yankee settlers who had no corned beef, so, poor things, had to substitute the omnipresent clams in their favorite hash. Clam hash has become a West Coast specialty, while corned beef hash is just a dish. (But what a dish!)

Like corned beef hash this is cooked pretty much by ear.

126

Fish and Shellfish

Chopped cooked potatoes you'll want (I think they're best if they've been baked rather than boiled), and chopped clams, butter, cream, onions, salt and pepper. Compose your own, or use 2 cups each of clams and potatoes, ¼ cup of minced onion sautéed in 3 tablespoons of butter. Mix together, season with salt and freshly ground pepper, put into a hot frying pan containing 2 tablespoons of melted butter. Spread evenly over the bottom and allow to brown. After about 10 minutes, pour on ½ cup of cream. When well browned (about a half hour over a very slow heat), fold like an omelet and serve on a hot platter, with parsley and lemon. This is as good for dinner as it is for breakfast.

2 cups chopped clams
2 cups chopped cooked
    potatoes
½ cup cream
¼ cup minced onion
5 tablespoons butter
Salt and pepper

NOTE: *Clam Balls.* Mix chopped clams with mashed potatoes, parsley, and egg. Roll in balls, then in flour, and fry in deep fat. Small-sized ones are tops for hors d'oeuvre.

❪ Coos Bay Clam Cakes

This could be stuck in a split buttered bun and called a clamburger, but let's not.

Mix 2 cups of ground clams with 2 beaten eggs, ½ cup of dried bread crumbs, ½ teaspoon of salt, ¼ teaspoon of ground thyme, or thyme seasoning powder, and 2 tablespoons of grated onion. Form into cakes, dust lightly with crumbs, and fry quickly in butter until brown. THIS MAKES SIX SMALL CAKES, OR A COUPLE OF DOZEN TINY ONES TO SERVE WITH DRINKS.

2 cups ground clams
2 eggs
½ cup dried bread crumbs
½ teaspoon salt
¼ teaspoon ground thyme
2 tablespoons grated onions
Crumbs
Butter

ℂ Winchester Bay Clam Soufflé

This is made with canned minced razor clams, Pioneer Brand, long a favorite on this coast. The story goes that a newcomer, having a hard time feeding his family, couldn't talk them into eating the razor clams that were so abundant near his home. He finally hit upon a manner of preparing them that pleased his fastidious family, and pleased his neighbors, too. By 1894, there was such a clamor for his clams that he started canning them, and we have all been clamoring for them ever since.

Cook ½ cup of minced onion in ¼ cup of butter until pale gold. Add ¼ cup of flour, cook 2 minutes, then pour in 1½ cups of milk and 2 cans of Pioneer minced clams, drained. (Use the juice for clam consommé.) Cook until thick, beat in 4 well-beaten egg yolks and cook another minute, stirring well. Cool slightly, then fold in the beaten egg whites, and season to taste (thyme, basil, or ground caraway may be used). Bake in a buttered dish at 350° for about 40 minutes, or until firm. SERVES 6.

¼ cup butter	2 cans Pioneer minced
½ cup minced onion	clams
¼ cup flour	4 eggs
1½ cups milk	Thyme, basil, or caraway

NOTE: *Clam Stew.* Another way with Pioneer minced clams is to dump a can into 2 cups of rich milk, add a lump of butter and salt and pepper, and heat. RESULT IS ENOUGH WONDERFUL CLAM STEW FOR 3 GENEROUS SERVINGS.

ℂ Baked Clams Elizabeth

This is a recipe from Sam's Grill, now on Bush Street but formerly in the old California Market. It is a favorite eating place with those who know their San Francisco and their seafood.

"Recipe for one portion: Open about 12 to 14 clams. Place them on the half shell in a flat silver platter or similar dish. Retain all the juice when opening the clams and place it in a bowl. To this add about 2 ounces of sherry or white wine, and squeeze in 1 lemon. Pour all of this over the clams and into the platter. Next, mix about ½ cup of stale milk bread (passed through a strainer for fine crumbs) together with some finely chopped chives or green onions and some fresh chopped parsley. Place this dry mixture over each clam, top off with a liberal sprinkling of good grated Italian cheese, and lastly add some melted butter to each clam over the cheese and bread mixture. Bake in a moderate oven for about 15 minutes — or until brown on top."

12–14 clams (in shell)	Chives or green onions
2 ounces sherry or white wine	Parsley
	Grated Italian cheese
Juice of 1 lemon	Melted butter
½ cup stale milk bread crumbs	

(Copalis Clam Pie

There are as many recipes for clam pie as there are varieties of clams — each one, according to its sponsor, the *only* one. The pioneer pie was apt to have potatoes in it, but this was the way one "old" family made it.

Line an 8-inch pie dish with pastry and sprinkle it with a tablespoon of minced parsley. Sauté ¼ cup of chopped onions in 3 tablespoons of butter until wilted. Add 3 tablespoons of flour and cook 2 minutes. Then add 1½ cups of milk or cream (part clam juice may be used), and cook until thick. Season lightly, remembering that clams are salty. Now alternate layers of chopped clams (1½ cups in all) with the cream sauce, sprinkle another tablespoon of minced parsley on top, cover with a crust, and bake in a hot oven (425°) until brown. SERVES 6.

Pastry for a 2-crust, 8-inch pie	3 tablespoons butter
	3 tablespoons flour
2 tablespoons minced parsley	1½ cups milk or cream
	Salt and pepper
¼ cup chopped onions	1½ cups chopped clams

❲ Quick Clam Ramekins

This is one of the reasons why canned minced clams are a West Coast pantry requisite.

Two 7-ounce cans of minced clams, not drained, are mixed with 3 chopped hard-boiled eggs, 2 tablespoons each of chopped onion and green pepper sautéed in 3 tablespoons of butter, ½ cup of bread crumbs, ½ cup of cream, and salt and pepper. This is put in individual ramekins or baking shells, topped with a mixture of minced parsley, crumbs, and butter, and browned in the oven. SERVES 6.

2 7-ounce cans minced clams	½ cup bread crumbs
3 hard-boiled eggs	½ cup cream
2 tablespoons chopped onion	Salt and pepper
2 tablespoons chopped green pepper	Minced parsley
	Crumbs
3 tablespoons butter	Butter

❲ Fried Razor Clams

Perhaps the most popular of all the ways with clams. Mud clams, too, may be prepared like this.

Put clams in a colander or frying basket, and plunge into boiling water. As soon as they open, plunge into ice water. Remove from shells, cut off the necks and remove all the black parts, using a sharp knife. Split the clams right down the front and through the foot, and lay them open on paper toweling to drain. Dust the clams with seasoned flour, dip in egg, then in fine crumbs, and pan-fry in butter until amber. Don't cook too fast or too long, and you will have a dish that is a dream of tenderness.

❲ Boiled Cod with Oyster Sauce

This was a favorite pioneer way with cod. Old recipes didn't say whether they used "true" cod, ling cod, or tom cod, a considerable relief to this harassed female, who has been trying to straighten out the marine nomenclature of the Pacific Coast. The ladies of early Oregon liked salt cod, too. One

Fish and Shellfish

recipe for salt cod with beets was called "Recipe Given by Mrs. General Babbit to Mrs. General Sprague." Its greatest charm lies in its name. Another recipe for codfish balls, quoted in its entirety from another old cook book: "Take what is left, make into balls, and fry. Serve for breakfast."

Steam a 3- or 4-pound piece of fresh cod in court bouillon until done. While it is cooking, heat a cup of small oysters in their own liquor until they are plump. Pour juice into a cup measure, and fill with cream to the top. Make a roux with 2 tablespoons each of flour and butter, add the cup of liquid, and cook until thickened, seasoning with salt and pepper. Return oysters to the sauce, and serve hot with the steamed fish, which has had the skin removed and has been sprinkled with minced chives. SERVES 6 TO 8.

3–4 pounds fresh cod	2 tablespoons flour
Court bouillon	2 tablespoons butter
1 cup small oysters	Salt and pepper
Cream as needed	Minced chives

NOTE: Pickled cod tongues were considered a great delicacy in early days, and so, for that matter, was pickled cod, a sort of Yankee escabeche.

NOTE: "Codfish tea" — does that stop you? There's a recipe for it in the *Berkeley* (California) *Cook Book*, 1884, and it's salt codfish steeped in hot water.

⟨ Crabs

There are several kinds of crabs on the West Coast. The most renowned is the Dungeness crab, the most spectacular the gargantuan King crab, and the most ubiquitous the smaller, but delicious rock crab. The Dungeness crab is large compared with its Eastern cousin, producing about six times as much meat from each shell, but the mighty Dungeness becomes a midget when compared to the King crabs of northern waters. These enormous creatures sometimes measure ten feet from claw to claw. They live in Alaska, but are flown south to our

131

fancier restaurants and markets, where they are featured as a West Coast specialty. Our enthusiasm for the King crab does not blind us to the charm of our own Dungeness, the crab that comes to market at San Francisco's Fisherman's Wharf, where part of the fishing fleet anchors. The crabs are boiled alive in huge vats set up on the sidewalks.

(Barbecued Crab

This is a favorite in the Northwest, and rightly so, though I object to its being called "barbecued." But I know I am in the minority on that one. It seems that anything that has a spicy sauce dabbed on can now masquerade under that name. Here, if you can find it, is a recipe for a crab that's really barbecued, and one that is a pretender.

First, for the sauce: crush a large clove of garlic in a teaspoon of salt. Add a tablespoon each of soy sauce and curry powder, ¼ cup of catsup, 2 tablespoons of lemon juice, and 2 cups of fish or meat stock. Simmer 5 minutes before using. For both the oven and the grilling method, clean the crabs, Dungeness preferred, allowing a half for each serving. Crack the claws and cut the body in halves or quarters. Either grill over charcoal, or cook in a casserole, in the oven, in either case basting constantly with the sauce until done. It is best to use live crabs, but if they are not available, cooked crabs will do. TWO CRABS AND THIS AMOUNT OF SAUCE WILL SERVE 4 PERSONS. The latter should be well swathed in towels or wearing bibs.

1 large clove garlic	¼ cup catsup
1 teaspoon salt	2 tablespoons lemon juice
1 tablespoon soy sauce	2 cups fish or meat stock
1 tablespoon curry powder	2 crabs

(Broiled King Crab Legs

Here's a recipe that should be numbered among the world's classics, and no doubt will be when it becomes better known. The King crab has only recently taken to the air, but already

132

Fish and Shellfish

some West Coast restaurants are featuring it. They are expensive, but some good things in life *do* come high.

Use the large middle section of the leg, one for each serving. Split the shell with a heavy pointed knife (a boning knife) the length of the leg (the shell is tough, not brittle, rather like heavy celluloid) and make a cross cut in the middle. Lay back the shell just enough to allow the entrance of the sauce, which is a simple one: equal parts of melted butter and lemon juice. Broil the crab legs over glowing charcoal, cut side up, and baste several times with the sauce during the process. (Your crabs will probably be precooked, so this takes only long enough to allow the bottom side to become nut brown.) Serve in the shell and eat in reverent silence. This same dish has been served flambé, but why try to improve perfection?

❨ Crab Legs Palace Court

The Palace! Everyone knows it, everyone loves it. Most famous of all San Francisco's famous eating places, most truly allied with the romantic history of San Francisco. The Palace Hotel, born in bonanza days, was destroyed in The Fire, but was rebuilt and is now greater than ever. Many a famous recipe has been created here. Green Goddess dressing (page 318), Oysters Kirkpatrick (page 148), Strawberries Romanoff (page 75). Because of its greatness, the Palace shares its secrets generously.

"Fill heart of artichoke (page 360) to level with fresh vegetable salad (cut string beans, cauliflower, asparagus tips, and peas). Dress 5 or 6 crab legs on it, garnish with 2 strips of red and green peppers.

"Dress on a plate a bed of shredded lettuce with a slice of tomato on it. Sprinkle chopped eggs around, and press same against lettuce to form a little nest. Set artichoke on top and serve with Thousand Island dressing.

"You can also dress on artichoke three slices of lobster, chicken, or shrimp."

⟨ Crab Louis

Just which Louis invented this West Coast specialty I am not prepared to say, but only because I don't know. I do know, however, that it was served at Solari's, in San Francisco, in 1914, for Clarence Edwords gives their recipe for it in his epicure's guide, *Bohemian San Francisco*. That version, incidentally, has chopped mustard pickle in the sauce, as well as Worcestershire. This recipe may not be that of the mysterious Louis, but it is one well liked in Seattle and Los Angeles, as well as San Francisco.

Arrange the body meat of a large crab, preferably a Dungeness, in a bed of lettuce. Pour over it the Louis dressing and garnish it with the crab legs, quartered tomatoes, and quartered hard-boiled eggs, arranged symmetrically. Sometimes artichoke bottoms are included, too. The Louis dressing — my version, that is — is made by combining a cup of mayonnaise, ¼ cup each of heavy cream, chili sauce, chopped green pepper, and chopped green onion, and 2 tablespoons of chopped green olives. Add salt and lemon juice to suit your taste. SERVES 2.

1 large crab	*¼ cup chopped green onion*
1 cup mayonnaise	*2 tablespoons chopped green*
¼ cup heavy cream	*olives*
¼ cup chili sauce	*Salt*
¼ cup chopped green pepper	*Lemon juice*

⟨ Pacific Cracked Crab

Some like it hot and some like it cold, but we all like it. In fact, so devoted are we to this West Coast treat that we usually make a meal of it, having little else but hot French bread and chilled white wine. That's West Coast eating at its best.

Plunge live crabs into boiling salted water, bring again to the boil, then turn heat down and simmer from 10 to 25 minutes, depending upon the size of your crabs. Remove apron, a portion of the shell that you will recognize from its name. Separate shells and discard stomach. Remove claws

134

Fish and Shellfish

and crack them with a gentle thwack with a mallet, and cut the body into 4 pieces with a heavy knife. Pile on a preheated platter and serve at once with melted butter. Or chill and serve on cracked ice with mayonnaise, made freshly with lemon juice. In either case, serve nutcrackers and picks to help dig out every last morsel of savory meat.

(Tarantino's Deviled Crab

Tarantino's, on Fisherman's Wharf in San Francisco, is a comparatively new restaurant, but its fame is no less great than many older ones. This is one of their popular seafood dishes, one that may be prepared far from the Bay area, using frozen crab meat. "Deviled," quite obviously, means hot as the devil, and so this famous Tarantino recipe is just that. So, unless you know that you can take it, add the mustard a little at a time, and taste as you add. (I hope that Messieurs Sweeney and McAteer will forgive my meddling!) Here is their recipe:

1 pound of crab meat, or	1 small can pimientos
4 whole cooked crabs	1 ounce Worcestershire
6 hard-boiled eggs	sauce
4 teaspoons French mustard	2 tablespoons butter
2 teaspoons dry mustard	½ cup flour (or less)
1 pint milk	

"Heat milk but do not boil. Place butter in saucepan and melt. Add flour until you have a medium roux. Do not brown. Add hot milk until you have a thick cream sauce. Add chopped hard-boiled eggs, French mustard, dry mustard, pimientos chopped finely, and Worcestershire sauce. Salt and pepper to taste. Cook for 5 minutes, stirring often. Remove all the meat from legs and body of salt-water hard-shell crab. If crab in the shell is not available, use 1 pound of crab meat. Add the crab meat to the sauce, stirring gently so as not to break the meat and legs. Now, place in crab shells or casseroles. Sprinkle top with Parmesan cheese, and bake 20 minutes at 450°."

([Dan & Louis' Fried Jumbo Crab Legs

Dan & Louis' Oyster Bar, in Portland, is noted for their wonderful ways with Olympia oysters, but they also know their other shellfish intimately. And here's a restaurant where you can dine like a king without paying his ransom. This recipe is as they gave it.

"Mix whole eggs, milk, salt, and flour into a batter. Add garlic salt to batter and mix thoroughly. Add crab legs to batter and gently turn them over until each crab leg is covered with batter. Drain off excess batter and gently roll legs in pilot meal until dry. French fry legs for one minute, or pan fry until a golden brown. Serve with tartar sauce and lemon slices. SUFFICIENT FOR 6 PORTIONS."

40 select jumbo crab legs	¼ cup flour
(from precooked crabs)	¼ teaspoon Schilling's garlic
4 eggs	salt
1 pint milk	1 quart pilot meal
1 pinch salt	(cracker dust)

([Gobey's Crab Stew

Fish stew was a specialty at the Auction Lunch, a San Francisco restaurant where the Empire Builders were wont to gather at noon. Another favorite restaurant was Gobey's, and there the specialty was this:

Remove and flake meat and fat from 2 large cooked crabs, and soak it in ½ cup of California sherry for 3 or 4 hours. Crush a clove of garlic and heat it with 2 tablespoons of butter. Remove garlic, add a tablespoon of flour, a pinch of rosemary, ½ cup of minced onion, ¼ cup of minced green pepper, 1 large peeled tomato, chopped, and salt and fresh ground pepper. Cook this 5 minutes, then add the crab meat, a cup of cream, and the sherry in which the crab soaked. Cook all together for a few minutes more, adding more cream if necessary, and correcting the seasoning. Serve with toast. This is, obviously, perfect for a chafing dish. SERVES 6.

2 large crabs	1 pinch rosemary
½ cup sherry	½ cup minced onion
1 clove garlic	¼ cup minced green pepper
2 tablespoons butter	1 tomato
1 tablespoon flour	Salt and pepper
1 cup cream (or more)	

(Crab Notes

Crab and Avocado. This seems to be a favorite combination, particularly in California. Halves of avocados are filled with crab salad or, and better, hot creamed crab is poured over slices of avocado which are neatly arranged on toast.

Oregon Stewed Crab. This is an old one, and a honey. Heat big hunks of crab meat in rich milk, add a piece of butter, salt and pepper, and serve with pilot biscuits.

Crab and Mushrooms Oregonian. Add sautéed mushrooms to a rich cream sauce flavored with sherry. Put in a casserole and completely cover the top with breaded fried crab legs. Don't skip this one!

Crab Meat in Browned Butter. This is for a chafing dish. Brown ¼ pound of butter, add the meat of a Dungeness crab, heat, sprinkle with chopped parsley, and serve at once with lemon. Ah!

Chafing Dish Crab. Brown 2 tablespoons of minced shallots in ¼ cup of butter. Add 2 tablespoons of flour, 1¼ cups of milk, and 2 tablespoons of sherry. Cook smooth, then add the meat of a Dungeness crab.

(Willamette Spiced Crawfish

Lillian Russell was so fond of these tiny fresh-water crustaceans that she was suspected of lacing lightly when she knew they were to be on the menu. This was when she was visiting the Northwest. Catching "crawdads" is as much fun as eating them, and there's considerable skill involved in both. The crawfish are usually boiled in a highly spiced court bouillon and served, either hot or cold, in portions of about a dozen, though many a trencherman has disposed of more than double that number. The crawfish is separated from its tail and the juices sucked from its body. The tail end is treated in the same manner. That gastronomical rite having been performed, the real business begins: the green fat is scraped from the body and spread on crackers. This is eaten with the tail and claw meat. Sometimes the fish are shelled in the kitchen and served with mayonnaise or Louis sauce, or breaded and deep fried — a sissy business, but a mighty pleasant one. This recipe comes from an Oregonian who does not approve the very highly seasoned liquor in which crawfish are often cooked. I agree.

For 4 dozen crawfish, have a gallon of water, 2 cups of white wine, 2 whole oranges, chopped, skin and all, 3 cloves of garlic, 3 tablespoons of salt, a teaspoon each of rosemary, whole cloves, and peppercorns. The fish are cleaned, then simmered in this liquid until they are bright red, or about 15 minutes. They may be served either hot or cold.

4 dozen crawfish	3 cloves garlic
1 gallon water	3 tablespoons salt
2 cups white wine	1 teaspoon rosemary
2 oranges	1 teaspoon whole cloves
1 teaspoon peppercorns	

(Frogs Legs Castellar

Frogs legs are found in some parts of the Northwest, but it's a lot easier to look for them in your frozen food market. This recipe is from Los Angeles.

Allow from 2 to 6 pairs of frogs legs per serving, depending on the size of the legs and the guests. Marinate them (12 pairs) in a pint of white wine, with an herb bouquet (rosemary, parsley and bay), and a crushed clove of garlic, for 6 hours. Drain and dip in seasoned flour and sauté a lovely gold in ¼

138

pound of butter. Remove them to a hot platter. Cook a ¼ cup of chopped shallots in the butter that is left in the pan, and, when they are a light brown, add 3 tablespoons of flour and a cup each of cream and the marinade, strained. Cook until smooth, correct seasoning, and serve with the frogs legs that have been sprinkled with minced parsley and garnished with lemon quarters.

12 pairs frogs legs	*¼ pound butter*
1 pint white wine	*¼ cup chopped shallots*
1 herb bouquet	*3 tablespoons flour*
1 clove garlic	*1 cup cream*
Minced parsley	

NOTE: A recipe very much like this one is for a chafing dish. The marinade is the same. The frogs legs (small ones, for this) are browned in the chafing dish. When they have colored, a jigger of brandy is poured on them and set aflame, then a cup of very heavy cream and ½ cup of the marinade are poured in and heated with the legs. The sauce is seasoned and served from the chafing dish. This is a bachelor's delight, and so there is always much ad libbing with the seasonings. . . .

NOTE: A simple way with frogs legs is to dip them in cream, then in seasoned flour, fry in butter, and serve with lemon and parsley. . . . Or, swill out the pan with red or white wine, pour on the legs, and sprinkle with parsley. In either case, the herbs of your desire may be added to the flour — powdered, of course.

(*Grunions*

It is not a gag, this business of grunion hunting. The tiny fish, a kind of silversides, do actually come right up on the beaches to spawn. They perform a fantastic sort of dance, digging holes in the sand with their tails, and in them depositing their eggs. Their run is so regular that their time of arrival can be charted fairly definitely, so people by the hundreds gather and catch them bare-handed. It's a fun game, enjoyed by everyone, including California's Governor Warren and his family. Grunions are cleaned, and cooked in deep fat like smelts. They should be very crisp, these slender little fish, so dipping them first in egg or milk, and then in corn meal is in order. They are highly prized for food as well as fun.

(Lobsters

Our West Coast lobsters are spiny lobsters, the langoustes of France. Unlike the Eastern lobsters (homards), they do not have the two large claws, and are usually smaller in size. It is a bit difficult to obtain live lobsters on some parts of the coast, apparently because they die quite easily and the loss is therefore much less if they are sold already boiled. In many cases, as for salad, Newburg, and such, it doesn't matter, but for broiling or cooking in the Chinese manner, it is most desirable to have live lobsters. Perhaps if you order them ahead of time, you can persuade your fish dealer to co-operate.

(Stuffed Lobster Bok Quan

This recipe was given to me by Dr. Edgar F. Mauer, who acquired it from one of his Chinese patients, Jack Quan, sometimes known as the Mayor of Los Angeles's Chinatown. It may sound like a terrific chore to prepare, but it's worth every hour you spend on it, including the time it will take you to round up the ingredients. If there is no Chinese section in your vicinity, you'll have to skip the entire project. This recipe is for six small lobsters, which should be alive. This is the way it was given to me:

"Chop very fine 1 pound lean pork, 4 water chestnuts, a clove of garlic, a little green ginger, a bit of ham, 3 or 4 mushrooms. (If the dry kind, soak in water for 30 or 40 minutes to facilitate chopping.) Toss this together, add some whiskey, a little soy sauce, pepper, and a very small amount of sesame oil, but it has to be the flavorsome Chinese variety called 'My-Yu.' The bottle says 'sesamum-oiler.' Take 3 salted eggs,

140

the kind that come in black peat — wash them, then separate the eggs, adding the whites to the above. Also add some taste powder (M.S.G.). Cornstarch may be used for thickening if necessary.

"Now split your lobsters, clean them, and remove the meat, leaving the half shells intact. Cut the meat into smallish pieces, and add the other ingredients. Now mix all very thoroughly by hand and salt to taste if you are not afraid of trichinosis from the raw pork. When thoroughly mixed, replace the mixture in the shells and steam them for 20 to 30 minutes. Before steaming you should slice the hard yolks of the salt eggs and garnish the top of the filling with them and some green onion — these for flavor and color.

"Just before serving, remove the liquor from the bottom of the vessel containing the lobsters, and carefully spoon it back on top of the filling.

"If cooked lobsters are used there will be little liquor, so make a sauce with some bits of lobster meat and shell, add taste powder, soy sauce, salt and pepper. Heat for 10 minutes. Remove the meat and chop very fine, or it may be discarded. Pour carefully over the stuffing and serve very hot.

"NOTE: Here are the amounts I used for this recipe (SERVES 6 TO 12):

"6 lobsters
1 pound lean pork
4 water chestnuts
1 clove garlic
2 teaspoons grated green ginger
¼ cup chopped ham
3–4 mushrooms
⅓ cup whiskey
2 tablespoons soy sauce
¼ cup toasted sesame oil
3 Chinese salted eggs
1 teaspoon M.S.G.
Pepper
Cornstarch"

NOTE: These salted eggs are duck eggs, and are to be had in any Chinese grocery store. They are covered with a thick black blanket, and are known to Occidentals as "100-year-old eggs." Actually, they are usually 2 or 3 months old, which makes them daisy-fresh compared to cheese and other foods we like aged.

❪ Chinese Garlic Lobster

Chow lung hai is what this is called, or so it sounds to me. It's a favorite among habitués of the best Chinese restaurants.

Chop a pound of cooked pork very fine, add 2 tablespoons of chopped green ginger (page 242), 2 cloves of minced garlic, and the meat of 2 live lobsters, which has been removed from the shell, cut in goodly chunks, and cooked in oil until red. (I'll settle for boiled lobster here, though it won't be *quite* as good.) Return this meat mixture to the cooked shells, and steam them in 2 cups of chicken stock for half an hour, basting once or twice. Before serving, thicken the juices with a little cornstarch mixed with cold water, and season with soy sauce. SERVES 4 AS A MAIN DISH — 8 TO 12 IF ON A CHINESE MENU.

1 pound cooked pork
2 tablespoons chopped green ginger
2 cloves garlic

2 lobsters
2 cups chicken stock
Cornstarch
Soy sauce

❪ Mussels, Fisherman's Style

Mussels have fallen into disrepute on the West Coast because of an unpleasant habit they have of poisoning us at certain times of year. During their unfriendly period, however, they are quarantined, so it is quite safe to eat them when they are in season. They may usually be had for the gathering, and are deliciously and highly flavored.

Soak and scrub and scrape 4 quarts of mussels, using a wire brush if possible. Put them in a large pot that has a cover, and add 4 chopped leeks, ½ cup of chopped parsley, 4 minced cloves of garlic, a few grindings of black pepper, and 1¼ cups of white wine. Cover and cook until they open, which won't be very long. Remove from the shells, pluck off the beards and the black parts, and put the mussels in a tureen, straining the hot broth over them. (Add ¼ pound of butter, if desired.) Serve with garlic bread. This broth may be served as sauce, and the mussels, with stomach and beards removed, may be

142

egged and crumbed and fried very lightly in butter until gold. Wonderful! SERVES 4 to 8, DEPENDING!

    4 quarts mussels   4 minced cloves garlic
    4 chopped leeks   Pepper
    ½ cup chopped parsley   1¼ cups white wine
              ¼ pound butter (optional)

(Oysters

The entire history of the West Coast is flavored with oysters. Kitchen middens, those ancient piles of shells left by the Indians after a gathering of the tribes, prove that even then oysters were eaten when there was whoopee to be made. These oysters were the native ones, the tiny *Ostrea lurida*, that were found from British Columbia to Mexico. In the Mother Lode country, oysters, though they were canned ones from the East, seem to have been as common as salt pork and slumgullion, but not as tiresome, for when gold-laden miners made an occasional break for San Francisco, they eagerly paid fantastic prices for more oysters. Actually, these canned oysters must have been exceptionally good. Dame Shirley, who knew a thing or two about food, says that they could not have been "nicer had they just slid from their shells on the shore at Amboy." Soon Oregonians, or at least those who hadn't taken off for the gold mines, discovered there was gold in those succulent little "natives" that grew up and down the coast. The first Shoalwater Bay oysters were sent to San Francisco in 1851, and soon the oyster boom was on. The oyster beds of Olympia and Yaquina were so crawling with adventurers, most of them disgruntled gold seekers, that a law was passed prohibiting nonresidents from gathering oysters. The Eastern oyster had been favored in San Francisco, particularly at the plush restaurants that began to crop up by the dozen, but finally the Palace, always champion of native products, began to feature the Western shellfish. Soon the little oysters of Washington, Oregon, and California began to gain the glory they deserved, and are now cultivated in tremendous quantities. The Eastern oysters (*Ostrea virginica*) are cultivated in a small way in

143

several areas; and the giant Japanese oyster (*Ostrea gigas*) in large quantities in Willapa bay.

The tiny Olympias are the very quintessence of oyster flavor, tasting as if all the goodness of the larger variety had been concentrated into this tiny morsel of delight. They are expensive, even near their birthplace, and no wonder, as it sometimes takes three hundred of them to make a quart. And don't let anyone tell you that they are *never* served on the half shell, for if you believe it you'll miss the treat of your life. A portion usually consists of three dozen oysters, but any gourmet worthy of his mettle can put away three times that amount without a quiver, except of pleasure.

The Japanese oysters, first planted here in 1902, are now called the Willapoint. They are enormous, sometimes as big as a man's hand. Wonderful for frying, bisques, scallops, and the like, but are seldom served in the half shell. So huge a "one-bite" morsel would prove too disconcerting, even when presented on its own plate of mother-of-pearl. These oysters are packed in jars and sent, iced, to all parts of the West.

❨ *Hangtown Fry*

This, most famous of our own oyster dishes, dates back to the days of the Argonauts. That we know, but we don't know just exactly how it got its name — it's too good a one not to have started many yarns a-spinning. A sure guess is that it had something to do with the town of that name (Hangtown was later renamed Placerville to appease some of its more fastidious citizens). One story is that a man about to be hanged asked that his last meal be "fried oysters with scrambled eggs on top and bacon on the side." A story that seems more likely is that the dish was named after Nick "Hangtown," whose nickname was acquired when he cooked for Mr. Studebaker, the wheelbarrow king, in Hangtown. (Mr. Studebaker was quite busy laying the foundation of his family's fortune.) Later Nick went to Collins & Wheeland, in San Francisco, where he became the cook, and introduced the famous oyster dish.

The shucked oysters are dried, dusted with flour, dipped in beaten egg which has been seasoned with salt and pepper, then rolled in cracker crumbs and browned on both sides in

144

butter, not more than a minute on each side. Beaten seasoned eggs are poured over the oysters and allowed to set, then turned, oysters and all, and browned on the other side. (About 4 medium oysters and 2 eggs to each serving.) This is served with bacon, and often fried onions and/or fried green peppers are an extra embellishment. An even simpler way to make this famous dish is to mix scrambled eggs with fried oysters and serve!

4 medium oysters	*Salt and pepper*
Flour	*Cracker crumbs*
Beaten egg	*Butter*

2 eggs

❨ Barbecued Oysters

With the advent of aluminum foil and the popularity of the charcoal grill, this recipe was born. May it live forever.

Scrub oysters well, and wrap them in aluminum foil, securing the edges well. For very large oysters, and goodness knows we have them in Washington, use but 1 to a package, for smaller ones 3 or 4, for baby Olympias 6 or 8. Arrange the oysters with the deep shell on the bottom, and place in that same manner on a bed of glowing coals. Let them roast about 6 minutes — for medium oysters, that is — and serve directly from fire to table, letting each man open his own. Melted butter is the only requisite except, perhaps, a pair of tongs for serving purposes. The oysters are eaten by splitting the aluminum, removing the top shell, which is open now, and baptizing the oyster with the butter. Clams and mussels may be barbecued in the same manner.

NOTE: A quite different way of doing oysters on the charcoal grill is to broil them. Dip shelled oysters, not too small, in melted butter, and then in crumbs. Put them in an old-fashioned toaster (the kind with the wires close together), and broil them over charcoal until brown, brushing them once on each side with melted butter. They may also be strung on skewers with mushrooms between, though in this case the crumbs are omitted and each oyster is wrapped in a piece of bacon.

⟨ Oysters Poulette

The Maison Dorée, an early and beloved restaurant in San Francisco, took great pride in this dish, and no wonder. Here again a chafing dish is in order. With the oysters serve smoked turkey, toasted English muffins, and a salad of diced celery and cucumbers, dressed lightly with mayonnaise and garnished with cress.

Make a sauce poulette by cooking 2 tablespoons of minced shallots or green onions in 4 tablespoons of butter until they are transparent. Add ¼ cup of sliced fresh mushrooms, and ¼ cup of white wine, and allow the liquid to reduce. Stir in 3 tablespoons of flour, cook another couple of minutes, then pour in a cup of chicken stock and a cup of heavy cream. Season with salt, pepper, and a grating of nutmeg. Cook smooth and thick, whip in 2 egg yolks, then fold in a quart of small oysters that have been heated just enough to plump, then drained. The classic poulette sauce is made by adding egg yolks, cream, and lemon juice to a simple cream sauce, and often used for frogs legs. This, however, is the popular California recipe — I suppose we had to get that wine in somehow. SERVES 6 TO 8.

2 tablespoons minced shal-
    lots
4 tablespoons butter
¼ cup sliced mushrooms
¼ cup white wine
3 tablespoons flour

1 cup chicken stock
1 cup heavy cream
Salt, pepper
Nutmeg
2 egg yolks
1 quart small oysters

⟨ Pickled Oysters

A charming menu, printed on yellow silk, and dated 1863, is the bill of fare of the Inauguration Ball of California's Governor Frederick F. Lowe. It was held at the Pavilion, in Sacramento, and featured, among dozens of other things, *four* oyster dishes — raw, pickled, fried, and pâté. Here is the way to pickle them.

Cook a pint of oysters in their own liquor until the edges

146

curl. Drain them at once, saving the liquor, and plunge them into ice water. Again drain, and arrange on a flat dish, covering with transparently thin slices of onion and lemon. Heat ½ cup of white wine vinegar with the oyster liquor, add a teaspoon of pickling spices, and cook 10 minutes, then strain and cool and pour over the oysters. Sprinkle with salt and pepper and minced parsley, add a drizzle of olive oil, and relegate to the refrigerator for a day or two before serving on a bed of lettuce for a first course, or as a lagniappe at a buffet supper. SERVES 6.

1 pint oysters	1 teaspoon pickling spices
Sliced onion	Salt and pepper
Sliced lemon	Minced parsley
½ cup white wine vinegar	Olive oil

◖ Portland Oyster Rabbit

Portland has always been an oyster town. Dean Collins, in Volume I of his charming little book *The Cheddar Box* (Volume II was a block of fine Tillamook Cheddar, same size), says that oysters were packed over the Harris Trail to Portland for Keith's Oyster House, where the gay blades of the '50s ate oysters, drank wine, and made whoopee and goodness knows what all, until 3 o'clock and after. "And," says Mr. Collins, "the 3 o'clock was A.M., and very very wild in those days." Perhaps they sometimes had this Portland rabbit, too.

Cook a cup of small oysters in their own liquor until their edges curl. In a pan over hot water, melt a tablespoon of butter, add ½ pound of Oregon Cheddar, and a little salt and pepper. Stir and cook *slowly* while the cheese melts. Then add the oyster liquor, also slowly, and 2 beaten eggs. When smooth, stir in the oysters and serve at once on toast, and don't forget some ice-cold beer! SERVES 4.

1 cup small oysters	½ pound Cheddar
1 tablespoon butter	Salt and pepper
	2 eggs

([*Prescott's Olympia Pan Roast*

Oyster pan roast and pepper pan roast are as typical of the Northwest as the Columbia River. There are several schools of thought on just how they should be done — this is mine. These recipes call for the infant Olympia oysters, but the larger "Eastern" oysters are often used.

Melt ¼ pound of butter, add 2 cups of Olympia oysters, and sprinkle with salt and pepper. As soon as the oysters are plump, which is almost at once, dish up on toast and serve. (Save that oyster juice!) SERVES 4 TO 6.

NOTE: *Other Oyster Pan Roasts:* A more frequent recipe is this. Bring a pint of oysters just to the boil, and drain off the liquor. In another pan melt ¼ pound of butter, add 2 tablespoons of catsup, 2 teaspoons of vinegar, and a dash of Worcestershire sauce. Cayenne, too, if you wish. Add this dressing to the drained oysters, simmer 1 minute, and serve on toast. Restaurants often serve this in individual casseroles, doing the last minute of cooking in the oven. For the life of me I can't see why the oysters are drained, but four different cooks have given me almost identical recipes, all draining the oysters. So . . . suit yourself — or leave the oysters undrained and thicken the juices a bit, as some good cooks do.

NOTE: *A Pepper Pan Roast.* Cook ¼ cup each of minced onion and green pepper and a crushed clove of garlic in ½ pound of butter for 2 minutes. Remove garlic, add a pint of oysters and cook until plump. Serve, as with the others, accompanied by toast. Another pepper roast merely adds chopped green pepper to the second one, above.

([*Oysters Kirkpatrick*

New Orleans, with its Oysters Rockefeller, has nothing on us, with our Oysters Kirkpatrick. This dish was named in honor of John C. Kirkpatrick, onetime manager of the Palace, in San Francisco. It was, of course, conceived in their kitchen. Like all recipes of renown, this one has many versions — but

148

Fish and Shellfish

who am I to quibble with the Palace Hotel's own recipe, graciously sent for inclusion in this book.

"Open oysters on deep shell, put in oven for about 3 or 4 minutes until oysters shrink. Pour off the liquor, then add small strip of bacon and cover with catsup and place in very hot oven for about 5 or 6 minutes (according to oven) until glazed to a nice golden brown."

Here's another way it's done, or *am* I quibbling? Allow pie-plates or deep ovenproof plates, one for each serving, and fill them with rock salt within an inch of their tops. Put them into the oven to become very hot. The oysters, usually 6 to a serving, are opened and left in their deep shells, which are placed in little indentations made in the hot salt. On top of each oyster is spread a spoonful of tomato catsup which has been mixed with finely minced green pepper. On this goes a piece of partially cooked bacon, next some grated cheese, with a small dab of butter as the finishing touch. The pans are returned to the oven (450°) until the cheese is nicely browned.

NOTE: Apparently this entire — and very good — business of roasting oysters in a pan of salt was originally just that — an oyster salt roast. But chefs were bound to add their distinctive touches, it's the artist in them. One was called "Oysters à la Mali," and was a bit more elaborate than most. A sauce made with ¼ cup of cooked chopped spinach, a tablespoon of minced parsley, a tablespoon of minced tarragon, a clove of garlic, ¼ cup of butter, a teaspoon of salt, and a cup of white wine, was mixed with 12 ground and drained poached oysters. This mixture was spread on the oysters in their shells (see above). They were then sprinkled with buttered crumbs and baked until brown.

NOTE: Simplest of all is Oysters Yaquina, in which the oysters are baked in their shells with no adornment save chive butter.

NOTE: *Good Woman's Oysters (Ostras de la Buena Mujer).* The oysters were first poached, then ground and mixed with bread crumbs, parsley, minced onions, butter, and a few chopped anchovies, then returned to their shells and baked. This was an old California way.

149

(Treasure Island Oyster Loaf

Famous in the early days of San Francisco, as well as in New Orleans — who can say which city served it first? And who cares?

Slice the top crust, in one piece, from a loaf of white bread — homemade, if possible. Carefully remove crumbs from the center of the loaf, leaving a shell. Brush the inside very well with melted butter, and also brush the cut side of the top. Put both pieces in a moderate oven (350°) to brown lightly. Now, fry some oysters (you know — dry them, dip them in egg and then in fine seasoned crumbs, let dry a while, then either pan fry or deep fry until brown). Fill the bread case with the fried oysters and replace the top. Serve very hot. Sometimes a little melted butter or hot cream is drizzled over the oysters in their crusty bed, but this seems to detract from that wonderful crispiness.

NOTE: These used to be known as "peacemakers" in San Francisco's gaudy days, because erring husbands in that food-conscious city would bring one home to appease their spouses, instead of the more conventional flowers or candy. And if you've never tasted a sandwich made of fried oysters, toast and lettuce — that's a peacemaker in miniature.

NOTE: We don't stop at oyster loaves, though they are most traditional. We have shrimp and clam, lobster and crab loaves, often making them individually — using crusty French rolls as the case. The clams are breaded and fried, like the oysters, but the other fish need not be. Merely cooked golden in butter. They are good adjuncts to an outdoor meal, these loaves. Serve them with roast corn, grilled hamburgers, and Balboa Salad (page 315).

(Oyster Notes

Oysters Benedict has poached oysters substituted for the eggs in that classic dish, eggs Benedict. Split and toasted English muffins, slice of ham, poached oysters (one to a dozen, depending on their size), and hollandaise.

150

Fish and Shellfish

Oysters Meunière. The luscious bivalve is dipped in flour, browned quickly but gently in butter, served on toast with plenty of butter and lemon juice poured over.

Oysters Baked in Cream. The famous old Portland cook book, the *Webfoot,* mixed a pint of cream, a pint of oysters, 4 eggs, salt and pepper, and baked it like a custard. Good, too.

Oyster Balls. An early Puget Sound recipe. Mix chopped poached oysters with mashed potatoes, parsley, and egg yolks. Form in balls, flour, and fry in deep fat. The original recipe said *bear* grease!

Olympia Oyster Fritters. These, according to an old book, are frittered by "taking up several in a spoonful of batter and frying." The tiny oysters offered a similar problem in frying — it's quite a chore to do them one at a time. The *Webfoot Cook Book* solved it this way: "Egg them, then form 5 or 6 in a cake, and dip in crumbs."

Oyster Shortcake. Just what you'd guess. Biscuit dough with creamed oysters, plenty of them, and a sprinkling of parsley for color and flavor.

Oyster Sausage is not uncommon. Poached oysters, drained, ground, and mixed with suet, veal, crumbs, and herbs, then fried in cakes or stuffed in casings and browned in butter.

Oysters Maréchale are glorified fried oysters, popular with the smart set of San Francisco in the '90s. A thick sauce is made with oyster liquor, cream, truffles, and mushrooms, thickened with egg yolk and made piquant with lime juice. The oysters are masked in this, then crumbed, then egged, crumbed again, and fried in butter!

Fried Oysters. The Cliff House, overlooking the famous Seal Rocks near the Golden Gate, has long been a favorite eating place for San Franciscans. Before the turn of the century, they used to drive there in their carriages, and eat the Cliff House specialty, fried oysters, as they watched the famed old seal, Ben Butler, as he sported on the rocks.

151

([Rockfish en Papilotte

Or, as we are much more apt to call it, rockfish in paper. This recipe may be used for any firm fish. A San Francisco cook book of 1872, called *How to Keep a Husband,* had a recipe for salmon *en papilotte,* simply sauced with butter. Well, that's one way.

Cut parchment paper, writing paper, or aluminum foil into large, fat, heart-shaped pieces (an 8½ × 11-inch piece is the right size before cutting) allowing one sheet per serving. Also allow a 4-ounce piece of fish for each paper, as well as 1 shrimp and 1 good-sized mushroom. Rockfish, miscalled rock cod, or any firm-fleshed white fish will do. (If a thin fillet is used, it should be folded double.) For 6 servings make a sauce by sautéing 5 chopped shallots in ⅛ pound of butter, adding ¼ cup of flour, a cup of white wine, a cup of cream, and ¼ cup of chopped sautéed mushrooms. An egg yolk may be added, too. Season to taste and chill for easier handling. Spread a little of the cold sauce on one half of a paper heart, place a piece of the fish on it, top with a sautéed mushroom and a cooked cleaned shrimp. Then add a good dollop of the sauce (about ½ cup). Fold the paper and double fold the edges, crimping the paper firmly. Bake in a hot oven (450°) for 15 minutes, or until the paper is puffed and brown. For other delightful ways of cooking fish in paper, see page 158 and page 170.

1½ pounds rockfish	¼ cup flour
6 shrimps	1 cup white wine
6 large mushrooms	1 cup cream
5 shallots	¼ cup chopped mushrooms
⅛ pound butter	Salt and pepper
1 egg yolk (optional)	

NOTE: Rockfish is believed by some people to taste very much like crab, and is frequently used as a "stretcher" for that more expensive delicacy. A salad made entirely with rockfish and celery, with mayonnaise and perhaps a touch of curry, is very pleasant.

152

Fish and Shellfish

⟨ Barbecued Sablefish Steak

Sablefish is perhaps better known as black Alaska cod. It isn't a cod, but it's wonderful — rich, meaty, and flavorsome.

Broil steaks over charcoal, basting with white wine and melted butter, in equal parts. Serve with a cucumber and onion salad and plenty of toasted French bread.

⟨ Salmon

Salmon is king in the Northwest, and always has been. Long before the invasion of the white men, the Indians were wise in the ways of the fish, and pretty dependent upon it as an omnipresent source of food. They ate the first salmon of the year with great ceremony, believing that by so honoring it, plenty of its siblings would come rushing up the river asking to be speared. The surplus salmon they kept in various ways. Some was sun-dried, flaked, and packed in huge leaf-lined baskets which held a hundred pounds or more, but mostly it was smoked. It is said that the presence of an Indian could be detected at a distance by the odor of smoked salmon, and that when one entered a pioneer's cabin — always without knocking — for a *nanitch* or look around, the stench was more than most could take. But both red and white Americans could take plenty of salmon, and they did.

The Indian methods of smoking fish were famous, and the white men learned them all, and still use the Indian methods when cooking salmon out of doors. A modern adaptation of the Indian way is to remove head, tail, and fins of a whole salmon, and to split it, removing the backbone from the inside and being careful not to split through the skin. Now a long piece of sapling, a wood without an unpleasant flavor, is split down a little longer than the length of the salmon, the spread fish is inserted in this split all the way, from head to tail, with a bit of the split wood protruding beyond the fish. (The stick is where the backbone was.) Next three or four crosspieces of wood are thrust through the split and into the two belly sides of the fish, to hold it open, and the top end of the split is tied together to hold everything in place. It will look some-

153

thing like a flabby kite. The unsplit end of the wood is thrust into the ground at an angle, and close enough to a bed of glowing coals to cook it to a beautiful turn. This is called barbecued salmon, or salmon sluitum, and is salmon at its best, served simply with butter and lemon, roast potatoes and corn. A simpler way, perhaps, is to nail the salmon on a board and prop that near the fire.

There are five kinds of salmon in the Pacific Northwest. King salmon, called Chinook in its homeland, is the largest and choicest of them all. It sometimes reaches sixty pounds. Next comes the red or Sockeye salmon, a much smaller fish that averages seven pounds. It is excellent for canning. Cohu, a medium red salmon, is also called silver salmon, and is best when eaten fresh. They weigh up to thirty pounds. Pink or humpback salmon averages only four pounds in weight. Much of it is canned, and, though it's light in color, it is fine in flavor. Because of the decided preference for the red-fleshed salmon, this pink was once difficult to market. One canny packer solved the problem by labeling it "Genuine Pink Salmon, Guaranteed Not to Turn Red." Last on the list is the humble Chum, or Keta, or dog salmon. It may be at the bottom of the list, but it is still a fish of which we are proud, for it's fine eating, fresh or canned.

(Baked Whole Salmon, Washington Style

A hundred years ago a group of pioneers saw what they took to be the ominous sign of Indians on the warpath — a red flag flying from the top of a tall dead tree. Approaching cautiously, they found that it was an Indian sign, all right, but not a flag. A huge split salmon had been fastened to the tree to advertise fresh fish for sale. If they succumbed to this sales device, and took one home, the chances are that it was cooked in this old pioneer manner.

A 10- to 20-pound fish is rubbed with salt, pepper, and a little powdered thyme, then wrapped in several thicknesses of wrapping paper. Allow ½ pound of fish per serving. The salmon is slowly baked at 275° for 3 or 4 hours, depending on the size. (The modern way to be sure is to use a meat thermometer. When it reaches 160° internal temperature, that's it!) The paper is cut open at the top and pulled back, the skin along with it. The sauce is made with 4 chopped hard-boiled eggs, ½ pound of melted butter, and ½ cup of lemon juice. Boiled new potatoes, with this, and baby peas.

SAUCE

4 hard-boiled eggs   ½ pound butter
½ cup lemon juice

⟦ Rogue River Grilled Salmon Steak

Next to beefsteak, a good fresh salmon steak is as fine as anything can be, providing it's done correctly. Broiling any fish, indoors or out, depends on timing, being sure to have a very hot fire so the fish won't dry out. There's no use trying to give exact directions for charcoal grilling because too much depends on the heat of the fire, and the distance from the coals, but indoor broiling of a salmon steak has been worked out to a split second by Frances Cabot of the Fishery Council. She says to have the broiler heated, and set at 550°. If the salmon steak is ½-inch thick, it should be 2 inches from the flame and cooked 3 minutes on each side. If an inch thick, cook it the same way, but give it 2 extra minutes on the second side. The fish should be brushed with butter or oil before broiling. For the charcoal grilling, butter or oil may be used as a baste alone, or may be mixed with white wine or lemon juice or herbs. The simpler the baste or sauce, the better.

NOTE: *Salmon en Brochette,* or kabobs, is a good method over charcoal. In areas that are close to the salmon rivers the fish is quite inexpensive, especially if bought whole. The pieces that don't steak well are ideal for skewer cookery — cut in chunks, strung on skewers alternating with whole mushrooms, quartered tomatoes (optional), pieces of green pepper, sliced onions, and sometimes bacon. Marinate for 3 or 4 hours in 1 cup oil, ½ cup white wine, 1 teaspoon salt, and pepper. Then broil over charcoal until nicely browned, basting occasionally with the marinade. Brown rice is good with these, dressed with buttered crumbs, and a huge bowl of fresh fruit makes it a perfect meal.

155

(Salmon Mayonnaise

"Salmon like the red red gold," was the way Dame Shirley described this fish, if not this dish. Actually, the red red gold doesn't show until the salmon is cut, for it's completely and beautifully blanketed with the gold of mayonnaise.

A large piece of salmon, or a whole one if the occasion merits it, is cradled in cheesecloth and cooked in court bouillon until the internal temperature reaches 160°, or 10 to 11 minutes a pound. Cool and spread completely with mayonnaise that has been mixed with gelatin (a tablespoon of gelatin melted in ¼ cup of water for every 3 cups of mayonnaise). Garnish with rings of ripe olives, pieces of pimiento, and halves of blanched almonds, and surround with deviled eggs and cucumber cups filled with diced celery. Pass extra mayonnaise, homemade, please, with lemon juice instead of vinegar.

(Salmon Bonneville

When the famous Bonneville Dam was built — an engineering feat that has changed the future of the Northwest — there was much concern for the salmon. These fish, for reasons known only to themselves, always return to the water of their birth to spawn. And then they die happily. But how could they beat their way upstream when they had an enormous dam blocking their way? And if they couldn't make it, there would be no more generations of salmon swimming downstream to the ocean, no more good eating, no more salmon industry. Fish ladders were the answer, and the fish have taken to them complacently enough. After all, what's a little extra climbing when love calls?

Poach the salmon, in a 4-pound piece, as in salmon mayonnaise, but flavor the court bouillon with rosemary. Poach a pint of oysters separately, and in their own liquor. Add them, and ½ cup of halved pitted ripe olives, to 2 cups of hollandaise sauce — or cream sauce to which 3 egg yolks and 3 tablespoons of lemon juice have been added. Other good salmon sauces are anchovy and béarnaise. SERVES 8.

1 4-pound piece salmon
   Court bouillon
   Rosemary
1 pint oysters
½ cup halved pitted ripe
   olives

2 cups hollandaise (or 2
   cups cream sauce, 3 egg
   yolks, and 3 tablespoons
   lemon juice)

⟪ Salmon Notes

Broiled Smoked Salmon. Smoked salmon needs no introduction, but I wonder if it is as good anywhere as it is in our Northwest. We are positively gluttonous about it, and eat prodigious amounts as is, or couched on toast, with olive oil and fresh ground pepper, for a favorite appetizer. We also like it broiled or grilled. Have it cut ½-inch thick, dip in butter or olive oil, and broil until lightly browned on both sides. Serve on toast with lemon and parsley. Creamed potatoes seem just right with this, and a string bean salad spiced with dill.

Salmon Cheeks are a great delicacy, and not only because there are but two small ones to a huge fish. Simply egg and crumb them, and fry them in deep fat. Serve with any fish sauce, or with lemon.

Salmon Fillets are becoming more popular. They are made from the meat near the tail, too small to steak, but as rich and sweet as could be desired. They may be grilled or cooked in any method recommended for fillets. Another way is to bake them in sour cream.

Salmon Mulligan was and is a favorite with campers. The salmon is hunked and cooked with bacon, canned lima beans, tomatoes, corn, and whatever else is handy. It's surprisingly good, even without an outdoor appetite.

Kippered Salmon, steamed and then smoked, is quite different from smoked salmon, or lox. It is most often served as an appetizer or at a smörgåsbord, but it's also wonderful cooked in any way in which finnan haddie is prepared.

Salt Salmon was quite common in the early days of Oregon and Washington. It made good chowder, good fish cakes, and was good creamed — in other words, it took the place of salt cod. One early recipe called "Fish in a Dish" intrigued me by its name. A sauce is made by browning ¼ cup of butter, adding 3 tablespoons of *cornstarch* (I used 4 of flour), 2 cups of boiling water, ¼ cup of chopped parsley, ½ teaspoon of salt, pepper, and 3 beaten eggs. This was put in layers with flaked and soaked salt salmon, it had crumbs on top, and it was baked until brown.

Spiced Salmon. Three pounds of poached salmon covered with 1 pint of vinegar, ¼ cup of pickling spices, ¼ cup of sugar. Stand 24 hours before serving. A pioneer's escabeche de pescado (page 175).

❪ *Sand Dabs Meunière*

This tender, sweet little fish is one of the prizes of the Pacific. In San Francisco, where they know fish at its best, they prize it highly. What's more, they know it needs no elaborate saucing. Other sole — rex, for instance — takes just as well to this simple treatment.

The fish may or may not be skinned, but they should be trimmed. Dip them in seasoned flour, then pan fry quickly in butter. Remove the delicately browned fish to a hot platter, add a judicious amount of fresh butter to the pan, also some lemon juice and minced parsley. Heat and pour over the fish.

❪ *Sand Dabs or Rex Sole in Paper*

These two succulent little fish aren't related, but they look like identical twins to the uninitiated. We take great pride in them both, and in the ways we cook them.

Cut heart-shaped pieces of paper as in Rockfish en Papilotte (page 152). Butter the paper well on one side, and lay half of a skinned and filleted sand dab or rex sole on one side.

158

Fish and Shellfish

Sprinkle with salt and pepper, and add a small slice of boiled ham, 2 mushroom caps which have been lightly cooked in butter, and sprinkle with a mixture of chives and parsley. Fold paper and crimp edges as in the rockfish recipe. Bake in a hot oven until the paper is brown and puffy. SERVES 1.

½ sand dab or rex sole	1 small slice boiled ham
Salt and pepper	2 mushroom caps
Butter	Chives and parsley

❲ Sand Dab Notes

Broiled Sand Dabs. Simply brush with butter and broil quickly. Simple perfection.

Sand Dabs with Orange. Trim fish and dip in flour and pan fry, as for meunière. Slice oranges ¼-inch thick, dip them in flour also, and brown on both sides in butter. Serve with the sand dabs.

Fillet of Sand Dab in White Wine. Put fillets in a buttered baking dish, sprinkle with salt, pepper, minced shallots, and parsley. Add white wine and bake until the fish is done — it won't take long. Bind sauce with egg yolk and pour over the fish.

❲ Puget Sound Skewered Scallops

Scallops, like the other mollusks, cannot stand cooking too long — they shrivel, toughen, and lose their lovely flavor.

Dip washed and dried scallops in melted butter, roll in fine cracker meal that has been seasoned with herbs (a cup of meal, a tablespoon of *fines herbes* (mixed herbs), a teaspoon of salt). String on skewers, alternating with sautéed mushroom caps as nearly the same size as the scallops as possible. Broil under a hot flame, or over hot coals, until very lightly browned, turning so that all sides will color. Serve with lemon parsley butter. Or string them on skewers with a whole slice of bacon, weaving it back and forth between the scallops. (One side of one scallop is bacon-covered, the other side of the next — get it?)

(Scallop Notes

Sautéed Scallops are easy, too. Wash them quickly, dry them, then dip in milk and fine bread crumbs. Sauté in butter for 3 minutes, or until golden, turning several times during the cooking.

Chafing Dish Scallops are exceedingly simple, exceedingly good. Heat a pint of scallops, halved if large, in ¼ cup of butter for 2 minutes. Add ½ cup of heavy cream mixed with 3 egg yolks, a tablespoon of sherry, a grating of nutmeg, and a little salt. Stir until the sauce thickens, and serve at once on toasted muffins.

(Sculpin Serisawa

This Japanese recipe is the creation of Mary Serisawa, wife of the noted painter Sueo Serisawa. It is at its best with sculpin, but it is wonderful eating with any whole fish, and is particularly suitable for outdoor cooking. Sculpin is a strange-looking fish, a mottled pink with a large meaty head.

Have the fish split enough so that it can be opened out flat, but don't have the head removed or you'll miss the best part. Mash a large clove of garlic with a teaspoon of salt, rub it on the fish, and let it stand while you build a charcoal fire. When the coals are glowing, put the fish in a wire toaster, skin side down, over the hot coals. (This may be done indoors, in your oven broiler.) When the fish has been cooking about 5 minutes, baste with this sauce: mash a cake of Fu Yu (soy bean cheese, available in Oriental markets) or 2 tablespoons of blue cheese, and add 2 tablespoons of soy sauce, a teaspoon of sugar, and 3 tablespoons of sake (or sherry, brandy or whiskey) and ¼ cup of melted butter. Turn the broiling fish two or three times, and keep basting. When the fish is quite brown, sprinkle thickly with sesame seeds, turn, brown, and repeat on the other side. (You'll lose a few seeds when doing this over charcoal, but most of them will stick to the basted fish.) Serve with thick slices of orange, peel and all. (Mrs.

Fish and Shellfish

Serisawa served the oranges in a huge fluted white shell — a lovely sight, surpassed only by the lovely fish.) SERVES 4 TO 8.

1 sculpin
1 large clove garlic
1 teaspoon salt
1 cake Fu Yu, or 2 table-
    spoons blue cheese
2 tablespoons soy sauce

1 teaspoon sugar
3 tablespoons sake (or
    sherry, brandy, or whis-
    key) ˋ
¼ cup melted butter
Sesame seeds

(Barbecued Sea Bass

This recipe calls for the small white sea bass, seldom found on the market, but quite often toted home by proud fishermen. It is a delicious fish, cooked any way, but this way it is pluperfect. The same recipe may be used for any fish the right size for barbecuing whole.

Clean a 6-pound bass (or other fish) and remove scales, also the head if you think it's prettier that way. (If the fish is larger than this, split it.) Have a good hot bed of glowing coals ready, a rather deep one if the fish is large. Grease a large broiler (old-fashioned toaster) well, and put fish between the grids. Brush it with Japanese basting sauce (below) and cook it first on one side, then the other (skin side first if it is a split fish), until brown and crispy. This will take quite a long time, and constant basting is in order. The fish may, like the sculpin Serisawa, be sprinkled with sesame seeds towards the end of the cooking. It is tested for doneness in the same old indoor way — a fork thrust into an inconspicuous spot. If the fish flakes easily and has lost its "raw" look, it's done. SERVES 8 TO 12.

To make Japanese basting sauce, crush 2 large cloves of garlic in a mortar with a tablespoon of salt. Add to ½ cup each of soy sauce, sherry (or sake, to be really Japanese) and cooking oil or melted butter.

1 6-pound white sea bass
2 large cloves garlic
1 tablespoon salt
    Sesame seeds (optional)

½ cup soy sauce
½ cup sherry or sake
½ cup cooking oil or butter

161

❲ Fillet of Sea Bass with Almonds

As the black sea bass grows as large as six hundred pounds, we seldom cook it whole. Filleted, however, it is a favorite fish, and this is a favorite way of cooking it, or any other fillets.

Arrange 2 pounds of seasoned fillet of sea bass in a skillet and cover with 2 tablespoons of minced shallots, ½ cup of sliced mushrooms, ¼ teaspoon of rosemary, and a cup of white table wine. Poach the fish gently until it loses its transparent look. This doesn't take long unless the fillets are thick. Remove the cooked fish to a flat fireproof baking dish and reduce the sauce left in the pan, by cooking rapidly, to half its volume. Add a cup of heavy cream and correct the seasoning. Cook 5 minutes more, then pour over the fish, which has been kept warm in a low oven, and sprinkle with slivered almonds. Slip under the broiler to brown lightly, and serve at once. SERVES 4 OR 5.

> 2 pound fillet of sea bass
> 2 tablespoons minced
>   shallots
> ½ cup sliced mushrooms
> Slivered almonds
>
> ¼ teaspoon rosemary
> 1 cup white table wine
> 1 cup heavy cream
> Salt and pepper

❲ Bass with Bean Sprouts and Ginger

Don't shy away from this recipe until you read it through. I admit it sounds very exotic, which of course it is, but Occidentals delight in it, too. It is Chinese, of course, and I don't mean to further scare you by telling you that they cook it in the dish in which it is to be served, putting it in a *wok* and covering it with a huge steaming lid. We can do the job quite nicely in an American pan, with a cover. (A so-called "chicken fryer" is a good type.)

Put a 3- or 4-pound piece of fish, or a whole one if small, in a pan with ¼ cup of chopped green onions, 3 tablespoons of soy sauce, 3 tablespoons of sherry, a tablespoon of slivered green ginger (page 242), 3 tablespoons of peanut, sesame, or other bland oil, and a cup of water. Cover tightly

162

and bring to a rapid boil, then allow to simmer for about 45 minutes, or until done. In the meantime, cook a pound of bean sprouts in 2 tablespoons of oil and 1 tablespoon of soy sauce for 5 minutes. When the fish is done, add ½ cup of its juices to the sprouts, cook another 5 minutes, put on a large platter, top with the steamed fish, and pour on the remaining juices, if any. Serve with rice and Chinese peas. SERVES 6.

3-to-4 pound piece of sea bass	1 tablespoon slivered green
¼ cup chopped green	ginger
onions	5 tablespoons bland oil
4 tablespoons soy sauce	1 cup water
3 tablespoons sherry	1 pound bean sprouts

❲ Baked Shad Sacramento

Shad was planted here in the Sacramento and other rivers, and has multiplied tremendously. When the run is on it is very inexpensive, probably because Westerners don't appreciate its bones. (Recently it has come to the market filleted, which ought to bring it the popularity it deserves.)

Have a whole shad, about 4 pounds, scaled and cleaned. Wash and wipe dry, then stuff ⅔ full with dressing made by adding ¼ cup of chopped almonds, ¼ cup of chopped green olives, and ¼ cup of butter, to 1½ cups of bread crumbs. Season with salt, pepper, and a little crushed fennel seed, and moisten slightly with white wine. Sew fish together. Rub with oil, place on oiled paper, aluminum foil, or cheesecloth, in a shallow pan and bake until done, about an hour. Surround fish with little bunches of dried herbs and set alight just before serving — if you like the idea, that is. SERVES 6.

1 4-pound shad	¼ cup butter
1½ cups bread crumbs	Salt and pepper
¼ cup chopped almonds	Crushed fennel seeds
¼ cup chopped green olives	White wine to moisten

NOTE: A can of minced clams may be added to the stuffing.

⟨ Cantonese Shrimp Balls with Chinese Peas

Grind together a pound of cleaned raw shrimps and a pound of raw pork. Add ½ cup of minced water chestnuts, fresh or canned, ½ teaspoon of M.S.G., an egg, a teaspoon of salt, and a tablespoon of cornstarch. Roll into balls about the size of Oregon Bing cherries (that's large), then roll in sesame seeds, and brown all over in oil. Set aside and prepare ½ pound of Chinese peas (page 375). Cut 4 pieces of celery — the outside ones do nicely — in *very* diagonal ¼-inch slices, if you see what I mean. Cook the celery in 2 tablespoons of oil for 2 minutes, add the peas, stir to mix well, and remove completely from the fire. Put the shrimp balls with the vegetables, and to the shrimp pan add 2 cups of well-seasoned chicken stock and 2 tablespoons of cornstarch dissolved in ¼ cup of cold water. Cook until clear, pour over the shrimps and vegetables, and return to the fire just long enough to reheat, but *do not* cook. Serve at once with boiled rice. SERVES 6.

SHRIMP BALLS

1 pound shrimps	*1 egg*
1 pound pork	*1 teaspoon salt*
½ cup minced water chestnuts	*1 tablespoon cornstarch*
½ teaspoon M.S.G.	*Sesame seeds*

Oil

VEGETABLES

½ pound Chinese peas
4 pieces celery
2 tablespoons oil

SAUCE

2 cups chicken stock
2 tablespoons cornstarch
¼ cup water

⟨ Broiled Garlic Shrimp

Shell and remove sand veins from the backs of a pound of green jumbo shrimps. Heat ¼ cup of butter with a crushed clove of garlic. Dip shrimps in it and broil in a preheated broiler for about 5 minutes, turning once during the process. This may be done outside, over charcoal, and if the shrimps are strung on skewers, the turning will be simpler. Jumbo shrimps (or prawns) run about 12 to 16 to a pound, and 4 to a serving should be enough for indoor appetites, twice that for outdoor hungers. (A chafing dish improvisation is to sauté the shrimps in this same garlic butter.) Serve shrimps with big wedges of lemon.

> 1 pound jumbo shrimps
> ¼ cup butter
> 1 clove garlic

⟨ Celestial Shrimps with Walnuts

The Chinese have a particular fondness for shrimps, and they cook them exquisitely.

Boil 2 pounds of shelled cleaned shrimps in 3 cups of salted water for 5 minutes. Drain, but save the liquid. Put ½ pound of perfect walnut halves in a very hot oven (450°) for 4 or 5 minutes, then rub off their brown outer skins. (Or use blanched split almonds, if you prefer.) Make a sweet and sour sauce, using 1¼ cups of the shrimp water, ½ cup of sugar mixed with 2 tablespoons of cornstarch, and ½ cup of vinegar. Season with salt or soy, add shrimps, split if very large, and a green pepper cut in long strips. Cook 3 minutes, then add the nuts which have been kept hot. Chunks of canned pineapple may be added, too. Serve this with Chinese peas, or broccoli cooked Chinese style (page 370). SERVES 6 TO 8.

2 pounds shrimps	2 tablespoons cornstarch
3 cups salted water	½ cup vinegar
½ pound walnut meats	Salt or soy sauce
½ cup sugar	1 green pepper
Canned pineapple (optional)	

⟨ Chinese Fried Shrimps

Here is one dish that every Chinese restaurant has to serve, whether or not the proprietors approve. The demand for it is too loud and insistent to be ignored.

Shell and clean green shrimps but leave tail on. Allow 4 jumbo shrimps to a serving. Dip into a batter made by mixing 1 large or 2 small eggs, slightly beaten, with a cup of flour, a cup of water, 2 tablespoons of cornstarch, ¼ cup of corn meal, ¾ of a cup of milk, and ½ teaspoon each of salt and baking powder. Fry in deep fat at 390° until lightly browned. Serve with Chinese mustard and catsup. The Chinese mustard is hot: mix dry mustard with water until fairly thin. The Chinese use little dishes like old-fashioned butter chips in which they pour catsup, then put a spoonful of this hot mustard on one side (about 3 tablespoons of catsup to 1 of mustard). The shrimps are dipped in this or these sauces before they are eaten. Finger food, of course. . . .

Green shrimps	*¼ cup corn meal*
1 large egg (or 2 small eggs)	*¾ cup milk*
1 cup water	*½ teaspoon salt*
1 cup flour	*½ teaspoon baking powder*
2 tablespoons cornstarch	*Chinese mustard*

NOTE: Another way is simply to dip the shrimps in egg and then in flour, and fry.

⟨ Shrimp Tempura

A Japanese version of the Italian fritto misto — fish and vegetables dipped in batter and deep fried. It is served, in Japan, with a sauce made with dried bonito, an ingredient difficult to procure even when living near a Japanese settlement. So the Japanese here usually use a sauce made by combining ½ cup of sherry (or sake) with ¼ cup of soy sauce, a tablespoon of grated ginger, and a teaspoon of sugar.

Shell and clean a pound of jumbo shrimps and dip in a batter made with a cup of flour, 2 tablespoons of soy sauce, 2 eggs, and ⅔ of a cup of milk. Fry in deep fat at 370° until brown. Serve with a sauce made as above. String beans and other vegetables are often so frittered and fried with the shrimps, as are pieces of other fish. SERVES 4.

SHRIMP

1 pound jumbo shrimps	2 tablespoons soy sauce
1 cup flour	2 eggs
	⅔ cup milk

SAUCE

½ cup sherry (or sake)	1 tablespoon grated ginger
¼ cup soy sauce	1 teaspoon sugar

⟮ Shrimps Nob Hill

This recipe may be done in the chafing dish. Heat 4 tablespoons of butter with a crushed clove of garlic for a minute or two. Discard garlic, and add 2 cups of canned tomatoes, ¼ cup of cream, ¼ cup of sherry, a tablespoon of minced parsley, and salt and pepper to taste. Simmer slowly for 5 minutes, then add 1½ pounds of cleaned boiled shrimps. When the shrimps are hot, serve with toast. SERVES 6.

4 tablespoons butter	¼ cup sherry
1 clove garlic	1 tablespoon minced parsley
2 cups canned tomatoes	Salt and pepper
¼ cup cream	1½ pounds shrimps

NOTE: Joe Tilden's famous shrimp sauté, also good for a chafing dish, was made by adding green shrimps to browned butter, saucing with white wine, anchovy paste, and lemon juice, and binding with egg yolk.

⟮ Shrimps Victoria

Sour cream and mushrooms are a happy combination. When they are joined by shrimps, the result is sheer bliss. A chafing dish may be used here.

Shell a pound of green shrimps and remove the black veins. Sauté them, along with 2 tablespoons of minced shallots, in ¼ cup of butter until the shrimps are pink. Add ½ pound of cleaned mushrooms and cook 5 minutes, adding another tablespoon of butter if necessary. Now sprinkle with a tablespoon of flour, ½ teaspoon of salt, and some fresh ground pepper; add 3 tablespoons of sherry and 1½ cups of sour cream. Correct the seasonings. Cook gently until hot, and serve with wild rice. SERVES 6.

1 pound shrimps	1 tablespoon flour
2 tablespoons minced shallots	½ teaspoon salt
¼ cup butter (or more)	Pepper
½ pound mushrooms	3 tablespoons sherry
1½ cups sour cream	

◖ Columbia River Smelts

These are the famous "candlefish" of the Indians, the Eulachon. They're so rich that the aborigines dried and burned them, like candles, and they gave a lovely light. The Jack smelt, a different fish entirely, is more apt to be found in California. It, too, is delicious, but not always so; it sometimes gets too close to tideland drilling and tastes as if it should make good fuel for diesel trucks.

Smelts are good egged and crumbed, and either pan fried in butter or deep fried. They are also wonderful when broiled over charcoal (crumbed first), and drizzled with butter during the grilling. After cooking, by any method, the fish may be opened up at the belly and the entire bone structure, head and tail, lifted out all of a piece. The pioneers, during the smelt run when there was a plethora, would spice them for future use.

◖ Fillet of Sole King Edward

This version of the classic recipe comes from an old San Diego cook book. It was almost certainly named during Edward VII's visit to America.

Fish and Shellfish

Fillets are arranged in a well-buttered baking dish, and sprinkled with salt and pepper. For 2 pounds of them, ¼ pound of butter is creamed and mixed with ¼ cup each of chopped almonds and chopped raw mushrooms. This is spread on the fillets, ½ cup of white wine is poured around them, and they are baked at 400° for 12 minutes, or until done. They are served from the same dish with fried potato balls on the side. SERVES 6.

2 pounds fillet of sole	¼ cup chopped almonds
Salt and pepper	¼ cup chopped raw mushrooms
¼ pound butter	½ cup white wine

NOTE: *Fillet of Sole Bercy* was, according to some, created at the St. Francis Hotel. It is sole poached in white wine with shallots, chervil, and parsley, and served with a white wine sauce.

NOTE: Fillets may be dipped in flour, sautéed in butter, and served with slivered almonds that have been cooked golden in more butter. Lemon juice with this.

⟨ Fillet of Sole Santa Monica

Dip 2 pounds of fillet of sole in melted butter and arrange on a flat baking dish. Sprinkle with salt and pepper. Add 2 cups of white wine, ¼ cup of minced shallots, and a very little rosemary (about ½ teaspoon minced, if fresh, ¼ teaspoon if dried). Cover and poach for about 8 minutes, or until the fish looks white clear through. Drain the wine from the dish into a saucepan and cook rapidly until reduced one half, then whip in a cup of heavy cream that has been beaten with 2 egg yolks. Heat gently, then pour over the fish and garnish with sautéed mushroom caps or pitted ripe olives that have been heated. SERVES 6.

2 pounds fillet of sole	¼ cup minced shallots
Salt and pepper	Rosemary
2 cups white wine	1 cup heavy cream
2 egg yolks	

ℂ Tarantino's Sole en Papilotte

The two Irish ex-GIs who run this famous restaurant on Fisherman's Wharf have devised a fine version of the famous New Orleans dish, using sole instead of California pompano (which isn't pompano at all). This recipe, incidentally, is good for any filleted fish, so take time out and memorize it.

"Roll fillet of sole lengthwise. Place in saucepan in rows. Cover with water, juice of lemon, and white wine. Cook 10 minutes or until firm. Melt butter in saucepan. Add flour until you have a firm roux. Don't brown. Then, add liquid from cooked fillet of sole until you have thick cream sauce. Salt and pepper to taste. Add mushrooms and green onions chopped finely. Fold paper upper left edge to lower right edge, forming a diagonal crease. Open the paper. Grease inside of paper with butter. Place 3 rolled fillets of sole just to the right of the crease in the center of the paper. Cover fillet of sole with sauce. Fold paper over fillet of sole. Start at top of paper, fold in about 1 inch at a time. Each fold locks the preceding fold all the way around paper from top to bottom. The package will then form half of a circle. Put on a pie tin and place it in a 400° oven and bake until it 'puffs up' and forms a ball."

4 pieces of parchment paper	2 green onions
(14 × 14 inches)	1 lemon
1½ pounds fillet of sole — 12	¼ pound mushrooms
pieces	1 tablespoon butter
2 ounces white wine	½ cup flour
Salt and pepper	

ℂ Stuffed Squid

Squid is more popular with the Italians and Japanese than with the rest of us, but we are beginning to learn how wonderful it is, stewed, or done this way, which is Japanese and called "ika."

Remove the innards from 6 squids, and the shell, which is *inside* the fish, and looks like a lovely leaf made of Pliofilm.

170

Leave the tentacles on. Make a stuffing with ½ cup of chopped raw carrot and ½ cup of minced onion, cooked in ¼ cup of butter until soft, then mixed with 2 cups of bread crumbs, and salt or soy sauce to taste. Moisten with sake, or sherry, and stuff squids, then fry a deep brown in butter. The tentacles become wonderfully crisp, and are the prize portion of this prize dish. SERVES 6.

6 squids	*2 cups bread crumbs*
½ cup chopped carrot	*Salt or soy sauce*
½ cup minced onion	*Sake or sherry to moisten*
¼ cup butter	*Butter*

⟨ Steelhead Baked in Paper

The steelhead, a giant rainbow trout, is a fish that anglers like to cope with, and to eat. It may be cooked by any method suitable for salmon, or in this manner.

Cut pieces of parchment paper, or if cooking over charcoal, of aluminum foil, the size of typewriter paper (about 8½ × 11 inches). Make an herb butter by adding a tablespoon each of minced chives and parsley, and a teaspoon of oregano, to a cup of creamed butter. Spread each piece of paper rather thickly with this mixture, allowing 1½ inches of unbuttered border all around. Put a piece of boneless steelhead (or any other fleshy fish), from ⅓ to ½ pound, on each piece, salt and pepper it, and squeeze on a little lemon juice. Then fold in half and double-fold the edges to seal the juices in. Bake in a hot oven (425°) for about 25 or 30 minutes, or roast over charcoal, keeping the packages fairly high above the flame. Serve, in either case, in the paper. THIS IS ENOUGH FOR 8 PACKAGES.

1 cup creamed butter	*8 pieces steelhead (⅓ to ½*
1 tablespoon minced chives	*pound)*
1 tablespoon minced parsley	*Salt and pepper*
1 teaspoon oregano	*Lemon juice*

❨ Baked Sierra Trout

Most fishermen prefer to dip their trout in corn meal and pan fry it in bacon fat, then eat it near the stream from which it came so recently. But with good fisherman's luck, there will be some to take home and cook this good way.

Dip 4 trout in melted butter, season with salt and pepper, and arrange on a baking dish. Add a cup of white wine, ½ pound of sliced mushrooms, a few sprigs of fresh tarragon, and 2 tablespoons of butter. Bake 30 minutes at 350°–375°. SERVES 4.

4 trout	*½ pound mushrooms*
Salt and pepper	*2 tablespoons butter*
1 cup white wine	*Tarragon*

❨ Poodle Dog Trout

The Poodle Dog, an early restaurant of Gold Rush days, later moved to larger and more magnificent quarters and became the talk of San Francisco. There were special private rooms upstairs, and a special private entrance through which heavily veiled ladies could enter. All very intriguing to the populace at large. The Poodle was as famed for its food as for its guests, and rumor says that it had the latter only because of the former. Could be.

Six brook trout are dipped in melted butter, then in corn meal, and broiled on both sides until brown. A sauce made with ½ cup of butter, ¼ cup of lime juice, and ¼ cup each of chervil and chives is served with it, and the garnish is souffléed potatoes and fried crab legs. SERVES 6.

TROUT

6 brook trout
Butter
Corn meal

SAUCE

½ cup butter	*¼ cup chervil*
¼ cup lime juice	*¼ cup chives*

172

Fish and Shellfish

(Tuna

Tuna, or "chicken of the sea," is best known, even on the West Coast, in cans. Nevertheless, many fishermen do come home with large amounts of it that have to be prepared, and the fresh fish markets often have it during the summer and fall season. Tuna is cooked in various ways: baked, broiled, steamed or barbecued, though it is most popular baked. The fish is usually skinned before cooking, and the outside fat is removed. A parsley-egg sauce is the favorite one, though some good cooks prefer tomato. Albacore, of the tunas, has the whitest meat and brings a higher price than the other canned tunas. For sandwiches, sauces, stuffing tomatoes and cucumbers, and similar uses, the "grated" tuna may be used. Incidentally, such tuna, the meat being in small pieces, was looked down upon until someone got smart and dubbed it "Bite Size" (or "Chunk") tuna. Now it's very popular, and rightly so.

NOTE: *Mukozuki,* a Japanese dish resembling eggs foo yung, may be made with canned tuna fish. Blanch ¼ pound of bean sprouts in salted water for a minute, drain and cool. Mix with a medium onion, sliced, the slices halved and separated, a can of flaked tuna fish, 5 slightly beaten eggs, 2 teaspoons of shoyu (soy sauce). Cook like an omelet, in hot oil, browning on both sides. This is truly delicious. SERVES 4.

(Cioppino

This is one of California's most famous dishes, and one that we can claim is ours, all ours. It is a versatile dish, as it was invented by fishermen who made it with whatever the ocean was inclined to yield, so of course there are dozens of ideas on how it should be done. Exponents of the various schools of cookery get quite fussed — and fussy — about how to make cioppino. Red or white wine, or sherry? Shrimp and crab, clams, or just a mixture of fish? The best way is as you like it. This recipe is for a combination of fish, but it's basic enough to be used with lobster alone, or with crab, or with practically anything that comes from the sea.

173

You'll need 1½ pounds of firm-fleshed fish — shark is good, and so is sea bass or rockfish. Also ½ pound of green shrimps, a large crab, and a dozen medium-sized clams or cockles, or mussels, or oysters. Have the fish cut in good-sized pieces, the shrimps shelled and their black veins removed, the crab cleaned, and the body cut in pieces, shell and all, the legs cracked for easier later picking, the clams well scrubbed and left in their shells. Now make a sauce: cook together ½ cup of olive oil, a teaspoon of minced garlic (more if you're a garlic fiend), a cup of chopped onions, a cup of chopped green onions, ½ cup of minced green pepper, an 8-ounce tin of tomato sauce, a No. 2½ can of tomatoes, 2 cups of red table wine, ¼ cup of minced parsley, a teaspoon of salt, ¼ teaspoon of coarsely ground pepper, ¼ teaspoon each of oregano and basil. Cook 5 minutes. Now arrange the fish, crab, and shrimps in layers in a big casserole or pot, pour over the sauce, cover, and cook on a low flame or in the oven for 30 minutes, or until the fish is done. Add the clams, or whatever mollusks you have chosen, and, as soon as they open up, sprinkle the whole with another ¼ cup of minced parsley, and serve forth in the casserole or in a tureen, with oodles of hot garlic bread. Bibs are in order, too. SERVES 6 TO 8.

1½ pounds fish	1 8-ounce tin tomato sauce
½ pound green shrimps	1 No. 2½ tin tomatoes
1 large crab	2 cups red table wine
1 dozen clams	½ cup minced parsley
½ cup olive oil	1 teaspoon salt
1 teaspoon minced garlic	¼ teaspoon coarsely ground
1 cup chopped onion	pepper
1 cup chopped green onion	¼ teaspoon oregano
½ cup minced green pepper	¼ teaspoon basil

NOTE: I have been told, and on good authority, too, that the Portuguese fishermen always thicken their cioppino sauce with a potato or two, and that they use *much* more garlic than is in this recipe.

NOTE: One story says that San Francisco's fishermen did *not* introduce cioppino to California, but that an Italian named

Fish and Shellfish

Bazzuro, who ran a restaurant on a boat anchored off Fisherman's Wharf, is responsible. What's more, it was supposed to have been an old recipe, well known in Italy. This back in the 1850s. I refuse to believe it!

⟨ *Escabeche de Pescado*

One of the most entrancing of all the recipes that we have inherited from the Mexicans is this soused fish, served cold. A perfect adjunct to a summer meal, escabeche is a method of preparation, a sort of pickling, and is done with venison and other meats as well, with beautiful results. (The Mexican stuffed chilies "escabeche" are a great treat for those who were born south of the border, but living north of it seems to diminish the insulation of the alimentary canal, and we just can't take it.) Fear not, this dish is not hot.

Lightly brown 2 pounds of fillet of any small fish in a little butter, and arrange them carefully in a flat dish, keeping them whole. Make a sauce with ½ cup of olive or salad oil, 2 tablespoons of vinegar, ¼ cup of orange juice, 2 teaspoons of salt, ¼ teaspoon of cayenne, 2 tablespoons of the zest of orange (the very outside, orange part of the skin) cut in tiny slivers, 2 tablespoons of green pepper, cut in the same size pieces as the orange, and 2 tablespoons of minced green onion or shallots. Pour over the fish and let stand in the refrigerator for 6 or 8 hours, or longer, basting the fish with the sauce once or thrice. At the same time chill thick slices of unpeeled orange in French dressing, and garnish the finished dish with them. SERVES 6.

2 *pounds fish fillets*	2 *tablespoons slivered orange*
Butter	*zest*
½ *cup olive or salad oil*	2 *tablespoons slivered green*
2 *tablespoons vinegar*	*pepper*
¼ *cup orange juice*	2 *tablespoons minced green*
2 *teaspoons salt*	*onion*
¼ *teaspoon cayenne*	*Orange slices*

175

(Fish Mariposa

Light as a butterfly, that's the way they look.

Use any small fish fillets for this. Season them and arrange on a flat buttered pan, bake 5 minutes but do not turn. Now beat 2 egg whites stiff, fold in a cup of mayonnaise and ¼ cup of grated cheese, pile on the fish fillets, and cook under the broiler until brown and puffy. SERVES 6 TO 8.

2–3 pounds fish fillets   1 cup mayonnaise
Salt and pepper   2 egg whites
¼ cup grated cheese

(Turbans of Fish, Olivos

Any fillet of fish will do for this, though it shouldn't be too thick. Cut in pieces about 8 inches long by 2 inches wide, dip them in melted butter, and coil them around in greased custard cups. Put a large pitted ripe olive in the center of each curled fish. Sprinkle with salt and pepper, stuff minced parsley and chives in each olive, pour a tablespoon of white table wine in every cup, cover with greased paper. (Put them all on a cookie sheet and cover with one sheet — of paper, that is.) Bake for about 20 minutes at 350° or until the fish lose their transparent look. Turn out on a hot dish, and garnish with French fried parsley and lemon quarters. Serve with ripe olive sauce.

For each piece of fish
1 large ripe olive   Salt and pepper
Butter   Minced parsley and chives
1 tablespoon white wine

176

Foreign Cookery

◖ *Chinese Cookery*

On the Pacific Coast we have some of the very finest Chinese restaurants in the world, and the food they serve has become so popular with us that many of their dishes are appearing on Occidental tables. Their spareribs, fried shrimps, eggs foo yung, and fried rice have actually become West Coast dishes, and many of their other creations are so well liked that cooks up and down the Coast are learning to cook with a Chinese accent. This is good, particularly when it comes to vegetables. No one cooks them as beautifully as the Chinese. The cooked vegetables have the crispness of the raw ones, with a color even more intense, and a flavor that is unsurpassed. The Chinese method is simple — it's a combination sauté-steaming process that is easy and quick, and must win the approval of nutritionists because the vitamins and minerals have no chance to make their getaway. The vegetables are first cut in little pieces. (All Chinese food is in small pieces as it has to be eaten with chopsticks.) Often they are sliced in thin diagonal slivers, sometimes cubed, sometimes cut in small odd-shaped pieces by turning the vegetable as it is sliced diagonally, and sometimes chopped with the huge cleaverlike knives that the Chinese think are paring knives. (They are, for them. They can even peel a water chestnut with one.) Some oil, preferably sesame, but any bland vegetable oil will do, is put into a heavy pot — about 2 tablespoons for 1½ pounds of vegetables. The oil is heated, the prepared vegetables are added and are stirred for a minute. If the vegetable does not have sufficient juices of its own, a tiny amount of water or

177

chicken stock is added, the pot is covered, and the vegetables allowed to steam for 2 or 3 minutes. The cover is then removed and the vegetables cooked, stirring occasionally, until done. This time varies — with spinach no further cooking is necessary, with broccoli another 5 minutes is probably in order. Anyway, you'll never taste such vegetables!

There were Chinese restaurants in the early days of California, Oregon, and Washington, but they weren't much because the proprietors served what they thought the customers wanted — chop suey and, apparently, fried steaks. Many of the Chinese who came to help build the railroads stayed on to work in the kitchens of the Westerners. Like those who cooked in the restaurants, they usually produced Occidental food because they wanted to please the "missy." The housewives appreciated the efficient — and cheap — help of the Chinese, and didn't realize what they were missing in the way of good eating. And so the tremendous interest that we have in Chinese food is a pretty recent one, but at the rate it's developing, we may all end up eating with chopsticks.

The method of Chinese cooking is so completely different from our own that cooks are apt to be frightened by it, but once the basic principles are learned it is as simple as our own — actually simpler. Much as I'd like to, I can't go into it here, except in describing the methods used in the Chinese recipes herein. (See Index.) I can't resist, however, telling just a little about a Chinese meal and how it's cooked. It's a fascinating subject. Chinese meals come in two sizes — the family-style meal and the banquet. At home the meal usually consists of several different dishes, all served at one time; one perhaps a steamed dish, one a soup, the others meat or fish cooked in combination with vegetables. And always rice. Each member of the family has a bowl of it, and helps himself from the common dishes on the table with his own chopsticks. The morsels so acquired are usually dunked in the rice bowl so that the savory sauces will lend their flavor to that staple food. The banquet is quite another matter — a ritualistic one, with the dishes arriving four at a time. It is a meal that few Occidentals have the opportunity of enjoying, but the food com-

178

monly served at fine Chinese restaurants is more banquet than family fare. Most Chinese dishes require a lot of last-minute attention, which is why even the Chinese themselves, unless they are very well staffed, have their banquets at a public place. It's one time when too many cooks most certainly do not spoil the broth. To kibitz in a Chinese kitchen when one of these elaborate meals is being prepared is fun. Everything is prepared ahead of time. Long tables are lined with baskets of peeled and cut foods: water chestnuts, bamboo shoots, green onions, almonds, bean sprouts, Chinese peas, ginger, and all the other things that go into the various dishes. Shrimps will be cleaned, pork roasted, garlic peeled. *Woks*, which are Chinese frying pans (large shallow metal bowls, with handles), will be everywhere, and in all sizes. And above the stove, hanging by chains from the ceiling, will be big tin affairs that look for all the world like upside-down milk pans. These are steamers, or reflectors. They are lowered over the *woks* when steaming is in order, as it frequently is (see lobster bok quan, page 140). Cooking shovels, which are Chinese spatulas, are at hand, and ladles, and the aforementioned knives. Then there are the skimmers, beautiful gadgets, looking like metal spider webs with bamboo handles — these for lifting fried foods from the deep fat. When the get-ready-to-serve signal comes, everything happens at once. Each cook knows his job — or I should say *jobs*, for he seems to be doing six at once. Miraculously, in a matter of minutes, all is ready. Each masterpiece is beautifully arranged on a Chinese compote or colorful serving dish, its rich brown or pink or white meaty morsels contrasting with the green of its vegetable, and all shining under the glorious transparency of the sauce — and quite as wonderful to eat as it is to behold.

(*Mexican Food*

Mexico has done many and wonderful things for our cuisine. In the earliest days of California, our food was largely from that country. The Spaniards who made the trek northward had, for the most part, been around Mexico long enough to have picked up their eating habits, and they were good habits.

Mexican cooking is old — nobody knows how old. But we do know that many everyday taken-for-granted dishes — tomatoes, potatoes, chili peppers, corn, chocolate, avocados, and such — have come to us from Central and South America by way of Mexico. Today many of our foods have a definite Mexican heritage, but they are so usual that we often forget that fact. The beans that we serve with our barbecue meals, the guacamole that is almost a staple with cocktails, the chili powder and "Spanish style" sauce that we toss into dishes whether Mexican or Yankee or French, all came to us across that southern boundary. Mexican restaurants are thick in California, and though they thin out as we progress up the Coast, they are still well known in Oregon and Washington. Most of them, happily, cater to our Northern palates; although their food is genuinely Mexican, they rarely turn on the full heat of their chili pots. Mexican food need not be searing to be good, and unless we were suckled on a hot pepper — as some Mexican children apparently are — we find that the lighter seasoning is easier on our palates.

The first Californian food, "Los Comidas California de Antes," was a wondrous mixture of the Mexican and the Indian. Native seeds, nuts, and berries were given to the Mission Fathers by the Indians, and the compliment was returned by gifts of Mexican seeds for the Indians. The everyday food of the Dons was said to have been very plain, and it was only on feast days, or when all the rancheros for miles around gathered for a rodeo, that the tables were really laden with fine foods. Before too many years had passed, the Indians learned to like these foods, and before long their native gruels, atole and pinole were practically unknown. In those days, as I have said, the Mexicans were great meat eaters, but they also had their beans, and their dishes made from nixtamal or parched corn. (See tortillas, page 43.) In some places, where wheat grew better than corn, the tortillas were made with flour (tortillas de harina, page 44). Today our people most recently from Mexico, and we have many, still eat largely in the Mexican manner, but the rest of us have it just occasionally, and enjoy it when we do. Those of us who know Mexican

Foreign Cookery

cuisine usually have pretty definite opinions about what we like best. For those of you to whom it is new, the so-called Mexican plate, usually consisting of a taco, an enchilada, a tostado, sometimes a tamale, and always some beans, is a good sampler, though it is pretty formidable in size unless you have the appetite of a trencherman. Once you've learned which Mexican dishes you like best, you can prepare them at home, and easily. This book contains a few of the most usual and most popular dishes, but if you want to become an expert in *la cocina,* you'd do well to get a Mexican cook book. The best one I know — the one that has a place of honor on my shelves — is *Elena's Famous Mexican and Spanish Recipes.*

⟨ Other Foreign Cookery

Italian Cookery has had a tremendous influence on our eating habits. Italian restaurants were among the first to appear in California — most of the gold-mining towns had at least one of them. One early Italian eating place was on a ship, anchored in San Francisco Bay. It was run by a man named Bazzuro who, some claim, introduced cioppino to the country. It was his place, or one like it, that had a sign reading "Coffee and Doughnuts, $1.00; a Square Meal, $1.50; a Regular Gorge, $2.50." Whether Mr. Bazzuro's cuisine was all Italian is a question — certainly doughnuts aren't. Today road signs from San Diego to Spokane proclaim Italian food, and testify to its popularity.

French Cookery also first came to us by way of the restaurant. In the Golden and Champagne Days of San Francisco, when no coin smaller than a quarter was ever seen, French restaurants opened up everywhere. An early one, the Poodle Dog, was perhaps most famous of them all. When it first opened, in 1849, it was like the other eating places of the time, a crude place with sanded floor, rough wooden tables, and, of course, a bar. But its food was extra good and by the turn of the century it, or its successor, was operating in a huge six-story building with rococo *décor,* giving the "most artistic, refined, and elegant effects," and still serving French

181

food, though by now not the simple fare of the peasant but the recherché creations of the imported chefs. Other French restaurants, in those gala days of San Francisco, were also famous: Blanco's, Marchand's, the Pup, Campi's, and the *bon vivants* of the day usually made the rounds of them. A song, to the tune of the "Marseillaise," was often heard when they were on the loose:

> Marchand's, Marchand's;
> The Maison Riche;
> The Poodle Dog, the Pup.

By the time these fabulous days were over the taste for French cookery had become general. Men who had bribed the recipes from some chef handed them over to their wives or cooks. Soon the cook books put out by Ladies' Clubs in Washington, Oregon, and California were including them along with the recipes for Election Cake. Purées, soufflés, and croquettes got the most space, but beef à la mode, galantines, and even blanquette de veau sometimes made the grade. Today, as in any civilized place, we have thousands of dishes that came to us by way of France. Few of them are included here for the simple reason that, being classics, they are in all good general cook books.

Scandinavian Cookery has shown its greatest influence in the Northwest, where great numbers of Finns came to fish, Norwegians and Swedes to lumber, and Danes to go into dairying or farming. Although such dishes as lutefisk and rodegrod have not wandered far from the families of Scandinavian ancestry, the smörgåsbord, that fabulous feast of good food, has won the complete and enthusiastic approval of the entire West Coast. It's really a natural for us — it's perfectly adapted to informal entertaining, which is what most of us go in for, and it gives a good cook the chance to strut her stuff, and still be a relaxed and charming hostess. We serve any of our favorite dishes, usually a couple of them hot, and if they deviate from the Scandinavian way too much, we simply call the affair a collation rather than a smörgåsbord.

Foreign Cookery

(A California collation was a very popular way of entertaining in the early days of California. One description says they were feasts of cold delicacies, baked hams, roast fowl and game, sandwiches and salads, with plenty of champagne. "Any such feast was called a collation whether it was served at noon or midnight.")

Japanese Cookery is becoming more popular, but so far it really hasn't contributed very much to our regional cuisine. We like sukiyaki and tempura and the crispness of their vegetables, and those of us who know it are quite mad about the way they charcoal broil their fish (see sculpin Serisawa, page 160). Still, Occidental palates balk at raw fish and dipping meat into raw egg at table, though both dishes are really excellent. The Japanese have two other culinary customs that we would do well to adopt and adapt: the little charcoal brazier which sits on the table and is used for sukiyaki and other last-minute cooking should lend charm to any cocktail party; and their presentation of food — the exquisite way in which they serve even the humblest meal.

Fruits

❪ Wild Fruits and Berries

The first white men to arrive on the West Coast found it lush with wild fruits and berries. Except for the acorn, the Indian's "daily bread," they utilized and enjoyed them all. Although they are now considerably less abundant, many of them are still highly prized by those lucky enough to come upon them.

Oregon Crabapples, found in Northern California and Washington as well as in Oregon, make a tart jelly that is most pleasing with meats and game. *Wild Cherries* produce exceptionally fine preserves, and *Ground Cherries,* found east of the Cascades, are usually used in combination with other fruits for a sweet spread. *Elderberries* are most popular for Granny's tonic, though they, too, make a good jelly. *Wild plums* yield marvelous jelly to serve with game, and gourmets find them preferable to the cultivated variety for eating out of hand. *Wild Blackberries* grew profusely in the early days and were found to be unsurpassed for pies, cakes, jams, jellies. They can still be enjoyed, for an old pioneer family, the Dickinsons of Portland, have not only transplanted them successfully, but make a wonderful pie filling that retains all the flavor of the fresh wild berries. The wild blackberry is one of the parents of the famous loganberry. *Wild Raspberries,* or thimbleberries, and *Salmonberries* are still abundant and popular in the Northwest. *Wild Strawberries,* undeniably the most perfect berries in all the world, grow in all three states, though unhappily not as abundantly as when the Willamette Valley was "red with them." The tender shoots of *Wild Gooseberries* and *Currants* were used by the pioneers as a "salad," and *Wild Cranberries* were used as the cultivated kind are

184

today. *Huckleberries,* from the Redwoods and points north, still sometimes come to market. Douglas, of fir fame, thought so highly of them that he sent the seeds to England — this more than a century ago. The *Oregon Grape,* that state's official flower, is really a barberry. It makes a fine jelly and a base for fruit punch. Another barberry, the *Nervosa,* has a large berry, and is even more popular for jelly. *Wild Grapes* were said to have been growing profusely when the white men first arrived on the Coast. Many of the vines now wild were probably planted by birds which had robbed the Mission gardens. The wild grape stock was once used as a phylloxera-resisting root for imported wine grapes. *Salal Berries,* favorite of the Indians, were used for pies by the pioneers. They still are today, and are particularly well liked when combined with huckleberries. There are other wild berries and fruits that were and are still used on occasion: *Bearberries, Buffalo Berries, Serviceberries, Lemon Berries, Black Strawberries* (or *Sea Figs*) and *Wild Rose Hips* are all edible in various degrees. So is the *Manzanilla,* or "little apple," and the *Manzanita Berry.*

(*Brandied Fruits*

With all manner of fruits and plenty of California brandy at hand, it was inevitable that brandied fruits should become very popular. Actually, they were popular *before* we had either the fruits or the brandy. The gold miners had a passion for them and, as money was no object to many of them, they were happy to pay huge prices to have this luxury sent to them around the Horn. So common was it in the Mother Lode country that jars in which brandied fruits had come were used as makeshift windows in the miners' cabins — a jar taking the place of a section of log.

(*Dried Fruit*

One of our major industries is the drying of fruits — peaches, apricots, pears, prunes, apples, cherries, figs, and of course raisins, tons and tons of them. This has been going on for a century. The early settlers found that the drying of fruits was the simplest way of husbanding them for later use. The pioneer women, who had precious few luxuries, picked the wild blackberries and strawberries with which the land was carpeted, and dried them. One early traveler to the wilderness was given dried mountain raspberries when he dined at a log cabin on his route. His diary says "they were the best thing I ever tasted," and that is easy to believe. Wild berries always have more flavor than the cultivated ones, and when that flavor is further concentrated in the drying, it must be the quintessence of all that's good about a berry — which is plenty.

The Franciscan Fathers dried what fruits were available *when* they were available, and so did the women in the mining towns, or at least those few who were there for domestic reasons. Dried fruits that weren't home-grown were also mentioned early in the history of our states. In the antepioneer days of 1845, the Belgian nuns of St. Paul's on the Willamette spoke of using dried apples "from Belgium." Peaches were dried, we know, because of the story of the greedy Indian who, having eaten too much of the dried peach pie so kindly offered by an early housewife, had the most frightful pains in his belly and was sure that he'd been poisoned. Cherries were dried and used in baking, and so were pears and apricots and figs, in those places where they grew. By 1868 raisins were being marketed, and by the '80s, dried fruits were apparently common on the entire West Coast. Today California produces more dried fruit than any place in the world, and in both Oregon and Washington it is a flourishing industry.

(*Apples*

Apples may not be native sons, but they certainly have become valuable citizens. Who can grow them better than the State of Washington? Oregon apples are superb, too, but, in a whisper, California's fruit leaves much to be desired. Yet it was in California that the first apples were grown — planted, as if you couldn't guess, by the Franciscan Fathers. The Rus-

186

sians planted apples in California, too, at Fort Ross in 1812. Cuttings were made from some of these, and one species of apple found in Sonoma County is still called "Russian apple." Sutter, of gold discovery fame, had apples, too, but they didn't amount to much. The apples of Oregon Territory are a different story, and quite a story. A young English lady, very beautiful of course, was the dinner partner of a gallant sea captain who was about to set forth on the perilous journey to Oregon. She gave the seeds of her dessert apple to Captain Simpson and idly bade him plant them when he reached the "wilderness." Months later, when the captain donned his dress suit for the first time since leaving London, he found the forgotten seeds in his pocket. That night he was dining with Dr. McLoughlin, famed Hudson's Bay Company factor at Fort Vancouver, which was the only place in all the Territory where one dressed for dinner. He gave the seeds to the good doctor, who was delighted. He and his gardener, Bruce, planted them at once and pampered them for many months. Finally one lone apple put in a forlorn appearance. Small and green and sour, it was nonetheless meticulously sliced into many portions, that all might enjoy this miracle of nature. The next year the apples were more plentiful, and they were *red!* Soon Fort Vancouver had a flourishing orchard. A pretty story, but it was the trees and cuttings that were hauled across the prairie that started the Northwest's enormous fruit industry. The Luelling brothers and William Meek, nurserymen, made the first significant plantings. They lugged 700 young trees with them on their trek to Oregon Territory, trees carefully packed in boxes built within their covered wagons, and watered even though men and cattle went thirsty. The trees reached their destination in beautiful condition, and were soon bearing magnificent fruit. In 1851, four boxes of apples brought $500 — in San Francisco, of course. That looked like good business to many of the pioneers, so more trees were started — hopefully. But it wasn't until the '90s that "apple fever" hit the populace. The Hood River Valley in Oregon was known as a great apple center by 1910, the Wenatchee and Yakima Valleys in Washington, a little later. A ridiculous number of apple trees were planted, and before long it was a lucky grower who stayed out of the red. Then came long years of struggle and finally the depression of the '30s. At that time Washington apples sold for under a dollar a box, the only stock the small businessman could afford to carry, and which he sold on the street corners of the country for a nickel apiece. But today the Washington apple industry is a flourishing one; hard work, expert merchandising, and advertising, and the fact that Washington apples are as fine as any grown anywhere, have done the trick. Rome Beauties, Winesaps, Jonathans, Yellow Newtons, and the most beautiful to look upon if not to eat, Delicious, are the principal varieties. A famous by-product of the apple, other than cider and vinegar, is Aplets, a confection not unlike a Turkish paste, made from apples, nuts, sugar, and I suppose, gelatin — at least a remarkably reasonable facsimile can be made in that manner. Aplets are made by the Liberty Orchards Company, Cashmere, Washington.

❨ Notes on Apples

Apples and Cranberries. Apples cooked in cranberry juice are a pleasant change from the cinnamon candy technique. The flavor is better and so is the color, if you care.

Apple Sauce with Coriander. Try this delightful spice instead of the more usual cinnamon or nutmeg — it's particularly good when served as a vegetable.

Apple Sauce with White Wine. Use white table wine instead of water when making apple sauce to serve with pork.

Apple Sauce at Its Best. Use tart apples, cook them with a minimum of water and sugar. Mash lightly, and add a good dollop of butter before serving.

❨ Apricots

California has a monopoly on apricot growing for both canning and drying, but her sister states of Oregon and Washington grow the beautiful fruit as well. The apricot industry has not increased as rapidly as other Western fruits, which is strange as it is a fruit whose flavor improves in the drying or the cooking, at least for my palate. It is unsurpassed as a filling for dessert pancakes or as a glaze for tarts made of other fruits, and is absolutely right whenever a very flavorsome sweet-tart flavor accent is needed.

❲ Dried Apricot Notes

Apricot-Macaroon Trifle. Alternate layers of stewed dried apricots and stale macaroons soaked in sherry. Top with toasted almonds, chill, and serve with whipped cream.

Apricot Pancakes. Make thin pancakes, spread with stewed dried apricots which have been forced through a sieve, flavor with rum (optional), and serve with sour cream.

Apricot Omelet. Make a sweet omelet, fill with stewed dried apricots, quite sweet, and sprinkle top with sugar. Slip under broiler to glaze, and serve flaming with brandy, or rum.

Apricot Glaze. Stew dried apricots as usual and, when very soft, force through a sieve. Add sugar to taste. This purée should be the thickness of a medium cream sauce. Arrange fruits in cooked tart or pie shells and paint with the glaze. Allow to stand a few hours before serving.

Apricot-Almond Ice Cream. Combine 1½ cups of sieved stewed dried apricots, 1 tablespoon of gelatin dissolved in ¼ cup of water, and melted over hot water, ½ teaspoon of almond extract, 1½ cups of cream, whipped, a pinch of salt, and ½ cup of toasted chopped almonds. Freeze in ice trays.

Dried Apricots may be used in bread, muffins, pies, soufflés, stuffings, and compotes. Fresh apricots are most popular eaten out of hand, or stewed, and canned apricots are eaten as they come, or brushed with butter or French dressing and broiled as an accompaniment to meat or poultry.

⟨ *Avocados*

Just why the avocado was so long in coming to California is a mystery. Mexico has always given generously of her secrets of good food, and it has been a favorite there since the days of the Aztecs. Actually, though, it wasn't until 1871 that Judge Ord, of Santa Barbara, was really successful in raising them in California, not until 1924, when the Growers Exchange was formed, that the avocado began to be generally known.

Henry E. Huntington was one of the famous Californians who gave the avocado a boost on its road to fame. He was served one at Los Angeles's Jonathan Club, and was so intrigued that he pocketed the seed and took it home to plant in his fabulous gardens in San Marino. That was the beginning of the avocado grove at the world-renowned Henry E. Huntington Library. Today, at least on the West Coast, the avocado is accepted as casually as the tomato or the onion, and we are always in the midst of working out new recipes for its use. The growers co-operative, which has dubbed its avocados "Calavos," will allow only 14 of the 99 common varieties to bear that label and, besides that, their fruit must meet other high standards. An avocado by any other name *may* taste as good, but not necessarily so. To be a Calavo, it *has* to be good.

Avocados are at their best when eaten fully ripe. We have learned that it is better to purchase them when they are still hard, and ripen them at home at a temperature of between 55 and 70 degrees — this because thoughtless marketers will test an avocado's ripeness with careless thumbs that leave it bruised and discolored for later purchasers. Harassed greengrocers have been known to display a coconut near their stock of avocados, with the suggestion that those with an urge to pinch use *it!* Avocados are properly tested for ripeness in two ways: if the seed rattles inside, they are almost ripe; if they give slightly when pressed between the palms of both hands (gently!), they are ready to eat. An avocado is most easily peeled by cutting it through the middle as you would a peach, then stripping off the skin. If only half is to be used, leave the pit in the remaining portion, and rub the cut surface with butter or lemon juice to prevent discoloration.

Connoisseurs prefer the avocado on the half shell, with salt, or the juice of lemon or lime, or possibly with a tarter-than-usual French dressing. Another way they approve is to serve it with a decanter of light rum, and with halves of lime, allowing the guests to add each in judicious amounts — this for a first course *or* a dessert. To sweeten or not to sweeten is a controversial subject; most gourmets believe that the avocado loses in the act. However, avocado ice cream is popular and good. But as for cooking the fruit, all experts agree that it is ruinous. Not only does the magnificent flavor of the avocado disappear entirely, a distasteful one takes its place. However, the avocado may be added to many cooked dishes just before serving — warming it does it no harm. And so we add them, diced, to creamed chicken or crab meat or lobster, we fold them into mashed potatoes, or add them to consommé or tomato bisque. We serve them on the half shell, as a cup for jellied madrilene, and some of us use them as a receptacle for crab meat, or salad, or fruit cocktail, or even caviar.

(*Berry Pie*

When berries are made into deep dish pies we have berries at their best. Simply fill a deep dish with them — any kind — and sugar them to taste. Dot with bits of butter, cover with a rich, not too thinly rolled crust, slash the top in two or three places, and bake in a hot oven until the crust is gorgeously brown. Serve neither hot nor cold, but comfortably warm. This will be runny; if you don't appreciate that luscious juiciness, a tiny sprinkling of flour may be mixed with the berries, but don't — please — use too much, or make it all gummy with cornstarch. The Western cooks of seventy-five or a hundred years ago sometimes used "risen pastry" for their deep dish berry pies. Try it, and try it also for strawberry shortcakes. Risen pastry is nothing more than a rich roll dough that has been allowed to rise, then rolled thin. For strawberry shortcake, make two thin layers, spreading butter between them, before a second rising and baking.

ℂ Strawberry Notes

With Orange Juice. Brillat-Savarin liked strawberries with orange juice. Try it for breakfast and you'll see why.

With Champagne. Put a huge whole strawberry in a glass of chilled champagne or white wine — a lovely summer toast.

With Gamay. Use whole perfect berries, with stems still intact. Arrange berries in individual plates around a mound of confectioners' sugar, and serve with a glass of Gamay or Cabernet. The berries may be dipped in the wine, or the wine sipped with the sugar-dipped berries — a perfect dessert for a sultry day.

ℂ The Loganberry and Other Western Berries

The loganberry was born in California in 1881. This is a true native because it was developed out here by Judge J. H. Logan of Santa Cruz, and is a cross between our wild blackberry and a red raspberry. It was a "chance hybrid" says Wickson, and has proved a most valuable fruit. The berry is very large, the shape of a blackberry, and of a dark red color, and the flavor is that of a sublimated blackberry.

The youngberry is a cross between the phenomenal berry and a dewberry. A large and very dark red berry, it is very well liked.

The last of these Western berries is the boysenberry, a hybrid of the blackberry, the raspberry, and the loganberry. It is the most popular of all, even though it has only been in the market for about fifteen years. It is extra large, has an exceptionally fine flavor, and fewer seeds than most berries of its type. This berry was propagated by Rudolph Boysen, and popularized by Knott's Berry Farm, near Buena Vista, California, a onetime roadside fruit stand which is now a tourists' mecca, specializing in serving meals featuring berry pies, and jams and jellies made with berries from their own farm.

192

❨ *The Cherimoya*

The cherimoya, or cherimoyer, is also called a custard apple, and is a fascinating fruit, usually the shape and size of a beef heart, and with a surface made up of a series of flat planes or facets. Its color varies from pale green to almost black, and its creamy white flesh has many black seeds. The flavor is slightly reminiscent of both banana and pineapple, if you can imagine that combination, and is very good if seeded, and put into a fruit mélange or compote. Cherimoya when served in combination with strawberries and with sour cream, is dreamy.

❨ *Cherries*

Our cherries are fabulous, that nobody will deny. Whether from California, Oregon, or Washington, they are huge, sweet, juicy affairs that usually require two or three bites in the eating! An Eastern fruit grower, who shipped some trees of his own propagation to our coast, did not recognize the cherry when he visited here a few years later. It was unbelievable to him that this giant was his own creation. The Mission gardens, strangely enough, had no cherries, but the Russians did, perhaps as early as 1812. The Luelling brothers were greatly interested in the fruit, probably because they were so delighted at the size and quality they attained in their new home. Henderson Luelling developed two new varieties of cherries in Oregon, both now world-famed. One is the Bing cherry, and Luelling named it after his Chinese houseboy. The other cherry, the Black Republican, was named, quite literally, after a political group. His brother, also in politics, developed a cherry which he named the Lincoln. Today our principal cherries are: Bing, Black Republican, Lambert, Royal Ann, and Tartarian.

❨ *Oranges and Other Citrus Fruits*

California and oranges are almost synonymous and have been ever since the orange industry really got under way. It all started, of course, at the Missions, where orange trees grew in most of the gardens. The first orchard of any size was planted at San Gabriel Mission, near Los Angeles, about 1805, and by 1863 there were enough orange trees around so that some families had a surplus — at least Californians were urged to make an orange preserve "as made in Scotland and known as Scotch marmalade." It was ten years later, in 1873, that the orange industry really got going. The United States Department of Agriculture acquired some navel orange seedlings in Bahia, Brazil, and sent a couple of them to the Tibbetts family, who lived at Riverside. The trees flourished, and the wonderful seedless oranges they bore were the talk of the state. Soon grafting buds from the trees were selling for a dollar apiece, and orange groves sprang up everywhere. Later, the Valencias were also planted in great quantities, particularly in the cooler sections nearer the coast. Then came lemons and grapefruit and the less common citrus fruits — limes, kumquats, tangerines, limequats, citrons, tangelos, and calamondins. Before long everyone was growing citrus fruit but everyone wasn't selling it. Times were tough and probably would have become tougher if the growers hadn't formed a co-operative. In 1893 the California Fruit Growers Exchange was organized. Today they handle 75 per cent of the state's lemon, orange, and grapefruit crops, which they market under the world-known name of Sunkist. They not only co-operate in the care of the groves and the picking, packing, and marketing of the fruit; they are largely responsible for the fact that most American children take breakfast orange juice for granted, and most cooks consider lemons as indispensable as onions or sugar.

Oranges. Here on the West Coast we do not limit our orange consumption to a healthful fruit beverage. We use them in much of our cooking. We float thin slices of them on clear soups and we even make the entire soup of them. We add them to salads, sauces, puddings, beverages, and breads, and more and more we use them as a pleasantly edible garnish for fish and for meat.

Fruits

Lemons. As for lemons, they have graduated from the tea tray and fish platter to every meal, every course. We have learned that there's magic in the squeezing of a lemon, and that its piquant juices bring out the flavor of soups, meats, vegetables, and salads, as well as the full goodness of other fruits.

Grapefruit. The grapefruit, though still used primarily as a table fruit and a beverage, is beginning to get around a little more. Grapefruit juice, we have found, makes a good base for fruit gelatin dishes, and for fish aspics, too, if the sugar is forgotten. Grapefruit sections rival lemon and orange as a garnish for various fish and meat dishes. Try them poached and served hot with roast pork or duck, and you'll see why.

Kumquats. Kumquats grow in California and they're a favorite with the Chinese, which makes them doubly eligible for inclusion here. Kumquats are the size of large olives (super-colossal supreme, that is) and are the shape of a pecan in its shell. They may be thinly sliced and used as a piquant touch with fruit cocktails or salads or compotes. Or they may be made into a particularly delightful marmalade, or preserved whole and served as a dessert at a Chinese dinner, or as an exotic and charming accompaniment for poultry and game.

Tangerines. Tangerines are perhaps best eaten out of hand, or in the never-to-be-forgotten manner told by M. F. K. Fisher in her fascinating book, *Serve It Forth.* They also take beautifully to poaching in a light syrup and spiking with rosemary, then serving chilled for a cool dessert on a sultry day. The Japanese are now canning mandarin oranges (which *are* tangerines). They make a nice breakfast fruit, or, when flavored with preserved ginger or ground coriander, an exotic dessert.

Limes. Limes are certainly indispensable to the bartender and to the gourmet. Like lemons they add a sprightliness to a number of dishes. Wedges of lime, when served with avocado, melon, or other fruits, accentuate their character. Sliced limes with soups, halved limes with fish, whole limes squeezed into salads, limes everywhere that lemons go — lime marmalade, lime pie, and limeade for some.

195

❲ Orange Notes

Oranges and Tequila. Slice oranges thin, skin and all. Arrange in a glass dish in layers, with sugar between each layer, then pour over tequila and allow to stand in the refrigerator for several hours before serving.

Oranges and Curaçao. Peel oranges deeply, so that no white remains. Slice thin and sprinkle lightly with sugar, then pour over curaçao to taste. Chill before serving.

Orange Shortcake. This is an old and wonderful idea: bake rich shortcake dough in pie tins. It should be ½-inch thick when baked. Split, butter very generously, and pile sugared slices of orange between layers. Serve with whipped cream.

❲ Cranberries

Cranberries grew wild in Oregon and Washington — still do, though they are small and insipid compared to the huge and wonderful berries now cultivated in Oregon. In early days, however, they were highly prized by both Indian and white. One story tells of Mrs. Birnie, Indian wife of an English officer of the Hudson's Bay Company, who, although she played the part of the *grande dame* in Astoria, took off once a year to do her "marketing." She, with only Indians along, traveled to Shoalwater Bay in a huge canoe that could hold seventy people. There she loaded up with elk meat, clams, and cranberries and, though she was undoubtedly pleased with this provender, her Indian friends could easily have brought it to her. The truth probably is that she wanted to get away from it all. . . .

Today the cranberries grown in Oregon and Washington are spectacular. Recently I happened to be passing through Bandon, on the coast of Oregon, when their annual Cranberry Festival was in progress. The cranberries were the size of grapes, each one perfect. And the foods that the ladies of Bandon had made with them! Pies, cakes, muffins, bread, cookies, puddings, jellies, relishes, aspics, and even candies. I felt then that with those enterprising Westerners behind it, the cran-

196

berry had a very good chance of getting somewhere besides on the Thanksgiving and Christmas dinner table. Certainly it's a fruit that, for flavor alone, deserves to be served all the year round. Then there's that color, that ease of preparation, and that low cost. All this, and vitamins, too.

❰ *Cranberry Notes*

Cranberry Soufflé. Grind 2 cups of cranberries, cook with 1 cup of sugar and 2 tablespoons of lemon juice for 2 minutes. Cool, add 4 egg yolks, beaten stiff, ¼ teaspoon salt, 4 egg whites, also stiff. Bake at 350° about 35 to 45 minutes. Serve with whipped cream.

Cranberry Pancakes. Spread hot pancakes with cranberry sauce. Roll. Serve with sour cream, or with creamed turkey.

Cranberry Ham Glaze. Bake ham as usual, skin, score, and paint with cranberry sauce that has been forced through a sieve. Stick in the inevitable whole cloves, if you wish, and return to the oven for 20 minutes, basting with extra cranberry sauce.

Cranberry Sauce with Game. This combination is a natural, providing, of course, that wine is neither used in the cooking of the game, nor served with it. Venison is particularly good when served with cranberries.

Cranberry Dessert Sauce. Strain ordinary cranberry sauce (recipe in every cook book), dilute with a little hot water, cool, and use as a sauce for peaches or cottage puddings.

❰ *Dates*

The date industry in California really never got going until 1890, or thereabouts. Date palms had been planted much earlier than that, but they never amounted to much, though there are some survivors at the San Diego Mission. Then Uncle Sam got busy and sent experts to get shoots of the famous date palms of Babylonia and Arabia. The Arabs were unco-operative, and I can't say that I blame them — they didn't

197

want any competition in the date business. It is said, and we should whisper it, that the shoots had to be "taken out in the dead of night," whether with or without permission we'd better not ask. Someone succeeded in getting shoots of the Deglet Noor, the prize of them all, and that is the date that now grows so profusely in the Coachella Valley of California, and makes 90 per cent of our output.

The Coachella Valley, not far from glamorous Palm Springs, is a desert below sea level. Here the date palm has ideal living conditions, with its "head in the sun and its feet in the water," for dates need great heat and much irrigation. Date palms are planted in harems, forty-nine females to one male, but they need no special insect for pollenation for it is a comparatively simple dusting job for man. Dates have been hand pollenated ever since men discovered their value as food. Not so simple the harvesting. Each huge cluster of fruit is covered with a paper hat to protect it from heavy desert rains, and when the fruit ripens the clusters must be hand-picked about four times. When the trees are young this is within man's reach, but as the palms grow, ladders have to be used. Today huge traveling platforms go down between the rows of palms, and two crews of pickers work from either side.

Most California dates, though technically fresh, are only semiperishable, for they will keep for months at moderate temperatures. We have three main varieties: the Deglet Noor, the Golden Saidy (Zah-hee'-dee), and the Khadrawi (Kahdrah'-wee).

The California dates are not dried, though actually they are both hydrated and dehydrated to produce uniform moisture content. They are marketed by the United Date Growers of California, a co-operative that is doing much to popularize our Western fruit. They may be used in any recipe calling for dried dates, but we like them best eaten as is, a truly delightful confection.

(Date Notes

Date Appetizers. Dates stuffed with Cheddar cheese — don't stick up your nose until you've tried it. Surprising. Or

198

stuff dates with green olives, wrap in bacon and broil, or stuff with sausage meat and broil. Strange sounding and better than they sound, really.

Dates with Cream. Believe it or not, pitted, cut in halves, and served with sugar and cream, they are delicious.

Dates with Brandy. Soak dates in California brandy for a few days, adding sugar if you wish. Serve over vanilla ice cream.

❰ *Figs*

Figs have been around since Mission days in California, where they grew in the gardens and were dried by the Padres for future use. These early figs were named "Mission," not unnaturally, and that variety, dark purple when fresh, black when dried, are favorites on the West Coast. Although Californians dried their own garden figs, this was not done commercially to any extent until the First World War, and even after that many of them were imported from Smyrna. The Second World War, and the curtailment of imports, gave the dried fig industry another boost. Now it is conceded that California figs are the best in the world — by us, anyway.

The story of the Calimyrna fig is a fascinating one. The original Mission fig and the more recently introduced White Adriatic fig bore profusely, but not so the Smyrna, also a white fig. (*White* figs are green when ripe, amber when dried.) That fig was introduced in 1882, in the hope that we could produce a fig comparable to the dried one which came from Turkey. Nothing happened — or at least not enough. The trees grew and bore fruit, but the figs dropped before they ever matured. This was a considerable blow to California orchardists, who were firmly convinced that everything flourished in California. Obviously something was wrong. It was finally realized that it was all a matter of pollenation and, after much to-do, it was decided that the wild Capri fig — a tree which bore no edible fruit but which did grow near the Smyrna in its native habitat — was the papa fig tree, and was essential for little figs. So the wild fig was imported and planted near the cultivated trees. Still no results. Finally, in 1890, a Mr. Roeding succeeded in producing by hand pollination some of the highly desired figs, but as each fig had to be handled separately it was decided that playing Cupid to the fig trees was hardly a paying proposition. What was the secret? It finally came out — a wasp so minute that it could barely be seen with the naked eye, the fig wasp, Blastophaga, a wasp, worse luck, that couldn't be found in California. Numerous persons tried to secure the insect from abroad, without luck. The United States Government tried; no soap. It could be that the Turks were farsighted enough to see the end of their fig industry if they allowed the little fly to get out of the country. There is one story, highly apocryphal, that has a Californian orchardist, disguised as a Turk, smuggling a few Capri figs, Blastophagas and all, from Smyrna. Anyway, by some means, fair or foul, the wasp finally arrived in 1899, and Mr. Roeding succeeded in raising Californian Smyrna figs, which he christened "Calimyrna." An anticlimactic discovery was made soon after. These wasps, whose acquisition had had the fruiterers in a turmoil, had been living happily in the San Joaquin Valley for at least twenty years.

We eat many dried figs on the West Coast, both as a decidedly delicious confection and in pies, puddings, breads, cookies, and such, but our biggest thrill is the fresh fig when it is in season. These plump, ripe, juicy fruits are very fragile, and so cannot be shipped any distance except by air. That makes them come high in the rest of the country. Kadotas are the favorite for eating fresh. Fresh figs are picked dead ripe, and when marketed are carefully packed in berry baskets, and sometimes even in little paper cups, like *petits fours.*

(Dried Fig Notes

Stewed Figs. Put 1 cup of dried figs in 1 cup of cold water and bring to a quick boil. Cook 35 to 45 minutes, or until tender, adding another cup of water during the cooking. A tablespoon of sugar may be added during the last 5 minutes. These make a delicious breakfast fruit. Some like sliced lemon or orange cooked with the figs, and I think a speck of salt lends them character.

Figged Muffins. Stuff a cooked fig (stem snipped off) with a walnut. Make ordinary muffin batter, put a little in the muffin tins, add the figs, cover with more batter, bake as usual. Or cut cooked or soaked figs in pieces and mix with muffin batter, adding a little grated orange rind as well.

Fig Turnovers are made by stuffing figs with a little hard sauce, then folding them in piecrust and baking until brown. Delightful!

Fig Appetizers. Steam figs, split, and stuff with cream cheese or Cheddar cheese, seasoned with herbs or olives or such. Well?

Fig Pickles. Boil a pound of dried figs for 15 minutes. Drain and cook in 1 cup of vinegar, ½ cup of sugar, with whole cinnamon, cloves, and allspice for 45 minutes.

Figs and Bacon. Soak dried figs overnight, egg and crumb, and fry in bacon fat. Serve with bacon — try it.

Figs and Brandy. Stuff dried figs with nuts, soak in brandy, then heat in the brandy in a chafing dish, add butter, and serve with meat.

(*Fresh Fig Notes*

Figs and Cream. Peel ripe figs and slice with a very sharp knife. Serve with cream and sugar, or lemon, for an enchanting breakfast fruit.

Figs and Port. This is a favorite dessert. Peel ripe figs and put, whole or sliced, in sherbet glasses. Pour on a mellow port wine to cover.

In *Fruit Salad,* or in fresh fruit compotes, figs combine well with oranges, tangerines, strawberries, and pineapple.

(Feiojas

The feioja, a subtropical fruit, is nicknamed pineapple guava, apparently because it tastes like strawberries (or bananas, some say). It is tremendously and deliciously fragrant. Olive-shaped and the size of a pullet's egg, with a beautiful dark green skin and a silvery bloom, it has a juicy flesh and seeds that are so small they are insignificant, an advantage that it has over the guava. The feioja makes superb jelly and marmalade, particularly when in combination with the peel and juice of a lemon. The fruit is also delicious to eat as is, or sliced in a fruit cocktail or compote, or for breakfast with sugar and cream.

(Granadillas

The granadilla, or passion fruit, put the Franciscan Fathers into a temporary tizzy when they found the Indians eating it. They believed it was a holy fruit, for in its flower they saw the symbols of the Crucifixion: the corona was the Crown of Thorns, the stamen and pistil the nails, the five petals and five sepals, the ten faithful Apostles. But the Indians liked the fruit and ate it whenever the stealing was good, and the poor Fathers suffered at every purloined bite. Then came the light. They, the Padres, had been wrong — was not this great craving for the fruit a sign from Heaven that the heathens longed for Christianity? And so the consumption of the fruit was approved, and so, quite naturally, it lost a bit of its flavor. . . . Passion fruit, purplish in color and mildly and pleasantly acid, makes a fine jelly, but its chief use is for syrup, a base for fruit punch.

(Guavas

We have two guavas that are grown quite extensively, the strawberry guava and the lemon guava — both are delicious. There is considerable botanical confusion about the California guavas. Suffice it to say that strawberry guavas are red, and lemon guavas are yellow, and that their real names are something else again. Both are very fragrant and usually sweet with a hint of tartness. Utterly delectable when sliced and added to a mélange of fresh fruit. Guavas are used for jellies and jams and, like quince, they turn a lovely amber rose in the cooking. Guava paste, dear to our Mexicans, is just as popular with everyone who has served it for dessert with Monterey Jack or Teleme cheese. Stewed guavas are delicious, too, and a purée of them, poured over sliced peaches and topped with sour cream is exotic and delightful.

Guava Dumplings are made by rolling quartered and sugared guavas in biscuit dough, baking, and serving with hard sauce or whipped cream cheese.

(*Jujubes*

The jujube, or Chinese date, was first introduced in the Sonoma Valley in 1876, but it does rather better in drier areas. The fruit is usually date-sized and a little fuller, but it sometimes grows as large as a hen's egg. Fresh or dried, they are eaten out of hand, but they are also made into bread, cookies, and puddings, even as a true date. The Chinese make mi-tsao, or honeyed jujubes, a sort of glacé that is quite pleasant.

(*Loquats*

The loquat, sometimes called the Japanese medlar, is an insignificant-looking fruit that grows on a striking tree. Huge woolly gray-green leaves almost hide clusters of round or oval yellow fruit that varies in size from a prune to an egg. Loquats are eaten fresh, and are said by their fans to taste like cherries, an opinion that would certainly be challenged by any loyal Oregonian. Loquat jelly is good, and preserves, when spiced and sharpened with lemon juice or vinegar, are popular.

(*Mangoes*

Mangoes were introduced into California around 1880 but, though they do grow here, those on the West Coast markets come from Florida. Those who grow them, or have the price to buy them, use them for chutney and eat them raw or stewed for dessert.

❰ Melons

Melons, all kinds of melons, grow in all three Far Western states. There was a lot of early talk about them, too. We know they grew at Fort Walla Walla in 1836, and that the pioneers, always hungry for sugar, which was unprocurable, succeeded in making sugar from the juice of watermelons, which were plentiful.

The cantaloupe rates highest, yet it isn't a cantaloupe at all, but a muskmelon. Honeydews are our next favorites, then we have honeyballs, casabas, Cranshaws, Persians, and, of course, the watermelon, either plain or striped. The Chinese also have a couple of melons that are of interest. One, the winter melon, is a large round vegetable, used for the famous winter melon soup (page 354); the soup is cooked right in the melon. The other, the bitter melon, is well named, and one has to have an Oriental palate to really appreciate it.

We usually serve melons in the shell, or cut into balls for fresh fruit cocktails — combining several different varieties of melon, or using one or two kinds with other fruits. A favorite first course is an ice-filled tray piled with wedges of the various melons, with their harmony of flavor and color — salmon pink, pale green, warm yellow, deep rose — a pretty dish to set before a guest.

❰ Papayas

The papaya, or papaw, has only recently been grown here in any quantity. It is quite a bit like a melon, with salmon-colored flesh and numerous black seeds. It should be ripe when eaten, and well chilled, and, though usually served as one does a cantaloupe, it is nice diced and added to fruit cocktails and such. A drizzle of lime or lemon juice goes well with it. Some connoisseurs believe that the flavor is improved by scoring the fruit lightly, two or three days before eating, thus allowing some of the juices to run off.

Fruits

(*Peaches*

Peaches were just another of the fruits that Father Serra and his boys brought along on their famous junket to California, though one person, Sir Francis Drake's scribe, claimed that peaches were in "New Albion" long before that — in 1648. That the Missions had them is sure. Vancouver saw them at Santa Clara and San Buenaventura, and both Robinson and Bryant say that they were at other missions. Luelling, in 1847, brought peach trees to Oregon Territory, as did other pioneers, and the peach trees planted in Monterey began to bear in 1850. They were planted in the gold country, too, and one tree in Coloma, where Marshall made his famous discovery, bore 450 peaches in 1854, which sold for $3.00 apiece. Thirteen hundred and fifty dollars for a couple of days of picking had even the gold miners talking about easy money.

By 1860 peaches were being put up in glass, and a couple of years later tin was used — the beginning of the enormous canned peach industry in California. Ninety-eight per cent of the nation's canned peaches and all of its dried peaches come from California. Our fresh peach output is exceeded only by Georgia, but both Oregon and Washington produce large numbers.

There are two main types of peach — the freestone and the cling. The cling peach is the one that is usually canned. It's firmer than the freestone, and keeps its shape better, though many connoisseurs prefer the flavor of the freestone peach.

Especially popular peaches include the Babcock, the Indian peach (a "blood cling," which has a wonderfully tasty red flesh) and, when it can be found, the saucer peach — a flat, almost misshapen fruit that is the quintessence of peach flavor. It is the same as the Chinese peen-to.

(*Peach Notes*

Canned peaches are used mostly as is, though the California Foods Research Institute has developed a number of interesting other ways to use the canned cling peach.

205

Peaches Jubilee. Drain peaches and combine with pitted black cherries that have been soaked in brandy. Serve flaming or not, as desired.

Baked Peaches. Fill peach halves with chopped filberts mixed with a little butter and brown sugar. Bake until lightly browned, and serve warm with cold sour cream.

Broiled Peaches. Brush with melted butter and broil, to serve with meats as a garnish. Chopped almonds may be sprinkled on top before browning.

Peach Melba, upside-down cake, and condé are also popular, as is, apparently, peach salad with cottage cheese.

❰ Pears

The three Pacific States have recently joined to market our growing winter pear crop — the Bosc, the D'Anjou, the Du Comice, and the Nelis — and the summer pear, the Bartlett. Bartlett trees are the oldest deciduous fruit trees in California, and grew in the Mission orchards. It is today the chief California pear, and the one that is canned and dried in enormous quantities, and also sent fresh to all parts of the world. This pear need not be ripened on the tree to achieve full flavor, in fact it is better if picked before completely soft, and ripened at controlled temperatures. The D'Anjou and Comice pears, as well as the Bosc and Nelis, all winter pears, are primarily the pears of the Northwest, and have but recently come into prominence. Their original names — Beurre d'Anjou, Beurre Bosc, and Doyenne du Comice — proclaim their French origin. The story goes that the French gentry of a century ago tried to outdo each other in the growing of pears. Hundreds of new varieties were developed, most of them since forgotten. Three of the best, mentioned above, were planted in the Northwest, and, to no one's surprise, at least no Westerner's, grew to far greater size and flavor than ever before. Until World War II these pears were imported to the United States from France, and a pretty price they brought, too. Now they are available at every greengrocery, and at no great cost. We are particularly partial to them for dessert, especially with cheese, or poached in wine and served with a simple cake or cookie. Canned pears, which are almost invariably Bartletts, are served as a compote, or fancied up in one manner or another.

⟨ *Persimmons*

Persimmons — they're an autumnal rite with me. I purchase them when they are hard so that I can enjoy their full beauty before they reach the eating stage. I arrange them lovingly in a huge shallow bowl and give them a place of honor on the dining table. I watch them change their color, soften, reach that degree of transparency and utter ripeness at which they are at their very best, I am told. And then, when they've become of more than passing interest to the fruit flies, I throw them, ever so reluctantly, into the garbage can. But don't listen to me. Listen to the thousands of gourmets who eagerly await the persimmon season, for it *is* a popular fruit on the West Coast.

Persimmons are various colors depending on both variety and degree of ripeness — some lemon yellow, some a deep red-orange, many with a beautiful blue-purple bloom. The shape is rather like a tomato, with a pointed bottom, more the shape of a china nest egg than anything else I can think of.

They were first planted near the American River in 1876, and marketed mostly in San Francisco, a few being sent to New York, Philadelphia, and Boston. We have been taught to like the persimmon by the Japanese, who also taught us a curing method by which improperly ripened fruit can have its astringent quality removed. Persimmons should be utterly ripe when eaten; you'll regret it if they're not, although new varieties have been developed which never *do* pucker up the mouth. Connoisseurs of persimmons eat them by cutting a little slice from the top, and eating the flesh out with a spoon; they feel it needs no embellishment. Others serve them on lettuce, with French dressing. A Thanksgiving salad that is so popular as to be almost a classic, is made by combining grapefruit sections, sliced avocado, and peeled ripe persimmons, all cut in approximately the same sizes, and arranged on romaine, with French dressing. Persimmons are also peeled and sliced and eaten with sugar and cream, like peaches, or served whole for dessert, along with a fruit knife and fork, and some crackers and cheese. Cream cheese, or Sierra breakfast, or teleme, are the usual choices. Persimmon pudding and pie are not uncommon, and persimmon ice cream is well liked though not well known.

(Persimmon Notes

Persimmon Jam has to be made with pectin. It also needs lemon juice and, for my taste, some rosemary or cloves, for added zest.

Persimmon Cup. Peel, put point down in a fruit cocktail glass, open and scoop a little out of the top, and fill with tart fresh fruits — oranges, grapefruit, cherries, or such. Sour cream topping, if you wish.

(Pineapples

At one time or another, pineapples have been grown in California, but the pampering required makes it unfeasible as a commercial crop, so we are content to get the fruit from Hawaii and from Mexico. In the early days, when the only travel was across the prairies or by ship around the Horn, Hawaii was our closest neighbor, and we had a sizable trade with the "Sandwich Islands." Kanakas, or native Hawaiians, were fairly numerous in the early days, working in the kitchens as well as in the mines. They no doubt taught us our way to prepare fresh pineapple, on the half shell, in sticks, shredded — three ways which we still favor highly. As for canned pineapple, we use it in huge quantities, both as a dessert and as an ingredient in Chinese cooking.

(Pomegranates

Pomegranates grew in the gardens of San Gabriel Mission very early in our history, and they have been grown here ever since. Today California is the only state where they are raised commercially. The tree, the blossoms, and the fruit are all beautiful to behold. Although the fruit is sometimes very pale, almost white, and sometimes brownish-yellow, it is the bright red variety that is popular. It is "obscurely six-sided," as Wickson says, with a tough skin and a crownlike calyx that adds to its beauty. The tougher the skin the better the fruit, for that shows that the pulpy flesh around the seeds is well developed and the juices abundant. The reddish juice is used in making grenadine, and also for a most delightful jelly. The fleshy seeds are often used in fruit salads and in compotes, and they add a piquant touch to them. The Mexicans use pomegranate seeds in a wonderful Christmas salad that contains fruit and nuts as well. They sometimes put the seeds in their guacamole. The fruit is also served as a dessert, with fruit knives and forks, spoons too, for those who like to scoop out the juices and seeds. A finger bowl is almost a must. A pomegranate, like a persimmon, always adds its beauty to centerpieces of autumn fruits. Its beauty is exceeded only by its flavor.

❪ *Pomegranate Notes*

Pomegranate Jelly. The juice may be extracted by cutting the fruit in half and using an orange reamer. When making jelly, pectin must be used — follow the directions that are given for low-pectin fruits, which is what this beauty is.

Pomegranate Sherbet. This is one of the most deliciously refreshing sherbets imaginable. Soak 2 teaspoons of gelatin in ¼ cup of cold water, then melt over hot water. Add to 3 cups of pomegranate juice, 2 cups of water, 1 cup of sugar (more if you want it sweet). Partially freeze to a mush in refrigerator tray, then fold in 2 well-beaten egg whites. Return to freezer, and stir a couple of times during the rest of the freezing.

Pomegranate Syrup (Grenadine). Squeeze juice, measure equal parts of juice and sugar, and let stand together for 3 days. Bring to a boil, simmer 5 minutes, strain, and pour into sterilized jars and seal.

(Prunes

Both California and Oregon produce delicious prunes. The Santa Clara prune, named after the valley (largest fruit canning and drying center in the world) where it is grown, is considered one of the best of them all. The prunes came to Santa Clara in 1856, from France. They were cuttings of the famous French prune, which were stuck into raw potatoes, then in sawdust, and packed in two leather trunks in which they made the long trip around the Horn. This packaging precaution proved wise, as the cuttings reached Louis Pellier, of San Jose, in beautiful condition. He grafted them to the rooting stock of the wild plum, and so the French prune came to the West Coast. The Luelling brothers later developed the golden prune in Oregon.

Prunes are allowed to become so ripe that they fall of their own sweet juicy weight, landing in softly harrowed ground that receives them gently. From there on their processing is highly scientific. The cook's main interest is the finished prune. We use them in many of our West Coast dishes — muffins, breads, puddings, even pot roasts and stuffings for game or goose, and as a very popular meat garnish. We also consume a goodly quantity of prune juice, probably for health's sake, and we and our children love to eat them raw, either from the box in the kitchen, or when they have been pitted and specially treated as a confection.

(Rhubarb

Rhubarb cuttings were one of the few things that the pioneer women managed to smuggle across the plains. Because of the lack of space in the covered wagons, they were supposed to carry nothing worth less than a "dollar a pound," but though the fruit was practically worthless in the East, it was priceless when it produced in the wilderness — anything for a relief from the monotonous diet of salmon and boiled wheat. Little Alice Clarissa Whitman, two-year-old daughter of the famous missionaries, was given a piece of rhubarb the day she drowned. She called it "apple" and the pleasure it gave her shows how few treats these pioneer children had.

⟨ *Raisins*

The Spanish Padres dried what grapes they didn't use for wine, so of course they get credit for producing the first raisins, but it wasn't until 1868 that they were dried commercially. These were muscat grapes, and in those early days they were marketed seeds, stems, and all. Ten years later a Mr. Thompson brought a Turkish grape, the Sultanina, to California. This is a seedless grape and makes as fine raisins as it does poor wine. This grape, now known as the Thompson Seedless, is used for the small seedless raisins and for a table grape, while the big plump muscat is used for seeded raisins, and for muscatel, so dear to the heart of the wino. Raisins are, today, a major industry in California. All Westerners use them extensively, in the usual ways. We also use them in many Mexican dishes and some Oriental ones, and raisin sauce for ham can almost be said to be a California classic.

⟨ *Sapotes*

The sapote is a peachlike fruit that is coming into favor. For many years there seemed to be a difficulty in growing them, although Wickson tells of two old trees in Santa Barbara, one of which dated back to Mission days. It is called the "peach of the tropics" because it looks like a peach, but with greenish-yellow skin, and with seeds like an orange. It should be ripened on the tree, but only the fruits that attain that state during August and September are edible. Those, of course, are the ones that go to market. Sapotes are lacking in tartness, so they need lemon or lime juice when served as a breakfast fruit, and they combine well with fresh oranges and grapefruit in a fruit cocktail or fruit salad.

⟨ *Tuna*

The tuna, or prickly pear, is the fruit of the cactus *Opuntia occidentalis*, and is sweet, flavorsome, and juicy. It is egg-shaped and a lovely yellowish-rose when ripe. A prickly pear may be eaten in two ways. One: peeled, sliced, chilled, and served with lemon juice, or lemon juice and sugar, or even with cream and sugar, and very good it is, too. The other is a bit more dramatic: the fruit is served whole on a dessert plate, with fruit knife and fork. The ends are sliced off and an incision made the full length of the tuna. The skin is then laid back and the pulp eaten "on the half shell." Luther Burbank thought it worth spending much time on the fruit to develop a prickleless variety, though whatever became of that one, I can't seem to discover.

Game

THE WEST COAST *is game country, which is a pleasure for hunter and gourmet alike. For the first settlers it was life itself. The country was loaded with deer, elk, antelope, bears, mountain sheep and goats, squirrels, rabbits, and, apparently, even wild boar. Game birds there were, too, with quail, ducks, geese, sage hens, prairie chickens, doves, pigeons, and grouse the most numerous. In spite of all this superabundance, game was sometimes scarce — or perhaps just elusive. When that happened, the pioneers ate anything they could bag: 'possum, badger, skunk, racoon, and, it is said, crow. When they could be choosy, however, it was venison that was their first choice, as it was with the Indians.*

Gamy stories crop up in most accounts of early days. There are the descriptions of the sumptuous repasts served by Factor McLoughlin at Fort Vancouver. The good doctor, probably the first gourmet of the "wilderness," featured venison and wild duck at his affairs and, knowing that wine is the very soul of a game dinner, always included it. This, along with the full dress, the bagpipe music, and the general formality that was observed, was the forerunner of the many exquisite game dinners that have been served here ever since. The humbler — and hungrier — pioneers were less ceremonious at mealtime, but they were just as grateful for this God-given supply of fine meat, and, like the Indians, always served it when a feast was in order. One such time with the Chinooks, a potlach, *was a form of old age security. The host at such a party, usually an aged aborigine who had acquired considerable worldly goods, would invite the tribe to a banquet of venison and wapato, salmon and camas. He would then give away everything he owned. The deal was that he was thereby entitled to visit any of his guests at any time he chose, and stay as long as the idea pleased him. He also could ask for — and get — anything owned by a person who had attended his* potlach. *"Cast thy bread upon the waters . . ."*

It's surprising, considering the lack of game conservation in the past, that the supply lasted as long as it did. In the '50s there were still huge herds of deer and antelope not far from San Francisco, at Mount Diablo, and in the south and the north game was pretty much taken for granted. The stage stations on the Oregon road invariably had venison, and the butcher shops in the Gold Country, including Mr. Armour's first establishment, were more apt to have deer and bear meat than they were mutton or beef. The earliest restaurants served game because there was little else, and early cook books had recipes for it, apparently for the same reason — at least they used pheasant for "chicken salad," deer for "meat loaf," and sage hen for "fricasy." Later, when other meats were available, there was less game served until the fancy restaurants, led by the Palace Hotel, started to feature it — grizzly steak, valley quail, and saddle of venison appeared on many of the early Palace menus. As late as the '90s there was still so much game in this rich land that vendors were hawking it in the streets of San Francisco, and a whole wild goose could be bought for fifteen cents. Those happy days are gone, but we still have a goodly supply of wild life, and careful supervision of hunting is increasing rather than diminishing it.

Game

(Game Notes

Deer. There are deer in all three Far Western states, and several varieties of them at that. Perhaps because it is the best known of the big game animals, it is by far the most popular with both Nimrod and gourmet.

Elk, or wapiti, also lives in all three states. Its meat, which is venison, is particularly good eating, and is prepared in the same manners as other venison. The Roosevelt elk is found in the Olympic Mountains and the Tatoosh Range. It is the largest of the wapiti, and is highly prized.

Antelope is plentiful in Oregon, where it is native, but the imported herds in the other two states are completely protected, in the hope that some day there can be an open season on them.

Bear is another three-state big game animal. A bear, being a huge animal, has lots of delicious meat. The paws are considered a great delicacy, and bear steaks and saddle of bear rate high with connoisseurs. Bear meat tastes best when cooked rare. But because of the danger of trichinosis, this is ill-advised unless the meat has been held frozen at 0° Fahrenheit for three weeks or longer. Bears played an important role in the lives of the early settlers. The town of Monterey was once saved from starvation because of the meat, and to many pioneers it was staple food, for it was both plentiful and good. The grizzly bear, now thought to be extinct on the Coast, was not as good eating. One historian wrote, "Only the appetite of a famished hunter can relish the flesh of an old one." California was apparently once alive with grizzlies, or else early imaginations were very active. One lone hunter was said to have killed fifty-four of them near San Luis Obispo in 1837. And Colonel Frémont, on an expedition with less than fifty men, came upon a hundred of the beasts and killed thirty of them — or so the story goes. Although the grizzlies were unpopular as food, they provided much sport for early Californians, who, unarmed except for their *riatas*, loved to hunt

215

the ferocious beasts. This was excusable as the bears did tremendous damage to their cattle.

Mountain Sheep. Although the country was once so well populated with these animals that they greeted the Spaniards who first landed on the California coast, they have now almost disappeared. This is sad news for epicures, for everyone agrees that they are one of the best of all game meats. A small herd of thirty or so bighorns do occupy a game preserve in Oregon, but there's little hope that their number will ever greatly increase.

Mountain Goats. There are more of these animals in Washington than in any other part of the country, but that doesn't mean there are many. They abide in the rugged cliffs of the high Cascades, from just north of Mount Adams to the Canadian border. The meat of the very young animals is the best.

Wild Boar is, surprisingly enough, still found in parts of California, particularly on some of the Channel Islands and in the Imperial Valley. The islands are privately owned, a fact that sets hunters and cooks to drooling. But in the valley they may not only be hunted — there is no closed season on them! The meat of the wild pig is delicious, tasting very much like what it is — pork.

Wild Rabbits. These are the most plentiful, and therefore the least popular, of all our game. Perhaps fear of tularemia detracts from their desirability. However, if carefully handled, there is no danger of infection. Wild rabbit may be cooked in any of the ways suitable for the domestic rabbit. In this book the recipes are grouped together in the Game section. Anyone who wants a really delicious meat at low cost or easy hunting, should take this rabbit business more seriously.

Squirrel. One of the best of the small game animals from an eating point of view. It's mild in flavor and can be cooked in any of the ways in which rabbit is cooked. Broiled squirrel is an especial treat — simply brush it with butter, cook until crisp and brown, and serve with big juicy wedges of lemon.

Game

Sage Hens. This delectable wild bird, actually a sage grouse, is unfortunately not as plentiful as it used to be. It feeds on berries and seeds, including those of the sagebrush, which gives its flesh a delicate flavor of that herb. Delicate if it's cleaned the minute it's shot, that is, otherwise the flavor of sage becomes so unbearably strong that it tastes as if it has been cooked by an herbiculturist.

Wild Ducks. The most plentiful and most popular of all the game birds, ducks — several varieties of them — are found all over our West Coast. Perhaps because so many cooks have had their hands in the preparing of this water fowl, its cooking is a controversial subject wherever sportsmen meet. Although there are several recipes for it in this book, I think the best culinary advice that can be given is to cook it the way you like it best.

Wild Geese. There are still some of these birds around, but pathetically few when one realizes that not so long ago they were so thick that wheat growers had to hire men to drive them from the fields. Just as is the case with wild ducks, there is considerable variation of opinion as to how long they should be cooked. The answer is that if you like your duck rare, that is the way you'll like your goose.

Wild Turkey. If and when available, wild turkey is cooked in the same way as the domestic bird. It was much sought after for holiday dinners in the early days, and if it couldn't be found a wild goose was often substituted.

Pheasant. Now one of our favorite game birds, the Chinese pheasant is not a native. Introduced in Oregon in the '80s, it, like many of us, took to the new country at once. It now resides in all three Far Western states. Pheasant meat is gourmet's meat.

Partridge. The Hungarian partridge, another introduced bird, is now quite plentiful, for it has multiplied rapidly since coming to its new home.

217

Quail. We have several varieties of quail. The California or Valley quail is a native Californian, and was later introduced into Washington and Oregon. It is now quite numerous everywhere. The Mountain quail, native in Northern California and to the Columbia River in Oregon, was introduced in Washington at a very early date. By 1850 they were well established in the San Juan Islands. All the quails are wonderful eating.

Grouse. The blue grouse is native to Washington. Franklin's grouse, a smaller bird, is found high in the Cascades. They are called "fool hens" because they haven't sense enough to run when their enemy, man, approaches, and are often killed with a stick. The only reason that there are *any* left is because of the isolated areas they choose for their abode. The ruffed grouse is often called a native pheasant. They, like others of the grouse family, are as good eating as any game lover could hope to have.

Other Game. Prairie hens, sandhill crane, wild swans, snow geese, and other game birds were once plentiful on the Coast, but no more. Western terrapin was used, mostly for soups, in the San Francisco of the '60s. In the very early days when fur trapping was the industry of the Northwest, beaver was sometimes eaten. Even today those who have tried it say that the tail of that animal is a rare and wonderful treat. Actually, the truth seems to be that almost all game is good eating — the proof is in the cooking.

❲ *Barbecued Antelope Steaks*

Antelope steaks are cut thick and brushed with a mixture of 1 cup of olive oil, 2 tablespoons of red wine vinegar, a large clove of garlic, crushed, and salt and pepper. This is applied with a bunch of parsley or other herbs, both before and during the charcoal grilling.

BASTE

1 cup olive oil	1 clove garlic
2 tablespoons red wine vinegar	Salt and pepper

Game

⟨ Roast Saddle of Antelope

Oregon is the only one of our West Coast states that has an open season on antelope. Though herds have been started in both California and Washington, it will probably be a number of years before they will be sufficiently large to permit hunting. The meat is delicious, slightly stronger than venison.

Wipe a saddle of antelope and lard it liberally with salt pork. Sprinkle with salt and pepper, rub with flour, and start in a hot oven at 450° for 25 minutes. Reduce heat to 300° and cook for 1½ hours longer, or until the meat thermometer reaches 135° or 140° for rare meat. This same recipe may be used for a saddle of bear. SERVES 8 TO 12.

⟨ Bear Ragout with Red Wine

Cut 4 pounds of bear meat in sizable chunks. Roll in seasoned flour and brown in ½ cup of bacon fat or bear lard if you have it. Add 2 cups of red table wine, a cup of water, and an herb bouquet, and simmer in a Dutch oven or in a covered casserole for 2½ to 4 hours, or until tender. (A tough old b'ar will take longer than one just out of cubhood.) When the meat is beginning to get tender, add onions, turnips, and carrots, all of which have been peeled and browned in bacon grease. Add water if liquid has evaporated. When meat is tender, correct the seasoning and thicken the sauce with a little flour and butter rubbed together. SERVES 8 TO 12.

4 pounds bear meat	Onions
½ cup bacon fat or bear grease	Turnips
2 cups red table wine	Carrots
1 cup water (or more)	Flour
1 herb bouquet	Butter

⟨ Bear Notes

Bear Steak. Because of the danger of trichinosis, already mentioned, it is risky to cook bear steak rare, even though it tastes best that way. It can be done if the meat has been held

219

at 0° Fahrenheit for at least three weeks. Try instead treating it as if it were a Swiss steak, pounding seasoned flour into it, searing it in fat, and then adding stock or water and simmering slowly until done. A tart fruit jelly with this — perhaps of pomegranate, wild grape, or cranberry.

Bear Ham. This is a good way to cook a tough old bear ham. Put it in a kettle with a bottle of red wine, 1½ quarts of consommé, an herb bouquet, 2 tablespoons of juniper berries, an onion, sliced, and a large piece of fresh ginger, and salt and pepper to taste. Simmer for 4 or 5 hours, or until the meat is tender. Reduce stock to 3 cups, correct seasonings, and thicken with ¼ cup of butter cooked with ¼ cup of flour.

❨ *Ojai Dove Stew*

The mourning dove is found in every state in the Union. The band-tailed pigeon is found only in the Pacific States, Arizona, and New Mexico. This recipe may be used for either.

Dust 6 doves with seasoned flour and brown in ¼ cup of olive oil with 1 chopped onion. Add a cup of stock, a cup of wine — either red or white — and an herb bouquet with bay, parsley, and marjoram. Correct seasoning, cover, and stew gently until tender. Serve with brown rice and green olives that have been heated in their own juices. Braised leeks are a good accompanying vegetable. SERVES 6.

6 doves	*1 cup stock*
¼ cup olive oil	*1 cup wine*
1 onion	*1 herb bouquet*

❨ *Roast Doves*

Stuff doves with a dressing made by cooking ¼ cup each of chopped green pepper and onion in ¼ cup of butter until wilted, then adding ½ cup of chopped green olives and 2 cups of cooked wild rice. Season with salt and pepper and a little thyme, add enough butter to moisten slightly. (This is enough for 6 or 8 doves.) Roast uncovered at 450° for 10 minutes, brush with melted butter, reduce heat to 350° and cook for 25 minutes, or until tender, basting with butter several times. SERVES 6 OR 8.

6–8 *doves*
¼ *cup chopped green pepper*
¼ *cup chopped onion*
¼ *cup butter (and a little more)*

½ *cup chopped green olives*
2 *cups cooked wild rice*
Salt and pepper
Thyme

◖ Notes on Doves and Pigeons

Stewed Pigeons. This, from the first Los Angeles cook book, is worthy of note. Stuff a dozen pigeons with a "bottle" of green olives (1 cup), chopped fine with the livers, bread crumbs, ginger, and pepper and salt. Sew the birds up and wrap them in grape leaves. Brown flour in "a large lump of butter," add "some soup," stew the pigeons in this until done. "Take off the grape leaves and dish."

Broiled Pigeons. Split down the back, flatten the breast, and sprinkle with salt and pepper. Brush with melted butter and broil over hot charcoal or in the broiling oven. Serve on buttered toast with plenty of extra melted butter poured over, and wedges of lemon for squeezing over the birds.

Doves, Country Style. Clean doves, but leave them whole. Put a slice of onion in each cavity, truss the birds, dip them in milk and then in seasoned flour, and fry in bacon fat until well browned, turning a few times. (Or fry in deep fat at 350°, if it's easier.) Make a gravy by using 3 tablespoons of bacon fat for each 4 doves, adding 3 tablespoons of flour, blending and cooking a couple of minutes, then pouring in 1½ cups of rich milk. The chopped cooked livers, hearts, and gizzards are now stirred in and the sauce is seasoned to taste and cooked gently for 10 minutes. Serve these with tart jelly and hot biscuits.

❲ Ducks Pressed à la Paul

Paul's Duck Press, in Los Angeles, is a restaurant highly esteemed by Southern California gourmets. Paul della Maggiora named his place after the beautiful old duck press which occupies a niche of honor. The specialty of the house calls for wild ducks, and as game laws forbid its sale, the birds must be supplied by the sportsmen who have bagged them. At Paul's they are cooked to perfection this way:

"Stuff a wild duck with a bouquet of 1 rib of celery, ½ a carrot, 1 sprig of parsley, and 1 bay leaf. Truss legs together and roast in a hot oven (425°) for 15 minutes. Remove bouquet, cut off legs and set aside. Remove breast in one piece, slice thin, and arrange on a hot platter and cover. Now make the sauce by melting 3 tablespoons of sweet butter in a chafing dish, adding a jigger of brandy, a wine glass of dry red wine, salt, a dash of cayenne, and a touch of lemon juice. Heat sauce to the boiling point, now add the juice of the duck which has been obtained by putting the remaining duck (the carcass and legs) into the press and turning the pressure wheel until the carcass is dry. Stir until the sauce begins to thicken. Now add the breast slices, and return pan to flame until contents are heated through but not boiled."

❲ Wild Ducks with Olives

This recipe, popular in California before the turn of the century, has much to recommend it, though gastronomical purists insist that wild ducks should never be stuffed.

Rub inside and outside of ducks with a cut clove of garlic, and stuff with a dressing made by combining 2 cups of bread crumbs with ¼ cup of minced onions wilted in ¼ cup of butter, ½ cup of sliced ripe olives, 2 tablespoons of minced parsley, and a whole egg, with salt and pepper to taste. The ducks are roasted in a hot oven a bit longer than if they were not stuffed, and basted often with 1 part butter, 1 part olive oil, and 1 part "claret." (Use a California claret, or a Cabernet.) The sauce is made by utilizing the juices in the pan, and for each tablespoon adding 1 tablespoon of flour, ¾ of a cup of stock, ¼ cup of the same wine used in the basting, ¼ cup of sliced ripe olives, and a little marjoram. Salt and pepper to taste. SERVES 4.

STUFFING: *For each 4 ducks*

2 *cups bread crumbs*   ½ *cup sliced ripe olives*
¼ *cup minced onions*   2 *tablespoons minced parsley*
¼ *cup butter*   1 *egg*
Salt and pepper

BASTE

1 *part butter*   1 *part claret*
1 *part olive oil*

SAUCE: *For each 1 tablespoon of pan juice*

1 *tablespoon flour*   ¼ *cup sliced ripe olives*
¾ *cup stock*   *Marjoram*
¼ *cup claret*   *Salt and pepper*

❮ *Boca Chica Roast Wild Duck*

Clean and dress duck, wipe inside and out with a damp cloth, and in the cavity put a small piece of celery, leaves and all, ¼ of a small onion, ¼ of an apple, and a slice of orange. Rub breast with a mixture of soy sauce and olive oil, or Italian vermouth and olive oil, and roast at 450° for from 12 to 45 minutes, or as you like it. Remove stuffing before serving. Wine with wild duck is as essential as it is with all game. A California Burgundy, or a Pinot noir is a good choice — so is Zinfandel, Barbera, or Carignane, if a good one can be found. Wild rice is classic with wild duck, but not essential. Fried hominy squares, baked hominy grits, and brown rice are in hearty agreement with the gamy flavor, and barley browned in butter, and then cooked in stock is close to perfect, particularly if the chopped heart, liver, and gizzard are added. The vegetable may be braised celery, endive, or leeks, asparagus, green lima beans, or cabbage. Cress makes a salad that seems just right, particularly if combined with thinly sliced oranges.

NOTE: If you prefer to serve your ducks with a simple stuffing, chop onion, celery, and apple in equal parts, and add a little grated orange rind and minced parsley and marjoram.

◖ Notes on Wild Duck

How a duck should be roasted depends entirely upon *your* taste. However, I do hope that those who shudder at the sight of blood will some day close their eyes and taste wild duck rarer than they think they like it. If they don't find it juicier and tenderer and more flavorsome than that to which they are accustomed, they win the controversy. Actually, the consensus seems to be 17 to 18 minutes in a hot oven, though many very good cooks prefer 8 to 12, and some 45 or more.

Some excellent cooks marinate wild duck in California brandy before roasting, others in red wine, and some in a combination of the two. The best idea, when using brandy, is to burn a little over the ducks when they are halfway through their roasting period.

Broiled Wild Duck. Split wild ducks and brush with butter and/or olive oil. Broil over hot coals 7 to 10 minutes on a side, or to *your* taste. Serve with melted butter and halves of lemon.

◖ Roast Shoulder of Elk à la Don Becker

Elk, still plentiful in all three Far Western states, was a very important food in the early days. It had another use, too. Its hide, when tanned, was used extensively for clothing and moccasins. History also relates that Sacajawea, the young and attractive Shoshone squaw who was so helpful to Lewis and Clark, used a shank of elk as an effective weapon when a white man tried to get affectionate with her. One well-aimed swat with the ready-made billy, and his ardor cooled immediately.

Trim a shoulder of elk well and wipe it carefully with a cloth dipped in wine or lemon juice. Put it in an open roasting pan in a hot oven (450°) and cook for 15 or 20 minutes, then reduce heat to 350°. Baste several times with a mixture of ¼ cup each of olive oil and Italian vermouth. The herbs in the vermouth make any other seasoning unnecessary. If a meat thermometer is used, cook to 140° internal temperature — that's

224

rare. (130° is even rarer, but not too much so for lots of people, including me.) If you do *not* use a thermometer, cook to your taste by timing or by feeling or by poking with a fork, three usual but not always accurate methods. (Anywhere from 8 to 20 minutes to the pound has been recommended for rare shoulder of venison.)

ℂ *Grilled Elk Steaks*

Have elk steaks or chops cut ¾- to 1-inch thick, and brush them with olive oil a few hours before grilling. Cook over hot charcoal 3 or 4 minutes on each side. (Like deer meat they are far better rare, but if you can't abide color with your meat, go ahead and cook them longer.) Salt and pepper and a chunk of butter are all that are needed with these excellent steaks, but wedges of lemon, or a tart jelly may be served. Baked potato, dressed with sour cream and chives, and braised zucchini, would go well here.

ℂ *Roast Wild Goose*

Wild geese were so abundant in Monterey, around 1847, that the boys used to catch them by weighting both ends of a rope and throwing it into the air. It would twist around a goose (sometimes around two of them) and bring it to the ground. Much later, when there were many fancy restaurants in San Francisco, geese were still so plentiful that only the breasts were used.

Like wild ducks, wild geese are preferred cooked rare by those who know. A hot oven, and 35 minutes in it is recommended. A young goose is delightfully tender, an old one so tough that it should be relegated to the pressure cooker and made into soup. Prunes are good with wild goose, particularly if soaked overnight in red wine or brandy, and, if you want a rare delicacy, soak the breast of a wild goose in a light brine, herb flavored, then smoke it for three days.

225

(Clackamas Pheasant Casserole

Even an old toughie of a pheasant is good when prepared this way.

Truss the bird and brown it gently in butter, turning it so that it is colored on all sides. Sprinkle with salt. Peel and chop 6 tart apples and mix them with ¼ cup of melted butter. Put half the apples in a casserole, add the bird and the remaining apples, pour on ¼ cup of heavy cream, cover, and cook in a moderate oven (350°) for about half an hour, or until tender. SERVES 2 OR 3.

1 pheasant	6 tart apples
Butter	¼ cup melted butter
Salt	¼ cup heavy cream

(Pheasant with Cream Gravy

This is the way the pioneers of Oregon Territory served pheasant — and they served it as often as we serve chicken. In fact, it practically supplanted that bird on those early Western tables.

Disjoint a pheasant and dust with seasoned flour. Cook ¼ cup of diced salt pork until it is crisp, then remove from the pan and set aside. Sauté the floured pheasant in the remaining fat until brown and tender, turning several times. Cover towards the end to insure tenderness — the whole process shouldn't take more than 20 or 25 minutes. Remove bird to a hot platter, add 2 tablespoons of flour to the pan, cook a minute, add 1½ cups of thin cream, and salt and pepper. Cook until thickened. Add the cubes of crisp salt pork, and serve this gravy with the pheasant. SERVES 2 OR 3.

1 pheasant	2 tablespoons flour
Seasoned flour	1½ cups thin cream
¼ cup diced salt pork	Salt and pepper

(Pheasant Mateo

One of the best game cooks on the West Coast, at least for my money, is John Keller, of Larkspur, California. This is

226

his recipe for roast pheasant, and an intriguing one it is, too.

Make a dressing with 1 cup of chopped apple, 6 large green onions, chopped, 3 ribs of celery, diced, a clove of garlic mashed in a teaspoon of coarse salt, a little black pepper, and ½ pound of bean sprouts. (If fresh ones are not available, canned ones could be used, but they should be well drained.) This is sufficient for 6 pheasants. Stuff and truss and bake in a 375° oven for about an hour, basting with olive oil and adding ¾ of a cup of French vermouth towards the end. Mr. Keller says, "The bean sprouts are for eating purposes," and how right he is. He also suggests for the next day that the cold bird — if any — be reheated in a mixture of 6 teaspoons of tart jelly and ¼ teaspoon of hot mustard. Good, too. SERVES 6 OR 12, DEPENDING ON THE REST OF THE MENU.

6 pheasants

DRESSING

1 cup chopped apple	*1 clove garlic*
6 large green onions	*1 teaspoon salt*
3 ribs celery	*Pepper*

½ pound bean sprouts

BASTE

¾ cup French vermouth
Olive oil

❰ *Roast Pheasant*

Pheasant is a party bird, particularly when broiled, roasted, or sautéed, but only a young bird (with the tip feathers of the wing pointed, and with short rounded claws) should be prepared these ways. Pheasant is dry, so it is necessary to introduce fat during the cooking, either by larding or basting, or both.

Lard the breast of the pheasant with either salt pork or bacon, or cover with strips of salt pork and tie firmly in place.

Stuff or not, as desired. (If not stuffed, put a piece of butter inside the bird — this adds to its juiciness.) Truss and place the bird breast down in an open roasting pan. Roast at 350° to 375° for about 45 minutes, basting frequently with the pan drippings. Serve with hominy squares or with wild rice, or, if you must be traditional and can stand the stuff, with bread sauce. (The recipe can be found in any general cook book. It's a sort of extra soupy milk toast mush, and not very popular, praise be, on our Coast.) SERVES 2 OR MORE.

NOTE: Most wine connoisseurs choose Burgundy or claret with pheasant, but I find a full-bodied white wine, say a Sauvignon blanc or a Pinot Chardonnay, very agreeable with the delicate bird.

❲ Pheasant Notes

A *Young Pheasant,* split and broiled like chicken, is pleasant indeed. Baste frequently with butter, and cook 8 or 9 minutes on each side. Serve on well-buttered toast.

Smoked Pheasant is a new delicacy to hit the market. It will remain a delicacy only as long as it is carefully smoked over good wood, and tended by an expert. May they never come near liquid smoke!

Roast Pheasant with Bing Cherries is a spectacular dish. After roasting the bird, put it on a heatproof platter and bring to the table. Also have a chafing dish with a can or 2 cups of pitted Bing cherries heating. Pour ¼ cup of rum over the pheasant and set it alight. Add a jigger of rum to the cherries and pour them around the pheasant. Serve with crisp brown rice croquettes.

❲ Roast Quail Alameda

Allow 1 quail per person. Brush inside and out of dressed bird with olive oil or butter. Truss and bake in a hot oven for 25 to 30 minutes, basting with butter two or three times during the process. Season with salt, pepper, and, if you wish, a dusting of tarragon seasoning powder. Swirl the pan with white wine and pour over the quail, which has been put on buttered toast or a square of fried hominy. Serve with cream and wedges of oranges.

NOTE: Quail is the whitest of the game birds, and the one which calls for one of the heavier white wines — a Pinot blanc, perhaps, or a Pinot Chardonnay. A vin rosé suits it well, too.

(Quail Notes

Broiled Quail is spectacular. Split it and broil over glowing charcoal just as you would chicken or squab, but baste plentifully with butter. (Another method is to tie salt pork over the breast.)

Breakfast Quail. An old Los Angeles cook book suggests quail for breakfast, a thought that sets a gourmet drooling. "Split down the back," the directions say, "and bake till brown with lots of butter. Serve on toast."

Quail with Tarragon. Stew a cup of finely chopped onions in ¼ cup of butter and 2 tablespoons of minced tarragon. After 10 minutes, add 2 quails, cover, and simmer closely until tender. Put quails on a platter, pour the sauce around them, and sprinkle their tops with crumbs browned in butter.

Hunter's Stew. This recipe from Los Angeles (1881) begins, "Let those who would partake of a delightful repast prepare" 12 quail or doves, cooked in 3 quarts of water with 2 pods of red pepper, 2 slices of bacon, and salt and pepper. Boil an hour, then add "potatoes, tomatoes, onion, celery, and corn." It is assumed that the vegetables were cooked until done, and the juice thickened.

(Rabbit Paprika

Here in the Far West we not only eat a lot of rabbit, many of us prefer it to chicken. It is an inexpensive meat, and it may be used in as many ways as may poultry, and in the same ways. This recipe is good for chicken or turkey, or for veal, or elderly game birds.

Have a frying rabbit cut into serving pieces, dust it with seasoned flour, and brown it in 4 tablespoons of shortening. Remove to a casserole, and in the pan brown 2 large onions, chopped, the rabbit liver, and a crushed clove of garlic. (Remove garlic and discard.) Remove liver, chop, and return to pan. Add a teaspoon of salt, a tablespoon of paprika, a little fresh pepper, and 2 cups of stock. Cook a minute or so, then pour over the rabbit and bake at 350°, or simmer on top of the stove, until the meat is tender. How long depends upon how young your rabbit. When the meat is done, pour off the sauce, reduce it to 1 cup, add 1½ cups of sour cream, and correct the seasoning. Chances are that a little more paprika will be needed. Serve with noodles or rice and spinach timbales. SERVES 4.

1 *frying rabbit*	1 *tablespoon paprika* (*or*
4 *tablespoons shortening*	*more*)
2 *large onions*	*Pepper*
1 *clove garlic*	2 *cups stock*
1 *teaspoon salt*	1½ *cups sour cream*

NOTE: A Mexican touch is to substitute chili powder for the paprika — in smaller amounts, of course.

NOTE: Chicken or veal paprika. Use 2½ pounds of veal, cut in cubes, or a 4-pound chicken, disjointed. Otherwise, proceed as above.

(*San Francisco Rabbit Stew*

Cut a rabbit, tame or wild, in pieces for serving, and marinate in a pint of white wine, ½ cup of olive or table oil, an herb bouquet made with parsley, thyme, and bay, a small sliced onion, and a crushed clove of garlic, for 24 hours, turning once or twice during the process. Drain, dredge with flour, brown in 2 tablespoons olive oil with ½ pound of mushrooms, and add the marinade. Cook in a covered casserole until tender, then add a cup of heavy cream to the sauce. Serve with noodles and spinach.

1 rabbit	1 small onion
1 pint white wine	1 clove garlic
½ cup olive oil, or table oil,	Flour
and 2 tablespoons	½ pound mushrooms
1 herb bouquet	1 cup heavy cream

◖ Wild Rabbit with Wine

Have a rabbit disjointed, dust with seasoned flour, and sauté in 3 tablespoons of butter until a lovely topaz. Add a cup of red table wine, an herb bouquet made with parsley, celery tops, bay, and rosemary. Cover and simmer until tender, remove to a hot platter, add enough stock to the sauce to make a cupful, bind with a roux of 1½ tablespoons each of butter and flour, and pour over the rabbit. Sprinkle with minced parsley, and serve with wedges of lemon. SERVES 4.

1 rabbit	1 herb bouquet
Seasoned flour	Stock as needed
3 tablespoons butter	1½ tablespoons butter
1 cup red wine	1½ tablespoons flour
Minced parsley	

◖ Rabbit Notes

Rabbit Pie. In a hundred-year-old recipe for pie, the rabbit is stewed with sliced onions and green peppers, thickened with a bacon-fat roux, and seasoned with thyme. A thick crust of baking powder biscuit finishes this hearty and very tasty dish.

Fried Rabbit. This is done just like fried chicken, and served with lemon wedges.

Clark County Rabbit with Prunes. This recipe has a German air about it. Marinate disjointed rabbit in 1½ cups of red wine, ½ cup of red wine vinegar, with an herb bouquet. Dust in flour, brown in butter, and finish cooking in a covered casserole with the marinade and ½ cup of pitted prunes.

231

Conejo Casserole. Marinate in white wine with an herb bouquet. Flour and brown as above, and finish cooking with ½ pound of sliced mushrooms, 1 cup of pitted ripe olives, 10 small peeled onions, and 10 baby carrots.

Rabbit Rosemary. Do exactly as Chicken Tarragon (page 294), but substitute rosemary for that herb. Delicious.

Broiled Rabbit. Leave a young rabbit whole, but cut the back so that it can be opened flat. Baste with basil-flavored wine vinegar and oil, in equal parts. Sprinkle with salt halfway through the cooking, which may be done in the broiler or over charcoal.

⟨ *Braised Venison, Sour Cream*

Here's a good way with tougher cuts, or with any cut from an animal of advanced age.

Lard a 6-pound piece of venison with bacon or salt pork, then brown it very thoroughly in bacon fat. Put it in a casserole with 2 cups of peeled tiny onions, a bunch of baby carrots, scraped but left whole, 2 cups of red table wine, an herb bouquet of parsley, bay, and rosemary, 2 or 3 juniper berries, if available, and 2 cups of water. Cover and cook in a 350° oven for an hour, or until the meat is tender. Pour off the sauce, reduce to 2 cups by boiling rapidly, thicken with a roux of 2 tablespoons of butter and 2 of flour, cook smooth, and fold in 2 cups of sour cream. Correct seasoning, pour back on the meat, and serve in the casserole with wild grape jelly and corn bread as accompaniments. SERVES 8 TO 12.

6–pound piece of venison	*2–3 juniper berries (if available)*
2 cups peeled tiny onions	*2 cups water*
1 bunch baby carrots	*2 tablespoons butter*
2 cups red table wine	*2 tablespoons flour*
1 herb bouquet	*2 cups sour cream*

Salt and pepper

Game

NOTE: Dame Shirley spoke of "venison with a fragrant spicy gusto as if it had been fed on cedar buds." *Cooked* with juniper berries, more likely — that flavor has always been right with venison.

(Charcoal-broiled Venison Steaks

This is venison at its best.

Have steaks cut 1½ inches thick, rub with garlic if you wish, and brush with butter. Broil over hot coals for about 10 minutes, for a rare juicy steak that will rival any meat in the world.

NOTE: If you've dried grape shoots or trimmings at hand, try them for the fire. They actually impart a delicious flavor to the meat. Other fruit woods are good, too.

NOTE: Thinner steaks are better pan-broiled — if you like them rare, that is. Sear them quickly on each side.

NOTE: Venison steak is preferred marinated by many persons. An equal amount of red wine and olive or cooking oil is good. Too long a marinating period will allow the marinade to permeate the meat so that the flavor of the venison will be completely obscured. A happy thought for those who can live without game, but not for the rest of us.

(Napa Venison Hash

Cook ½ cup of minced onions in ¼ cup of butter. Add 2 cups of minced cooked venison, a tablespoon of flour, a cup of red wine, salt, pepper, and marjoram to taste. Heat gently and serve on fried corn meal mush, or on toast. SERVES 4.

½ cup minced onions	1 tablespoon flour
¼ cup butter	1 cup red wine
2 cups minced cooked venison	Salt and pepper
Marjoram	

❴ Roast Haunch of Venison with Chestnuts

This recipe is superlative.

Marinate a haunch of venison covered with a bottle of California claret or Burgundy, to which has been added a large onion, sliced, a crushed clove of garlic, a bay leaf, and three crushed juniper berries. (Remove the shank bone before marinating.) Allow the meat to stand overnight. Skewer meat into a compact form and lard with strips of fat bacon, using about 6 slices in all. Insert meat thermometer in the fleshiest part of the leg, making sure that it does not touch the bone. Put in a 450° oven for 20 minutes, then reduce heat to 325° and cook until the internal temperature reaches 140°. (This is rare, which is as it should be. If desired even rarer, cook only to 135°; if well done, to 150°.) During the roasting, baste occasionally with some of the marinade. The sauce, which is the important part of the recipe, is made by boiling 1 pound of chestnuts for 10 minutes, then removing shells and dark inner skins. (If this is done while they are still warm, the skins will come off easily.) Cover the chestnuts with 1½ cups of stock (canned consommé will do if no venison stock is at hand) and cook further until *just* underdone, not long enough for them to break into pieces. Drain, saving stock, and put aside. Clean a pound of mushrooms and remove stems if they are long, otherwise just cut a thin slice from the bottom so that there will be no danger of grit. If the mushrooms are large, cut them in quarters, otherwise leave them whole. Sauté gently in ¼ cup of butter for 5 minutes. Set mushrooms and their juices aside with the chestnuts, and to the pan in which they have cooked add ¼ cup of butter and 4 table-spoons of flour. Cook 2 minutes, stirring well, then add a cup of the stock in which the chestnuts cooked, and a cup of the marinade. As soon as this thickens, fold in 1½ cups of thick sour cream, correct the seasonings, then reheat chestnuts and mushrooms in this sauce, taking great care to keep the heat low so that the cream will not curdle. The sauce should be the consistency of heavy cream — if it is too thick, add a little more stock. Pour into a bowl with a large ladle, and serve with the venison. Red cabbage, broccoli, or asparagus would be good with this dish, as would be fried hominy squares, or mashed potatoes. A red wine is a *must* — either a California Burgundy or Pinot noir, or a California claret or Cabernet. Experts say don't serve currant jelly when you're serving wine, as it will ruin the latter — but be your own judge. SERVES ABOUT 12.

Haunch of venison   *6 slices bacon*

MARINADE

1 bottle red table wine   *1 clove garlic*
1 large onion   *1 bay leaf*
3 juniper berries

SAUCE

1 pound chestnuts   *4 tablespoons flour*
1½ cups stock   *1 cup marinade*
1 pound mushrooms   *1½ cups thick sour cream*
½ cup butter   *Salt and pepper*

❲ *H.D.'s Siskiyou Buck Stew*

An old-timer may be used for this, or the tougher parts of a young buck. Cut off all fat and cut the meat in big chunks. Dust 3 pounds of meat with seasoned flour and brown quickly in ½ cup of very hot fat, along with 3 cloves of garlic. Put in a Dutch oven, add a can of tomato sauce, 3 large green peppers, sliced, and 3 large white onions, chopped. Season with sweet basil and add mushrooms if available, and enough water to bring the liquid halfway up the meat. Cover and simmer for 1½ to 2½ hours, or until tender, stirring a few times during the cooking. SERVES 6.

3 pounds venison   *3 large white onions*
½ cup shortening   *Salt and pepper*
3 cloves garlic   *Sweet basil*
1 can tomato sauce   *Mushrooms (optional)*
3 large green peppers   *Water*

❲ Venison Hamburgers

Grind small pieces of lean venison which are unsuitable for broiling or roasting. For each pound mix in 1 tablespoon of chopped onion, a tablespoon of olive oil or other shortening, a tablespoon of red wine, and ¾ of a teaspoon of salt. Form loosely into cakes, and grill quickly, either indoors or out. SERVES 3.

For each 1 pound ground venison

1 tablespoon chopped onion   1 tablespoon red wine
1 tablespoon olive oil   ¾ teaspoon salt

❲ Venison Liver

The liver is one of the choicest parts of the venison, but, unlike the muscle meat, it must be eaten fresh. For this reason it is often enjoyed at camp, and few stay-at-home gourmets get a chance at it. It's so really wonderful that it's worth a tedious trip into the woods for just one little bite. Slice it ½-inch thick and pan-fry it *very* quickly in bacon fat. Serve with or without bacon or fried onions.

❲ Venison Notes

Elk Meat is considered venison, so the recipes for one or the other are interchangeable.

Soup. Use parts of venison too tough for stew, and any and all bones and scraps for soup. The stock may be made all at once and kept frozen until ready to use. It makes a very fine soup, right with any meal.

Jerky. Cut the flank in strips, with the grain of the meat, 1 inch by ½ inch by any length possible, and rub well with salt, or dip into boiling hot brine. The meat is then hung over wire and allowed to smoke for a day or so. (Don't let it cook!) A further drying in the sun is advisable. Another method is to soak the meat in brine for 2 days. The brine should be strong enough to float an egg. Jerky may be made without smoking

— the meat is dried in a hot sun. The jerky, eaten as is, is delicious as an outdoor appetizer to serve with beer. Its thirst-raising properties are tremendous, and so is its flavor.

Broiled Jerky. Jerky is wonderful when broiled over a camp-fire. Novices at jerky feasts should remember to take it easy. Like dried apples, jerky will swell in your insides and give you an awful stomach-ache.

Dried Venison in Cream. *The Webfoot Cook Book* of Port-land says that dried venison in cream is "a good breakfast dish." Well, rather!

Venison Chili with Beans. This is an interesting idea — it shows how native foods acquire the foreign touch. Made as for chili and beans, it is exceedingly good, a fine way to utilize the tougher parts of the animal.

Venison Loaf. Here's another old pioneer favorite. As venison was the beef of many of the early families, it was obviously used in exactly the same ways. Make this like a meat loaf then, using marjoram, thyme, or basil as the season-ing, and adding more than the usual amount of fat.

Saddle of Venison. Perhaps the choicest of all the cuts. Lard it well and bake it in a hot oven for 20 minutes. Reduce heat and finish cooking to 140° for rare, higher for better done.

Venison with Cherries. In the early days of the Northwest, cherries were often dried and used in the gravy served with roast venison. Also, in Gold Rush days, there is mention of using crushed cherries in the sauce for venison. Today's ver-sion is to use canned pitted Bing cherries.

Hunter's Pot Roast. Poke holes in the meat and stuff in slivers of garlic and salt pork. Brown in fat, put in a Dutch oven and add any desired vegetable, and either red wine, stock, or tomato juice, with an herb bouquet. Cover and cook until tender. Rectify seasonings, bind sauce slightly, and serve with potato pancakes. Turnips are usually one of the "desired vegetables," as are onions.

Oregon Meat Pancakes. Here again the pioneers showed the way. It's a sort of mincemeat pancake, actually for breakfast or for lunch, rather than for dessert. Mix together 1 cup of minced cooked venison, an apple, chopped, a green pepper, chopped, 2 tablespoons of raisins, chopped, 2 tablespoons of lemon juice, 2 tablespoons of butter, and a little salt and sugar. Make thin pancakes, put a spoonful of this mixture on each cake, fold, and when ready to serve warm gently in butter. Serve with wedges of lemon and powdered sugar for anyone who wants it. This tastes better than it reads.

⟨ Salmis of Game

A salmis was originally a dish of previously roasted feathered game. In less elegant terms, a way of reheating leftover game birds. Now it has come to mean a sauce for reheating any game, or any meat, for that matter. This recipe, a very simple one, is as good for lamb, beef, or mutton as it is for game.

Chop a bunch of green onions, including some of the green part. Cook them in ⅓ cup of butter until wilted. Stir in 3 tablespoons of flour, cook 3 minutes, then add ¾ of a cup of California claret, a tablespoon of lemon juice, 2 tablespoons of orange juice, a long sliver of orange rind, a cup of stock made from the trimmings of whatever meat is used, salt to taste, and a dash of cayenne. Cook a moment, then add slices of cold game or meat, leaving them in the sauce just long enough to heat. Do not boil. Put on a hot serving dish and sprinkle with minced parsley.

1 bunch green onions	*2 tablespoons orange juice*
⅓ cup butter	*Long sliver of orange rind*
3 tablespoons flour	*1 cup stock*
¾ cup claret	*Salt*
1 tablespoon lemon juice	*Dash of cayenne*
Slices of cooked meat	

NOTE: Another salmis, particularly good for duck, uses shallots instead of green onions, and includes a touch of rosemary and some sliced ripe olives.

Herbs and Spices

FROM THE TIME *the first white settlers in California found anise, yerba buena, and other herbs growing wild and used them in their cookery, our foods have been well flavored. The pioneer women of the Northwest brought sage cuttings with them on their journey over the Oregon Trail, and later, in their new homes, learned from the Indians which herbs were valuable for cooking, which for medicine. Gradually more and more herb roots, seeds, and cuttings arrived in the new world, were planted, and thrived. And the spices that we couldn't grow were brought by trading ships from across the Pacific or around the Horn. Today many of us have herb gardens, and those of us who have not know that we can often buy fresh herbs, and always good dried herbs and spices at the grocer's. The Spice Island Company, growers and packers of spices now world known, have proved in a few short years how superior are herbs that are grown in California. These herbs, raised mostly on the warm hillsides around San Jose and Los Gatos, or, as with the tarragon, near the fog-cooled coast, are packed in leaf form, not ground or crushed. The advantage is obvious — as with peppercorns or coffee beans, the essential oils are not released until the time has come for them to give their flavor to some dish.*

The recipes in this book call sometimes for fresh herbs, sometimes for dried — one may be substituted for the other. If the fresh herbs are called for, use from ⅓ to ½ that amount when switching to the dried, and soak the latter in a little of the recipe's liquid before adding. And, conversely, the amount of fresh herbs is doubled or tripled when used instead of the dried.

Herbs in cooking, indispensable as they are, can be overdone, so take it easy. And for goodness' sake, don't have every dish at a meal an herbed one. Although exact measurements have usually been given in these recipes, you can't beat the old culinary cliché, "season to taste" — like spices, herbs that have been around too long lose strength.

❬ Herb Notes

Herb Bouquet. Unless otherwise noted in the recipe, by an herb bouquet I mean a piece of bay, 2 or 3 sprigs of parsley, and one of the mints, usually thyme or marjoram. Sometimes more herbs are included — it's all a matter of taste.

Fines Herbes. In West Coast parlance this means a mixture of herbs — usually parsley and chives in addition to one or more of the following: tarragon, basil, marjoram, rosemary or any other pungent herb.

❬ Chili Powder

Chili powder, which is sometimes the pure dried chili pepper, ground, and sometimes has other spices blended with it, is a must in West Coast cooking. Although first-generation Mexican Americans still start from scratch with the chili peppers, most of the rest of us use the powder. Besides using chili in most Mexican dishes, try these ways:

Mix butter with salt, pepper, and chili powder (1 teaspoon to each ¼ pound), roll in balls, and serve with corn on the cob. Add chili powder to mashed avocado along with onion salt and garlic vinegar for a wonderful cocktail spread (use 1 teaspoon of each per avocado). And put chili powder on the breakfast table when you serve boiled eggs — you'll know why once you've used it.

Herbs and Spices

❨ Coriander

The seed of coriander, either whole or ground, is the best known part of the plant, but on the West Coast both the Chinese and the Mexicans make enchanting use of the leaves. Known to the Chinese as Yinsöi, Ts'oi, or Chinese Parsley, it is the very soul of some Chinese dishes — chicken wrapped in paper (page 288), for instance — and though it may be an acquired taste, once acquired it can come close to being an addiction. And it's not just the Chinese who know and love it. The early Californians and the Mexicans called the herb cilantro, and used it frequently. In fact, the Californians of Mexican and Spanish heritage still do.

❨ Curry Powder

Curry powder is a mixture of various spices, blended according to the packer's, or the cook's, own formula. Besides using it for curries, try a dash in French dressing, in scrambled eggs, in deviled eggs, in cream soups. Curried carrots are good, and a teaspoon of curry powder in ½ pound of butter for boiled potatoes, for broiled fish, or for lima beans, is spectacular.

❨ Garlic

Few West Coast cooks can get along without garlic. Sometimes we use it subtly, so that its presence is not even suspected, and at other times we use it with abandon, allowing its fragrance to dominate the dish, as in our favorite garlic bread, or garlic spareribs. Few green salads are without it, and it perfumes our basting sauces and our "dunking" mixtures. This love of garlic comes to us naturally, for we inherit it from the Mexican in us, and from our Italian and Chinese ancestors as well. Blessed, we think, is garlic. We use a trick taught us by our Spanish-Mexican ancestors. We grind it with some salt to get all its wonderful flavor without danger of biting into a burning piece of it. We don't use a *metate* now, rather a mortar and pestle, but the trick is the same.

241

(*Ginger*

Because green (fresh) ginger is available here wherever there is a Chinese population, we use it often, particularly when preparing Oriental dishes. Its brownish skin is scraped off and the ginger is grated or cut into minute slivers. It's hot, so watch it. For those living where green ginger is unheard of, I suggest using preserved or crystallized ginger. It won't be the same, but it's better than soaked ginger root. The ground ginger won't do at all, as it's largely the crispness of the root that lends the character. When using the preserved or candied ginger, wash as much syrup or sugar from it as possible; it will be sweet, but as sweetness is often a characteristic of Oriental meat and fish cookery, it won't matter too much.

Meat

To THE EARLY SETTLERS *in the Northwest, meat meant game. To those in California, the Spanish and Mexicans, it meant beef. There were cattle in the Northwest, at Fort Vancouver, but that didn't mean anyone could enjoy a steak. Dr. McLoughlin wanted to build up a large herd, and he wasn't going to have any butchering — though just what he did with the surplus bulls, history doesn't say. He himself served venison and wild duck at his sumptuous dinners, and the guests found them delicious. . . . The pioneers who made the tough trek across the prairie ate buffalo meat on the way. In California, particularly in the southern part, there was plenty of beef for the Mexicans. In fact, more than plenty, because the animals were raised for their hides and their tallow, and what meat wasn't eaten was left for the pleasure of the vultures. This plethora of beef lasted until the great drought of the '60s, when thousands of head of cattle perished, and cattle king Abel Stearns, as well as others, was ruined.*

During the Gold Rush meat, like everything else that was edible, was scarce. Some preserved meats and hams were shipped around the Horn. They apparently weren't always appreciated. Dame Shirley wrote, "We have had no fresh meat for nearly a month . . . there is no danger of famine, for have we not got wagon loads of hard dark hams whose indurate hearts nothing but the sharpest knife and the stoutest arm can penetrate?" In those first days of the Gold Rush meat was the foundation of more than one

243

fortune. Philip Armour — and you know that name — started a butcher shop in Placerville, then Hangtown, selling venison and what beef and mutton he could get. And he wasn't the only one who tossed aside the pick and picked up the cleaver. The Bixby cousins started a meat shop at Volcano, and later two of them returned to the East and drove a flock of 1800 sheep across the country. They well knew the value of the animals, and wouldn't kill a single one for their own sustenance on the journey, instead buying venison from the Indians. They themselves saw no deer, so they couldn't help but admire the hunting skill of the Indians. That was before they woke up to the fact that the number of venison they purchased from the scamps always corresponded with the number of ponies that had been lost the day before.

(Beef Stew with Olives

Of course our beef stews are as varied as everyone else's, but we do have an occasional touch that is different. This one combines green olives and vermouth, a flavor combination that is as good with beef as it is with gin.

Cut 3 pounds of lean stewing beef into cubes, roll them in seasoned flour, and brown in ¼ cup of olive oil with a crushed clove of garlic. Remove garlic, add a cup of dry vermouth and enough water to barely cover the meat. Cover and cook until tender. Just before the beef is done, add a dozen and a half large green olives, the meat having been cut from the stones in a spiral. Add salt to taste (remember olives are salty) and cook long enough for the olives to heat thoroughly. Serve with crusty Italian bread, heated. SERVES 6 OR 8.

3 pounds lean stewing beef	1 cup dry vermouth
¼ cup olive oil	Water as needed
1 clove garlic	18 large green olives

Salt

244

NOTE: Topping a stew with pastry has always been a popular way of dressing up this lowly dish. The early cooks in Oregon often used "risen paste," which was bread or roll dough, rolled thin and allowed to rise on the stew before it was baked. This is a trick worth reviving — the flavor of fresh-baked yeast bread is so right with rich savory gravy.

❨ *Beef with Oyster Sauce*

This is a Chinese recipe, at least it's cooked in the Chinese manner. It's a fine way to use the last bits of that roast of beef, and the oyster sauce is a wonderful companion to the beef.

Cut cooked beef in long strips, across the grain. Assuming you have 2 cups of strips, split 8 green onions in quarters, lengthwise, and then in 2-inch pieces, and cut a cup of water chestnuts (or less) in slices. Soak 4 dried mushrooms (the large Chinese black mushrooms, preferably) in water to cover, then cook until tender and cut in strips. Save the liquid. Now heat 2 tablespoons of cooking oil (not olive — preferably peanut or sesame oil), add the onions, mushrooms, and water chestnuts, stir-fry for 2 minutes, add the meat and a cup of mushroom stock, ½ of teaspoon of M.S.G., and 4 teaspoons of cornstarch moistened in a tablespoon of water. As soon as the sauce is clear, turn out on a dish which has been lined with broccoli or spinach leaves, and pour over about ⅓ cup of warmed oyster sauce (available in Chinese markets, or at fancy grocery stores). The oyster sauce may be served separately, if desired. Rice with this, and whatever other Chinese dishes suit your fancy. (See Chinese Dishes, index.) SERVES 6.

2 cups cooked beef, cut in strips	2 tablespoons cooking oil
8 green onions	1 cup mushroom stock
1 cup water chestnuts (or less)	½ teaspoon M.S.G.
4 dried mushrooms	4 teaspoons cornstarch, in 1 tablespoon water
	⅓ cup oyster sauce

❨ Braised Beef with Red Wine

Wine plays a double role in this recipe. It makes the tough cuts deliciously tender, and makes an everyday dish party fare.

Have a 6-pound piece of beef from the round or chuck or rump larded with ½ pound of salt pork. Brown it in ¼ cup of beef dripping or olive oil, put it in a casserole, add 2 cups of red wine, 4 chopped shallots, 2 cloves of garlic, 2 whole cloves, an herb bouquet, and salt and pepper. Cover and cook in a slow oven (325°) for 2 hours. Now pour on ¼ cup of brandy, and add a pound of baby onions, peeled, 2 bunches of baby carrots, left whole but scraped and trimmed, and a pound of mushrooms, left whole, but the stems trimmed off if very long. Add a cup of stock and continue to cook uncovered until the vegetables and meat are done, basting them so that they will glaze and color, and adding more liquid if necessary. This should take at least another hour. Serve with a good red wine. SERVES 8 TO 10.

6 pounds beef (in one piece)
½ pound salt pork
¼ cup beef drippings or olive oil
2 cups red wine
4 shallots
2 cloves garlic

2 cloves
1 herb bouquet
Salt and pepper
¼ cup brandy
1 pound baby onions
2 bunches baby carrots
1 pound mushrooms

1 cup stock

❨ Braised Short Ribs Zinfandel

It's a pity that this dish isn't served oftener — its richness and flavor are worthy of more attention.

Have 4 pounds of beef short ribs cut in serving pieces, dust them with seasoned flour, and brown on all sides in shortening. Put in a casserole, add a dozen small peeled onions, 8 small scraped carrots, and a cup of sliced celery. Pour in 2 cups of Zinfandel or other robust red table wine, add an herb bouquet of parsley, bay, and marjoram, and salt and pepper.

246

Cover and cook in a moderate oven (350°) for 1½ to 2½ hours, or until tender. Serve with mashed potatoes or noodles. SERVES 4.

4 pounds beef short ribs	1 cup sliced celery
12 small onions	2 cups Zinfandel
8 small carrots	1 herb bouquet

Salt and pepper

(Braised Oxtails

There's nothing humble about this dish. Its rich sauce, spiced with herbs and perfumed with wine, is so good that you'll want lots of fresh crusty bread so that not a precious drop will be wasted.

Have an oxtail disjointed and roll the pieces in seasoned flour. Brown the meat in 3 tablespoons of shortening or drippings, then remove to a casserole. In the same pan brown a cup of sliced carrots, a crushed clove of garlic, and a dozen small peeled onions. Remove garlic, add vegetables to the casserole, along with 2 cups of red table wine (Cabernet, Gamay, or Zinfandel would all do nicely), and an herb bouquet (parsley, savory, marjoram, and bay). Add stock or tomato juice to come to the top of the meat, and salt and pepper. Cover and cook at 350° for 2 to 3 hours, or until the meat is tender. Mushrooms may be added during the last half hour of cooking. SERVES 4 TO 6.

1 oxtail	2 cups red table wine
3 tablespoons shortening	1 herb bouquet
1 cup sliced carrots	Stock to cover
1 clove garlic	Salt and pepper
12 small onions	Mushrooms (optional)

(Carne a la Vinagreta

This is, of course, meat vinaigrette, with a Spanish accent, and close to perfect for a hot summer day. The old, and the foreign recipes for cold meats put most of our "cold cuts" to shame.

247

Simmer a 3-pound piece of boneless beef or veal with salt and a clove of garlic until the meat is tender. Cool and slice and arrange symmetrically on a fairly deep dish. Chop a bunch of green onions and a green pepper, and mix with ¼ cup of minced parsley, a cup of olive oil, ⅓ cup of wine vinegar, and salt and pepper and cumin to taste. Pour over meat and let stand 24 hours before serving, cold. SERVES 6 TO 8.

3 *pounds beef* (*in one piece*)	¼ *cup minced parsley*
Salt	1 *cup olive oil*
1 *clove garlic*	⅓ *cup wine vinegar*
1 *bunch green onions*	*Salt and pepper*
1 *green pepper*	*Cumin*

([Carpetbag Steak

You can guess the vintage of this recipe because of its name. It's quite a dish — guaranteed to please the men.

Have tenderloin steaks cut 2½ inches thick. With a sharp knife split the steaks through their middles, but not all the way, making a sizable pocket with as small an opening as possible. For each steak cook four medium-sized oysters in a teaspoon of melted butter until they are just warmed through, then insert them (drained) into the pocket, and sew up the opening. Brush on both sides with melted butter, then broil to the degree of rareness that is your choice. This is a filling dish, so unless your guests have gargantuan appetites, keep the rest of the meal light. A salad, perhaps, with fruit and cheese for dessert, and soup, if there is to be any, clear. Here's one time when a red wine tastes right with oysters!

([Grenadin de Boeuf, Grand Veneur

This is another recipe from the Palace Hotel, in San Francisco, so of course it's superb.

"Marinate tenderloin steaks for 2 days in red wine with spices, carrots, celery, and onions. (One bottle California red table wine, a bay leaf, 2 sprigs of thyme, a few sprigs of parsley, and 2 each chopped carrots, onions, and celery ribs.)

Drain, sauté in olive oil for about 8 minutes, salt and pepper, and serve with gnocchi instead of potatoes."

Tenderloin steaks	*Parsley*
1 bottle red wine	*2 carrots*
1 bay leaf	*2 onions*
2 sprigs thyme	*2 celery ribs*
Salt and pepper	

(*Grenadine of Beef Flintridge*

Grenadine of beef is now very much the vogue in the best West Coast restaurants, and cooks, formerly awed by it, have found that preparing it at home is nothing of a trick.

Brush thick tenderloin steaks with olive oil and broil them to your taste. Serve with a sauce made by adding ¼ cup of Madeira (or sherry) and ¼ cup of tomato purée (not paste) to a cup of sauce Espagnole or brown gravy. To this add ½ cup each of sliced sautéed chicken livers and sliced sautéed mushrooms. Season to taste. For sauce Espagnole see any classic cook book. My personal bible of sauces, any and all, is *The Wine Cook Book* by the Browns. (I am sad to say that they are no relation.)

Thick tenderloin steaks	*½ cup sliced sautéed chicken*
Olive oil	*livers*
¼ cup Madeira	*½ cup sliced sautéed mush-*
¼ cup tomato purée	*rooms*
1 cup sauce Espagnole	*Salt and pepper*

NOTE: Broil meat as above, and serve with béarnaise sauce. Garnish with asparagus tips and ripe olives that have been heated in their own liquor.

(*"Lawry's" Roast Beef*

The Prime Rib in Beverly Hills is famous because of its roast beef, which is served on a cart in the manner made famous by Simpson's-in-the-Strand, London. They serve this beef with a marvelous spinach (page 396), and with Yorkshire pudding, baked Idaho potatoes, and horseradish sauce.

"The secret of the superb beef is a double one. First, buy only the very best and properly aged beef. Second, cover the entire roast (of many ribs, you may be sure) with a thick coating of moist rock salt, and start in a 475° oven immediately after salting. This fuses the salt and keeps the juices in. Keep the oven fairly hot for rare or medium-rare beef; for well done, reduce heat and cook longer. The salt will come off in huge sheets, and will not impart saltiness to the roast."

◖ Portland Popover Pudding

These are really individual Yorkshire puddings, which is why they appear in the meat section. Yorkshire pudding with a difference!

Mash a large clove of garlic very thoroughly with a teaspoon of salt. Beat 2 eggs well, add the garlic, a cup of milk, and a cup of flour, and beat some more. Heat large custard cups (the ovenproof kind that are bowl-shaped), pour enough hot beef or pork drippings into each cup to cover the bottom, fill ⅔ full with batter, and bake at 450° for 15 minutes, then reduce oven to 350° and finish cooking — about 20 minutes longer. Pierce with a knife to allow steam to escape the minute they are taken from the oven. This makes four huge popovers, and are they ever good! They are just as wonderful with roast pork as with roast beef.

1 large clove garlic	1 cup milk
1 teaspoon salt	1 cup flour
2 eggs	Beef or pork drippings

NOTE: Another version of these fabulous creatures is to use herbs instead of, or along with, the garlic. A tablespoon of minced parsley, or a teaspoon of mixed dried herbs is about right.

⟪ *Mexican Beef with Oranges*

Here again the Mexicans show us a thing or two about really fine cooking. Don't forget this one next time you plan a summer party. Round out the meal with Shrimps Nob Hill (page 167), molded guacamole (page 43), tortillas or corn bread sticks, fried beans (page 366), and, for dessert, Jack cheese, guava jelly, and fruit. The appetizers, to keep the Mexican theme intact, empanaditas. (The shrimps, though not from south of the border, have a Spanish air about them.)

Simmer a 4-pound piece of boneless beef with 2 cloves of garlic, a bay leaf, an onion, and a teaspoon of coriander and salt. When tender, cool, slice, arrange on a platter, and cover with thin slices of orange, skin and all. Pour on enough orange juice and olive oil, in equal parts, to cover and marinate for 24 hours before serving. SERVE COLD TO 10 OR MORE PERSONS.

4 pounds boneless beef (in one piece)	*1 teaspoon coriander*
	Salt
2 cloves garlic	*Orange slices*
1 bay leaf	*Orange juice and olive*
1 onion	*oil to cover*

⟪ *Olive Pot Roast*

Olives have attained a place of honor on the shelves of West Coast cooks. Ripe or green, we find they add charm to almost every course.

Make about 12 holes in a 4-pound rump roast with an ice pick, working it so that the holes are large enough to take stuffed olives. Insert the olives, then plug the holes with pieces of bacon or salt pork. Proceed as usual for a pot roast, flouring, searing in fat, then cooking covered. For the liquid use tomato juice, seasoned with salt and pepper, thyme or dill. When the meat is done, correct seasoning and thicken gravy slightly, if necessary. Serve with potato pancakes. SERVES 6 TO 8.

4-pound rump roast	*Tomato juice*
12 stuffed olives	*Salt and pepper*
12 pieces bacon or salt pork	*Thyme or dill*

(Pot Roast Californian

This is a recipe from the California Food Research Institute, an organization that has done much to better our Western cuisine. It is concerned with the promotion of typical Western foods — dried fruits and ripe olives being a couple of their babies. Here prunes and olives are combined with most gratifying results.

Rub a 4-pound pot roast with salt, pepper, and ⅛ teaspoon of ground ginger. Chop 2 cloves of garlic fine, slice 3 onions, and cook in ½ cup of oil. Add meat and brown on all sides, then add ½ cup of water. Cover tightly and simmer for 1½ hours. Turn frequently. While the meat is cooking, soak ½ cup of dried mushrooms and 1½ cups of prunes in 1½ cups of water. Add prunes, mushrooms, soaking water, and a cup of pitted ripe olives to the meat, and continue cooking another hour, or until tender. Remove meat to a platter and surround with olives and prunes. The sauce may be thickened if desired. SERVES 6 TO 8.

4–pound pot roast	½ cup oil
Salt and pepper	2 cups water
⅛ teaspoon ground ginger	½ cup dried mushrooms
2 cloves garlic	1½ cups prunes
3 onions	1 cup ripe olives

(Steak Solera

This is dreamily good.

Have tenderloin steaks cut about 1½ inches thick and pan fry them quickly in butter. Put each steak on a piece of hot buttered toast that has been topped with a thin slice of ham (preferably a Virginian ham, or at least one that is not "tenderized"). Put on a hot platter and in the oven. For each steak add 1 tablespoon of butter and 1 of Madeira or sherry to the sauté pan. Heat and pour over the steaks before serving.

For each tenderloin steak

1 piece buttered toast	1 tablespoon butter
1 thin slice ham	1 tablespoon Madeira or sherry

Meat

Spanish Steak

This is the way the Spanish and Mexican Californians really did it.

Remove the veins and seeds from 6 dried chili peppers, and cover them with 2 cups of boiling water. Soak until tender, then scrape the pulp with the water, discarding the skins. Rub 3 pounds of round steak with seasoned flour and brown it in ¼ cup of lard or beef drippings. Add the chili water, 2 whole cloves, a clove of garlic, and a sprig of thyme. (These may be tied in cheesecloth, if you wish.) Cover and simmer until the steak is tender. Correct seasoning and serve with re-fried beans or rice. SERVES 4 TO 6.

6 *dried chili peppers*	¼ *cup lard or beef drippings*
2 *cups water*	2 *cloves*
3 *pounds round steak*	1 *clove garlic*
Seasoned flour	1 *sprig thyme*
Salt	

NOTE: *Smothered Venus* — that was the name given a steak smothered in onions, in an old Los Angeles cook book. But the steak was *boiled,* so we can only hope it was a toughie to begin with.

Japanese Broiled Meat

Pound round steak and score it, then cut in serving pieces. Marinate for 5 hours in ½ cup of sherry or sake, ½ cup of soy sauce, and a tablespoon of shredded green ginger. Drain and broil over charcoal. This is also a good marinade for thicker American steaks.

MARINADE

½ *cup sherry or sake*	1 *tablespoon shredded green*
½ *cup soy sauce*	*ginger*

Steak with Oyster Blanket

This combination of steak and oysters shows up in most of the old recipe books from all three states. The rich robust

253

flavor of the steak, and the incomparable delicacy of the oysters, make a happy pair — a dish that should definitely be snatched from the past.

Broil steaks in your usual manner. While they are cooking melt a tablespoon of butter (for each serving) with a whisper of garlic, and add ½ cup of oysters. Cook until the oysters plump, remove garlic, and ladle the oysters over the broiled steak, sprinkling with parsley. Serve a wedge of lemon as a garnish.

NOTE: Another way: broil steak rarer than wanted, spread raw oysters on top, sprinkle with salt and pepper, douse with melted butter, and put under the broiler until the edges of the oysters begin to curl.

❲ Brains Benicia (Stuffed Peppers)

You've never tasted really *good* stuffed peppers until you've tasted these.

Soak a set of calf's brains in cold water for an hour, rinse, remove membrane, and cook in acidulated water for 20 minutes. Plunge into cold water to chill, then chop coarsely. Add a cup of ground cooked veal, ½ cup of grated cheese, 3 eggs, 3 tablespoons of melted butter, salt and pepper, and marjoram to taste. Stuff 6 green peppers with this mixture, sprinkle the top with more grated cheese or buttered crumbs, put in a baking dish, pour a cup of seasoned tomato juice in the dish, and bake at 350° until the peppers are just tender and the tops brown. SERVES 6.

1 set calf's brains	Salt and pepper
1 cup ground cooked veal	Marjoram
½ cup grated cheese	6 green peppers
3 eggs	Grated cheese or crumbs
3 tablespoons butter	1 cup seasoned tomato juice

❲ Ham and Ham Notes

All the early settlers on the West Coast who could kept a few pigs. They needed the fat for candles and soap, as well

254

as for lard, and of course they used the meat for bacon and ham. (That some kept more than a few swine is evident in a recipe in the first Los Angeles cook book, giving directions "To Cure 1000 Hams!") One pioneer woman saved a precious ham from a thieving Indian because she happened to be stirring a pot of corn meal mush when she discovered the rascal cutting the ham from the rafter where it hung. One large spoonful of very hot mush on a very bare bottom did the trick.

Ham with Brindle Gravy is a sheepherder's dish. Water is added to the pan in which ham has been fried. This makes a strange "brindle" colored gravy which is poured, unthickened, over sourdough biscuits and served with the fried ham. Good, too, the kind of simple dish that will be long remembered.

Braised Ham Chinese. Marinate a thick slice of ham with soy sauce and sherry wine in equal parts. Brown in oil, add ½ cup of sliced green onions, 1 teaspoon of grated ginger, and ½ cup of water. Cover with marinade and cook until ham is tender, adding more water if necessary. An unbelievably wonderful combination of flavors, this.

⟨ *Ham Inglenook*

Skin a partially cooked ham, and return it to a 350° oven, basting it more or less constantly with 2 cups of red table wine, 1 cup of consommé, and ¼ cup of sugar. In the pan have a cheesecloth bag containing 3 whole cloves, a large clove of garlic, crushed, and a bay leaf. See that this is wetted down with the basting sauce. When the ham is glazed, skim every vestige of fat from the basting sauce, add 2 tablespoons of lemon juice and ¼ cup of sherry, and serve as a sauce with the ham. And serve plenty of the same red wine — say a Napa Gamay — with the meal.

1 ham	3 cloves
2 cups red wine	1 clove garlic
1 cup consommé	1 bay leaf
¼ cup sugar	2 tablespoons lemon juice
	¼ cup sherry

❨ Ham Steak with Cherries

While Californians use wine or raisins for saucing their ham, some of their northern neighbors favor cherries. The tartness of the fruit, and the zest of ginger, do wonderful things with the richness of the ham.

Trim fat from two ¾-inch slices of ham and score the edges. Pit 3 cups of Bing cherries and cook them with ½ cup of water until the juices run. Pile the cherries on the ham slices, and to the juices add a tablespoon of chopped candied ginger, 2 tablespoons of sugar, ⅛ teaspoon of salt, and a tablespoon of flour mixed with 2 tablespoons of water. Cook this until thick, pour over the ham and cherries, and bake at 350° for an hour, or until the ham is done. SERVES ABOUT 6.

2 *slices ham* (*¾-inch thick*)	2 *tablespoons sugar*
3 *cups Bing cherries*	⅛ *teaspoon salt*
½ *cup water*	1 *tablespoon flour in 2 table-*
1 *tablespoon chopped can-*	*spoons water*
died ginger	

❨ Ham and Oyster Pie

Ham and oysters are often found together, and were even back in Gold Rush days, though the hams were "hard and black" and the oysters canned. Dame Shirley describes a general store in an early mining town: "Flannel shirts and calico ditto — the latter starched to an appalling degree of stiffness — lie cheek by jowl with hams, preserved meats, and oysters."

A rich crust for this, but just a top one, and it is baked separately from the pie. Two cups of flour, ⅓ cup each of butter and lard, a teaspoon of salt, and water. Roll thin, spread with softened butter (1 tablespoon), fold in quarters, roll again, spread with another tablespoon of butter, and again fold. Chill. Roll thin, let rest on the board for a few minutes, then cut the size of the top of a 2-quart casserole or a little larger. Prick and bake on a cookie sheet. The filling is made by cooking 3 large chopped shallots in ½ cup of butter, stirring in ½ cup of flour, cooking 3 minutes, then adding a quart of milk (part cream), salt, pepper, and a little Spice Islands Thyme Seasoning Powder. When the sauce is thick, add 3 cups of cubed cooked ham and heat some more. Slip the pie-crust in the oven to reheat. Add a pint of drained oysters to the sauce and as soon as they begin to crinkle pour the whole mixture into the aforementioned casserole. Lift the crust, which is now hot, onto the top with a couple of spatulas and a prayer, and serve forth this gorgeous dish. The reason for baking it this way is that if the crust is cooked over the filling, it sometimes overcooks the oysters. However, if you want to do it that way, go to it. SERVES 6 TO 8.

CRUST

2 cups flour	⅓ cup lard
⅓ cup butter, and 2 tablespoons	1 teaspoon salt
Water	

FILLING

3 shallots	Salt and pepper
½ cup butter	Thyme seasoning powder
½ cup flour	3 cups cubed cooked ham
1 quart milk	1 pint drained oysters

(Ham Vina Blanca

And the vina blanca is not champagne, but a California white table wine — say a Pinot blanc. Joe Tilden, famed *bon vivant* and amateur chef, always boiled his hams in champagne — we settle, more modestly, for this.

Skin the ham when partially cooked, and baste with 2½ cups of white wine while baking in a 325° oven. When the ham is done, make a sauce: cook 3 tablespoons of chopped shallots in 3 tablespoons of butter, add a cup of rich stock, a cup of the white wine, a whole lemon, sliced paper thin, then the slices quartered, a pinch each of cloves and cayenne, a tablespoon (or more) of sugar, and salt to taste.

1 ham	1 cup rich stock
2½ cups white wine	1 lemon
3 tablespoons chopped	Pinch of cloves
shallots	Pinch of cayenne
3 tablespoons butter	1 tablespoon sugar (or more)
Salt	

❨ Broiled Lamb Kidneys with Herbs

Remove skin from 12 lamb kidneys and split from the round side without cutting through. Make a paste with ¾ of a cup of finely chopped parsley, a tablespoon of minced tarragon, 6 green onions, chopped fine, ¾ of a cup of butter, and salt and pepper. Open kidneys flat, divide the paste among them, spreading it over the cut surfaces, and broil under a hot flame for 5 to 8 minutes. Don't overcook. SERVES 6.

12 lamb kidneys	6 green onions
¾ cup finely chopped parsley	¾ cup butter
1 tablespoon minced tarragon	Salt and pepper

❨ Simi Kidney Sauté

Wash, skin, and clean a pound of lamb or veal kidneys, and slice them thin. Chop 4 shallots or green onions, and sauté them in ¼ cup of butter until wilted. Add the sliced kidneys and cook quickly for a minute or two on each side. Add ¼ cup of red table wine, a little salt and fresh ground pepper, and 3 tablespoons of minced parsley. Serve at once on crisp buttered toast. Kidneys toughen if overcooked, so watch it. They should cook only long enough so that the blood stops running. SERVES 3 OR 4.

1 pound lamb or veal kidneys	¼ cup red table wine
4 shallots	Salt and pepper
¼ cup butter	3 tablespoons minced parsley

❨ Kidney Notes

With Potato. Put a little herb butter into cleaned kidneys. Cut top off baking potatoes, cut out part of insides, insert kidney, dot with more herb butter, tie on top of potato, and bake slowly until potatoes are done.

Kidney Rolls. Spread bacon with a mix of crumbs, butter, minced chives and parsley, and raw egg. Wrap around cleaned kidneys, secure, and bake for 20 minutes.

Kidney with Oysters. Grill lamb kidneys and slice. Put slices on a round of buttered toast, top with an oyster, brush with butter, and return to the broiler to plump the oyster.

Sautéed Kidneys. Try flavoring them with a little grated orange rind and using orange juice as the liquid. There's a Californian touch!

⟨ Barbecued Lamb Steaks

Don't skip this way with lamb. It's one of our better tricks at the charcoal grill, one which will satisfy even the inveterate beef eater.

Have steaks cut from a leg of lamb, the thickness depending upon your taste. A 1-inch steak is best for well-done meat, but a 2-inch one is better if you like your meat charred on the outside and pink and juicy within. Grill them over very hot coals, basting them with garlic oil (a crushed clove of garlic to ½ cup of olive oil), using a bunch of "yarbs and simples" for a basting brush — tie some celery leaves, a few branches of parsley, and a good sprig of rosemary or marjoram together in a faggot. (If the herbs aren't all available, settle for parsley and celery.) For further notes on barbecuing, see page 24.

⟨ Roast Lamb with White Wine and Olives

Once more wine and ripe olives join to add charm to a simple dish. Lamb, roasted this way, is lamb at its best. Serve it with pan-roasted potatoes and string beans combined with sautéed mushrooms, and flavored with snips of fresh dill.

Put a dozen peeled cloves of garlic in the roasting pan with a leg of lamb. Pour over a whole bottle of white wine, jab the meat well with an ice pick, and baste at least a dozen times during the cooking. The garlic thickens the sauce and perfumes the lamb in a heavenly manner. Just before serving, heat 2 cups of pitted ripe olives in the sauce and serve with the roast. SERVES 8.

1 leg of lamb	1 bottle white wine
12 cloves of garlic	2 cups pitted ripe olives

(Breast of Lamb, California Style

This is a good dish and pleasantly easy on the budget.

Have 3 pounds of breast of lamb cut in 4-inch pieces, the width of the rib. Prepare a marinade with 2 cups of red wine, a large onion, sliced, a bay leaf, a teaspoon of sweet basil, and a crushed clove of garlic. Marinate the lamb at least 12 hours, turning as many times as you think of it. Pour off the marinade and bake the meat in an open pan at 400° until some of the fat has cooked out and the meat is beginning to brown. Pour off the fat, pour on the marinade, reduce heat to 325°, sprinkle the meat with salt and pepper, and continue cooking until the meat is tender, brown, and crispy. Remove to a serving dish, skim the marinade of fat, reduce to a cup by cooking quickly, and pour over the ribs. SERVES 4.

3 pounds breast of lamb   *1 bay leaf*
2 cups red wine   *1 teaspoon sweet basil*
1 large onion   *1 clove garlic*
Salt and pepper

NOTE: These ribs, after the marinating, may be charcoal grilled. In this case it's better to have them cut in larger pieces.

(Frontera Braised Lamb Shanks

This is a man's dish, a Western dish, a superlative dish. We usually use lamb shanks, but those of mutton are as good if not better, though they do need a longer sojourn in the oven.

Allow 1 lamb shank for each serving unless you've trenchermen about. Then allow a few extras. Do not have the shank bone cracked — it will be unsightly if you do. Rub the shanks with flour seasoned with salt and pepper, and, for six shanks, brown them carefully in ⅓ cup of shortening with a clove of garlic. Put them into a large casserole. To the pan in which they've browned, add 2 tablespoons of flour, a cup of either red or white table wine, and ½ cup of stock or water. Cook a minute, then pour over the lamb shanks. Add an herb bouquet of parsley, bay, and rosemary, cover, and bake at 350° for an hour, or until tender, turning once or twice during the cook-

260

ing. Vegetables — turnips, carrots, onions, and celery — may be cooked with the meat.

6 *lamb shanks*	1 *clove garlic*
Seasoned flour	1 *cup red or white wine*
⅓ *cup shortening*	½ *cup stock or water*
2 *tablespoons flour*	1 *herb bouquet*

⟪ Braised Leg of Mutton, Oyster Stuffed

There's not a meat eaten on the Pacific Coast that isn't, sooner or later, and happily, combined with oysters. This one was *sooner,* as it appears in the first cook books of the area.

Have a leg of mutton skinned and the gland and bones removed. Chop a pint of oysters — and here's a good time to use those giant Willapoint oysters from Washington — and mix them with a cup of dry bread crumbs, ⅓ cup of melted butter, and 2 tablespoons each of minced parsley and grated onion. Season with salt and pepper and a teaspoon of lemon juice. Stuff into the bone cavity and sew or skewer the opening securely. Now brown the mutton in ¼ cup of shortening and put in a deep casserole with 2 cups of California white wine and a couple of cloves of garlic. Toss in an herb bouquet, cover, and cook in a slow oven (300°) for 2½ to 3 hours, uncovering for the last 15 minutes.

1 *leg mutton, boned*	2 *cups white wine*
¼ *cup shortening*	2 *cloves garlic*
1 *herb bouquet*	

STUFFING

1 *pint oysters*	2 *tablespoons minced parsley*
1 *cup dry bread crumbs*	2 *tablespoons grated onion*
⅓ *cup melted butter*	*Salt and pepper*
1 *teaspoon lemon juice*	

⟪ Saddle of Mutton Spokane

A saddle of mutton is a perfect roast. Have it skinned and rub it with garlic that has been ground with salt and marjoram.

Roast with the flank end up, basting it often with a mixture of olive oil and red wine in equal parts. When the meat thermometer has reached 140°, it is done. Serve with a purée of dried white beans cooked with white wine, or with beans and brandy.

<table>
<tr><td>1 saddle of mutton, skinned</td><td>Marjoram</td></tr>
<tr><td>Garlic</td><td>1 part olive oil</td></tr>
<tr><td>Salt</td><td>1 part red wine</td></tr>
</table>

NOTE: Saddle of mutton was held in sufficiently high esteem to be served for Christmas dinner at the Palace Hotel in 1894. May it again gain the prestige it so deserves.

❨ Char Siu (Chinese Roast Pork)

Char siu is the Chinese name for this wonderful roast pork, but chances are that if you order it by that name when at a Chinese restaurant your courteous waiter will write "roast pork" on his order pad. After all, he went to college, too.

Ask for a flat piece of boneless pork, about 2½ pounds of it. Marinate overnight in ¼ cup of soy, a tablespoon of honey, and ¼ cup of chili sauce. Roast slowly for 1½ to 2 hours. Serve sliced in strips with mustard and tomato sauce, or with ½ cup of toasted sesame seeds ground with 8 green onions, and ¼ cup of soy sauce. SERVES 6 TO 10.

2½ pounds boneless pork

MARINADE

¼ cup soy sauce	¼ cup chili sauce
1 tablespoon honey	

SAUCE

½ cup toasted sesame seeds	8 green onions
¼ cup soy sauce	

❨ Chinese Spareribs

Chinese roast spareribs are wonderful! There are several ways of doing them — all good, all popular with Occidentals. This way, strong with garlic, is perhaps the favorite. They do not have to be served with other Chinese food to be appreciated. They are entirely superb with mashed potatoes and succotash, both as un-Oriental as they come.

Mix ¼ cup of honey with ¼ cup of soy sauce, 1 cup of chicken stock or bouillon, 4 cloves of garlic, ground to nothing with 2 teaspoons of salt, and ¼ cup of tomato purée or tomato catsup. Marinate 4 pounds of pork spareribs (don't have the ribs separated) in this for several hours or overnight, turning two or three times. Roast in a hot oven (450°) for 10 minutes, then reduce heat to 325° and finish cooking, basting with the marinade. This usually takes about an hour — sometimes longer. Separate the ribs with a sharp knife, but leave them whole. Add enough water to the pan to make 1 cup of liquid, thicken with a tablespoon of cornstarch in a little water, and serve with the ribs. SERVES 4.

¼ cup honey	¼ cup tomato purée or
¼ cup soy sauce	catsup
1 cup chicken stock	4 pounds pork spareribs
4 cloves garlic	Water as needed
2 teaspoons salt	1 tablespoon cornstarch

(*Roast Pork and Beans Palo Alto*

Chef Mergenthaler, onetime chef at the Palace Hotel, said that the Empire Builders of the '60s had been mostly "pork and bean eaters." If this was the way they ate them, there was certainly no reason for sneering.

Soak a pound of dried white beans overnight, then simmer them with an herb bouquet and a clove of garlic until the skins burst when the beans are blown upon. Drain and season them with salt and pepper, and spread them in an open roaster. Top with a 5- or 6-pound loin of pork and bake at 350° for 4 hours, or until the meat thermometer reads 185°. Stir the beans several times during the cooking. If the fat from the pork does not give sufficient moisture, add some of the water that has been drained from the beans. Serve the roast surrounded with the beans. SERVES 6 TO 8.

1 pound dried white beans	1 clove garlic
1 herb bouquet	Salt and pepper
5–6 pound loin of pork	

❨ Mexican Roast Loin of Pork

Once more the Mexicans teach us a culinary trick worth learning.

Rub a loin of pork with 3 cloves of garlic that have been crushed with 2 teaspoons of salt, 1 teaspoon of oregano, and 1 teaspoon of cumin. Roast as usual. Remove pork to a platter, pour off fat, all but ¼ cup. Add ¼ cup of flour, brown, then add 2 cups of tomato purée, a tablespoon of chili powder, a cup of water, and any or all of the following: ½ cup of sliced ripe olives, ½ cup of seedless raisins plumped in hot water, ½ cup of chopped canned green chili peppers, ½ teaspoon of cumin seeds. Serve with the roast and with beans in the Mexican manner.

1 pork loin roast	*2 teaspoons salt*
3 cloves garlic	*1 teaspoon oregano*
1 teaspoon cumin	

SAUCE

¼ cup pork fat	*2 cups tomato purée*
¼ cup flour	*1 tablespoon chili powder*
1 cup water	

Any or all of the following:

½ cup sliced ripe olives	*½ cup chopped canned green*
½ cup seedless raisins	*chili peppers*
½ teaspoon cumin seeds	

NOTE: A quicker way. Rub pork with seasoning as above. Roast. Dilute canned Mexican chili sauce with water, and use as a baste.

❨ Pork Notes

Painted Ladies. Very daringly named, this recipe of the '80s was for whole small apples, poached in syrup, and with their cheeks painted with melted currant jelly. These were served with pork.

Lomo. An early Californian pork dish called lomo is made by marinating pork tenderloin in 1 cup of vinegar that has had

264

Meat

3 tablespoons of minced tarragon, 2 crushed cloves of garlic, and 1 each chopped onion and green pepper added. Turn a couple of times during the marinating period of 4 hours. Drain well, paint with olive oil, and broil. This is in many of the old cook books. SERVES 4 OR MORE.

(Chorizo

This is Mexican sausage, and is used by them for a seasoning in other dishes, as well as by itself. It's very good fried, then crumbled over fried beans, or added to scrambled eggs.

Grind 2 pounds of lean pork. Grind a clove of garlic with 1½ teaspoons of salt, add it and ¼ cup of vinegar, 2 tablespoons of chili powder, ½ teaspoon of oregano, and ¼ teaspoon of cumin, ground. Mix well and pack into casings, or just roll into a long roll and wrap in aluminum foil. This will keep nicely in the refrigerator for several weeks.

2 pounds lean pork *¼ cup vinegar*
1 clove garlic *2 tablespoons chili powder*
1½ teaspoons salt *½ teaspoon oregano*
¼ teaspoon ground cumin

(Sausage Pudding

Delicious. Roll a pound of sausage meat in small balls and cook in the oven until about half done. Pour over a batter made with 2 eggs, a cup of milk, a cup of flour, ¼ teaspoon of salt, and return to the oven (450°). After fifteen minutes reduce heat to 350° and cook until brown and puffy. Serve with corn on the cob and applesauce. SERVES 6.

1 pound sausage meat *1 cup milk*
2 eggs *1 cup flour*
¼ teaspoon salt

NOTE: Meat balls may be done in the same way, though extra fat will have to be added before they are baked.

(Sausage Notes

In Pancakes. Brown little pork sausages, roll each one in a thin pancake, return to oven to heat, and serve with applesauce.

With Potato. Leftover cooked sausage, mixed with leftover mashed potato, rolled in balls, egged, crumbed, and fried in deep fat.

Sausage Pie. Line a dish with mashed potatoes, top with well-browned sausages, sprinkle with bread crumbs that have been mixed with chopped parsley and chives and sausage fat. Bake in oven.

(Sweetbreads Jessica

This is a recipe from the Wine Institute, and is but one of the many superb ones developed by them.

Cook 1½ cups of rice in 3 quarts of boiling water until tender. Drain, dry, mix with 3 tablespoons of melted butter and a cup (packed) of coarsely chopped water cress. Butter a 1-quart ring mold and pack the rice into it, then turn out on a platter and fill the center of the ring with creamed sweetbreads. Cook 2 pairs of sweetbreads and separate into their natural divisions. Make a sauce by cooking a tablespoon of grated onion in ¼ cup of butter, adding ¼ cup of flour, then, after 2 or 3 minutes of cooking, 2 cups of thin cream, a teaspoon of salt, ¼ cup of California sherry, a tablespoon of lemon juice, and 2 egg yolks, beaten with a little of the hot sauce. Cook until smooth, add sweetbreads, taste for seasoning, heat gently, and pour into the rice ring which I hope has been kept hot all this time. SERVES 6 OR 8.

1½ cups rice	3 tablespoons butter
3 quarts water	1 cup chopped water cress
2 pairs	sweetbreads

SAUCE

1 tablespoon grated onion	1 teaspoon salt
¼ cup butter	¼ cup sherry
¼ cup flour	1 tablespoon lemon juice
2 cups thin cream	2 egg yolks

266

Meat

(Sweetbread and Oyster Pie

Oysters, as is their West Coast wont, combine with almost anything, including sweetbreads. The ladies of an earlier day thought this "very nice," and indeed it is, though the ingredients included in it may seem a bit overwhelming. Serve it at a buffet, with string beans vinaigrette, rice croquettes, and plenty of celery and olives.

Grind a pound of veal and ¼ pound of ham very fine, mix with ½ cup of bread crumbs, ¼ cup of milk, and an egg. Season with salt, pepper, and a very little thyme, and form into small balls, which poach for 15 minutes in 2 cups of veal stock. Cook 2 pairs of sweetbreads and cut into pieces about the size of the meat balls. Clean ½ pound of small mushrooms and sauté for 4 minutes in 2 tablespoons of butter. Make a quart of cream sauce (½ cup of flour, ¼ pound of butter, a quart of rich milk, salt and pepper to taste), add ¼ cup of sherry. Combine with the other ingredients, and a pint of small oysters. Put in a large baking dish (2½ quarts), top with rich pastry, and bake in a hot oven until the crust is done. THIS IS A PARTY DISH — IT WILL SERVE 8 OR 10.

1 pound veal	2 cups veal stock
¼ pound ham	2 pairs sweetbreads
½ cup bread crumbs	½ pound mushrooms
¼ cup milk	2 tablespoons butter
1 egg	¼ cup sherry
Salt and pepper	1 pint oysters
Thyme	Rich pastry

CREAM SAUCE

½ cup flour	1 quart rich milk
¼ pound butter	Salt and pepper

(Tongue

Some of the pioneers acquired a real love for tongue on the way across the prairies — buffalo tongue, that is. One early wag called them "engineer's tongue," claiming that these beasts were tops in that profession, always finding the shortest and easiest passes through the Rocky Mountains. Buffalo tongues

267

were available, at a price, in the Oregon Territory, as the traders brought them to the fur companies, and later, in San Francisco, they often appeared on early menus. The Occidental Hotel featured smoked buffalo tongue at a banquet in 1889, and other hotels served it, as well as venison tongue, and held them both in high esteem. Beef and sheep tongues were also well liked, if their inclusion in all the old recipe books is any indication.

◖ Braised Tongue Tulare

Cook a fresh tongue with an herb bouquet until almost tender — 2 to 4 hours (less in a pressure cooker — usually 35 minutes, but follow the manufacturer's directions). Cool the tongue and remove skin, then brown it all over in 4 tablespoons of butter, and remove to a casserole. In the pan in which it browned, add 2 tablespoons of flour, and ½ cup each of diced carrots and onions. Cook a minute or three, add a cup of white wine and ½ cup of tongue stock, season to taste, and pour over the tongue. Cook in the oven until the tongue is prettily glazed and very tender. Mushrooms may be added if desired. Serve with spoon bread. SERVES 8.

1 beef tongue	½ cup diced onions
1 herb bouquet	1 cup white wine
4 tablespoons butter	½ cup tongue stock
2 tablespoons flour	Salt and pepper
½ cup diced carrots	Mushrooms (optional)

NOTE: *Tongue Tarragon.* This same recipe is easily varied by using red wine instead of white, and adding 2 tablespoons of minced tarragon leaves.

◖ Tripe

Tripe apparently used to be a great favorite on the West Coast, for there are many recipes for it in early cook books. Today it is still popular with our Mexican Americans, who cook it beautifully in their menudo, but it is not often found in ordinary restaurants or homes. This is good — it keeps the price pleasantly low for those of us who dote on it.

Skinner's Chop House, Sacramento, a favorite with the Argonauts, served fried tripe apparently unadorned, and served it daily.

◖ *Menudo*

This is the wonderful tripe stew or soup that the Mexicans do so well, and we all love so well. Traditionally it is served at Christmas breakfast. Also traditionally it is made with nixtamal, or whole dried corn that is treated with lye and parboiled. Canned whole hominy makes a satisfactory substitute.

Cut 3 pounds of tripe into pieces, and put in a big pot with a knuckle of veal, cracked, 4 cloves of garlic ground with 2 teaspoons of salt, 2 cups of chopped onions, a teaspoon of coriander, 2 teaspoons of oregano, 2 teaspoons of chili powder, and a gallon of water. Cook slowly for about 6 hours, then add a large can of whole hominy. (If nixtamal is available, use 2 cups, and cook it from the beginning with the tripe.) Cook another half hour, or until the tripe is tender. Remove veal knuckle, correct seasoning. Serve from a soup tureen and pass minced green onions to be sprinkled on top. Tostados are in order, or tortillas. SERVES 8 TO 12.

3 pounds tripe	*1 teaspoon coriander*
1 veal knuckle	*2 teaspoons oregano*
4 cloves garlic	*2 teaspoons chili powder*
2 teaspoons salt	*1 large can whole hominy or*
2 cups chopped onions	*2 cups nixtamal*
1 gallon water	

◖ *Tripe and Oysters*

Here we go again, tossing oysters in the pot. This recipe shows up in almost all the older Pacific Coast cook books, in one version or another. This is one of the fancier ones.

Boil 3 pounds of tripe until tender and cut into rounds with a small biscuit cutter. (The odd-shaped scraps are fine for pepper pot soup or menudo.) Cook a chopped onion in ¼ cup of butter, add ¼ cup of flour, cook 3 minutes, then add a pint of rich milk (part cream), 3 tablespoons each of minced green pepper and pimiento, salt and pepper to taste, and ¼ cup of California sherry. Now heat the tripe rounds in this sauce, along with a pint of oysters. As soon as the oysters get curly around their edges, serve, on toast. This is a good dish for a chafing dish. SERVES 6 TO 8.

3 pounds tripe
1 pint oysters

SAUCE

1 onion
¼ cup butter
¼ cup flour
1 pint rich milk
3 tablespoons minced green pepper

3 tablespoons minced pimiento
Salt and pepper
¼ cup sherry

(Tripe with Green Peppers

San Franciscans go for this dish in a big way. Try it once and you, too, will be an addict.

Boil 2 pounds of tripe in salted water to cover, with an herb bouquet, a sliced onion, a clove of garlic, 3 cloves, and a few peppercorns. When tender — 2 to 4 hours (or less, of course, if you use a pressure cooker) — drain, save the stock (it's good for soup stock, and will jelly by itself), and dry the tripe well, cutting it in strips. Dip in flour, then in beaten egg seasoned with pepper and salt, and finally in crumbs. In the meantime, cut 3 large green peppers in strips and slice 3 large onions, and sauté them in shortening or bacon fat. Season with salt and pepper and arrange on a baking dish. Fry the tripe in deep fat (370°) until it is nicely brown, arrange on the bed of vegetables, and keep hot until serving

270

time. Sometimes this is served with a thin rich cream sauce poured over all. SERVES 6 TO 8.

2 *pounds tripe*	*Flour*
1 *herb bouquet*	1 *egg*
1 *sliced onion*	*Salt and pepper*
3 *cloves*	*Crumbs*
1 *clove garlic*	3 *green peppers*
Peppercorns	3 *large onions*
Shortening or bacon fat	

❨ *Willapa Veal Stew*

Here, once more, we have oysters married to meat, and happily.

Have 2 pounds of boneless veal cut in small cubes, dust them with flour, and brown in 3 tablespoons of shortening along with ¼ cup of minced onions. Add ½ cup of white wine and 1½ cups of stock, and simmer until the meat is tender. Pour off the juice, add a teaspoon of anchovy paste and a little pepper, salt if needed. Thicken with a roux of 3 tablespoons each of butter and flour. Return sauce to the veal, add a pint of small oysters or large ones cut in pieces, and as soon as they plump, serve sprinkled with minced parsley and accompanied by crisp buttered toast. SERVES 6.

2 *pounds veal*	1 *teaspoon anchovy paste*
3 *tablespoons shortening*	*Pepper and salt*
¼ *cup minced onions*	3 *tablespoons butter*
½ *cup white wine*	3 *tablespoons flour*
1½ *cups stock*	1 *pint oysters*
Parsley	

❨ *Albondigas*

Albondigas are meat balls with a Spanish accent. We like them as a main course and in soup. The early Californians brought this recipe from Mexico, and the early American ladies cooked it better than they pronounced it. It keeps popping up in early cook books as avonigas, abondegus, abondas — everything but albondigas.

Mix 1 pound each of ground beef and pork with a cup of soft bread crumbs, ¼ cup of milk, 2 eggs, 2 teaspoons of salt, ½ teaspoon of oregano, and, if desired, ½ teaspoon of cumin. When thoroughly blended, form into small balls. Now make a sauce by cooking ½ cup of minced onion in 2 tablespoons of fat for 3 minutes, then adding ½ cup of minced green pepper (or ¼ cup of minced green chili pepper), 2 tablespoons of flour, 2 cups of Spanish-style tomato sauce, a cup of water or stock, and salt, pepper, and chili powder to taste. Poach the meat balls in this sauce, covered, for about 40 minutes. SERVES 6 GENEROUSLY.

MEAT BALLS

1 *pound ground beef*	2 *eggs*
1 *pound ground pork*	2 *teaspoons salt*
1 *cup soft bread crumbs*	½ *teaspoon oregano*
¼ *cup milk*	½ *teaspoon cumin (optional)*

SAUCE

½ *cup minced onion*	2 *cups tomato sauce*
2 *tablespoons fat*	1 *cup water or stock*
½ *cup minced green pepper*	*Salt and pepper*
2 *tablespoons flour*	*Chili powder*

NOTE: Ground unblanched almonds, about ½ cup of them, may be added to the sauce.

❴ Chinese Meat Balls (*Jar Yook Tun*)

The Chinese seem always to do things just a little better than the rest of us — or at least we are so convinced when we compare their meat balls with the plain American kind.

Combine 1½ pounds of ground lean pork with a cup of chopped water chestnuts (canned or fresh), ¼ cup of minced green onions, a teaspoon of finely minced green ginger (page 242), a tablespoon of soy sauce, 2 whole eggs, and 2 tablespoons of cornstarch. (If this mixture is too wet to form, add a few bread crumbs.) Roll into small balls, then in cornstarch, and cook gently in peanut, sesame, or some other bland oil. Reheat these meat balls in sweet and sour sauce (page 17), or this sauce: in the pan in which the meat balls have cooked, brown a well-crushed clove of garlic. Remove and stir in 3 tablespoons of cornstarch and 2 cups of pork stock (or chicken stock). Cook until clear and season to taste with soy sauce. Green pepper strips, pieces of green onion, Chinese almonds, Chinese peas, or long diagonal slices of celery may be heated (not cooked) in this sauce before it is combined with the meat balls. The ginger may be omitted. SERVES 4 TO 8.

MEAT BALLS

1½ pounds lean pork	*¼ cup minced green*
1 cup chopped water chest-	*onions*
nuts	*1 tablespoon soy sauce*
1 teaspoon minced green	*2 eggs*
ginger	*2 tablespoons cornstarch*

SAUCE

1 clove garlic	*2 cups pork or chicken stock*
3 tablespoons cornstarch	*Soy sauce*

NOTE: Celery or mushrooms or sesame seeds may be added to these meat balls. Served without sauce, on toothpicks, they make a delightful appetizer.

◖ *Oregon Coast Meat Balls*

These are so named because they use little cubes of Oregon's famed blue cheese, Langlois, as a delightful filling.

Mix 2 pounds of twice-ground beef with 2 teaspoons of salt crushed with a clove of garlic, and 2 eggs. Mix well and form around cubes of this blue cheese. Dust lightly with flour, and sauté in ¼ cup of butter, then pour on a cup of red wine and simmer, covered, for 10 minutes. Serve with brown rice. SERVES 6.

2 pounds ground beef	*Cubes of Langlois blue*
2 teaspoons salt	*cheese*
1 clove garlic	*¼ cup butter*
2 eggs	*1 cup red wine*

(Seattle Swedish Meat Balls

There are a great many residents of Swedish birth or descent living in the Northwest, so it is quite natural that there are many dishes with the same ancestry. This one is a favorite for a main dish, usually served with brown beans, or as one of the dishes at a smörgåsbord.

Mix 2 pounds of thrice-ground beef with a pound of ground pork, also ground three times. Add 4 eggs, a cup of dried crumbs, 1½ cups of beer, a tablespoon of salt, ½ cup of onions browned in 2 tablespoons of butter, and either a teaspoon of ground ginger or one of dill. Form in balls, brown in ¼ cup of butter, remove to a hot dish. Add 3 tablespoons of flour to the pan, brown it, then pour in a cup of cream and 1¼ cups of stock. Cook until smooth and thickened, and pour over the hot meat balls. SERVES 8.

MEAT BALLS

2 *pounds ground beef*	1 *tablespoon salt*
1 *pound ground pork*	½ *cup onions*
4 *eggs*	6 *tablespoons butter*
1 *cup dried crumbs*	1 *teaspoon ground ginger or*
1½ *cups beer*	*dill*

SAUCE

Butter from above recipe	1 *cup cream*
3 *tablespoons flour*	1¼ *cups stock*

(Puchero

Here's another stew brought us by the Mexicans.

Brown a cup of diced salt pork, then add 2½ cups of lean beef cut in cubes, a crushed clove of garlic, ½ cup of minced onion, a cup of chopped cabbage, a teaspoon of oregano, ½ teaspoon each of coriander and cumin, a No. 2 can of tomatoes, 2 tablespoons of chopped parsley, ½ cup of soaked garbanzos, and ¼ cup of rice. When the meat is almost tender, add a cup of corn cut fresh from the cob, and salt and pepper to taste. The broth is strained from the meat and served in cups at the same time as the meat. A highly seasoned Mexican sauce

274

(page 264) is served with the meat and vegetables. SERVES 6.

1 cup diced salt pork	*½ teaspoon cumin*
2½ cups cubed beef	*1 No. 2 can tomatoes*
1 clove garlic	*2 tablespoons chopped pars-*
½ cup minced onion	*ley*
1 cup chopped cabbage	*½ cup soaked garbanzos*
1 teaspoon oregano	*¼ cup rice*
½ teaspoon coriander	*1 cup fresh corn*

Salt and pepper

NOTE: Joe Tilden's "perchero," no doubt fashioned after this dish, had beef, pumpkin, and other vegetables, and saffron — the last a seasoning more often found in Spanish than in Mexican dishes.

(*Estofada*

The early Californians liked their stews highly seasoned, but the American ladies who adopted their dishes often kept their names but not their seasonings. This comes from a cook book written in the '80s, and is typical. It says, "Use two pounds of beef ribs or mutton. A chicken is best."

So brown the meat, 3 pounds of stewing meat, or a small disjointed chicken. Use ¼ cup of fat, and brown with 2 onions and 2 green peppers (left whole, the recipe says, but better quarter them), a little garlic (one clove, crushed), thyme (½ teaspoon), vinegar (2 tablespoons), raisins (½ cup, seeded or seedless), olives (½ cup, green, cut from their stones), and a few tomatoes (2 cups, canned). Four slices of toast are also added for thickening, and the whole cooked to a salubrious stew. SERVES 6 TO 8.

3 pounds meat or	*½ teaspoon thyme*
1 small chicken	*2 tablespoons vinegar*
¼ cup fat	*½ cup raisins*
2 onions	*½ cup green olives*
2 green peppers	*2 cups canned tomatoes*
1 clove garlic	*4 slices toast*

NOTE: Two other Mexican dishes, olla podrida and sancocho, were also popular with the early Californians. The former, named after the *olla*, or clay pot in which it was cooked, was a wondrous stew of meats and vegetables, with as many variations as an Irish stew. It was made of beef or mutton, sometimes poultry and game, chick peas or beans, and vegetables, and usually had some chorizo added. The sancocho was also of meat, and had potatoes, corn, and other vegetables included. It was probably just another olla podrida.

⟪ Yeung Dong (Stuffed Mushrooms)

Clean a pound of large mushrooms and save stems. Mix ½ pound of ground beef and ½ pound of ground pork with a whole egg, ½ teaspoon of M.S.G., a teaspoon of soy sauce, ½ teaspoon of salt, a little pepper, 4 chopped green onions, ¼ cup of minced water chestnuts or celery and the stems, chopped. Form into balls, press them into mushroom caps, then dip the meat tops in sesame seeds. Into a skillet put ½ cup of chicken stock, 2 tablespoons of oil, and a teaspoon of soy sauce. Add mushrooms, stuffed side up, cover, and steam gently for 35 to 40 minutes. Add enough water to make ½ cup of liquid, and thicken with 2 teaspoons of cornstarch. SERVES 4.

1 pound large mushrooms	*½ teaspoon salt*
½ pound ground beef	*Pepper*
½ pound ground pork	*4 green onions*
1 egg	*¼ cup minced water chestnuts*
½ teaspoon M.S.G.	
1 teaspoon soy sauce	*Sesame seeds*

SAUCE

½ cup chicken stock	*2 tablespoons oil*
1 teaspoon soy sauce	*Water as needed*
2 teaspoons cornstarch	

⟪ Vitella Tonnato

Both the Italians and the Mexicans do fine things with cold meat dishes. This is the Italian masterpiece. (Escabeche de lengua, or carne a la vinagreta, the Mexican one.) This dish

276

is made from two to five days before serving, which makes it nice for a busy cook who has to plan ahead for a party.

Spread out flat a 4-pound piece of veal shoulder, bones removed, and on it lay 6 fillets of anchovies. Roll the meat and tie it firmly, and put it in a pan just large enough to hold it. Add a sliced onion, a sliced carrot, and an herb bouquet (bay, parsley, rosemary). Add enough stock (made from those bones you paid for) to come to the top of the meat. Cover and simmer slowly until the meat is tender (1½ to 2 hours). Cool, cut in slices, and arrange in a symmetrical manner in a shallow casserole. (An oblong Pyrex baking dish is the perfect shape.) Reduce the stock to 1 cup by boiling rapidly. Cool, add a 7-ounce tin of grated tuna, 6 chopped anchovies, a very well crushed clove of garlic, ½ cup of olive oil, ½ cup of lemon juice, and ⅓ cup of minced or sliced ripe olives. Pour this over the veal and let stand in the refrigerator for from 2 to 5 days. Serve cold, sprinkled with parsley. SERVES 8.

*4 pounds veal shoulder,
   boned
12 fillets of anchovies
1 onion
1 carrot
1 herb bouquet
   Stock to cover*

*1 7-ounce tin grated tuna
1 clove garlic
½ cup olive oil
½ cup lemon juice
⅓ cup minced or sliced ripe
   olives*

Nuts

THERE WERE *all kinds of wild nuts growing on the Pacific slope when white men first came. They were a staple food of the natives. In fact, the acorn, which was leached and ground into meal, was their daily bread.*

⟨ *Walnuts*

A hard-shelled nut, the *juglans Californica*, or California walnut, grew wild in the country, and the Madeira nut, or white walnut, was introduced at an early date. In 1849 one smart Argonaut founded his fortune by selling walnuts. Arriving in Sacramento broke, he bought a bag of "Madeira" nuts on credit, and sold them by the cupful. He cleared $50 in five days. It wasn't until the '50s that walnuts were planted extensively, and it was in 1867, when the Santa Barbara softshell was introduced, that the walnut industry really got under way. Today the nut that is still called the English walnut is grown extensively in California — in fact we furnish most of the nation's and much of the world's supply. The California Walnut Growers Association, like Sunkist and other co-operatives, is an organization that supervises the packing and marketing of much of the state's walnut crop, selling them under the famous brand name "Diamond." Walnuts, high in nutriment as well as flavor, are used pretty generally in West Coast kitchens and on West Coast tables. They are usually purchased shelled, when used in cooking, but in the shell when eaten out of hand. A favorite dessert is a huge bowl of California walnuts, usually in company with Washington apples, Oregon cheddar, or California wine, and sometimes with all three. Walnuts and port, a popular treat of old, has again come

278

into favor — a delightfully simple way of ending an elaborate meal.

❡ *Almonds*

The almond was introduced early in California history, and by 1853 quite a few trees had been planted, but they were erratic in their bearing, and many of them ended in the cookstove. Finally the perfect locations for the almond trees were discovered, and the almond came into its own. In 1910 the California Almond Growers Exchange was formed, and almonds graduated from their position as a holiday treat to the place they now hold — a pantry requisite.

❡ *Filberts*

Filberts are the latest, and one of the most delicious nuts to come out of the West. California tried cultivating filberts, but without any marked success. Then the Northwest tried it, and now the Northwest filberts are rivaling the almonds and walnuts of California. Filberts are terrific — their flavor is considered by many connoisseurs to be the very finest of the nuts. Northwest filberts are easy to slice and to blanch (bake them for 20 minutes at 275°, and the skins will rub right off), and may be used in any of the ways already popular with other nuts.

❡ *Pine Nuts*

This is a nut of many names — piñon, pignolia, Indian nut, or piñones. It is wild, growing in the huge pine cones that grow on several varieties of evergreens. The nuts are soft, and have a slight and delightful flavor of the pine itself. They go nicely in rice and paste dishes, the Italians using them with particular skill.

Olives and Olive Oil

THE FRANCISCAN FATHERS *first grew olives for their holy oils, but some of it undoubtedly ended up in their Mission pozoleras, for cooking purposes. Later it proved valuable for trading with the Yankees who occasionally put into coastal ports. At Mission San Diego, where they have been pressing oil since the early nineteenth century, a visiting Spaniard once noted that the olive oil was as good, or better than the Spanish. High praise, that, and still deserved.*

Processing ripe olives is a tricky business, but Californians after many trials and tribulations have learned to cure them properly and bring out their rich unctuous flavor. We have also learned to eat them, not only as a relish, but as a food — as a culinary requisite that adds charm and flavor to soups, sauces, entrees, and salads. California has a corner on the ripe olive market and has done well with it. Although ripe olives were unknown to the general public at the turn of the century, they are now found in every grocery store.

The nomenclature of olive packers is amusing: a large olive is not the smallest size packed, but close to it. There are a couple of midgets called "medium" and "select" that are even smaller. But those larger than the large olives are many — extra large, mammoth, giant, jumbo, colossal, supercolossal, and gargantuan. It all happened because California olives kept getting bigger and bigger; what will they do if this keeps up?

As for green olives, they may be an acquired taste, but

it's one that lots of Westerners have. We are now packing them as well as ripe olives. Good ones, too. Then there are our wonderful green ripe olives, considered by many to be the very finest eating in the world. All these olives, as well as the olive oil, are used in our kitchens, as the recipes in this book will show. The dishes that are not perfumed with the oil of the olive are very apt to be studded with the fruit.

❬ Garlic Olives

Ripe olives are even better than usual when prepared in this Californian manner.

Drain juice from a tin of ripe olives. Any size olives may be used, and they may be pitted or not, as you please. (Also they may be crushed gently, so that they burst open, or slit with a sharp knife.) Squash 2 or 3 cloves of garlic, put them in a jar with the olives, cover with olive oil, and allow to stand for at least 2 days before serving.

❬ Olive Notes

Spiced Ripe Olives are made by adding a small red chili pepper, a clove of garlic, and a sprig of dill, to olives in their own brine, along with some olive oil, usually 3 tablespoons to a pint. Sometimes oregano and bay leaf are used instead of dill. They are usually allowed to stand a few days before serving.

Green Olives, given the garlic treatment, are wonderful, too. Crush firm green olives enough to split them open. Put them in a quart jar, add several cloves of crushed garlic, a couple of hot green or red chili peppers, a few whole pickling spices, if you wish, or a head of fresh dill, ¼ cup each of olive oil and vinegar, and fill the jar with the brine in which the olives were packed. Good!

Try serving ripe olives *heated* in their own liquor, either as an appetizer, or as a garnish for meat or fish. Everyone is surprised by them, but pleasantly so.

Pickles and Preserves

EVERY PIONEER *housewife went in for preserving; she had no choice if she wanted to eat, come winter. Today it is usually cheaper and certainly easier to buy our condiments, though not always as satisfactory. A few of our favorites, however, are not always available on the market, so I include the recipes for them here.*

⟦ Cherry Olives

Norma Young, of KHJ, Los Angeles, is well known and well loved by Southern California housewives. This is her recipe — one of them, that is — so popular that she has to give it to her listeners every year. The cherry olives are served as appetizers.

Wash large black cherries, but do not remove either stems or pits. Drain them and put them into pint jars. To each jar add 1 teaspoon each of salt and sugar, and ½ cup of white vinegar. Fill jars to the top with water that has been boiled and cooled. Put on tops and rims, and forget about them for at least 2 weeks before serving.

For each 1 pint black cherries

1 teaspoon salt	*½ cup white vinegar*
1 teaspoon sugar	*Boiled and cooled water*

⟦ Northwest Chutney

We serve curries so often that we have concocted several chutneys from various native fruits to accompany them. This is a good one.

282

Pickles and Preserves

Mix a quart of cider vinegar, 3 cups of sugar, ½ pound of seedless raisins, 6 pounds of peeled and quartered sour apples, ¼ pound of garlic, peeled and cut in tiny slivers, ½ pound of green ginger, blanched and cut into pieces the size of pine needles, 6 chili peppers, peeled, seeded, and cut in slivers, and 2 tablespoons of salt. Cook this very gently until the apples turn into a thick transparent syrup. If too thick, add more vinegar. Taste and add sugar to suit, also cayenne, if you like your chutney hotter. Then add 6 pounds of the hardest, greenest pears you can find, peeled and cut into long segments. Simmer some more until the pears are transparent, but don't let them overcook — the pears are in frank imitation of mangoes, so we want them to keep their form. Pour into sterilized jars and seal.

*1 quart cider vinegar (or
   more)*
3 cups sugar (or more)
½ pound seedless raisins
6 pounds sour apples
¼ pound garlic
½ pound green ginger
6 chili peppers
2 tablespoons salt
Cayenne (optional)
6 pounds hard green pears

(Bodega Dill Beans

String tender young string beans and remove ends, but leave whole. Blanch them for 1 minute in boiling water, then pack in sterilized quart jars. To each jar add 1 chili pepper, a clove of garlic, peeled, and 1 head of dill. Fill with a mixture of 2 cups each of hot water and hot vinegar, and ¼ cup of salt. Seal and keep several weeks before serving. The smaller the beans, the better the pickle. Many persons serve these, well chilled, with cocktails.

For each 1 quart of beans
1 chili pepper   1 clove garlic
1 head dill

As much of this mixture as needed to fill jar
2 cups hot water   2 cups hot vinegar
¼ cup salt

283

⟨ Spiced or Pickled Figs

Many an Easterner has received these delicious figs from
California friends at Christmastime — it's an old favorite way
of preserving them. This particular recipe came from "Lucky"
Baldwin's family, and was given me by KHJ's food commen-
tator, Norma Young. The original recipe was pretty complicated — took seven days to make — but Mrs. Young simplified
it so that it can be made in a few spare minutes during the day.

Wash 4 pounds of firm figs, either black or white ones, and
leave on the stems. Cover them with boiling water and let
stand 5 minutes. Let the figs drain well, then prick each one
2 or 3 times with a fork. Make a syrup with 2½ pounds of
sugar, a cup of vinegar, a cup of water, and a little bag of
spices (either 1 teaspoon each of ground cloves and cinnamon,
or 4 sticks of cinnamon and a teaspoon of whole cloves).
Place over heat, stir until sugar is dissolved, bring to the boil,
and boil for 5 minutes. Now drop in the prepared figs, bring
to the boil, then lower the heat and simmer the figs for 1
hour. Let stand in the syrup for 5 hours, until the fruit is tender
and plump. Reheat to boiling. Pack figs in hot sterilized jars,
cover with boiling syrup, and seal immediately.

4 pounds figs	1 teaspoon ground cloves and 1 tea-
2½ pounds sugar	spoon ground cinnamon or
1 cup vinegar	4 sticks cinnamon and 1 teaspoon
1 cup water	whole cloves

⟨ Preserved Kumquats

This recipe I include because it's a hard one to find in most
general cook books. It was given me by Miss Essie Elliott,
long-time home economist for Sunkist, and long-time loved by
everyone in the food business. Miss Elliott quite naturally
knows her citrus fruits better than most.

Wash a quart of kumquats well and make ½-inch slit in
one side of each. Steam or boil gently for about 10 minutes to
tender the skins, then drain well. Make a syrup of 2 cups of
sugar and 3 cups of water, bringing them to a boil and boiling
for 5 minutes. Add the kumquats, bring again to a boil, then
remove from the fire and set aside overnight. Add ½ cup of

light corn syrup and again bring to the boil. Allow to stand overnight a second time. Repeat this process two or three times, adding corn syrup each time. (Miss Elliott says, "One can go on indefinitely adding syrup and letting the fruit plump and preserve. The very thin syrup at first prevents the shrinkage and collapse of the kumquats, which is so usual when the original syrup is too heavy. I usually stop after three additions of corn syrup and seal them.") These kumquats may be cooked down to the "candied" or thick preserve stage, and dried in the oven for eating as a confection. The seeds may be removed, and this can be done before candying, if desired. Miss Elliott likes them snipped into pieces and mixed into a sweet potato casserole.

1 quart kumquats	*3 cups water*
2 cups sugar	*1½ cups light corn syrup (or more)*

❨ *Onions Tiburon*

This is a pickled onion with the West Coast addition of raisins and white wine. Truly superb!

Put a quart of small white pickling onions in a moderate oven for 5 or 10 minutes. (This will enable you to peel them without a tear.) Peel and scrape, don't cut, the root ends, then cover with 3 cups of white wine and ½ cup of white wine vinegar. Add a tablespoon of tomato paste, 3 tablespoons of olive oil, 3 tablespoons of sugar, a chili pepper, a bay leaf, 3 cloves, and a sprig of thyme — the spices tied together in a cheesecloth. Add ½ cup of white raisins and simmer very slowly until the onions are tender and the sauce thick and golden. (If the sauce is not the right consistency when the onions *are* tender, cook it separately and return to the onions while boiling hot.) Don't let the onions cook too long. Put in sterilized mason jars, and seal.

1 quart small white pickling onions	*3 tablespoons sugar*
3 cups white wine	*1 chili pepper*
½ cup white wine vinegar	*1 bay leaf*
1 tablespoon tomato paste	*3 cloves*
3 tablespoons olive oil	*1 sprig thyme*
½ cup white raisins	

Poultry

❲ *Arroz Con Pollo*

Rice with chicken is a Mexican party dish with a Spanish ancestry. It's rich and filling, with a savoriness that makes it an ideal dish to serve a hungry and appreciative crowd.

Brown a cup of minced onion and a crushed clove of garlic in ½ cup of olive oil. Remove garlic and discard. Remove onion to a deep pot with a cover. Brown 2 cut-up frying chickens in this oil and put in the pot with the onions. Add 1½ cups of rice and brown it in what's left of the oil, stirring carefully. Add it to the chicken, also a cup of fresh or canned tomatoes, 3 cups of water, salt and pepper, and, if you like it, a pinch of saffron, chili powder, or cumin. Cover and simmer ever so slowly until the rice is tender and fairly dry. SERVES 10 TO 12.

1 cup minced onion	*1½ cups rice*
1 clove garlic	*1 cup tomatoes*
½ cup olive oil	*3 cups water*
2 frying chickens	*Salt and pepper*
Pinch of saffron, chili powder, or cumin (optional)	

❲ *Breast of Chicken, Palace*

Here's another recipe generously shared by the Palace Hotel in San Francisco, a hostelry which we on the West Coast will stack up against any in the whole wide world.

"Season breast of chicken and sauté in butter for 10 minutes. Do not permit it to color too much. Allowing 1 slice of Virginia ham for each breast, fry in the same pan for ½ minute only. Add cream (I'd say ⅓ cup to a serving), and, as soon as it comes to a boil, remove chicken breast and ham. Reduce cream to ½ its volume, and add a speck of cayenne and some sherry wine (1 tablespoon to a serving). Finish with a little hollandaise sauce (I use a tablespoon or a little more). Put ham on a piece of buttered toast, top with chicken breast, then three large sautéed mushrooms. Pour on sauce and serve under glass."

For each chicken breast

Butter to sauté   1 tablespoon sherry
1 slice Virginia ham   1 tablespoon hollandaise
⅓ cup cream   3 large sautéed mushrooms
          Speck of cayenne

⟨ Chicken and Chestnuts

Cook a stewing hen until tender. Boil a pound of chestnuts for 8 or 10 minutes. Peel while still warm; the inner skins should come off easily as well as the shell. If not sufficiently tender, cook them in a little chicken stock until they are. Put a layer of chicken, boned and cut into good-sized pieces, in a casserole, then add a layer of chestnuts. Next a layer of diced cooked ham (1 pound), and a layer of tiny parboiled onions (a dozen). Finish with another layer each of chicken and of chestnuts. Pour over a sauce made by cooking ⅓ cup of rendered chicken fat or butter with ⅓ cup of flour, for a couple of minutes, then adding 3 cups of rich chicken stock, a cup of white table wine, and 2 tablespoons of tomato paste, with salt and pepper to taste. Reheat gently in a slow oven. Mushrooms may be used instead of, or as well as, the ham. SERVES 6.

1 stewing hen   ⅓ cup flour
1 pound chestnuts   3 cups chicken stock
1 pound cooked ham   1 cup white wine
12 tiny onions   2 tablespoons tomato paste
⅓ cup chicken fat or butter   Salt and pepper
          Mushrooms (optional)

❬ Chi Bow Gai (*Chicken in Paper*)

This is one of the most entrancing of Chinese dishes. The tender juicy chicken, the delightful seasonings, and the charm of the little paper wraps are all appealing. Though it's to be had at most Chinese restaurants, there are few homemakers who attempt it — a pity, as it's easily made.

Cut pieces of parchment paper, cellophane, or bond paper, or even aluminum foil, into 5-inch squares. Have about 18 of them. Cut pieces of raw (and tender) chicken into chunks about 1-inch square, ½-inch thick. (There should be no gristle or bones, but some of the skin may be left on. Use the bones for a super soup.) Marinate the chicken for 2 or 3 hours in a mixture of ¼ cup of sherry, a crushed clove of garlic, ¼ cup of soy sauce, a tablespoon of cooking oil, and a teaspoon of very finely slivered green ginger. (Otherwise use preserved ginger, rinsed of its syrup, or a little ground ginger.) Turn the meat during the marinating. Rub the center of the paper squares lightly with oil, and put a piece of the chicken in the center of each piece of paper. Top with a tiny leaf of parsley, preferably Chinese (see coriander, page 241), and fold in the following complicated-sounding, but very simple manner. Fold the bottom corner over the chicken so that its point comes 1½ inches below the top corner. Fold first the left and then the right corners over in the same manner, then fold down the top corner and tuck it in at the bottom to secure it between the first fold and the two side folds. Get it? It's really easy, and is a Chinese trick used for all manner of packaging — saves string. Just before serving, fry these papers in deep fat at 350° for 2 minutes. They may be kept warm in the oven for a few minutes, but are better if not reheated. Of course, everything but the frying part may be done hours ahead. SERVES 4.

1 small chicken	¼ cup soy sauce
Squares of paper (5-inch)	1 tablespoon cooking oil
¼ cup sherry	1 teaspoon slivered green
1 clove garlic	ginger

Chinese parsley

Poultry

(Chinese Chicken Wings with Ginger

The wings are apparently looked down upon by dealers in "chicken parts," because they usually sell for the lowest price. That must be because everyone doesn't know this wonderful Chinese way with them.

Marinate a pound of chicken wings for 4 hours in a mixture of ¼ cup of soy sauce, ¾ of a cup of sherry, 2 tablespoons of very finely minced green ginger (or ½ teaspoon of ground), and 2 cloves of thoroughly mashed garlic. After the marinating, drain the wings, dust them with flour, then dip in a batter made by adding 1 egg and ⅓ cup of the marinade to ½ cup of flour. (If this seems too thick, add a bit more of the marinade.) Fry in deep fat at 360° until the chicken is well browned and tender, and the coating crisp. Serves four if it is the only entree.

1 pound chicken wings

MARINADE

¼ cup soy sauce   2 tablespoons minced green ginger or
¾ cup sherry   ½ teaspoon ground ginger
2 cloves garlic

BATTER

1 egg
⅓ cup marinade (or more)
½ cup flour

(Chicken Casserole St. Helena

This recipe does not come from the *St. Helena Cook Book,* published in 1883. The chicken recipes in that little book, which is also titled *How to Win a Heart,* consist of a rule for baked chicken, which turns out to be broiled, one for chicken pie that is very dull, and *three* for chicken croquettes. Lovisa Thompson, who wrote the book, apparently didn't approve of wine in her cooking, but then Napa, at that time, hadn't the famous wineries that it has today.

Have 2 frying chickens disjointed, roll them in seasoned flour, and then sauté in ¼ cup each of olive oil and butter, with a clove of garlic. Make a bed in your largest casserole — a bed of a large onion, sliced, 2 tablespoons of minced parsley, 1 sliced carrot, 2 chopped stalks of celery, and an herb bouquet. Discard garlic, arrange chicken on this herb bed, swirl the sauté pan with 2 cups of white table wine, and pour over the chicken. Cover and cook in a 350° oven until tender, turning once or twice during the cooking. While the chicken is in the oven, make about 18 potato balls and parboil them until just *under*done. Peel the same number of baby onions — walnut-sized — and cook them until also *not quite* done. Sauté 18 mushroom caps — good-sized ones — for 3 minutes in 2 tablespoons of butter. Now your chicken is done. Remove it from the casserole and, carefully as possible, slip out the bones. Put them to simmer with a cup of water. Now strain off every bit of juice in the casserole, pressing it from the vegetables in a strainer, but not forcing it through. Discard these cooked vegetables. To the juices add the water on the bones and enough more white wine and butter to make 4 cups. Season to taste, and bind with a roux of ¼ cup each of butter and flour. Arrange the boned chicken in a casserole and top with the vegetables, having a ring of the potatoes around the outer edge, then the mushrooms, then the onions. (If you wish, you may put green peas in the very middle.) Pour on the sauce and when ready to serve, heat in the oven, basting a little of the sauce over the vegetables so that they will become prettily glazed. This is a one-dish meal. SERVES 6 TO 8.

CHICKEN

2 *frying chickens*	2 *tablespoons minced parsley*
¼ *cup olive oil*	1 *carrot*
¼ *cup butter*	2 *stalks celery*
1 *clove garlic*	1 *herb bouquet*
1 *large onion*	2 *cups white wine*

VEGETABLES

18 potato balls	*18 mushroom caps*
18 baby onions	*2 tablespoons butter*

SAUCE

Chicken bones	*¼ cup flour*
1 cup water	*¼ cup butter*
Juice from chicken	*Salt and pepper*
White wine and butter as	
needed	

《 Chicken Lomas del Rio

This is the recipe of Robert Lawrence Balzer, an authority on California wines, cookery, and fine groceries. Author of *California's Best Wines,* he has shared his vinous knowledge with me generously.

Have a 3-pound frying chicken disjointed, sprinkle it freely with salt and freshly ground pepper, and brown it on all sides in ¼ pound of butter. Remove the chicken to an earthenware casserole and add 2 tablespoons of flour to the pan, smoothing out any roughness. Pour on a bottle of Pinot blanc or similar white wine, add a dozen small onions and an herb bouquet, and add this mixture to the chicken. Cover and cook slowly, either on top of the stove, or in the oven, until the chicken is tender. Rectify the seasonings, bind the sauce with a roux of 3 tablespoons each of flour and butter, cook another minute or so, and serve with plenty of French bread for dunking purposes. SERVES 3 OR 4.

1 3–pound frying chicken	*5 tablespoons flour*
Salt and pepper	*1 bottle white wine*
¼ pound and 3 tablespoons	*12 small onions*
butter	*1 herb bouquet*

《 Chicken Marangot

This recipe is adapted from one in the section called "French Department" (many old cook books had foreign "departments") in the first Los Angeles cook book, *Los Angeles*

Cookery, 1881. It is obviously a recipe for chicken Marengo with a Californian touch. It could be made, said the donor, with rabbit or leg of lamb.

Have a frying chicken cut in serving pieces. Heat a clove of garlic in 2 tablespoons each of olive oil and butter, remove garlic, then brown chicken in this mixture. Remove chicken to a casserole, add 2 tablespoons of butter to the pan, and in it lightly brown ½ pound of mushroom caps. To this add a cup of fresh chopped tomatoes, a cup of California white wine, and salt and pepper. Pour a jigger of California brandy over the chicken, light it, and allow the flames to die out. Pour the other mixture over the chicken and cook in the oven until the meat is tender. Sprinkle with minced parsley before serving. The only way it isn't like the classic chicken Marengo is that there are no heart-shaped croutons or fried eggs as a garnish. SERVES 3 OR 4.

1 frying chicken	*½ pound mushroom caps*
1 clove garlic	*1 cup chopped tomatoes*
2 tablespoons olive oil	*1 cup white wine*
4 tablespoons butter	*Salt and pepper*
1 jigger brandy	

⟨ Mexican Chicken Cazuela

A *cazuela* is an earthenware pot, used by the Mexicans for many cooking purposes. It has a rounded bottom and handles at either side, and is placed directly over the heat. We find it a useful vessel for salads, and for casseroles as well. This recipe, named after the pot itself, was not baked in the early days, but stewed, and the peppers then used were of the chili variety.

Have a frying chicken cut into serving pieces, brown lightly in 4 tablespoons of chicken fat, remove chicken to another pan, cover with water, add a clove of garlic and salt, and boil until the chicken is tender. In the pan in which the chicken was browned, put 2 chopped onions and 2 chopped green peppers. Cook until wilted, then add 2 tablespoons of flour, a cup of the chicken broth, and 2 cups of stewed tomatoes. Add a cup of pitted ripe olives. Grate 8 large ears of corn and put a layer of it in a buttered baking dish. Now add a layer of chicken (pulled from the bones in as large pieces as possible), then a layer of the tomato mixture. Repeat until the ingredients are used, ending with a layer of corn. Put slices of bacon over the top, and bake until all is hot, and the bacon crispy. SERVES 3 OR 4.

1 frying chicken	2 tablespoons flour
4 tablespoons chicken fat	1 cup chicken broth
1 clove garlic	2 cups stewed tomatoes
Salt	1 cup pitted ripe olives
2 onions	8 ears corn
2 green peppers	Bacon

(*Chicken Sauté with Artichokes*

Have a 3- to 4-pound frying chicken cut in serving pieces, dust with salt and pepper, and sauté in ¼ cup of butter. In the meantime, cut 3 artichokes in quarters, lengthwise, remove chokes and all the tough bottom leaves, and cut off the tops halfway or more down. When the chicken is lightly browned, add the artichokes, 2 tablespoons of olive oil, and a clove of garlic. Also add 1¼ cups of white table wine, cover, and cook until the artichokes are tender, about half an hour or a little longer. (If the chicken is done before the artichokes, remove it temporarily — nothing's worse than overdone poultry.) Now artichokes and chicken are removed to a hot platter, and the garlic fished out of the sauce. Three egg yolks are beaten with a cup of heavy cream and added to the sauce, along with a teaspoon of lemon juice. It is cooked gently until thickened, the seasoning corrected, and it is poured over the chicken and artichokes which are, I hope, still hot. SERVES 3 OR 4.

3–4 pound frying chicken	1 clove garlic
Salt and pepper	1¼ cups white wine
¼ cup butter	3 egg yolks
3 artichokes	1 cup heavy cream
2 tablespoons olive oil	1 teaspoon lemon juice

⟨ California Chicken Tarragon

Tarragon is a favorite herb on the West Coast, as you've no doubt discovered by now. We use it in many ways, but of all of them, we like it best with chicken.

Have a tender frying chicken cut in serving pieces and dust it with flour that has been seasoned with salt and pepper (1 teaspoon salt, a few grindings of pepper, to ½ cup of flour). Brown gently and evenly in ¼ cup of olive oil, or butter, or a combination of the two. When the chicken is nicely browned and all but tender, add ½ cup of white table wine, and a tablespoon of fresh tarragon leaves, minced fine. Cover and finish cooking the chicken, but don't cook to a dry and stringy state. If it is a young one, and it should be, it will take 20 to 26 minutes. Now arrange the chicken on a hot platter, strain the sauce over it, and garnish with whole leaves of fresh tarragon. If the fresh herb is unavailable, use half the amount of the dried, soaking it in a couple of tablespoons of white wine. The garnish, in that case, will have to be omitted. SERVES 3 OR 4.

1 frying chicken   ½ cup flour
1 teaspoon salt   ¼ cup olive oil or butter
Pepper   ½ cup white wine
        1 tablespoon minced tarragon

⟨ Chicken Raphael Weill

This is a famous chicken recipe named after a famous San Franciscan businessman and amateur chef. He was founder of the White House, still one of the San Francisco's leading department stores. A member of the Bohemian Club, he followed in Joe Tilden's footsteps as a cook of real talent, and his portrait, complete with chef's cap and apron, still hangs in that club. There seems to be some question as to whether this dish was created by Mr. Weill or named in his honor. There is no doubt, however, that he was capable of creating such a dish — he personally arranged the menus of many of the most important dinners at the Bohemian Club. He was also entrusted to select the wines for the great who visited San Francisco, among them two charming ladies — Melba and Bernhardt.

Have a 3-pound chicken disjointed. Squash 2 cloves of garlic or 4 shallots, and put them to "melt" in ¼ cup of butter. Add the chicken, seasoned with salt and *white* pepper, but do not brown. Flame with a jigger of brandy, then add ½ cup of chicken stock, ½ cup of white wine, and an herb bouquet with parsley and tarragon. Cook until tender in a covered casserole, and serve with a sauce made by adding 1½ cups of heavy cream to what's left of the juices in the casserole, seasoning with 2 tablespoons of sherry and salt and pepper (again white — this is a white dish), and thickening with 3 egg yolks. (Heat cream, beat a little of it into the egg yolks, then add the yolks gradually to the rest of the cream, whipping the while.) Minced parsley is sometimes sprinkled on the chicken before it is sauced. Today many San Francisco restaurants include mushrooms in this dish, a perfectly reasonable addition, though some call it unauthentic. SERVES 3 OR 4.

1 3–pound chicken	*1 jigger brandy*
2 cloves garlic (or 4 shallots)	*½ cup chicken stock*
¼ cup butter	*½ cup white wine*
Salt and white pepper	*1 herb bouquet*

SAUCE

1½ cups heavy cream   *Salt and white pepper*
2 tablespoons sherry   *3 egg yolks*
Juices in casserole in which chicken has cooked

(*Chicken Portola*

Don Gaspar de Portola, first governor of the Californias, was not smitten with the charms of his bailiwick. In spite of this California continues to respect his memory, and has even named a dish in his honor. Several cooks have claimed to have originated this recipe, but there seems little doubt that credit belongs to Coppa, a famed restaurateur of prefire days in San Francisco. Anyway, this version is his, more or less as it appeared in *Bohemian San Francisco*, by Clarence Edwords.

Allow 1 coconut for each serving. Saw off the top, about ⅙ of the way down. (It's worth hunting up a power saw for this job, but it can be done by hand.) Using a very strong spoon, scoop out a good part of the coconut meat. Try to do this evenly, leaving about ¼-inch lining of coconut meat in the shell. For each 4 servings, allow 1 frying chicken, cut so that the breast is in 4 pieces, and the legs and thighs separated. Brown the chicken lightly in ¼ cup of olive oil and set aside. To the oil remaining in the pan add 4 slices of bacon, cut in dice, a large onion, chopped, a large green pepper, also chopped, and a clove of garlic that has been ground in a mortar with a teaspoon of salt. Let this cook quietly until the vegetables are limp, then add 3 cups of peeled chopped tomatoes (or canned, if you must), a few grindings of black pepper, and salt if needed. Simmer 30 minutes, then add 3 ears of green corn, grated, and ⅓ cup of the coconut meat, also grated. Divide the chicken among the shells in your most judicious manner — a piece of dark meat and a piece of white to each shell. Fill with the sauced vegetables, and cover the rim of the coconut with a paste made of flour and water, and replace top. Set the shells in a pan containing an inch or so of water, and bake at 350° for 1½ hours, basting with water once or twice so that the shells won't get too dry. The original recipe strained the vegetables, all but the coconut, from the sauce, but I can't see why. SERVES 4.

4 coconuts	1 clove garlic
1 frying chicken	1 teaspoon salt (or more)
¼ cup olive oil	3 cups chopped tomatoes
4 slices bacon	3 ears corn
1 large onion	⅓ cup coconut meat
1 large green pepper	Pepper

Flour and water

NOTE: *Chicken in a Shell,* another early San Francisco specialty, was quite different. It was chicken in a sherry-flavored sauce, which was made with cream and egg yolks. Sliced sautéed mushrooms were added, and the mixture was served in cockleshells!

(*Chicken Notes*

Chicken with Vermouth. Add pitted ripe olives and blanched almonds to creamed chicken. Flavor with French vermouth to taste.

Chinese Chicken with Oyster Sauce. This is quite different from the pioneer version, naturally. The chicken is boned and cut up in small chunks, then marinated in soy sauce, sherry, green onions, and a tiny bit of honey. It is then dusted with cornstarch and fried until tender (a very short time), and served with Chinese oyster sauce — available in Chinatown.

Sweet and Sour Chicken. Steam chicken, then brown in oil, cut in pieces, combine with pineapple chunks, blanched almonds, green pepper cubes, and sweet and sour sauce.

Walnut Chicken. Cook chicken as in Chinese Chicken with Oyster Sauce. Blanch a cup of walnuts. Make sauce with soy sauce, sherry, green onions, chicken stock, and cornstarch. Combine. Almonds may be used instead of walnuts.

Occidental Chicken in Paper. This couldn't be more unlike the Chinese dish and still be chicken in paper. A half of a very small chicken is placed on a slice of cooked ham and topped with minced shallots, mushrooms, and parsley. A goodly hunk of butter is added, and the whole wrapped carefully in parchment paper. Bake in a hot oven about ½ hour, and serve in the paper.

Broiled Chicken. Remove backbone from split broilers before grilling. (Throw them in the soup pot.) This will make them prettier and easier to eat.

❬ Chicken Liver Ring

Grind 1 pound of chicken livers, then push them through a sieve to remove veins. Mix with a cup of hot cream, 2 tablespoons of sherry, 6 eggs, ½ teaspoon of tarragon seasoning powder, ½ teaspoon of salt, and some pepper. Put in a well-greased ring mold, put mold in a pan half filled with hot water, and bake at 325° until it is set. Unmold and fill center with creamed mushrooms or creamed asparagus. SERVES 6.

1 pound chicken livers	½ teaspoon tarragon seasoning
1 cup cream	powder
2 tablespoons sherry	½ teaspoon salt
6 eggs	Pepper

❬ Chicken Livers with Pineapple, Chinese Style

Cut a pound of chicken livers in halves, dip them in soy sauce, and brown lightly in ¼ cup of bland oil. Add 4 pineapple slices, cut in chunks, and ½ cup of split blanched almonds, or Chinese almonds. Heat for a minute, then pour on a sauce made by thickening 1¼ cups of pineapple juice, ¼ cup of vinegar, ¼ teaspoon of salt, and ¼ cup of sugar, with 2 tablespoons of cornstarch. Add prepared Chinese peas, about a cup of them, if available. Cook 2 minutes, and serve with rice. But good. SERVES 4.

1 pound chicken livers	¼ cup oil
Soy sauce	4 slices pineapple
½ cup split blanched almonds	

SAUCE

1¼ cups pineapple juice	¼ cup sugar
¼ cup vinegar	2 tablespoons cornstarch
¼ teaspoon salt	1 cup Chinese peas (if available)

❬ Chinese Pressed Duck

Here's another of those celestial dishes.

Have a duckling split down the back, and boil it in water to cover, but don't drown it. When tender, remove the bones very carefully, flatten the meat out on a pan, put another pan on top, and weigh it down with an iron or something else that's good and heavy. Let stand until very cold, then dust with flour and brown in oil. Make a sauce with ½ cup of the duck stock, ¼ cup of sherry, and 2 tablespoons of soy sauce, and thicken it with a tablespoon of cornstarch and ½ teaspoon of almond extract. Cut the duck in neat-as-can-be squares, paint with the sauce, and sprinkle very thickly with coarsely chopped toasted almonds. SERVES 6.

1 duckling	2 tablespoons soy sauce
Oil	1 tablespoon cornstarch
½ cup duck stock	½ teaspoon almond extract
¼ cup sherry	Chopped toasted almonds

NOTE: Another Oriental way with duck is to skin and bone it (or just skin it, if that suits you better), cut it in serving pieces (right through the bone), and marinate in ½ cup of California sherry, 2 tablespoons of soy sauce, and 2 tablespoons of honey. Cook, covered, until tender, then uncover and finish in a moderate oven until brown.

❨ Duck with Olives

Have a 5-pound duck disjointed and cut into convenient pieces for serving. Cover wing tips, feet, giblets, and neck with water, add an herb bouquet and an onion, and simmer until a rich stock is obtained. Add the duck liver and cook another 10 minutes. In the meantime, dredge the duck in seasoned flour and brown in 3 tablespoons of butter. Remove to an earthenware casserole. Chop the liver and giblets and return them to the stock, which has been disembarrassed of the other ingredients, and pour over the duck, along with ½ cup of white wine. Cook in a 350° oven until the duck is almost tender. Skim the sauce of all fat — using one of those giant eye-dropper basters if you have one — and to it add 1¼ cups of green olives, cut from their stones. Correct seasoning, pour back into the casserole, and cook for another 15 minutes. SERVES 4 OR 5.

1 5-pound duck	3 tablespoons butter
1 herb bouquet	½ cup white wine
1 onion	1¼ cups green olives
Salt and pepper	

⟨ Duck with Oranges

Orange and olives, both Californian of course, each claim top billing when prepared with duck. Which wins is a matter impossible to decide. Both are so completely delicious.

Roast a duck, stuffed with quartered orange, at 350° for 2 to 2½ hours, basting a few times with orange juice. Make a sauce by cutting the zest (very outside orange skin) from 2 oranges, and cutting it in strips the size of halved toothpicks. Poach them for 5 minutes. Now peel the 2 oranges deeply, and cut them in segments, discarding seeds. Make a roux in the duck pan — pour off excess fat, leaving but two tablespoons, add two tablespoons of flour, brown well. Then stir in a cup of orange juice, a tablespoon of lemon juice, and ½ cup of consommé. Strain, add zest, correct seasonings, then add orange segments just long enough to heat them. Serve duck garnished with the segments, and pass the sauce. SERVES 4 OR 5.

1 duck
1 orange
Orange juice

SAUCE

Zest and segments from 2 oranges
2 tablespoons duck fat
2 tablespoons flour

1 cup orange juice
1 tablespoon lemon juice
½ cup consommé
Salt and pepper

⟨ Chinese Squab with Asparagus

Not surprisingly, there were few squab recipes in early cook books, and they weren't mentioned in the hotel menus of the last century, at least in those which have come to my attention. The Hotel del Coronado, in 1896, has a "squab à la casserole," and a recipe for "squab en casserole" appears in a book of the '90s, but doesn't seem worth perpetuating. Not so, the Chinese recipes for squab. They cook it exquisitely.

Cut 3 squabs into 2-inch pieces without removing their

300

bones. (Do this with a heavy sharp knife, or a pair of poultry shears.) Brown them in ⅓ cup of oil until tender. Add a cup of sliced mushrooms, a cup of sliced water chestnuts, and a cup of asparagus, sliced diagonally; also a cup of chicken stock, cover, and cook 4 minutes, then remove squab and vegetables to a hot serving dish. Make a sauce in the same pan by adding enough stock to make 1½ cups, ¼ cup of sherry, 2 tablespoons of soy sauce, and 2 tablespoons of cornstarch. Pour over squab and vegetables, and serve. SERVES 3 TO 6.

3 squabs	*1 cup chicken stock (and*
⅓ cup oil	*more as needed)*
1 cup sliced mushrooms	*¼ cup sherry*
1 cup sliced water chestnuts	*2 tablespoons soy sauce*
1 cup sliced asparagus	*2 tablespoons cornstarch*

❨ *Squab Felipe*

Allow ½ cup of cooked wild rice, a shallot, and 4 mushrooms for each jumbo squab. Chop shallot and mushrooms, and sauté in a tablespoon of butter. Add a slice of bacon, diced and fried crisp, and a teaspoon of minced parsley, along with the rice. Stuff squabs, truss them, and brush with melted butter. Bake at 350° for 45 minutes, or until tender, basting with a mixture of melted butter and white wine.

For each 1 jumbo squab

½ cup cooked wild rice	*1 tablespoon butter*
1 shallot	*1 slice bacon*
4 mushrooms	*1 teaspoon minced parsley*

BASTING SAUCE

1 part melted butter
1 part white wine

NOTE: The stuffing made with bean sprouts, as in Roast Pheasant Mateo (page 226), is superb with squab.

❨ Turkey

An early Thanksgiving menu, dated 1882, does not include turkey, but that noble bird appears on the Palace Hotel New Year's Day dinner for 1882, and at the Raymond Hotel, Pasadena, in 1886 and 1888. Even earlier, in 1872, a Sacramento banquet, given in honor of the Japanese Embassy, featured turkey, cranberry sauce, and *brown oyster sauce*, so once more oysters turn up in combination with other meats.

As everybody knows, or can find out, how to roast a turkey, it seems pretty silly to give a conventional recipe for one here. The only difference in ours — and at that in only some — is that we are apt to baste the bird with wine. And all of us, except teetotalers, serve wine with our holiday birds. We like plain dressing, or that made with oysters, chestnuts, almonds, or walnuts, and recently we have discovered the charm of water chestnuts added to the stuffing.

Today turkey is an all-the-year-round food in our Far Western states. It is plentiful and comparatively inexpensive — particularly the large toms — so it's apt to appear at party meals, even on July the Fourth!

❨ Barbecued Turkey Steaks

These are a new departure and can be very good indeed. A large tom turkey, and it has to be a frozen one, is cut in cross-section slices, 1-inch thick, on a power meat saw. Thus you have steaks, some of which are all white meat, some part dark meat, and some all dark meat. (And there's one time when I think the white meat is far superior to the dark; so, as I think dark meat is far better when cooked in other ways, I don't have that cut in steaks, but bake or steam it, and use it in other turkey dishes.) Marinate the steaks for 3 or 4 hours in one part oil and one part white wine — herbed if you wish. Broil over charcoal, basting with the marinade. The time is usually about 10 minutes, more or less, depending on the heat of your fire.

302

Poultry

(Broiled Baby Turkey

These are becoming tremendously popular, particularly at the barbecue. Weighing from 6 to 8 pounds, these plump little babies are split and broiled with a basting of white wine, melted butter, and the herb of your choice — ours is apt to be tarragon. They may be done indoors, but, not surprisingly, they taste better when done at the barbecue, or at least over charcoal. A good baste is 1 cup each of white wine and melted butter (or oil), and ¼ cup of minced fresh tarragon.

(Turkey Cabrillo

This is a popular dish made with breast of turkey, which can often be purchased separately.

Steam a turkey breast until tender, but don't let it overcook and dry out. Arrange a bed of cooked and seasoned broccoli on a platter, cover with a cup of mornay sauce. (Did you know that that sauce was supposed to have originated in San Francisco, at the famed Bohemian Club?) Slice the turkey breast, arrange on the broccoli, completely cover with more mornay sauce, sprinkle with Parmesan, and brown under the broiler.

NOTE: A recipe for mornay sauce, which is a rich cheese sauce, can be found in any good cook book — except this one, that is.

(Mole de Guajolote (Turkey Mole)

The story goes that this complicated dish was evolved by some Mexican nuns who wanted to give their all to a visiting church dignitary. Their all was everything in the kitchen, including three kinds of chili peppers and innumerable spices and chocolate. Elena Zelayeta, an expert on Mexican cooking, and one of the finest cooks on the West Coast, has a wonderful recipe for it in her *Elena's Famous Mexican and Spanish Recipes* — a very complicated one, too. At the end of the recipe Elena adds, characteristically, "P.S. If this seems too much trouble, you can buy canned mole sauce at Mexican food stores!" Amen.

⟪ Walnut-Fattened Turkey

This, from the first Los Angeles cook book, shows that the geese of Perigord hadn't much on us when it came to stuffing: this poor bird was stuffed before and after it was killed. I think it's amusing enough to quote the recipe exactly, particularly as the "stuffing" (used before the bird was killed) was seasoned, as well as the "dressing," used afterwards.

To Fatten a Turkey, Make the Dressing, and Roast It.

Get your turkey six weeks before you need it; put him in a coop just large enough to let him walk, or in a small yard; give him walnuts — one the first day, and increase every day one till he has nine; then go back to one and up to nine until you kill him, stuffing him twice with corn meal dough each day, in which put a little chopped onion and celery, if you have it. For the dressing, use bread, picked up fine, a table spoonful of butter, some sage, thyme, chopped onion, pepper, salt, and the yolks of two eggs, and pour in a little boiling water to make it stick together; before putting it in the turkey pour boiling water inside and outside, to cleanse and plump it; then roast it in a tin kitchen, basting all the time. It will be splendid, served with a nice piece of ham and cranberry sauce.

A "tin kitchen" was one of those tin ovens that was placed on top of the range — or at least that's *my* guess.

⟪ Notes on Stuffings

Oyster Stuffing. A favorite, quite naturally. Add 2 cups of chopped raw oysters to the basic dressing, omitting vegetables, if you wish.

Almond or Walnut Stuffing. Add 1 cup of slivered toasted almonds, or 1 cup of coarsely chopped walnuts to the basic stuffing.

Green Olive Stuffing. Add 1 cup of chopped green olives to the basic stuffing, and omit green pepper.

Cranberry Stuffing. Add 2 cups of ground raw cranberries to the basic stuffing, along with ¾ cup of sugar. Omit vegetables and poultry seasoning, but add nuts if desired. Good for duck or goose.

Mushroom Stuffing. Add a pound of sautéed sliced mushrooms to the basic stuffing, but omit green pepper and half the onions.

Water Chestnut Stuffing. This is a new favorite with us all. Add a cup or 2 cups of coarsely chopped water chestnuts to the basic stuffing, but omit poultry seasoning, using instead 2 teaspoons of grated fresh ginger.

Ripe Olive Stuffing. Add 1 cup of sliced ripe olives to the basic stuffing, and use half olive oil and half butter. Omit poultry seasoning, and use ½ teaspoon of oregano instead, and crush a clove of garlic with the salt.

Liver and Walnut Stuffing. Add ½ cup diced cooked liver and ½ cup of walnuts to the basic stuffing. Moisten with ¼ cup of California brandy.

Prune Stuffing. Add 2 cups of soaked prunes, chopped, to half of the basic stuffing. Omit high seasoning and onions, but use red wine to moisten.

Orange Stuffing. Add grated orange rind instead of poultry seasoning to the basic stuffing. Also ¼ teaspoon of rosemary or basil if desired.

Salads

VISITORS *to our Coast never fail to be impressed by our salads. Whether it's their excellence, which we modestly acknowledge, or the fact that we serve them as a first course which awes them, we are not sure. Actually, that salad-first custom, though almost invariably followed in restaurants, is not so common at home; we are quite as apt to serve them with or after the entree, as before it. Still it would be fun to know what started the restaurants on this curious habit, and when. Menus are of little help in the matter, because they simply don't agree. The very earliest menus, such as that of the Fashion Restaurant in San Francisco, in 1859, doesn't even mention salad. A Sacramento menu of 1863 lists it after the oysters but before the roast, as do the Lick House and the Occidental Hotel in 1876. Yet the Palace, that same year, and again at later dates, lists the salad after the roast. "Ma Tante," who ran a restaurant in early San Francisco in which she served food family-style, always appeared first with a huge bowl of salad — probably to keep hungry men at peace until the table was completely filled. As for cook books, they are no help. One called* How to Win a Heart, *published in San Francisco in 1883, lists salad as mandatory after the main course at lunch, but omits it entirely for dinner. The other old cook books simply give a few "salad" recipes, mostly for chicken salad, boiled dressing, and mayonnaise, but never mention how it was served.*

Today everyone on the Coast likes salads, even the chil-

dren, and most of them eat at least one a day. We make the ordinary ones just as they are made elsewhere, but our own salads — the salads that we have created or improved upon — are those in which we take such pride!

⟪ Abalone Salad

Cook abalone lightly (or use canned), cut in cubes, marinate in French dressing, and serve with mayonnaise that has had chopped lemon pulp and minced parsley added. (Use the pulp of half a lemon, seeded, and a tablespoon of parsley, to each cup of mayonnaise.)

⟪ Avocado Salad

Avocados on the half shell, their centers filled with a dressing made with ½ cup each of wine vinegar and olive oil, and 2 tablespoons each of minced parsley, green pepper, and green onions, is a fine dish, either as a first course or as a salad.

DRESSING

½ cup wine vinegar	2 tablespoons minced green
½ cup olive oil	pepper
2 tablespoons minced parsley	2 tablespoons minced green onions

⟪ Bean Sprout Salad

Our markets usually have fresh bean sprouts for the Oriental populace, but we find that they can be used in dishes other than Chinese and Japanese. This salad is an example of how East and West can meet.

For 1 pound of bean sprouts, make a dressing with 3 tablespoons each of soy sauce, sherry wine, and lime juice, and ⅔ of a cup of salad oil, 3 tablespoons of minced green onion, and a teaspoon of grated fresh ginger. Pour over raw bean sprouts, mix well, and top with toasted slivered almonds. Allow to stand a few hours before serving. SERVES 8.

1 *pound bean sprouts*	3 *tablespoons minced green*
3 *tablespoons soy sauce*	*onion*
3 *tablespoons sherry*	1 *teaspoon grated fresh*
3 *tablespoons lime juice*	*ginger*
⅔ *cup salad oil*	

NOTE: If "sesamum oiler," which is a Chinese oil made from toasted sesame seeds, is available, use ⅓ cup of it and ⅓ cup of plain oil. The bean sprouts should be blanched for 30 seconds in boiling water if it is desired to serve the salad without standing. If the roots have started to form on the sprouts, it will be necessary to pick them off, otherwise washing is sufficient preparation.

❲ *Caesar Salad*

And now we come to it — the most talked-of salad of a decade, perhaps of the century. Like all recipes that have become widely known, several chefs and restaurateurs have claimed to have originated the salad. Actually many of them *have* had a hand in promoting it, though not necessarily as a Caesar. As for its origin, the best guess seems to be that the whole thing started in Tia Juana, during prohibition, but whether it was actually created by one named "Caesar," or just named for him, is a matter of considerable discussion. The salad is at its best when it is kept simple, but, as it is invariably made at table, and sometimes by show-offs, it occasionally contains far too many ingredients. This is a simple version.

Crush a clove of garlic and add it to ¾ of a cup of olive oil. Let stand overnight. Brown 2 cups of croutons, made from stale sourdough French bread, in ¼ cup of this garlic oil, stirring them carefully so that they will color on all sides. Drain on paper toweling. (Or, if you prefer, merely toast the bread cubes brown in a slow oven.) Now break 2 large or 3 small heads of romaine into a large bowl, grind on a good generous amount of fresh black pepper and add ½ teaspoon of salt, then dress with ½ cup of the garlic oil. Turn the salad until every leaf is glossy with oil, then break 2 eggs, cooked *one* minute, plunk into the middle of the salad. Now, before the mixing is resumed, squeeze the juice of a big fat lemon directly over the egg (if the lemon is small, use 1½ or even 2 of them!), and mix so that there is a thick creamy look to the lettuce. If you wish to include fillets of anchovies, and many say you *must*, here is where they are added — 6 or 8, snipped into bits. Now taste it, and don't hesitate to use your fingers. More salt? More lemon? Add them, or vinegar if you wish, plenty of experts do so. (And others insist on a slug of Worcestershire!) The seasoning is now as you want it, so a good ½ cup (at least) of grated Parmesan is tossed in, the salad mixed some more, and finally the croutons are added, and the salad served at once so they won't become limp and soggy. Like any salad of this kind, the artist adds (or subtracts) as he goes along, so Caesar salad, as *you* make it, is all your own! SERVES A DOZEN, MORE OR LESS.

1 clove garlic	*Pepper*
¾ cup olive oil	*2 eggs*
2 cups croutons	*Juice of a large lemon*
2–3 heads romaine	*6–8 fillets of anchovies (optional)*
½ teaspoon salt	*½ cup grated Parmesan*

NOTE: *Commonwealth Salad.* This just shows what can happen when someone starts playing around with Caesar Salad: Dress 2 heads of romaine, broken into pieces, and a large cucumber, diced, with a cup of sour cream, a teaspoon of salt, 2 tablespoons of melted butter, some fresh ground pepper, a 1-minute egg, the juice of 2 lemons, ½ cup of grated Parmesan, and a cup of croutons, toasted, not fried, brown. This is good and would still be good if the cheese were omitted.

ℂ Celery Victor

Here's a world-famous salad that was originated by Chef Victor Hirtzler, of the superb St. Francis Hotel of San Francisco. This is the recipe as they gave it to me, and as they now serve it at the hotel.

"Take a head of celery, cut the stem and scrape the leaves. Wash well and parboil for 5 minutes. Cool off and drain. Lay the celery in a pot and cook in good chicken broth with onions, carrots, and kitchen bouquet. Salt to taste. When cooked, let cool off in broth. Drain and dish up on a plate and arrange on top of celery a slice of hard-boiled egg, a slice of tomato, another slice of egg, and another slice of tomato (alternately), and serve with French dressing. Also can be served with crab legs."

NOTE: Sometimes chef's recipes seem a little vague to the layman. Just in case, here's an explanation or two. Hearts of celery are usually used for Celery Victor, and they are often split in half, the root end trimmed nicely, and the leaves, all but the baby ones, removed. The celery is cooked lying flat in a shallow pan with enough well-seasoned chicken stock to cover, and an herb bouquet. When it is just tender, it is allowed to cool in the stock, which is then drained off (there's a wonderful soup!) and as much excess stock as possible pressed from the celery. It is arranged in a serving dish, or on individual dishes, sprinkled with coarsely ground fresh pepper, and chopped chervil and parsley. It is then covered with French dressing made from 1 part of tarragon vinegar to 2 parts of olive oil. Chill, and serve as a salad or first course. It may be garnished as above, with tomato and egg slices, or with crab legs. It is also often served with a couple of anchovy fillets crossed over it, and sometimes pimiento strips.

NOTE: Idwal Jones, gourmet and author of *Vines in the Sun,* tells me that Victor himself always used a very sharp white wine vinegar when making his most renowned dish.

NOTE TO THE THRIFTY: A very reasonable facsimile of Celery Victor may be made with the *outside* stalks of the celery. Scrape them, cook in the seasoned stock as above, then stack 2 or 3 pieces together, one inside another, and cut them diagonally into neat parallelograms. Dress as above, using 2 or 3 pieces to a serving.

(Chestnut Salad

This is a salad from an old Californian cook book — one that should be revived.

Combine 1 pound of boiled sliced chestnuts with 2 cups of sliced celery, and mix with 1 cup each of mayonnaise and sour cream, seasoned with a few drops of lime juice, some salt, and a speck of cayenne. Serve on lettuce. Nice idea, don't you think? And wouldn't a garnish of stuffed green olives be good? SERVES 10 OR 12.

> 1 pound chestnuts
> 2 cups sliced celery
> 1 cup mayonnaise
> 1 cup sour cream
> Few drops lime juice
> Salt
> Speck of cayenne

(Almond Cucumber Salad

Peel and slice 2 cucumbers thinner than you think possible, then sprinkle them with salt. Make a dressing of 1 cup of sour cream, ¼ cup of chopped almonds, 2 tablespoons of minced chives, a teaspoon of lemon juice, and ½ teaspoon of salt. Drain cucumbers, pour on dressing, and serve. SERVES 6.

> 2 cucumbers
> ½ teaspoon salt (and more as needed)
> 1 cup sour cream
> ¼ cup chopped almonds
> 2 tablespoons minced chives
> 1 teaspoon lemon juice

(Cold Cucumbers, Chinese Style

This is as close as the Chinese ever come to a salad.

Slice unpeeled cucumbers very thin, and marinate them in equal parts of soy sauce, vinegar, and bland vegetable oil.

> *Unpeeled cucumbers*
>
> MARINADE
>
> 1 part soy sauce   1 part vinegar
> 1 part bland vegetable oil

NOTE: Cauliflower, raw and sliced, or radishes, either sliced or *crushed*, may be dressed in the same manner.

⟪ White Cucumber Salad

This is one of the world's best salads — it is particularly good with fish, but is also a fine "extra" salad, when more than one is wanted at a buffet. The salad is devoid of greenery, which will stop those characters who mutter about rabbit food and Nebuchadnezzar.

Slice peeled cucumbers very thin. For each large cucumber add a tablespoon of grated onion to ½ cup of mayonnaise. Arrange a layer of cucumbers in a shallow bowl, sprinkle with salt, and spread with the mayonnaise mixture. Continue until all is used, ending with mayonnaise on top. (If necessary, plain mayonnaise may be used for the top layer.) Stand in the refrigerator for 12 to 24 hours before serving. The dressing will thin and turn white in the standing, the flavors will mingle, and the cucumbers will wilt. But don't let that stop you — that's the reason the salad is so good.

> *For each large cucumber*
> *1 tablespoon grated onion*
> *½ cup mayonnaise*
> *Salt*

NOTE: If so desired, the cucumbers may be alternated with paper-thin *slices* of onion.

⟪ Fruit Salads and Fruit Salad Plates

Apparently many people, including several writers of cook books, think that on the West Coast we all but live on fruit salads. Actually, they are a rarity, though a favorite lunch, both summer and winter, is a "fruit plate," usually consisting of a mound of cottage cheese surrounded by various fruits in season. Here are a few combinations. Serve any of them with or without cottage cheese, and with sour cream or French dressing, or mayonnaise.

Sliced peaches, raspberries, sliced oranges, and cubed cantaloupes.

Pineapple fingers, pitted Bing cherries, thinly sliced feijoas, and peeled plums.

Salads

Peeled apricots, halved strawberries, grapefruit segments, and green gage plums.

Orange segments, sliced persimmons, peeled white grapes, and sliced pears.

Peeled figs, sliced nectarines, Cranshaw melon balls, and blackberries.

Fresh dates, peeled muscat grapes, sliced apples, sliced avocado, and pomegranate seeds.

Pitted peeled plums, seedless grapes, peach halves, and cassberries.

Tangerine segments, pear halves, pitted prunes, and halves of apricots.

(Mixed Green Salad

This has been the Number One salad on the West Coast for the past score years, and probably always will be, though there have been many admissions of late, first whispered, then outspoken ones, that this everlasting green salad tossing is becoming something of a bore. So — to vary it — we make it in the classic manner but toss in other ingredients at will — nuts, cheese, olives, croutons, slivers of orange peel or anchovies, or anything else that seems reasonable.

(Lichi Nut Salad

This is an Occidental way of using canned Chinese lichi nuts. Chill and drain them, arrange 2 or 3 on a leaf of lettuce, dress with French dressing, and serve very cold. They are often stuffed with cream cheese, too, or with almonds — nuts stuffed with nuts. These lichi nuts, which are canned when fresh, are actually a fruit, and are good in fruit compotes, too, or served speared with toothpicks and in a bed of ice, as an exotic ending for a Chinese dinner. (Fresh lichi nuts have been, and are, grown in California, but I have yet to see them on the market.)

❨ Mexican Salad (Ensalada)

There are numerous salads popular with the Mexicans of today, but, as with the rest of us, the one of mixed greens rates high with them. Romaine, cress and escarole is a combination well liked, and often sliced radishes, cucumbers and green peppers are included. The dressing is apt to be tarter than a classic French one — 2 parts of oil to 1 of vinegar. Minced onions and chili powder are often added for extra zip.

❨ Olympia Oyster Salad

Serve this for a lunch salad, with popovers. It is also good for a first course, or at a buffet with, say, sliced ham and potatoes au gratin.

Simmer a pint of small Olympia oysters in their own liquor until they plump — this doesn't take more than a minute or two. Add 2 tablespoons of vinegar, and salt and pepper, and allow to chill. Drain and mix with mayonnaise that has been flavored with a touch of anchovy sauce. Dress on lettuce. SERVES 4 TO 6.

1 pint Olympia oysters   Mayonnaise flavored with
2 tablespoons vinegar   anchovy sauce
Salt and pepper

❨ Sweetbread and White Grape Salad

This was a party salad in the '90s, at least in the Northwest, and it is worth reviving.

Cook a pound of sweetbreads, clean well, and separate in pieces. Combine with ½ cup of finely cut celery, ¼ cup of sliced filberts, a cup of peeled and halved white grapes, and enough mayonnaise to moisten. Salt should be added. Serve in lettuce cups. SERVES 6 TO 8.

1 pound sweetbreads 1 cup peeled and halved white grapes
½ cup chopped celery   Mayonnaise as needed
¼ cup sliced filberts   Salt
Lettuce

314

Salads

⟨ California Potato Salad with White Wine

Boil 5 large potatoes until *just* tender, slice or dice, and dress, while warm, with ⅔ of a cup of white table wine mixed with ⅓ cup of salad oil, a tablespoon of white wine vinegar, ¼ cup of minced green onions, 2 tablespoons of minced parsley, salt and pepper to taste, and ¼ cup of melted butter. Let marinate for several hours before serving. SERVES 8 TO 10.

5 *large potatoes*	¼ *cup minced green onions*
⅔ *cup white wine*	2 *tablespoons minced parsley*
⅓ *cup salad oil*	*ley*
1 *tablespoon white wine vinegar*	*Salt and pepper*
	¼ *cup melted butter*

NOTE: Boiled halved chestnuts, mixed with this salad, make an interesting dish, and one that will have everyone guessing.

⟨ Balboa Salad

Summer eating, this, and good with fish or at barbecues.

Peel the largest ripest tomatoes that can be found, and slice them rather thick. Arrange flat or just slightly overlapping on a large platter or tray, and sprinkle with salt. Now take oregano and, rubbing it between your hands, powder it in a thin dust over the tomatoes. A drizzle of olive oil will finish this salad. Vinegar is *not* necessary because of the acid in the tomatoes, and the oregano eliminates the need for pepper. Serve very cold. For a superfine variation, cross tomatoes with anchovy fillets, and serve as a first course.

NOTE: *Tomatoes with Brandy.* Another version of this salad starts with the slices of tomato arranged in the same way, but they are dressed with minced sweet basil (fresh, please), olive oil, and, of all things, *brandy!* (½ cup oil to 3 tablespoons California brandy.) Amazingly good! Salt and pepper with this, which is fine for a first course.

(Zucchini Vinaigrette

We like zucchini on the West Coast, but only, I suspect, because we have learned to serve it in every possible way except *plain* boiled. This is a pleasant salad.

Select zucchini of uniform size, preferably not more than 4 inches long. (We eat all our summer squashes when they are mere infants.) Scrape off any fuzz, trim ends, split them lengthwise, and steam until they are tender but still firm. Arrange in a flat dish and pour over vinaigrette sauce, then allow to chill for at least 4 hours before serving.

(Salad Notes

Trinity Church Salad. "Chicken, grouse, quail, or pheasant with celery and mayonnaise." That's the way they did it in Portland, sixty years ago.

Breakfast Salad. A token salad is often served on West Coast breakfast plates, and a pleasant habit it is, too. A slice of red ripe tomato, a segment of rich green avocado, perhaps a piece or two of sliced oranges or a peeled peach half, any one of which is nestled on a curly leaf of crisp lettuce — !

"The Mystery" was the name of a salad served in Portland in the '80s, if we can believe that old cook book, the *Webfoot*. Slice tomatoes, put in layers with bell or chili peppers, celery, and onions, all "reduced to impalpable shreds." Spread with mayonnaise. And this, you gastronomes, is very good indeed!

Another salad in the *Webfoot Cook Book* is a bit dubious. Called "cucumber salad," it contained that vegetable with onions, cayenne, mace, Madeira, salad oil, and vinegar. "Put in jars," it said. A relish?

Ripe Olive Salad. This is an exotic idea that came from an old San Francisco family. Put a cup of diced stale bread in a jar with a dried chili pepper, screw top tight, and let stand for several days. Remove chili and discard, add a cup of ripe olives (pitted, I hope!), 3 tablespoons of chopped green pep-

316

per, and ½ cup of mayonnaise. Mix quickly, and serve on lettuce.

Palace Court Salad. Shredded lettuce, thick slices of ripe tomato, heart of artichoke filled with crab salad. Serve with Thousand Island dressing, and garnish with chopped hard-boiled egg yolk.

Onion and Tomato Salad. Slice sweet onions and marinate in ice water and vinegar, half and half. Drain, arrange on a bed of parsley with sliced tomatoes. Serve with oregano-flavored French dressing.

Cucumber and Shad Roe Salad. Cooked shad roe, cut carefully in slices, arranged on lettuce and dressed with cucumber dressing.

Lobster Salad. Marinate large firm pieces of lobster meat in French dressing made with red wine vinegar. Drain, mix lightly with a few strips of the red part of radish, green pepper, and ripe olives, cut the same size. Dress with mayonnaise, flavored lightly with curry powder.

Smoked Salmon Salad. Tiny shreds of smoked salmon and fillets of anchovies are mixed with a salad of green leaves, and dressed with oil and vinegar.

⟨ *Langlois Dressing*

Named, of course, after our famous Oregon blue-veined cheese.

Mix ½ pound of Langlois blue cheese with ½ teaspoon of salt that has been crushed with a large clove of garlic, then blend in ½ cup of wine vinegar and 1¼ cups of olive or salad oil and a few grindings of black pepper. This is wondrous on peeled sliced tomatoes or on lettuce. If desired, it may be diluted with red wine.

½ pound blue cheese	*½ cup wine vinegar*
½ teaspoon salt	*1¼ cups olive or salad oil*
1 large clove garlic	*Black pepper*

(Avocado Salad Dressing

Good on hearts of lettuce or romaine.

Force the pulp of 2 ripe avocados through a sieve, add the juice of a lemon, a tablespoon of grated onion, and salt and pepper to taste.

2 avocados	1 tablespoon grated onion
Juice of 1 lemon	Salt and pepper

(Green Goddess Dressing

There have been innumerable imitations and variations of this famous salad dressing since it was first created at the Palace Hotel, in honor of George Arliss, who was opening in William Archer's play *The Green Goddess*. This recipe is one given me by the Palace Hotel, and who should know better than they how it is prepared? The parenthetical notes are mine, added egotistically for fear that laymen may find the chef's directions a trifle vague.

"Mince 8 to 10 fillets of anchovies with 1 green onion, add minced parsley (¼ cup) and minced tarragon (2 tablespoons), 3 cups of mayonnaise, a little (¼ cup) of tarragon vinegar, and finely cut chives (¼ cup). Mix in a bowl that has been rubbed with garlic."

8–10 fillets of anchovies	2 tablespoons minced tarragon
1 green onion	3 cups mayonnaise
¼ cup minced parsley	¼ cup tarragon vinegar
¼ cup finely cut chives	

NOTE: There is a growing tendency to add sour cream to Green Goddess dressing, as there is to add it to almost everything. Do so if you wish, and cut down substantially on the mayonnaise.

NOTE: Another version of Green Goddess: 1 cup of mayonnaise, ¼ cup of minced parsley, ¼ cup of tarragon vinegar, 2 teaspoons fresh (or 1 of dried) tarragon (the latter soaked in the vinegar and strained out). To this add 4 minced anchovies or 2 tablespoons of anchovy paste, and either 2 tablespoons of minced green onions or chives. Thin with a little cream if desired.

❲ *Corte Madera Sour Cream Salad Dressing*

Next to French dressing and possibly mayonnaise, this is our favorite salad dressing.

Mash the yolks of 2 hard-boiled eggs, work in 2 tablespoons of lemon juice, and mix with a cup of sour cream. Add salt and pepper to taste.

2 egg yolks, hard-boiled	*1 cup sour cream*
2 tablespoons lemon juice	*Salt and pepper*

NOTE: *Quick Sour Cream Dressing.* Add lemon juice or vinegar, salt and pepper to taste, to sour cream.

NOTE: *Mayonnaise and Sour Cream.* Also quick! Just combine the two in equal parts — good for fruit salad.

NOTE: *Dill Dressing.* Add chopped fresh dill to sour cream dressing, for cucumbers, shrimps, string beans, or lobster.

❲ *Wine French Dressing*

For those who don't like their salad dressing either oily or tart, this is a happy solution.

Mix ½ cup of California red table wine and ¼ cup of red wine vinegar, with ¾ of a cup of salad oil. Season with a teaspoon of salt, some fresh ground pepper, and, if you wish, garlic.

½ cup red wine	*1 teaspoon salt*
¼ cup red wine vinegar	*Fresh ground pepper*
¾ cup salad oil	*Garlic (optional)*

Sauces

OUR WEST COAST *is a land of sauces — not the intricate compounded sauces of* la haute cuisine, *but the simple sauces that we whip up casually in the course of our everyday cooking. Some we learned from the Mexicans, whose sauces are red and rich and redolent with herbs and spices. Some we learned from the Chinese, subtler sauces, these, usually contrived to glaze and combine meats and vegetables in a harmony of flavor and of color. Some we learned from other nationalities, and some we conceived ourselves — either sauces for our game or seafoods, or for the charcoal-broiled meats we love so well. And as for these last — we have created an infinite variety. Some like them hot, some like them mild, some like them not at all. Some like them as marinades, some as bastes, some as actual sauces. It's one of those things that each man will have to decide for himself. All I can do about it is to give you a few sauces from which to choose.*

❰ Blue Cheese Sauce for Steaks

This is almost a spread. Blend ¼ pound of Langlois blue cheese with ¼ cup of olive oil and a clove of garlic that has been macerated in a tablespoon or two of brandy or Worcestershire sauce. Broil a thick steak, slice, spread with this mixture, and slip under the broiler just long enough to melt the cheese. This works well with hamburgers, too.

¼ pound Langlois blue
    cheese
¼ cup olive oil

1 clove garlic
1–2 tablespoons brandy or
    Worcestershire sauce

⟨ Herb Barbecue Sauce

This is said to be a very old California recipe. It is not hot, in fact it has not a bit of pepper in it, so have no fear.

Cook together a ½ cup of vinegar, a cup of water, ¼ cup of chopped onion, 3 cloves of minced garlic, a tablespoon of minced rosemary, and ¼ cup of minced mint leaves, ½ cup of oil or butter, and a teaspoon of salt. Simmer 10 minutes, strain, and use. Pepper steak or whatever you're grilling just before serving.

½ cup vinegar
1 cup water
¼ cup chopped onion
3 cloves garlic

1 tablespoon minced rose-
    mary
¼ cup minced mint leaves
½ cup oil or butter
    1 teaspoon salt

⟨ Hottish Barbecue Sauce

Squash 4 cloves of garlic with a tablespoon of salt. Add a cup of olive oil or salad oil, ½ cup of vinegar, a small onion, minced, a small green pepper, minced, a tablespoon (that's a lot!) of chili powder, a cup of tomato juice, and a teaspoon of oregano. Simmer this for 10 minutes, and strain before using. (This will keep well — if you want to keep it.) There's nothing to prevent your adding Worcestershire, tabasco, mustard, cayenne, smoked salt, or even sugar to this recipe if that's what you want — but I won't have any part in it.

4 cloves garlic
1 tablespoon salt
1 cup olive oil or salad oil
½ cup vinegar

1 small onion
1 small green pepper
1 tablespoon chili powder
1 cup tomato juice
    1 teaspoon oregano

❲ Wine Barbecue Sauce

This is a simple sauce which may be used as a marinade *and* a baste, or just for basting.

Crush 2 cloves of garlic (or more. How well do you like it?) in 2 tablespoons of salt. Add a cup of red wine, ¼ cup of red wine vinegar, 1¼ cups of olive oil (or part olive oil, part cooking oil), and a few twists of the pepper mill. Add herbs of your choice — oregano, perhaps, for beef, rosemary for lamb, thyme for fish, tarragon or marjoram for poultry — using 1 teaspoon, if dried (freshly dried, that is!) or 2 if green. Or use a bunch of herbs for a basting brush — parsley if you can't find any other.

2 *cloves garlic*	1¼ *cups olive oil*
2 *tablespoons salt*	*Fresh ground pepper*
1 *cup red wine*	1 *teaspoon dried herbs or*
¼ *cup red wine vinegar*	2 *teaspoons green herbs*

❲ Cherry Sauce for Meat

Oregon, the land of cherries, quite naturally uses this delectable fruit in particularly exciting ways. This sauce should be served with roast lamb or veal, with game, or with mutton. For boiled mutton, it is a considerable improvement over the caper sauce, once so popular.

Cook ¼ cup of minced onions in ¼ cup of butter until wilted, then stir in a tablespoon of flour and cook for 3 minutes. Boil 2 cans of consommé until reduced to 1 cup liquid, and add this to the onion mixture. Now add ⅓ cup of California sherry and 2 tablespoons of California brandy, and cook 3 or 4 minutes longer. Next comes ½ pound of pitted Bing cherries. As soon as the cherries are hot, serve the sauce.

¼ *cup minced onions*	2 *cans consommé*
¼ *cup butter*	⅓ *cup sherry*
1 *tablespoon flour*	2 *tablespoons brandy*
½ *pound Bing cherries*	

322

Sauces

❨ West Coast Cocktail Sauces

1. 1 cup of mayonnaise, 2 tablespoons of anchovy paste, 1 cup of sour cream, 1 tablespoon of lemon juice.

2. 1 cup of mayonnaise, ¼ cup of canned green chili sauce (salsa), 1 tablespoon of vinegar. (This is hot, so should not be used on fish with a delicate flavor. Good for leftover cooked fish.)

3. 1 cup of mayonnaise, ½ cup of cream, ½ cup of tomato purée (or catsup), 1 teaspoon of sweet basil if fresh, ½ teaspoon if dried, salt and cayenne.

4. ½ cup each of chili sauce, sour or sweet cream, and mayonnaise, 1 teaspoon of curry powder, salt and lemon juice to taste.

5. 1 cup of mayonnaise, ½ teaspoon of coriander, ¼ teaspoon of cumin, 1 tablespoon each of minced green onion and green pepper, 2 tablespoons of lemon juice.

6. ½ cup of catsup, ¼ cup of sour cream, ¼ cup of lemon juice, salt and cayenne to taste.

❨ Lemon Tartare Sauce

I hate to call this tartare for fear it will be mistaken for that chopped-sweet-pickle-and-mayonnaise abomination that is served at some restaurants, usually plunked on a wilted leaf of lettuce, or worse, in a pigmy paper cup.

Peel a lemon, remove the white part and the seeds, and cut it fine, using a very sharp knife so it won't be crushed. Mix it with a cup of mayonnaise, ¼ cup each of minced green onions and parsley, and, if you wish and I hope you do, 2 tablespoons of tarragon. Chopped green olives may be added instead of the onion.

1 lemon
1 cup mayonnaise
¼ cup minced green onion
(or green olives)

¼ cup minced parsley
2 tablespoons tarragon
(optional)

323

⟨ Lemon-Wine Steak Sauce

Cook ¼ cup of minced onion and a crushed clove of garlic in 2 cups of Pinot noir (or any red table wine) until the liquid is reduced one half. Remove garlic, add 2 tablespoons each of butter and olive oil, ¼ cup of lemon juice, salt, pepper, and a tablespoon of minced parsley.

¼ cup minced onion	2 tablespoons olive oil
1 clove garlic	¼ cup lemon juice
2 cups red wine	Salt and pepper
2 tablespoons butter	1 tablespoon minced parsley

⟨ Mexican All-Purpose Sauce

Cook a clove of garlic and a chopped onion in 2 tablespoons of lard. Remove garlic, add 2 tablespoons of flour, 2 cups of tomato purée, 2 tablespoons of chili powder, and ½ teaspoon of salt. Cook 5 minutes. Oregano, cumin, and/or coriander may be added. More salt may be needed and it may be thinned with water as desired.

1 clove garlic	2 tablespoons chili powder
1 onion	½ teaspoon salt
2 tablespoons lard	(or more)
2 tablespoons flour	Oregano, cumin, or cori-
2 cups tomato purée	ander (optional)

⟨ Green Olive Sauce

Melt ¼ cup of butter with a clove of garlic, remove garlic, and add 2 tablespoons each of minced parsley and shallots, 2 tablespoons of flour, 1¼ cups of white wine, and ⅓ cup of chopped stuffed green olives that have been rinsed with hot water. Cook 4 or 5 minutes, and serve with fish.

¼ cup butter	2 tablespoons minced shal-
1 clove garlic	lots
2 tablespoons minced	2 tablespoons flour
parsley	1¼ cups white wine
⅓ cup chopped stuffed green olives	

Sauces

(Marinade for Game

Combine 1 bottle of red table wine (California claret, or Burgundy, or Gamay, or Barbera, or Zinfandel) with ¼ cup of red wine vinegar or lemon juice, a few peppercorns, an herb bouquet of parsley, bay, and marjoram or rosemary, a large onion, 2 carrots, and a few celery leaves, all chopped, and 3 juniper berries. It is better to add salt during or after the cooking, rather than in the marinade, but for those who don't agree, 2 teaspoons may be added here.

1 bottle red table wine
¼ cup red wine vinegar or
*   lemon juice*
Peppercorns
1 herb bouquet
1 large onion
2 carrots
Celery leaves
3 juniper berries

(Orange-Ginger Sauce

This is a sweet and sour sauce, well suited to pork cooked in the Chinese manner, or to their meat balls. It also is wonderful on broiled spareribs, or on ham.

Cook 2 tablespoons of butter or ham drippings with 2 tablespoons of cornstarch. Add a cup of orange juice, ¼ cup of vinegar, ¼ cup of sugar, ¼ cup of sherry, 3 tablespoons of soy sauce, and 2 teaspoons each of slivered orange peel and slivered green or crystallized ginger. Cook until clear and thickened.

2 tablespoons butter
2 tablespoons cornstarch
1 cup orange juice
¼ cup vinegar
¼ cup sugar
¼ cup sherry
3 tablespoons soy sauce
2 teaspoons slivered orange peel
2 teaspoons slivered green ginger

(Oxnard Orange Sauce for Duck

This sauce is good for either wild or domestic duck, or for goose. It's also amazingly good with roast pork, ham, or veal.

Slice the zest (the very outer orange skin) from half of an orange. Cut it in slivers, cover it with water and simmer for 3 minutes, then drain and discard the water. Add a cup of orange juice, a cup of port wine, and a cup of the rich, but skimmed, juices that come from the pan in which your duck was roasted. Season with salt, a little cayenne, 2 tablespoons of lemon juice, and a little pinch of rosemary.

Zest of ½ orange	Salt
1 cup orange juice	A little cayenne
1 cup port wine	2 tablespoons lemon juice
1 cup meat juices	Small pinch rosemary

NOTE: *Kumquat sauce* is even more exciting. Make in the same manner, using orange and lemon juices, but substitute four ever-so-thinly sliced kumquats (seeds discarded) for the zest.

(Raisin-Almond Sauce

Brown ¼ cup of butter, then stir in 3 tablespoons of flour. Add 1½ cups of rich stock, ⅔ of a cup of seedless bleached raisins, ½ cup of blanched slivered almonds, ½ cup of California sherry, 6 very thin slices of lemon, cut in halves, and ¼ teaspoon of ground cloves. Boil gently until the raisins are plump, and serve with smoked tongue or ham.

¼ cup butter	½ cup blanched slivered
3 tablespoons flour	almonds
1½ cups rich stock	½ cup sherry
⅔ cup seedless bleached	6 thin lemon slices
raisins	¼ teaspoon ground cloves

(Alki Point Shrimp Dip

Alki Point, one of the first settlements in Washington, was planned as a great metropolis called "New York." It never made the grade, so the early settlers tacked the name "Alki" — Chinook for "by-and-by" to its name. The "New York" was subsequently abandoned. This sauce was created somewhere near Alki Point (now within Seattle's limits), and it is a dream that *does* come true.

Mince, as fine as possible, 3 hard-boiled eggs, 3 green onions, (white, and tender green part) 3 sprigs of parsley, a clove of garlic, 6 stuffed olives, and ¼ of a green pepper. Mix this with 2 cups of mayonnaise, along with 2 tablespoons of anchovy paste and 2 tablespoons of tarragon vinegar. Taste and add salt if necessary, and a dash of tabasco if the idea appeals to you. Dunk shrimps in this, or use it as a sauce for any shellfish, including scallops and mussels, or for a fish salad.

3 hard-boiled eggs	2 cups mayonnaise
3 green onions	2 tablespoons anchovy paste
3 sprigs parsley	2 tablespoons tarragon vine-
1 clove garlic	gar
6 stuffed olives	Salt, if necessary
¼ green pepper	Dash of tabasco (optional)

❨ Salsa

Salsa means sauce, but the name has become attached to this particular one. Of all the sauces we have, it is the most original and the most refreshing. It was used in very early days in California, and it's used today up and down the coast. A bit like gazpacho (page 344), it is served cold with steaks or fish, either on the side of the plate, or in little individual bowls.

Peel and chop 4 red ripe tomatoes, a large red onion, a large bell pepper, ½ a small red chili pepper (very fine, this). Mix with a teaspoon of salt, ¼ teaspoon of fresh ground pepper, and 2 tablespoons of lemon juice or red wine vinegar. Taste for seasoning, and add more salt if necessary. Chill well.

4 tomatoes	1 teaspoon salt (or more)
1 large red onion	¼ teaspoon pepper
1 large bell pepper	2 tablespoons lemon juice or
½ small red chili pepper	red wine vinegar

⟮ Vermouth Basting Sauce

This is one of the easiest and one of the best of basting or marinating sauces. It is a favorite of one of California's best cooks and best hunters, John M. Keller, grandson of Mateo Keller, one of California's first vintners.

The sauce is equal parts of sweet vermouth, Californian of course, and olive oil, also Californian.

⟮ Walnut Fish Sauce

Combine a cup of sour cream, a tablespoon of lemon juice, ½ teaspoon of salt, and ¼ cup each of chopped walnuts and grated horseradish.

1 cup sour cream	½ teaspoon salt
1 tablespoon lemon juice	¼ cup chopped walnuts
¼ cup grated horseradish	

⟮ Yerba Buena Sauce

Yerba Buena, the early name for San Francisco, was also the "good herb," a wild mintlike plant that ran wild over all the hillsides. The Indians used it in cooking, and the whites, if sufficiently hard pressed for seasoning. We prefer a gentler flavor, like the chervil or parsley, and tarragon, used in this herb sauce, which is good with poached eggs, sweetbreads, chicken, chicken livers, squab, and other light meats.

Simmer 2 tablespoons of minced shallots in 3 tablespoons of butter, then add 2 tablespoons of flour. Cook a minute or two, then pour in ½ cup each of chicken stock and white wine, a tablespoon each of minced parsley or chervil, and tarragon. Cook 3 minutes, then season to taste.

2 tablespoons minced shallots	1 tablespoon minced parsley or chervil
3 tablespoons butter	
2 tablespoons flour	1 tablespoon minced tarragon
½ cup chicken stock	
½ cup white wine	Salt and pepper

Soups

THE PACIFIC COAST *is great soup country. Settlers from every land, of every race, tossed their national favorites into our regional soup pot. Even the Indians made a soup of sorts, boiling a basketful of water and game and wild roots by throwing in hot stones. There were many chowders eaten in Oregon Territory; the abundance of both shellfish and Yankees made that inevitable. Lobscouse was introduced by seafaring men, and was a concoction of bully beef or jerky and pilot biscuit. The famous epicure, Joe Tilden, many years later still numbered lobscouse among his favorites. He made it with corned beef, salt pork, onions, and potatoes, and used pepper with a generous hand, and always thickened it with "sea biscuits." Slumgullion was a stew or soup of anything that was edible — and this meant crows, or muskrats, or gophers, or even skunk if food was scarce. In California, the soup varied from the atole to the really fine sopa a la Espagnola, a rich beef or mutton broth, thickened with garbanzos, cabbage, rice, and sometimes small dumplings made of masa, which was enjoyed by the well-to-do families. There was also the wondrous olla podrida, a concoction of meat and lentils and greens — so hearty that perhaps it should be called a stew. A like creation, puchero, was both soup and stew, for the broth was served first, and then the meat, re-sauced with a savory tomato and pepper mixture. Later, in the Bonanza Days of San Francisco, more elaborate soups were introduced. Chefs, imported from France by the new rich, introduced their potages and veloutés and bisques. Fortunately for our cuisine, they often used native products, either by choice or by necessity, so we have other soups to add to our really fine collection.*

⟨ Abalone Chowder

The Yankee touch is apparent in this chowder, though the addition of wine has a hint of the West.

Simmer 1½ pounds of abalone — whole or sliced — in 3 cups of chicken stock or salted (1 teaspoon) water, with an herb bouquet of thyme, parsley, and bay. When tender enough to pierce easily with a fork, drain, reserving the liquid, and grind the meat. Dice ¼ pound of salt pork and cook it until it's a beautiful crisp amber. Remove the pork and save, then add a cup of sliced onion to the fat, and cook it until it colors. Two cups of diced raw potatoes come next, and the abalone with its liquid is simmered with the vegetables, along with salt and pepper to taste. When the potatoes are done, 2 cups of cream (milk will do, but not as nicely) and a cup of white wine are poured in, the pork cubes are returned to the chowder, and the seasoning is corrected. The chowder is poured into a tureen and sprinkled with parsley. That's all, except for some pilot biscuits — and an appetite. SERVES 6 to 8.

1½ pounds abalone	1 cup sliced onion
3 cups chicken stock	2 cups diced raw potatoes
(or salted water)	2 cups cream
1 herb bouquet	1 cup white wine
¼ pound salt pork	Salt and pepper
Minced parsley	

⟨ Chinese Abalone Soup with Chicken or Pork

Canned abalone stars here, so you don't have to live in California to enjoy it. Though the soup is Chinese, it's right with any meal except one featuring abalone. Abalone is canned in Mexico, and is available in most gourmet shops — or should be.

Pour the juice from a 1-pound can of abalone, and to it add enough water to make 2 cups. Combine this with 2 cups of unsalted chicken or pork stock. (This is one way to use pork

330

bones, and a surprisingly good way.) A teaspoon of soy sauce and a tablespoon of sherry are next in order, and ¼ cup of the abalone, cut into match-sized pieces. Heat, correct the seasoning, and serve with pride. You'll have abalone left over, so see the recipe for abalone and pork (page 122), or eggs foo yung (page 81). SERVES 4 TO 6.

Juice from 1-pound can of
   abalone
Water as needed
2 cups chicken or pork stock

1 teaspoon soy sauce
1 tablespoon sherry
¼ cup slivered abalone
Salt and pepper

❨ *Almond Soup with Coriander*

Almond soup was being made in England before Sir Francis Drake discovered "New Albion," but it took West Coast cooks to devise this version — a superior one, we like to think.

Pound a cup of blanched almonds in a mortar, or put them through the meat grinder, using the finest knife. (Blanch them by covering with cold water and bringing to a boil. Drain and put in a bowl of cold water. Rub them between the hands, and they will practically skin themselves.) Add 3 cups of chicken stock (an old Los Angeles recipe uses veal stock, so suit yourself), a small onion, and ½ a bay leaf, and simmer gently for a half hour. Remove and discard onion and bay, and add ½ teaspoon of ground coriander (more if it isn't fresh from the grocer's shelf) and a cup of heavy cream. Bind with the yolks of 4 eggs, or, if that is too much for the budget, with 2 tablespoons each of butter and flour, made into a roux. Taste for seasoning, and, if you wish, add 2 or 3 drops of almond flavoring. Strain, or not, and garnish with slivered toasted almonds, or minced chives, or grated orange rind. This soup is quite as good served cold as hot, so think of it as a substitute for Vichyssoise ubiquitous in the West, too! SERVES 6.

1 cup blanched almonds
3 cups chicken stock
1 small onion
½ bay leaf
½ teaspoon ground coriander
Almond flavoring (optional)

1 cup heavy cream
4 egg yolks or
   2 tablespoons flour and
   2 tablespoons butter
Salt and pepper

331

(Santa Cruz Artichoke Soup

Here's a soup that will have everyone guessing — and hinting for a second serving.

Wash 2 large artichokes and cut them in half from top to bottom. Don't trim or remove any of the stem. Cook them in 3 cups of chicken stock. (I use so much in soup making, that I make it up a gallon at a time and freeze it. Or use chicken concentrate or chicken bouillon cubes.) Add the juice of half a lemon and, as soon as the hearts are tender, pull them from the leaves and drop them in acidulated water (p. 358). Boil leaves more, until almost mushy. Scrape the pulp from the leaves, an easy job when using a teaspoon, mash the stems, and return to the stock. Cook a tablespoon of minced shallots or green onions in 2 tablespoons of butter, add a tablespoon of flour and cook 4 minutes, then add the stock, and a cup of thin cream. Season with salt and pepper to taste, strain, and add the hearts, cut into tiny dice. If you've been careful not to let the artichokes stand around, they should retain their color. But if they should darken, I think a drop or two of green coloring is excusable — but for goodness' sake, take it easy, no one must ever suspect. This is another soup that takes to chilling. SERVES 6.

2 large artichokes	2 tablespoons butter
3 cups chicken stock	1 tablespoon flour
Juice of ½ lemon	1 cup thin cream
1 tablespoon minced shallots or green onion	Salt and pepper

(Avocado Bisque

There are several ways of using avocados in soup, all of them good, all of them avoiding the actual cooking of the avocado. This first comes closest to being a full-fledged recipe.

Cook a tablespoon of minced onion in a tablespoon of butter. While it is simmering slowly, make a cup of cream sauce (1 cup cream, 1 tablespoon each of butter and flour). Press the pulp of a large ripe avocado through a sieve, add it to the onion, stirring briskly for 30 seconds, then combine with the cream sauce and a cup of chicken stock. Season with salt and pepper and a squeezing of lemon juice or a little sherry, and serve with croutons. SERVES 3 OR 4.

> 1 tablespoon minced onion   1 large ripe avocado
> 1 tablespoon butter   1 cup chicken stock
> 1 cup thin cream sauce   Lemon juice or sherry
>   Salt and pepper

⟨ Avocado Summer Soup

This, quite naturally, is cold. It's also rich, easy, and highly satisfactory.

Add a cup of sieved avocado to 1 cup of hot chicken stock. Mix well and strain through a hair sieve, then combine with a cup of very heavy cream and ½ cup of white table wine. Add 2 teaspoons of lemon juice, salt and pepper, and a tiny speck of cayenne. Chill well, and serve sprinkled with chives or chopped fresh dill. Fritos, or whatever they call corn chips in *your* part of the world, seem just right with this. SERVES 4 TO 6.

> 1 cup sieved avocado   ½ cup white table wine
> 1 cup chicken stock   2 teaspoons lemon juice
> 1 cup heavy cream   Salt and pepper
>   Speck of cayenne

⟨ Avocado Soups in Brief

1. Combine equal parts of puréed avocado, jellied consommé, and cream. Serve cold!

2. Put jellied consommé in one side of a bouillon cup, guacamole (page 10) in the other. (Separate with a spoon or spatula while pouring.) Top with a blob of sour cream. Each diner does his own mixing.

3. Again use sieved avocado, jellied bouillon, and sour cream, equal parts of each, but mix them before serving. Thin with a little white wine or lemon juice, and be sure it's well seasoned. Chives with this.

4. This one's hot. Three cups of hot chicken stock with 1 puréed avocado stirred in just before serving. Sherry added or not, as you will. Salt you'll want.

5. Another hot one, this with garlic. Crush a small clove of it in ¼ teaspoon of salt. Combine it, a cup of bouillon, and a cup of sour cream with ½ cup of puréed avocado. Salt and chili powder for seasoning. Tomato juice may be substituted for the bouillon. Diced avocado for a garnish, or a few dill seeds. Heat carefully or the sour cream will curdle.

And don't forget that avocado dice make fine garnishes for various soups — plain or tomato bouillon, clam broth, cream of chicken soup, and many others.

❲ Jellied California Borscht

Quite certainly the first Russians on our Coast did *not* bring this recipe with them, nor would a modern Russian admit that it was borscht. Perhaps it isn't, but it was adapted *from* borscht, and it's very, very pleasant.

Cook together 3½ cups of beet juice (use either the juice from canned beets or cook 4 large chopped beets in a quart of water) and 2 cups of veal stock or consommé (again, use either the canned or the homemade variety, though as this is a hot-weather soup, the quick and easy method is my usual indolent choice), with 3 whole cloves, a chopped onion (medium), a couple of cabbage leaves, and 1½ tablespoons of wine vinegar. After 10 minutes of simmering, strain and add a tablespoon of gelatin which has been mixed with 2 tablespoons of cold water. Chill, and serve in glass bowls with a dollop of sour cream and a few dill seeds on top of each serving. This will be just *barely* jellied. If you prefer to have it stiffer, add 2 tablespoons of gelatin, but I think it's nicer this way. Hot fish piroshki (page 12) are the perfect accompaniment, and even if it is hot weather, you *could* have made them in advance and kept them in your freezer, ready to reheat. SERVES 6 TO 10.

3½ cups beet juice
2 cups veal stock or con-
   sommé
3 whole cloves
1 medium onion

2 cabbage leaves
1½ tablespoons wine
   vinegar
1 tablespoon gelatin in 2
   tablespoons water

(Oakland Chestnut Soup

We grow some chestnuts on the West Coast, but even if we didn't we'd no doubt use them — they are so right with our game and with many of our vegetables. Right, too, in one of our favorite soups. This soup is plenty rich as is, but a San Diego recipe for it calls for a garnish of whipped cream!

Boil ½ pound of chestnuts for 8 minutes, drain and peel while still warm. Both shells and inner skins will come off easily. Now cook the blanched chestnuts until soft in 2 cups of chicken or veal stock, then mash them through a sieve. Make a cream sauce with 2 tablespoons of butter, 2 of flour, and 2 cups of milk. Combine with the chestnuts and the stock in which they have cooked, and season with a teaspoon of ground coriander (or grated lemon peel), a teaspoon of lemon juice, salt, and ¼ cup of sherry. Strain through a fine sieve before serving. If it seems too thick, don't hesitate to thin it with milk or water. This is a good soup to serve before some simple meat — a grilled chop, perhaps, or some cold roast veal. SERVES 6 TO 8.

½ pound chestnuts
2 cups chicken or veal stock
2 tablespoons butter
2 tablespoons flour

2 cups milk
1 teaspoon ground coriander
1 teaspoon lemon juice
Salt

¼ cup sherry

(Tillamook County Soup

Named after Oregon's famed Cheddar, it also has California's ripe olives as an ingredient. It, with a salad or a fruit, will make a mighty salubrious meal.

335

Cook 2 tablespoons of onion in 2 tablespoons of butter until wilted. Add a cup of mashed potatoes, a cup of stock or potato water, and 2 cups of milk. Whip smooth, then add ½ teaspoon of oregano, crushed fine. Let cook slowly for 4 or 5 minutes before adding ¾ of a cup of grated Cheddar cheese. Now continue cooking and whipping until the cheese is melted and the mixture smooth. Season with salt and cayenne, add ½ cup of sliced ripe olives, and serve at once. SERVES 4 TO 6.

2 tablespoons onion	½ teaspoon oregano
2 tablespoons butter	¾ cup grated Cheddar
1 cup mashed potatoes	Salt
1 cup stock or potato water	Cayenne
2 cups milk	½ cup sliced ripe olives

ℂ Oregon Cherry Soup

Oregon is proud of her cherries, and this is a good fruit soup — not too sweet to serve at the beginning of a light summer meal or even with it. There are some who even serve it as dessert, but why?

Pit 2 pounds of ripe red cherries and cook them in 2 cups of water with a piece of cinnamon, 2 cloves, about 2 drops of almond extract, and ¼ teaspoon of salt. When soft, rub through a sieve and add 2 cups of red wine (a Cabernet or a California claret) and a tablespoon of brandy, as well as sugar to taste. (Not too much, for my taste.) Return to the fire, bind with 2 egg yolks, and cook until slightly thick. Serve well chilled. SERVES 6 TO 8.

2 pounds cherries	¼ teaspoon salt
2 cups water	2 cups red wine
Cinnamon	1 tablespoon brandy
2 cloves	Sugar
2 drops almond extract	2 egg yolks

ℂ Don Far Tong (Chicken and Cress Soup)

Quite obviously Chinese, and quite obviously good only if the stock is rich with chicken. (My only quarrel with Chinese food is that even at some of the best Oriental restaurants the soup is often watery. I confess that I have been tempted, even while complimenting some Chinese restaurateur on a wonderful meal, to quote an old Chinese saying: "He who makes soup of thistles is ill qualified to discuss the savor of a stalled ox.")

Slice 3 green onions, the white and the tender green part, and cook them in a quart of rich, well-seasoned chicken stock (hope you have it in your freezer!) for 3 minutes. Beat 2 eggs slightly, just enough to mix, and add to them a teaspoon of soy sauce. Now bring the soup to a merry boil, pour in the egg mixture, and stir, not too vigorously, until the egg sets in long threads. Add a cup of water cress leaves, and serve at once from a soup tureen. SERVES 6 TO 8.

3 green onions	*2 eggs*
1 quart chicken stock	*1 teaspoon soy sauce*
1 cup water cress leaves	

❰ Cazadero Chicken Liver Soup

Because we're very fond of chicken livers, we sometimes wish that our poultry suffered from the Strasbourg "liver complaint." This soup uses two other favorites, tarragon and sherry.

Slowly cook a cup of cleaned cut chicken livers in a tablespoon of butter, with ½ cup of minced onion. Force through a strainer, add a teaspoon of chopped tarragon (½ teaspoon, if dried), or a tablespoon of parsley if you prefer, a cup of cream, 3 cups of chicken stock, and salt to taste. Strain once more, and, if you wish, point up the flavor with ¼ cup of sherry. SERVES 6 TO 8.

1 cup chicken livers	*1 cup cream*
½ cup minced onion	*3 cups chicken stock*
1 tablespoon butter	*Salt*
1 teaspoon chopped tarragon or parsley	*¼ cup sherry (optional)*

([*Chicken Tarragon Soup*

Chicken consommé, if heavy with the flavor of the fowl, is always well liked, no matter what the garnish. Patti consommé, created in honor of that lady herself by the Palace Hotel chef, was garnished with chicken forcemeat balls, spaghetti, and hearts of artichoke. Another for which we have a great fondness is this tarragon-flavored soup.

Sacrifice a whole fowl for this, an old hen or a rooster will do nicely. (Pull off any fat before cooking, and render it for use in other dishes.) Cover the bird with water, add a sliced onion, a teaspoon of salt, and an herb bouquet, and cook, slowly, until the meat is literally falling from the bones. (What you do with the meat is your problem. It won't be very good, so you'll have to dream up some way of saucing it. Or give it to the cat.) Allow the stock to stand overnight in the refrigerator, remove all fat, reheat, then strain through double cheesecloth. Put to heat with 2 tablespoons of fresh minced tarragon. (Or 1 tablespoon of dried, if it is *freshly dried!*) There should not be much more than a quart of stock, and it should be so rich that it can almost float a spoon. Simmer for 20 minutes, then strain out the tarragon, correct seasoning, and serve with 3 or 4 fresh tarragon leaves in each dish. SERVES 6 TO 8.

1 fowl	*1 teaspoon salt*
1 herb bouquet	*2 tablespoons minced fresh*
1 onion	*tarragon*

([*Clam Wine Soup*

We like wine in any or all of our soups — there's no doubt that that's what makes them extra good. This soup is light, which makes it perfect for any meal that is to feature a rich entree of meat, game, or fowl.

Make some fish stock by covering 3 pounds of bones, trimmings, and heads of fish with water and simmering for half an hour. Strain through cloth. To one quart of this stock add

1 can of minced clams (7 ounces), a cup of white table wine, 2 stalks of celery, a clove of garlic, crushed, ½ an onion, 2 cloves, and salt and pepper to taste. Simmer gently for 15 minutes, strain, pressing out all the good in the clams, then strain again through cheesecloth. (This may be cleared with egg white, if desired.) Correct seasoning and serve, topped with unsweetened whipped cream or a very thin slice of lemon. A few chopped water chestnuts make an interesting garnish. SERVES 6 TO 8.

1 quart fish stock	*1 clove garlic*
1 7-ounce can minced clams	*½ onion*
1 cup white wine	*2 cloves*
2 stalks celery	*Salt and pepper*

ℂ *Pismo Cream of Clam Soup*

If this soup is made from the clam whose name it bears, you'll have to go to Pismo Beach and dig your own, or buy the frozen kind from Mexico. Any edible clam will do, though, even those from the Atlantic.

Grind a pint of clams and save the juice. Cook 2 tablespoons of minced onion in 2 tablespoons of butter. Add the clams and juice, and either ½ teaspoon of thyme seasoning powder, or ¼ teaspoon each of thyme and M.S.G., also ½ cup of water. Simmer 10 minutes, pour in 2 cups of milk, and taste for salt and pepper. Bind with ½ cup of heavy cream mixed with the yolks of 2 eggs. Sherry is optional. SERVES 6 TO 8.

1 pint clams	*½ cup water*
2 tablespoons minced onion	*2 cups milk*
2 tablespoons butter	*Salt and pepper*
½ teaspoon thyme seasoning	*½ cup heavy cream*
* powder or*	*2 egg yolks*
* ¼ teaspoon each thyme*	*Sherry (optional)*
* and M.S.G.*	

❨ Pacific Clam Chowder with Rice

We view with amusement the Eastern controversy about clam chowder, and make ours with or without tomatoes or milk and enjoy it either way. We like it best, however, our own way, with a touch or two which makes it typically of the West.

Dice ½ pound of bacon and cook it crisp. Remove and drain, reserving the fat, in which you cook a large onion and a large green pepper, both diced. Now comes a cup of cooked rice (shocked?) and 2 cups of chopped clams with their juices, and 2 cups of canned tomatoes. A half teaspoon of thyme seasons the chowder, along with salt to taste and a goodly amount of fresh ground pepper. If this is too thick, add some water. Cook until the clams are just tender, add the diced bacon, and sprinkle with 2 tablespoons of parsley. Serve with tortillas or with pilot biscuit. An interesting variant is to use caraway seeds instead of thyme, for the seasoning. SERVES 6 OR MORE.

½ pound bacon	2 cups canned tomatoes
1 large onion	½ teaspoon thyme
1 large green pepper	(or caraway)
1 cup cooked rice	Salt and pepper
2 cups chopped clams	2 tablespoons parsley

NOTE: Another Pacific clam chowder is made in the Yankee way, with milk, but curry powder is used as a seasoning.

NOTE: The *Webfoot Cook Book* added chopped carrots and cabbage to a clam chowder, as well as potatoes, crackers, butter, and cream!

❨ Clam Soup Notes

Clam broth was said to have saved the life of many a pioneer child; it, or clam juice, was used as a substitute for mother's milk. Today we still like it, and the stronger it is the better we like it. At its best it is the pure juice of the clam.

1. Combine half clam broth and half consommé, and you'll have clam consommé. Garnish it with diced avocado.

2. Combine half clam broth and half chicken broth — this gives you consommé Bellevue, and a wonderful soup it is, too.

3. Combine clam broth and tomato juice in equal parts, and serve it hot or chilled.

4. Combine clam broth and celery broth in equal parts. Garnish, if you wish, with raw, finely sliced celery. The celery broth may be made from the leaves of the celery.

5. Clam broth may be frozen to a mush and served before or with the main course. This is delicious on sultry days.

6. For a quick clam bisque, cook a can (7-ounce) of minced clams with ½ cup of white wine and 1½ cups of milk for 10 minutes. Beat the yolks of 2 eggs with ½ cup of cream, and add a little of the hot mixture, then combine both, stirring well. Cook for 2 or 3 minutes more, gently, and serve.

Mussels, at the time of year when they are safe, may be used in any of these recipes.

⟦ California Claret Soup

A California claret, or a wine made with the grapes used for a Bordeaux — a Cabernet — makes this soup extra special. How the West Coast cooked during prohibition, I can't imagine! The *Webfoot Cook Book*, Portland, 1885, has sago in a claret soup, for thickening, and garnishes it with beaten egg whites. Could be.

To a quart of rich consommé or bouillon, add 1½ cups of claret and a teaspoon of sugar. Salt and pepper if needed. Serve hot with a thin slice of lemon in each cup. In hot weather, add a tablespoon of gelatin, dissolved in ¼ cup of cold water, and serve chilled. SERVES 6 TO 10.

1 quart consommé or bouillon	*1 teaspoon sugar*
1½ cups claret	*Salt and pepper*
	Lemon slices

❨ Dungeness Crab Bisque

Here's our famous crab again, this time done up as a fabulous bisque.

Chop 2 cups of crab meat very fine, and simmer it with a quart of rich milk (part cream is best) and an onion, for 20 minutes. Remove onion and bind the soup with a roux made with 2 tablespoons each of butter and flour. Season with salt and pepper, and a few gratings of nutmeg, also sherry, if you wish. For an extra touch, whip cream, salt lightly, and top each cup of soup with a dollop of it, then slip under the broiler so the top will brown lightly. This soup, served with tiny popovers and a fresh fruit plate, makes a dreamy lunch. SERVES 6 TO 8.

2 cups crab meat	2 tablespoons flour
1 quart rich milk	Salt and pepper
1 onion	Nutmeg
2 tablespoons butter	Sherry (optional)

❨ Iced Curry Soup

Many of the Orientals who came here to work on the railroads remained to invade the kitchens of the well-to-do. It was a welcome invasion for those who loved good food. The talented touch of these cooks is evident in many of the old and typical dishes of the Coast.

Season 2 cups of rich chicken stock with 2 teaspoons of curry powder and a teaspoon of lemon juice. Bind with 2 egg yolks in ½ cup of heavy cream, pour in serving cups, and chill. Serve sprinkled with very finely minced green onions, just a trace of them for color. SERVES 3 OR 4.

2 cups chicken stock	2 egg yolks
2 teaspoons curry powder	½ cup heavy cream
1 teaspoon lemon juice	Minced green onions

❨ Deep Sea Consommé

Round up 4 pounds of seafood — fishbones and head, the shells and small claws from a lobster or two, the same of crabs, and a few clams and oysters, or scallops, or even abalone. Cover

342

with 6 cups of water, add an herb bouquet (parsley, thyme, bay), a cup of white wine, celery leaves, and an onion stuck with a couple of cloves. Let simmer for a couple of hours. Strain and clear, correct seasoning, adding a little M.S.G. if the flavor needs emphasizing, and serve garnished with 2 or 3 small shrimps in each serving. This same soup, flavored with saffron, is perfectly wonderful — if you like saffron. SERVES 8 OR MORE.

4 pounds assorted seafood	*Celery leaves*
6 cups water	*1 onion*
1 herb bouquet	*2 cloves*
1 cup white wine	*M.S.G. (if necessary)*
Saffron (optional)	

❲ Wine Fish Chowder

This recipe is from the Wine Institute, the organization that takes such good care of vintners, wine drinkers, and cooks.

Cook 1½ pounds of fresh or frozen fish in 2 cups of water until tender. Flake, first removing bones and skin. Strain liquid. Sauté 1 large onion, sliced, and 1 cup of coarsely chopped celery in 3 tablespoons of bacon drippings for 5 minutes. Add fish liquid, 4 cups of coarsely diced raw potatoes, 2 teaspoons of salt and just enough water to cover. When potatoes are nearly done, add the fish and 2 cups of hot milk. Correct seasoning, and when the potatoes are tender, add ½ cup of California sauterne or Rhine wine. Reheat and serve with croutons and chopped parsley. THIS MAKES 2 QUARTS OF CHOWDER, 6 LARGE OR 10 SMALL SERVINGS.

1½ pounds fish	*3 tablespoons bacon drip-*
2 cups water (and more as	*pings*
needed)	*4 cups diced raw potatoes*
1 large onion	*2 teaspoons salt*
1 cup chopped celery	*2 cups milk*
½ cup sauterne or Rhine wine	

NOTE: Northwestern women of a century ago, trying desperately to add variety to their meals, cooked salmon and pork together, with potatoes. More of a stew than a chowder, and well liked.

(Gazpacho

A favorite summer soup with everyone who tries it, this is a West Coast version of the Spanish and South American variety. Almost a liquid salad, there is no better way to start a meal on a broiling summer day.

Rub a large bowl with a cut clove of garlic. Peel 3 pounds of very ripe tomatoes, remove their cores, and chop them in rather small pieces. Don't lose any of that precious juice — pour it and the tomatoes into the bowl. Peel and chop 2 medium-sized cucumbers and add them, along with ½ cup each of minced green pepper and onion, and 2 cups of tomato juice or ice water. Next comes ⅓ cup of olive oil, 3 tablespoons of vinegar, plenty of salt and pepper (taste it!), and either a dash of tabasco or a fresh hot red pepper minced into infinitesimal pieces. Chill this very thoroughly and serve with an ice cube in each dish. The Spanish version has lots of layered bread or toast, but we skip that out here. SERVES 10 OR 12.

1 clove garlic	⅓ cup olive oil
3 pounds tomatoes	3 tablespoons vinegar
2 cucumbers	Salt and pepper
½ cup minced green pepper	Dash of tabasco or
½ cup minced onion	1 small hot red pepper
2 cups tomato juice or ice water	

(El Centro Green Pepper Soup

A delightful soup, this, and as good served cold as hot.

Cook ½ cup of minced green pepper and ⅓ cup of minced onion in a tablespoon of butter until soft. Add 2 cups of chicken stock and ¼ teaspoon of oregano, and simmer 20 minutes, then force through a sieve. Combine with 1 cup of cream sauce (1 cup rich milk, 1 tablespoon each flour and butter), and season with salt and pepper. If served hot, garnish with whipped cream (1 cup) which has had 2 tablespoons of finely minced green pepper added. If served chilled, add the extra green pepper to the soup before chilling, and

344

fold in a cup of cream. This version will need extra salt. SERVES 4 TO 6.

½ cup minced green pepper
⅓ cup minced onion
1 tablespoon butter
2 cups chicken stock
¼ teaspoon oregano

1 cup cream sauce
2 tablespoons finely minced green pepper
1 cup whipped cream or 1 cup cream

Salt and pepper

❰ Cream of California Herbs

California's climate is just right for a lot of things, including herbs. They all flourish here, though one has to get pretty far north to have luck with chervil, I admit.

The base of this soup is lettuce — the outside leaves that are so often discarded. Wash them well and chop them. (Here's one time when it is not a gastronomical sin to use a knife on lettuce!) Two cups of them — well packed cups — are simmered with a quart of white stock, along with ¼ cup of minced parsley or chervil, ¼ cup of minced shallots or green onions, and a teaspoon each of minced tarragon and rosemary. (Or suit your own taste; any harmonious herbs will do — just don't overdo them.) Simmer gently for 10 minutes, then press through a strainer. If the color is not good, add a few leaves of spinach, ground to a paste in a mortar. Correct the seasoning, then bind with a cup of cream and 3 egg yolks. Chives on this, whether served hot or cold. SERVES 6 OR MORE.

2 cups chopped lettuce leaves
1 quart white stock
¼ cup minced parsley or chervil

¼ cup minced shallots
1 teaspoon minced tarragon
1 teaspoon minced rosemary
Salt and pepper
1 cup cream

3 egg yolks

❰ Mussel Soup

Early residents of the West, being blissfully unaware of any danger in eating mussels, used them often and well. Try this when it is safe (page 142).

Scrub 4 quarts of mussels very well, scraping the shells or using a wire brush. Put them in a pot with ½ cup of chopped onion, a chopped clove of garlic, 2 tablespoons of olive oil, and 2 cups of water. When the mussels open, remove them and strain the liquor very carefully through cloth heavier than cheesecloth. Remove the beards from the mussels (these you can't miss; that's what they look like — beards) and chop half the mussels, returning them to the liquor, and adding a cup of tomato juice, ½ cup of cooked rice, and a pinch of saffron. Salt and pepper to taste. A cup of white wine is also a good addition. SERVES APPROXIMATELY 8.

> 4 quarts mussels (about 48
> medium-sized ones)
> ½ cup chopped onion
> 1 clove garlic
> 2 tablespoons olive oil
>
> 2 cups water
> 1 cup tomato juice
> ½ cup cooked rice
> Pinch of saffron
> Salt and pepper
>
> 1 cup white wine (optional)

NOTE: The mussels not used in the soup may be eaten like steamed clams, dipping them in butter.

❲ Essence of Mushroom

Sometimes I think this is our very finest soup, but that's when I am forgetting another score of favorites. Because it's light, yet very flavor-rich, it's perfect for a party dinner.

Grind a pound of cleaned fresh mushrooms, stems and all. Cook a teaspoon of minced shallots in a tablespoon of butter until they get that transparent look, then simmer the mushrooms in the same pan. After 3 minutes, pour on a quart of stock, rich but not highly seasoned. Keep at a simmer for half an hour, then strain, pressing every bit of goodness from the mushrooms. (A ricer, lined with cloth, does this easily.) Season with salt only, and serve. Variations on this theme: sherry to taste, or a whipped cream garnish, or a few leaves of fresh tarragon for color and flavor. SERVES 6 OR 8.

> 1 pound mushrooms
> 1 teaspoon minced shallots
> Salt
>
> 1 tablespoon butter
> 1 quart rich stock

⟨ Onion Soup with Wine

We like it in the French manner, but we also like it in this way, which is entirely ours.

For each serving slice 1 medium-sized onion and "melt" it in 2 tablespoons of butter. Add a cup of very rich and well-seasoned chicken stock and ¼ cup of white table wine, and 3 tablespoons of grated Jack cheese. Pour into individual onion soup pots, top with a slice of toasted sourdough French bread, sprinkle lightly with a little more grated Jack, and put under the broiler until the cheese is melted and brown. Sometimes we use Camembert, instead of Jack cheese, and that's good, too.

For each serving

1 medium-sized onion
2 tablespoons butter
1 cup chicken stock

¼ cup white table wine
3 tablespoons grated Jack cheese
1 slice sourdough French bread

NOTE: Joe Tilden, famed *bon vivant* of San Francisco, perfected another never-to-be-forgotten onion soup: Cook onion long and slowly in butter, add rich stock *and* rich milk, and bind with egg yolks. Serve with Parmesan cheese.

⟨ Cream of Ripe Olive Soup

Here's a soup that is slated for fame — if it hasn't already gained it!

Use the ripe olives that come already minced — they're the least expensive. Cook 2 cans of them in 3 cups of stock, along with a clove of garlic, for 20 minutes. Remove garlic, add a cup of heavy cream and 2 egg yolks (or a cup of thin cream sauce), season to taste with salt and pepper, and serve, with or without a dash of sherry. SERVES 6.

2 cans minced ripe olives
3 cups stock
1 clove garlic
1 cup heavy cream ⎫
2 egg yolks ⎬ or 1 cup thin cream sauce
Salt and pepper
Dash of sherry (optional)

❰ Dan & Louis Oyster Stew

The ill wind that, in 1865, wrecked the schooner *Annie Doyle* on Yaquina Bay, was very good for Oregonian gourmets. Meinert Wachsmuth, who was stranded in the new country, went into the oyster business, eventually taking up squatter's rights at Shoalwater Bay (Willapa Harbor). His son, Louis, was brought up there and he, later, bought the famous oyster beds at Yaquina Bay. Now he is in the oyster business in a big way, including his famous Dan & Louis Oyster Bar in Portland. There, in a salty atmosphere, the tiny Olympia oysters are opened right before your eyes, and served, either on the half shell (page 144), in a cocktail, as an Olympia oyster fry, or in the celebrated oyster stew. I begged the recipe, and here it is:

1 *pint Olympia oysters*	⅛ *pound butter*
2 *quarts milk*	¾ *teaspoon Schilling's Savor*
½ *pint cream*	*Salt*
Salt and pepper to taste	

"Heat milk and cream in double boiler until piping hot. Stirring constantly, add butter, salt, pepper, Savor Salt. Drop oysters into pot and allow them to simmer for 5 minutes. Stir again and serve in deep bowls with a pat of butter. THIS RECIPE IS SUFFICIENT FOR 6 GENEROUS HELPINGS."

❰ Oysterville Bisque

This oyster bisque is rich, as a bisque should be, but by substituting milk for cream a very satisfactory oyster soup will result.

Drain a pint of oysters and save the juices. Cook 2 tablespoons each of diced green pepper, onion, and celery in 3 tablespoons of butter. When they are transparent, add the oysters and cook them very gently for 5 minutes. Add the resulting liquid to the first juices and put the oysters and vegetables through the grinder. Return to the liquid, add a blade of mace or a sprig of marjoram, salt and pepper to taste, and 3 cups of cream or milk. Cook another 10 minutes, add ½ cup

348

of white wine or ¼ cup of sherry. Strain, pressing the oysters through the sieve, and, if you wish, bind with a roux of 2 tablespoons each of flour and butter. Garnish with a little finely chopped green pepper. SERVES 6.

1 pint oysters	1 blade of mace or
2 tablespoons diced green	1 sprig marjoram
pepper	3 cups cream or milk
2 tablespoons diced onion	½ cup white wine or
2 tablespoons diced celery	¼ cup sherry
3 tablespoons butter	Salt and pepper
Butter and flour to bind (optional)	

❲ Richmond Beach Chicken and Oyster Stew

This is the way Mildred Oakes, one of the best cooks in Seattle, makes her oyster stew.

The large Willapa oysters are used for this. Cut a pint of them (sometimes that's only 4 or 5!) in pieces, and cook them gently in ¼ cup of butter for about 3 minutes, along with ½ cup of finely sliced celery. Add 3 cups of chicken stock and 1 cup of sauterne. Heat, taste for seasoning, and serve sprinkled with chervil or parsley. SERVES 6.

1 pint oysters	3 cups chicken stock
¼ cup butter	1 cup sauterne
½ cup finely sliced celery	Salt and pepper
Chervil or parsley	

NOTE: Another very different soup using Willapa Bay oysters is a chowder, made with the oysters, and with rice, green peppers, bacon, celery, and milk. The seasoning is cardamom, which makes it even more surprising.

❲ Voyageur's Split Pea Soup

A hardy lot, these skilled French-Canadian boatmen who traveled hundreds of miles in their bateaux, bringing furs to the Hudson's Bay Company post at Fort Vancouver. They carried salt pork and dried peas as standard equipment, for split pea soup was their staff of life. They apparently traded recipes as well as furs, for the pioneers learned to make this delectable soup. Today the state of Washington produces more dried peas than any other part of the world, some of which are used for this still-popular potage. And in Buellton, California, a man named Andersen made fame and fortune because of his mother's recipe for split pea soup. This recipe is in the French-Canadian manner.

Soak a pound of split peas overnight. Next day dice ½ pound of salt pork and cook it until brown. Remove and save pork, and in the fat cook a cup of chopped onion and 2 very finely minced cloves of garlic. Combine with the peas and 2 quarts of water or stock. (The water in which tongue or ham or corned beef has boiled is perfect.) A bit of bay and some celery leaves are added for seasoning, and some pepper. Cook until the peas are so soft they're a mush. Remove leaves, strain through a coarse sieve, pressing through all the soft peas, add the diced pork, correct the seasoning, and if necessary thin with water or stock, though this soup *should* be thick. Garnish with cubes of ham or croutons. SERVES 8 TO 12.

1 pound split peas	2 quarts water or stock
½ pound salt pork	Bay leaf
1 cup chopped onion	Celery leaves
2 cloves garlic	Pepper

(Joe Meek's Pumpkin Soup

When Dr. McLoughlin wrote his London headquarters that the pumpkin seed he had requested had not arrived, he was burning, and not because he craved pumpkin pie! He wanted the crop for pig food. The seeds apparently came shortly after, for many early pioneers, including the famous trail blazer Joe Meek, were soon eating pumpkin in their nutritious stews. Another early pumpkin incident apparently caused another slow burn. Joe Meek, who was to provision a pack trip, did so with nothing but a couple of pumpkins. His companions weren't amused. Whether or not the pumpkin was made into soup, history does not relate. This recipe is a modern adapta-

350

tion of the early one that called for "a piece of pumpkin the size of your two hands."

Heat a quart of milk with 3 cups of cooked mashed pumpkin, a tablespoon of sweet basil, ¼ cup of minced onions, 2 tablespoons of butter, and salt and pepper to taste. Cook in a double boiler for a half hour, strain, and serve, garnished with croutons. SERVES 6 TO 8.

1 quart milk	1 tablespoon sweet basil
3 cups cooked mashed pump-	¼ cup minced onions
kin	2 tablespoons butter
Salt and pepper	

❨ Bay Shrimp Stew

Here we go again with another superlative fish stew.

Shell and clean 1½ pounds of cocktail shrimps. If larger shrimps or prawns are used, cut them in small pieces, but leave the tiny Bay shrimps whole. In either case they should be cooked. Crush a large clove of garlic with ½ teaspoon of salt, add the shrimps, and cook them in ¼ cup of butter for 3 minutes. Pour in 3 cups of chicken or fish stock and 3 cups of cream. Season with salt and pepper, and a whole bay leaf, and cook gently for 20 minutes. Remove the bay leaf and put a small piece of butter in the tureen or soup bowls before pouring over the hot soup. This soup seems even better when reheated, as it gives more time for blending. It may be thickened slightly, if desired, and a garnish of minced chives is not amiss. SERVES 8 OR MORE.

1½ pounds shrimps	3 cups stock
1 clove garlic	3 cups cream
½ teaspoon salt	Salt and pepper
¼ cup butter (and more)	1 bay leaf

❨ Grant Street Soup

This recipe comes from Grant Street, in San Francisco's Chinatown, but just which of its many restaurants, I cannot say. For, like the recipe for boiled rice, it's everybody's property.

Cut a cooked pork chop (or about 5 ounces of roast pork) into narrow strips. Now rinse about 12 or 15 dried shrimps (the little ones, available in Chinese markets) and cook them in a quart of chicken stock for 10 minutes. Add the pork, cook a few more minutes, season with a tablespoon of soy sauce, and salt and pepper if necessary. Serve sprinkled with leaves of Chinese parsley — or, if that is too exotic for your palate, with our own variety, or with leaves of water cress. SERVES 6.

1 cooked pork chop   *1 quart chicken stock*
12–15 dried shrimps   *1 tablespoon soy sauce*
Salt and pepper

(Jellied Sherry Consommé

This is a very simple soup, but a very charming one.

Soak an envelope of plain gelatin in ¼ cup of cold water. Add it to 3 cups of boiling chicken stock (use hot water and chicken concentrate, if you wish), along with ¼ cup of dry sherry, and a teaspoon of lemon juice. Season with salt and pepper to taste, then chill. Serve in cups with a bit of minced parsley or chives to give it color. SERVES 4 TO 6.

1 envelope gelatin   *¼ cup sherry*
¼ cup cold water   *Salt and pepper*
3 cups chicken stock   *1 teaspoon lemon juice*

NOTE: If you wish, omit the sherry and substitute 1 cup of white table wine for 1¼ cups of the chicken stock.

(Venison Soup

There are as many versions of venison soup as there are hunters to make it. Some are thick mulliganlike creations, calculated to appease hunger made keen by the chase, others are meticulously skimmed and clarified affairs, suitable for the most formal table. Then there is this:

352

Crack a pound of venison bones and cut a pound of the meat into pieces (trimmings and tougher cuts do nicely) and brown them for 5 minutes in 3 tablespoons of shortening. Remove bones and meat to a stock pot, and in the remaining fat brown ¼ cup each of chopped onions, carrots, and celery. Combine with the meat and add enough water to cover, ½ cup of red wine, some salt, and an herb bouquet made with bay, marjoram, and parsley. Simmer very gently, skimming occasionally. When the meat is very tender, strain, cut meat into dice, and return to the soup. Season with a tablespoon of lemon juice, salt and pepper if needed. For an extra and pleasant touch, add a few cooked chestnuts, cut in quarters, or a little cooked wild rice. SERVES ABOUT 6.

1 pound venison bones	*¼ cup chopped celery*
1 pound venison	*Water to cover*
3 tablespoons shortening	*½ cup red wine*
¼ cup chopped onions	*1 herb bouquet*
¼ cup chopped carrots	*1 tablespoon lemon juice*
	Salt and pepper

❲ Ying's Variety Soup

Whether this soup, concocted by a Chinese cook employed on an early California ranch, was inspired by genius or by a lack of other meats, is not a matter of record.

A half pound of tripe is boiled in a quart of salted water with an onion until tender, then cut in tiny dice. To it is added a cup each of diced heart, kidney, and liver, and all is simmered together until done, with more water added to make 1½ quarts in all. The seasoning is salt, and a small red pepper, and just before serving some ½-inch pieces of green onion are usually added. SERVES APPROXIMATELY 8.

½ pound tripe	*1 cup diced kidney*
1 onion	*1 cup diced liver*
1 quart salted water	*Salt*
(and more)	*1 small red pepper*
1 cup diced heart	*Green onion*

❲ Winter Melon Soup

This is, to me, one of the most fascinating of soups. It is Chinese, but I can see no reason why it shouldn't be served at any meal — it's that good. It's a spectacular soup, as the melon itself plays the role of soup tureen!

Purchase a large Winter melon at a Chinese market. Wash it, cut a slice from the top, and scoop out the seeds. Put the melon on a rack in a large kettle, but not so large a one that the melon won't stand upright. Pour some hot water around the outside of the melon, and fill the inside with a soup made by simmering ½ cup of Chinese dried shrimps in 3 cups of water for an hour, then combining with 3 cups of chicken stock. (If this doesn't fill the melon, add more chicken stock.) Cover the pot and let the whole thing steam for an hour, or until the melon is tender. Don't overcook, though — if you do the whole beautiful thing will collapse. Lift the melon, soup and all, into a bowl that will hold it right side up. The Chinese handle it in a cradle or sling made of string. Add ¼ cup of water cress leaves, and ladle into individual bowls, scooping a little of the melon into each serving. This tastes better, somehow, if eaten with the Chinese soup spoons made of porcelain, and served from Chinese soup bowls. SERVES 8 TO 12.

1 large winter melon	*3 cups chicken stock*
½ cup Chinese dried shrimps	*(or more)*
3 cups water	*¼ cup water cress leaves*

NOTE: This may be made with any clear soup, though it should really have a Chinese character. A soup made by adding tiny dice of ham and water chestnuts to chicken soup would be good, or a duck soup with a few raw green peas. The main thing is to have it rich and well flavored.

❲ Fruit Soups

Except for those of us who are of Scandinavian or Central European extraction, we have had little taste for these soups until rather recently. Soups can be made from many of our

West Coast products: apples, oranges, cherries, cranberries, dried prunes, apricots, raisins, blueberries — any fruit, actually. The most usual method is to spice the fruit juice with cinnamon, cloves, and lemon peel, and thicken it with sago (2½ cups fruit juice, ¼ cup lemon juice, ¼ cup sugar, ½ cup sago, stick cinnamon and whole cloves, served chilled). Another way is to use arrowroot, or even cornstarch or rice as the thickening agent, or, and better I think, to serve it jellied (1 tablespoon of gelatin soaked in ¼ cup of cold water and added to 2¼ cups of the juice). Then there is the soup made with dried fruits, of which we produce such huge quantities. A half cup each of dried apples, raisins, apricots or your own assortment — snipped into bits and soaked overnight, then stewed in plenty of water until soft, with the cinnamon, cloves, and sliced lemon. This is thickened with 2 tablespoons of sago and mixed with an equal amount of chicken stock. The addition of the chicken stock gives a little "oomph" to the soup, making it rather better, I think, than those made with fruit only. Wine also adds character to these dessertlike soups, as in the Oregon Cherry Soup (page 336). That is one of the better fruit soups, but after all is said and done, I think fruit is best used in soup as a garnish:

Two cups of beef consommé, ½ cup of red table wine, garnish of pitted red cherries, 3 or 4 to a serving.

Two cups chicken stock, ½ cup cream, ½ teaspoon curry powder, salt and pepper. Diced raw apples as a garnish.

Any clear soup garnished with thin slices of lemon or lime.

Vegetables

THERE'S NOTHING DULL *about vegetable cookery on the West Coast. We have, and I do dare say it, the greatest variety of vegetables in the world, and we have most of them all year round. What's more, we have learned from the Chinese, from the Italians, and from talented cooks of the other nationalities that make up our populace, how to best cook them. We have come a long way since the days when the white man first came to the fertile land and found little in the way of edible vegetation — or at least little that was being eaten besides berries and nuts. True, the Indians of the Northwest did have wapato, a potato-like root that grew in the marshes and which the squaws dug with their toes. They also had camas, a bulb not unlike an onion, which they cooked in a pit, underground, very much as we roast clams today. The rancheros, when they first came to California, had their tortillas and their beans, but mostly they had meat. True, like the Padres, they had puchero, a meat and vegetable stew, and, on fast days, they had colache, a mixture of corn, beans, tomatoes, and squash or pumpkin. They, and the Indians also, had an occasional dish of nopales (cactus leaves, page 383) and quelites, or greens, but they could, apparently, live happily without them.*

In the Northwest the story was quite different. Dr. McLoughlin, chief factor of the Hudson's Bay Company, planted vegetables — onions, beans, peas, potatoes — almost as soon as he arrived at Fort Vancouver, and he gave

356

Vegetables

them generously to the early settlers in the vicinity who appreciated them.

Everywhere, in those early days, the supply of vegetables varied greatly, from famine to feast according to circumstances. Potatoes, for instance, were supposedly so plentiful that the pioneers blanched at the sight of them, yet, at a Fourth of July party in Portland in the '50s, the potatoes were "brought from Illinois." In the gold country, vegetables were at first almost nonexistent, until, in 1849, a man named Briggs realized that there was another kind of fortune in the tillable land around the Sacramento River. "Green gold" began to arouse interest in California as it already had in Oregon. There a pioneer named Spalding had discovered that eastern Oregon and Washington were right for growing "every kind of vegetable." And so began one of the biggest industries in the West.

❨ Artichokes

The globe artichoke is actually the bud of a giant thistle. The plant itself is a decorative one, as anyone who has seen the acres of them along the coast around Half Moon Bay knows full well. Almost all commercially grown artichokes come from this region, and from here they are shipped to all parts of the country. Artichokes, when first introduced in California, were a flop, too many people being of the opinion that they were more trouble than they were worth. The Italians, of course, knew better, but only because they knew so well how to cook them. Finally the Palace Hotel, in San Francisco, started to feature artichokes, and they immediately became very much the mode. Today they are standard fare, from Seattle to San Diego.

❨ Boiled Artichokes

Select artichokes that are bright green, with leaves that show no signs of opening, and that are so fresh that they actually squeak when squeezed. The baby artichokes are highly prized, but the larger ones can also be deliciously tender, and are more suitable for some methods of serving. Cooks do not agree on exactly how to trim an artichoke. Some slice an inch straight off the top and cut the stem close to the base; others clip the top of each leaf with scissors and peel the stem but leave it on; others trim all the tough leaves completely off and scoop out the choke by separating the inner leaves and digging it out. One thing on which cooks *do* agree is that as soon as the vegetable is cut, in any manner whatsoever, it is put at once into acidulated water (1 tablespoon of lemon juice or vinegar to a quart of water). It is also boiled in the same water, with salt added, unless otherwise noted. Artichokes take from 20 to 45 minutes, depending on their size and youth. They are done when the bottoms pierce easily with a fork, or when an upper leaf pulls out without resistance. Drain upside down.

NOTE: *Artichokes on the Half Shell*. This is an easy way to remove the choke. Split artichokes, any size, in half, from top to bottom, including the stem. Now you can see where the choke is hiding. Slice off the top of the artichoke about half way down and scoop out what little choke remains. Peel stem and trim off all the tough outside and bottom leaves. This leaves nothing but the edible portion of the artichoke — the part that can be eaten with a fork. Drop at once into acidulated water. Cook in the same way as above, and serve with melted butter or hollandaise.

NOTE: *Buttered Artichoke Bottoms*. This carries the recipe above just a little further. The artichoke is not split, but is sliced horizontally about an inch and a quarter or so (depending on the size of the vegetable) above the bottom. The stem is cut off, all the tough leaves trimmed away, and the "choke" (or the "internal filamentous portion," as an early California cook book says) that remains in the middle is scooped out. This gives you a big tasty artichoke bottom, surrounded by a few tender leaf ends. Cook as above, and serve hollandaise or mayonnaise in the little hollow in the middle. The Bohemian Club in San Francisco served artichoke bottoms Provençal in 1883; this means that they were cooked with garlic.

([Artichokes Barigoule

This may not be our recipe, but we've liked it ever since the Palace started serving it. It appears on one of their menus dated 1879.

Trim and boil 4 artichokes for 5 minutes, drain, and remove chokes, then put in cold acidulated water (page 358). Make a forcemeat with 4 slices of minced bacon, ¼ cup of minced shallots, ½ cup of minced mushrooms, a tablespoon of minced parsley, salt, pepper, and a little nutmeg. Stuff the artichokes, tie a string around each to keep the filling in, and brown on all sides in olive oil. Add ½ cup of stock or wine, or a combination of the two, cover, and bake until tender. Remove strings before serving to four persons.

4 artichokes   *1 tablespoon minced parsley*
4 slices bacon   *Salt and pepper*
¼ cup minced shallots *Nutmeg*
½ cup minced mushrooms *½ cup stock or wine*
            Olive oil

([Artichoke Ring

Cook 4 to 6 artichokes (in acidulated water, page 358) until soft, scrape the leaves with a spoon, and force the heart through a sieve. Combine 2 cups of the purée with a cup of cream, whipped, 4 beaten egg yolks, salt, and lemon juice to taste, and a hint of cayenne. Add the egg whites beaten stiff, and bake in a ring mold that has been set in a pan of water, for 30 minutes at 350°. Fill with creamed sweetbreads or shrimps. SERVES 6 OR 8.

            2 cups artichoke purée   *4 eggs*
               (4–6 artichokes)   *Salt*
            1 cup cream   *Lemon juice*
                     Cayenne

ℂ Artichokes in White Wine

Artichokes are one of the few vegetables that take to wine cookery, for which we bless them, and they go wonderfully well with fish, poultry, and eggs, and with meats that are not too rich.

Trim 1 inch from the tops of 6 artichokes, and remove the stems and tough bottom leaves. Into each heart thrust a small sliver of garlic and drizzle a teaspoon of olive oil, then stand them upright in a pot that has a tight-fitting lid. Add 2 cups of white table wine, and ½ teaspoon of salt to the pot, cover, and cook gently from about 30 to 45 minutes, or until tender. It may be necessary to add a little more wine. Serve hot with a mixture of melted butter and olive oil for leaf dunking. The Italians sometimes tuck a fillet of anchovy into the artichoke, along with the garlic. A wonderful idea when served with veal! SERVES 6.

6 artichokes	2 cups white wine
6 slivers garlic	(or more)
6 teaspoons olive oil	½ teaspoon salt
(and more)	Melted butter

ℂ Artichoke Cups

Cut artichokes horizontally across, a little below the middle. Discard top leaves, stems, and choke, as well as the tough outside leaves on the bottom. In other words, leave only the edible portion of the vegetable. Cook it in acidulated water, as in the preceding recipes, and drain. They may be served hot, filled with shad roe lightly mixed with hollandaise; or with chicken livers in white wine sauce; or with crab Newburg. Or they may be chilled and filled with chicken or lobster salad, or perhaps with a mixed vegetable salad of diced cucumbers, cooked peas, diced celery, and a little onion, dressed with mayonnaise.

ℂ Stuffed Artichokes

Artichokes may be stuffed with a variety of things. A bread dressing, or one with cheese, is most usual, but a fine and frighteningly rich one is this:

360

Vegetables

The artichokes have the tops cut off about an inch down, are then cooked until half done, and the chokes removed. The dressing is made by cooking ½ cup of chopped mushrooms, and ½ cup of chopped Italian ham in 3 tablespoons of olive oil flavored with garlic. A cup of cooked calf's brains, ½ cup of bread crumbs, and ½ cup of pine nuts are added. The whole is seasoned and put into the centers of the artichokes with the leaves spread well apart. (This is enough for six large ones.) Put in a baking dish, pour in a cup of white wine or artichoke water, and bake at 350° for about 20 minutes, or until tender. This is, of course, an entree. See index for other artichoke dishes. SERVES 6.

6 large artichokes	1 clove garlic
½ cup chopped mushrooms	1 cup cooked calf's brains
½ cup chopped Italian ham	½ cup bread crumbs
3 tablespoons olive oil	½ cup pine nuts
Salt and pepper	

⟮ Artichoke Notes

Artichoke Bottoms, cooked as on p. 358, may be egged and crumbed, and fried in deep fat, or sliced and sautéed in olive oil, with or without garlic, or sliced into shirred egg dishes, covered with cheese sauce and crumbs, and baked. They may also, according to an old cook book, be dried for future use, but I won't guarantee it.

Fried Artichokes. Raw artichokes may be fried, and very successfully. Cut them in quarters if small, in eighths if large, and trim off all the inedible parts. Fry gently in olive oil, with or without garlic or green onions. Add a little red wine vinegar or lemon juice just before serving.

Frittered Artichokes. Cooked artichoke bottoms, quartered, dipped in fritter batter, and fried in deep fat, are delicious.

Artichoke Bottoms may be diced and used in combination with seafood or poultry in cocktails, or creamed dishes, or omelets.

⟨ Asparagus

The rich delta lands of the Sacramento River supply nearly half of the nation's fresh asparagus, and 90 per cent of the *world's* canned, and now they're freezing enormous quantities as well. Other parts of the Coast, notably Porterville, in California, and Sunnyside in Washington, produce much fine asparagus, too, and many a home gardener considers the asparagus quite as important as the roses. Just how long asparagus has been this popular out here, I can't say. It appears in *Los Angeles Cookery*, 1881, and menus from both the Palace and the Bohemian Club list it in 1883, though it was probably grown to some extent long before that — certainly after that time, mention of it appears frequently.

⟨ Asparagus Vinaigrette

Asparagus is pretty tricky stuff to cook correctly. It should be green and tender and almost crisp — so that when held by the end for dunking, it won't droop desolately, like a wilted daisy. This is true whether it is to be eaten hot or cold. One way to accomplish this, at least for salad, is to stand over it while cooking, and the minute — no, the *second* — it is done drain it and rinse it with cold water. This stops subsequent cooking. Arrange the asparagus in a flat serving dish, pour over ¼ cup of vinaigrette sauce for each pound of asparagus, and marinate in the refrigerator. But please don't serve *too* cold. The flavor will be better if the dish is allowed to stand at room temperature for a short while before mealtime.

⟨ Tin How Asparagus

Many an early housewife, grateful for the "cheap Chinese labor" that she had in her kitchen, couldn't understand what Kearney and his ilk were making all the fuss about. These beloved Chinese housemen were quiet and efficient, and wonderful cooks. They prepared the food in the Occidental manner, as was desired, but they never lost their Oriental way with vegetables. Their "way" was simply a matter of timing, so that the vegetables though cooked, were crisp and colorful, with

362

their true fresh flavor. Today, much of our vegetable cookery, at least at home, still shows that good influence, even though the saucing be Occidental. This recipe goes Chinese all the way.

The skinny asparagus, usually much less expensive than the plumper kind, is ideally suited for this recipe. Snap the tough ends from 2 pounds of it and then, laying it on a board, chop it coarsely with a French knife in irregular-sized pieces, averaging the size of a large pea. (The Chinese would cut them with a huge cleaverlike knife, and at a sharp angle, turning as they cut.) Make a Chinese gravy by thickening ¾ of a cup of chicken stock with a tablespoon of cornstarch moistened in a tablespoon of cold water, and seasoning with 2 tablespoons of soy sauce. (A clove of garlic, too, if you wish.) Cook the asparagus in 2 tablespoons of cooking oil for 2 minutes, stirring so that it will be well mixed. Now add the Chinese gravy and cook the asparagus in it for another minute. It will still be bright green, and crisp yet tender. SERVES 6.

2 pounds thin asparagus	*2 tablespoons soy sauce*
¾ cup chicken stock	*2 tablespoons cooking*
1 tablespoon cornstarch in	*oil*
1 tablespoon cold water	*1 clove garlic (optional)*

⟨ Asparagus San Fernando

This is a very new way of cooking asparagus, and, I think, a perfect one. Any size of stalks may be used, and they need not be uniform, which means that "field-run" asparagus may be used. All that matters is that it be fresh. Snap off the tough ends where the snapping is easy. Wash and remove all the scales, then slice the asparagus in very thin diagonal slices. Make the cuts at a *very* oblique angle, so that they are several times longer than the diameter of the stalk. Get it? Put the asparagus in a frying basket and have the deep frying pan filled with boiling salted water. Just before eating, plunge the basket into the boiling water, cook 2 minutes, drain, and serve with melted butter, salt and pepper. And please don't reject this recipe without giving it a try. This is a good way to do asparagus for salad, too, rinsing it in cold water after draining, so that it won't cook any longer.

◖ Asparagus with Chicken Liver Sauce

This is exciting! It was inspired by a Chinese recipe, but the tarragon and the sieving are both Occidental touches.

Cook 2 pounds of asparagus, but not too long. Drain and serve with a sauce made by cooking ¼ cup of cut chicken livers and a tablespoon of chopped shallots in ¼ cup of butter for 6 or 7 minutes. Add a teaspoon of flour and ¼ cup of water or stock, salt and pepper to taste, and, if you wish, tarragon, then force through a strainer. Easy as that and superlative. Try it with fish or chicken or veal. SERVES 6.

2 pounds asparagus

SAUCE

¼ *cup chicken livers*	*1 teaspoon flour*
1 tablespoon chopped shallots	¼ *cup water or stock*
	Salt and pepper
¼ *cup butter*	*Tarragon (optional)*

◖ Barbecue Beans

Beans are a must with barbecues, and have been ever since the days when the Spanish Dons had their roundups, and pit-roasted whole beeves for the rancheros for leagues around. Today no two barbecue experts will agree on just how to cook the meat *or* the beans. Some like elaborate recipes, some the simplest, like this:

Soak 2 pounds of Mexican pink beans overnight, then, using the same water and adding more if necessary, boil with a ham bone, a large onion, 3 crushed cloves of garlic, a teaspoon of chili powder, and cook until tender but not mushy. Now salt to taste, and add chili powder to your taste as well. Some outdoor cooks insist upon an 8-ounce can of Spanish-style tomato sauce, too. Remove ham bone and simmer slowly until the desired consistency. SERVES 12.

2 pounds pink beans	1 teaspoon chili powder
1 ham bone	(or more)
1 large onion	Salt
3 cloves garlic	1 8-ounce tin tomato sauce
	(optional)

❲ Black Beans Rodriguez

This recipe, or at least the inspiration for it, came from Guatemala. The combination of hot, well-seasoned black beans and cold sour cream is superb.

Wash and soak a pound of black beans overnight. Next morning, add an onion, 2 cloves of garlic, 3 stalks of celery, a chili pepper, and a carrot. Also an herb bouquet of parsley, thyme, and bay. Cover with water and simmer slowly until the beans are almost tender. Remove the vegetables and herbs, add 3 tablespoons of lard and plenty of salt to the beans, and put them in a casserole along with the remaining juices. Add enough white wine to bring the liquid almost to the top of the beans. Cover and bake until tender, and serve with huge blobs of sour cream. SERVES 6.

1 pound black beans	1 carrot
1 onion	1 herb bouquet
2 cloves garlic	3 tablespoons lard
3 stalks celery	Salt
1 chili pepper	White wine as needed

❲ Frijoles Refritos

Beans, beans, and more beans was the order of the day in early California. Beans, fried beans, refried beans, morning, noon, and night, for they were served at every meal including breakfast, and are even today by families of Spanish and Mexican descent. The rest of us have learned how truly wonderful they are, and we have them at barbecues, at buffets,

365

and very often at our own family meals, *including* breakfast. (Try them, just once, on a crisp Sunday morning, served with broiled ham and huevos rancheros (page 84) and you too will be a convert.) Like the *marmite* of France, the *cazuela,* a large terra cotta vessel, with rounded bottom and sloping sides, is almost always simmering on the back of the Mexican stove, giving out with the tantalizing odor of slow-cooked beans.

Wash a pound of Mexican pink or red beans, or pintos, if you wish, and put them to simmer with 1½ quarts of water, stirring occasionally. (The beans do not have to be soaked unless they are very old.) Test them after a couple of hours, and salt them. If they are tender, but not mushy, it's time to fry them. Put ½ cup of lard or bacon or ham fat into a *cazuela* or heavy pot, and melt it, then add a few beans at a time, mashing them with a spoon, and adding some of the bean liquor. Continue this until all the beans and liquor are used. (Some people like *all* the beans mashed, some prefer most of them whole, just crushing enough to thicken the liquid.) Cook and stir until it is of the desired thickness. These are fried beans. They may be varied by adding garlic or onions or chili powder for extra seasoning, but this is the basic, and the best, way.

Refried beans (frijoles refritos) are even better. Just reheat and refry them with more lard or oil, until they are hot and little crispy bits appear here and there. SERVES 6.

⟨ *Frijoles Notes*

Refried Beans with Cheese. Frijoles refritos con queso are made by dicing Monterey Jack or other mild cheese and adding it to the refried beans which are cooked just long enough to melt the cheese. (This is a honey!)

Beans, California Style. An old Pasadena cook book has a like recipe by Helen Elliott Bandini, of a famous old California family. She says to use "2 tablespoons of lard for each pint of cooked beans," but tablespoons were large in those days. Otherwise her recipe is the same, except that she uses

366

a little cayenne and calls the recipe "Beans, California Style."

Canned kidney beans, seasoned with sautéed minced onion, and a little red wine, salt, pepper, and thyme, are a quick and easy barbecue accompaniment.

(String Beans with Celery

Carrots and peas are not a favorite with us, thank goodness, but other vegetable combinations are.

Remove the strings from a pound of green beans and "French" them, slitting each bean into four lengthwise pieces. Cut a small head of celery into pieces as nearly as possible the same size (save the heart for nibbling raw). Cook the vegetables, covered, in a cup of chicken stock, until they are tender but still a little crisp. Drain, but reduce what stock is left until there is but a spoonful or so, then add 3 tablespoons of butter and pour over the vegetables. Correct seasoning if necessary. Especially good with fish. SERVES 6.

> *1 pound string beans*   *1 cup chicken stock*
> *1 small head celery*   *3 tablespoons butter*
> *Salt and pepper*

(String Bean Notes

These suggestions are all for 1½ pounds of string beans, cooked, but not too much. They may be cut in pieces, sliced diagonally, French sliced, whole (if not too large), or chopped. All should have salt and pepper to taste.

String Beans with Bacon. Chop beans before cooking Dress with 4 slices of bacon cooked crisp and crumbled, the bacon fat, and a tablespoon of lemon juice or red wine vinegar.

String Beans with Mushrooms. Dress with ¼ to ½ pound of mushrooms that have been sliced or chopped and sautéed in ¼ cup of butter.

String Beans with Mushrooms and Sour Cream. As above, but add a cup of sour cream to the mushrooms.

367

String Beans with Mushrooms, Sour Cream, and Bacon. Chop beans, mushrooms, and bacon. Boil beans, sauté mushrooms, fry bacon, and drain. Combine with 1 cup of sour cream. Corn bread with this for a luncheon dish.

String Beans with Cream and Parsley. Make a cream sauce using 1 tablespoon of butter, ½ clove of crushed garlic (remove after cooking), 1 tablespoon of flour, and a cup of light cream. Add ¼ cup of minced parsley and mix with the beans.

String Beans with Parsley and Lemon. Dress with ¼ cup of melted butter, 2 tablespoons of lemon juice, ¼ cup minced parsley.

String Beans with Olive Oil and Cheese. Heat 3 tablespoons of olive oil with a clove of garlic. Discard garlic. Dress beans, sprinkle with grated cheese (Parmesan), a drizzle of lemon juice, and salt and pepper. Mix like a salad, and serve hot.

Fiesta String Beans. Add 2 or 3 canned green chilies, cut in strips and the seeds rinsed off, to the beans, along with 1 cup of tomato sauce.

String Beans with Dill. Add 2 tablespoons of minced fresh dill or 2 teaspoons of dill seeds, crushed in a mortar, to ⅓ cup of melted butter and 1 tablespoon of lemon juice. Pour over hot beans. Or dress with a sauce made by cooking a crushed clove of garlic in 3 tablespoons of butter, with ¼ cup of minced fresh dill or 1 tablespoon of crushed dill seeds, and 2 tablespoons of flour. After 3 minutes, add 2 tablespoons of lemon juice and a cup of chicken stock. Cook until thick and strain. This may be served hot or cold.

String Beans with Herbs. Dress with ¼ cup of butter, 1 teaspoon of lemon juice if you wish, and with a teaspoon of minced savory, thyme, marjoram, or basil, or 1 tablespoon of chives or chervil. Or use a mixture.

❰ Bean Sprouts

Though they are known primarily as an ingredient in Chinese cookery, I do not hesitate to predict that bean sprouts will become a favorite "green" vegetable. Already we are using them in salads, and those who have cooked them this way are wildly enthusiastic about them with fish or meat or eggs.

Melt ¼ cup of butter and in it cook ½ cup each of sliced celery, onion, and green pepper, for about 3 minutes. (A crushed clove of garlic may be added for flavor, then removed.) Add a pound of bean sprouts and a tablespoon of soy sauce. Cover and cook gently for about 8 minutes. Correct seasoning and serve, with or without chopped toasted almonds sprinkled over the top. Try this with Chinese spareribs (page 262) and rice for a delightful meal. SERVES 8.

¼ cup butter	1 pound bean sprouts
½ cup sliced celery	1 tablespoon soy sauce
½ cup sliced onion	Salt and pepper if necessary
½ cup sliced green pepper	
1 clove garlic (optional)	Chopped toasted almonds (optional)

NOTE: Cook bean sprouts in a little butter, just enough to get them a little limp. Cook shrimps in butter and sprinkle with M.S.G. Pile shrimps in middle of platter, surround with bean sprouts, and serve with rice. This is a Japanese dish, and a nice one.

⟪ Broccoli with Ripe Olives

Cook 1½ pounds of broccoli in salted water until almost tender. Chop coarsely (this may be done before cooking). Cook a crushed clove of garlic in ¼ cup of olive oil for 2 minutes, remove garlic, add a can of minced ripe olives, juice and all, and a teaspoon of lemon juice. Turn into the broccoli, correct seasoning, and stir over a low flame until done to your taste. SERVES 6.

1½ pounds broccoli	1 can minced ripe olives
1 clove garlic	1 teaspoon lemon juice
¼ cup olive oil	Salt and pepper

([Broccoli Salinas

Cook 2 pounds of the tender parts of broccoli in salted water until done, but still crisp and green, and serve with a sauce made by heating ½ cup of mayonnaise in a double boiler (easy on the heat!) with 2 tablespoons of tarragon vinegar and 2 chopped hard-boiled eggs. This with fish, veal, or ham. SERVES 6.

2 pounds broccoli   2 tablespoons tarragon vine-
½ cup mayonnaise   gar
          2 hard-boiled eggs

([Broccoli with Soy and Almonds

Here I go again with a vegetable cooked in the Chinese manner, but it is so good, and such a good way to use the tough stalks. The tender heads may be used as a salad, vinaigrette, or as a vegetable for another meal.

Peel 2 pounds of the heavy stalks of broccoli, being sure to remove the tough green part. Cut the rest in thin diagonal slices, and cook in boiling salted water for 2 minutes, or until tender but still crisp. Drain. Now heat ¼ cup of toasted sesame oil ("sesamum oiler," to be found in Chinese grocery stores), or use butter. Add a tablespoon of soy sauce and ¾ of a cup of chicken stock, heat, and thicken with a tablespoon of cornstarch mixed with ¼ cup of cold water. When clear and thick, pour over the broccoli, add ½ cup of blanched and split almonds, and heat. Serve with pork. SERVES 6 TO 8.

2 pounds broccoli stalks   ¾ cup chicken stock
   Salt   1 tablespoon cornstarch in
¼ cup toasted sesame oil   ¼ cup cold water
   (or butter)   ½ cup blanched and split
1 tablespoon soy sauce   almonds

([Brussels Sprouts with Walnuts

Of course we like brussels sprouts with chestnuts — who doesn't? But we also like them with other nuts, and we like

370

them firm and green, and delicate of flavor, not gray and mushy and odoriferous.

Select a pound of small firm sprouts and remove all loose and faded leaves. Then boil them in salted water until just tender — they will be bright green. Drain them very well. Melt ¼ cup of butter, add ½ cup of blanched walnut halves (page 165), and cook a couple of minutes so that the nuts will brown lightly. Add the sprouts, and salt and pepper to taste, and return to the fire just long enough to heat. Peeled and seeded white grapes are sometimes added instead of the nuts — this when served with turkey. SERVES 6.

1 pound brussels sprouts	*½ cup walnut halves*
¼ cup butter	*Salt and pepper*

NOTE: Brussels sprouts are also very good when served with sour cream, or with butter and herbs (tarragon, savory, or basil). Or with sautéed shallots, minced parsley, and a touch of lemon juice. Recently we have taken to eating brussels sprouts raw, in salad, quartering them and dressing them like cole slaw. Also very energetic persons have been known to scoop out their insides and stuff them with shrimp or herring salad. This, of course, as an appetizer.

⟨ Cabbage

Cabbage was apparently one of the first vegetables we cultivated out here. It was served often, in early days, and it must have been frightful eating, as the ladies of that time cooked it an hour or two. Squaw cabbage is also mentioned as having been eaten, but it turns out to be a plant of the mustard family whose juicy stem, when cooked, was quite palatable. Today our cabbage seems always to be young and tender and sweet. We have the green or white cabbage, the red, and the savoy — that gorgeous beauty with the dark crinkly green leaves — and the Chinese cabbage. We cook them in some unusual ways.

❲ Dilled Cabbage with Sour Cream

Cut a new cabbage in eighths, remove core, and cook quickly in salted water until tender — about 5 or 6 minutes. Drain very well and keep hot. Crush a tablespoon of dill seeds in a mortar, cook them for 1 minute in a tablespoon of butter, add a cup of sour cream and a tablespoon of vinegar, and salt and pepper. Heat and pour over the cabbage. SERVES 6.

1 new cabbage   1 cup sour cream
1 tablespoon dill seeds   1 tablespoon vinegar
1 tablespoon butter   Salt and pepper

NOTE: An old Oregon recipe for cabbage called "Aunt Ellen's Way of Cooking Cabbage," turns out to be cabbage simmered in sour cream.

❲ Red Wine Cabbage

Cook a sliced onion in ¼ cup of butter until wilted. Add a small shredded red cabbage, a cup of red table wine, a teaspoon of sugar, salt, pepper, and ¼ teaspoon of ground allspice. Mix, then cover and cook until the cabbage is tender. Serve with roast pork. SERVES 4 OR 5.

1 onion   1 cup red table wine
¼ cup butter   1 teaspoon sugar
1 small red cabbage   Salt and pepper
        ¼ teaspoon ground allspice

NOTE: Red cabbage is quite often combined with chestnuts, particularly when served with venison.

❲ Cardoons

This is a close relative of the globe artichoke, but it is the midriff and stem, not the bud, that is eaten. The flavor is very much like that of the artichoke bottom — in other words, delicious — but it is hard to find except in Italian and other foreign markets. A pity, for it deserves more attention.

372

Vegetables

◖ *Carrots Quan Dai*

The Chinese cook even carrots well.

Scrape a bunch of them and cut in slices ¼-inch thick, cutting on the diagonal so that the slices will be quite large. Cook in 2 tablespoons of vegetable oil, covered, for 3 minutes. Cover with ½ cup of sweet and sour sauce (page 17), and add ½ green pepper, cut in slices. Cook until the pepper is bright green, and serve at once. Here's a good vegetable for tongue. SERVES 4.

1 bunch carrots	*½ cup sweet and sour sauce*
2 tablespoons vegetable oil	*½ green pepper*

◖ *Cauliflower Notes*

Cauliflower with Shrimp Sauce. Add ½ cup of diced cooked shrimps to 1 cup of cream sauce, and serve with cauliflower.

Cauliflower with Nuts. Brown ½ cup of any kind of nuts in the same amount of butter, and pour over cauliflower.

Japanese Cauliflower. Slice cauliflower and cook for about a minute or two in boiling salted water. Drain and serve, while still crisp, with a sauce made by cooking 2 tablespoons of chopped onion in ¼ cup of cooking oil for 1 minute, then adding ¼ cup of soy sauce.

Cauliflower with Sour Cream. Add ¼ cup of chopped walnuts to a cup of sour cream, season with salt and pepper, and serve cold on hot or cold cauliflower.

Cauliflower with Herbs. Savory, tarragon, thyme, parsley, chervil, oregano, and marjoram, all go well with cauliflower. Add any of these to melted butter, with a little lemon juice, and pour over flowerets.

Cauliflower with Pine Nuts. Make a sauce for cauliflower with crushed pine nuts, garlic, salt, olive oil, and lemon juice. Thin with water. Wonderful!

❨ Brentwood Braised Celery

A fancy recipe from a fancy place — home of Hollywood's elite.

Select 3 young heads of tender celery and split them in half, right through from top to bottom. Wash well, then dry, and cook, cut side down, in ¼ cup of butter until they acquire a lovely golden color. Turn over carefully. Add a cup of rich brown stock or bouillon, ½ cup of sherry, and cover and cook slowly until the celery is tender, basting occasionally during the cooking. The sauce should reduce considerably during the process. Lift celery from the pan carefully, arranging it on a hot platter and stripping with pimiento. Reduce the sauce further, until almost a glaze, and paint the celery with it. Garnish with small whole mushroom caps that have been sautéed in butter, and diced chicken livers, also cooked in butter. SERVES 6.

3 heads celery	½ cup sherry
¼ cup butter	Pimiento
1 cup brown stock	Mushroom caps
Chicken livers	

❨ Celery with Tarragon

Cut celery in matchlike pieces, about 2 inches long, and cook 2 cups of them in a cup of chicken stock, with a teaspoon of dried tarragon tied in a little cheesecloth bag. When the celery is just tender, drain it, add enough white wine to the stock to make 1 cup of liquid, and thicken it with a tablespoon each of butter and flour. Season with salt and pepper. Return the celery to the sauce just long enough to reheat, and serve, sprinkled with minced fresh tarragon. Serve with eggs, or lamb, or fish. SERVES 6.

2 cups sliced celery	1 tablespoon butter
1 cup chicken stock	1 tablespoon flour
1 teaspoon dried tarragon	Salt and pepper
White wine as needed	Minced fresh tarragon

Vegetables

(Chayote

This is a strange vegetable inasmuch as it has nothing much to offer in the way of flavor, yet everything when it comes to consistency, because it keeps its form even if it's overcooked. A pale green squashlike affair, it's roughly pear-shaped — very roughly, that is — and has but one seed. It has a very low starch content so it is sometimes used in place of potatoes in salad, or in scalloped dishes. Chayotes need not be peeled, though some prefer to do so. They are boiled just like potatoes.

The innards of a boiled chayote may be scooped out, mixed with sausage, returned to the shell and baked. Or buttered crumbs and herbs and onions may be mixed with the flesh; or chopped green pepper and tomato sauce; or crisp bacon, or ripe olives, or anything with *flavor*. Or the chayote may be partially hollowed out and used as a receptacle for creamed crab meat, or curried shrimps, or chopped ham and sour cream. Or the chayote may be diced or sliced before or after cooking, and dressed with garlic butter, or cheese sauce, or tomato sauce, or just with butter, minced parsley, and lemon juice.

(Chinese Peas

Chinese peas are one of our most delicious vegetables. We have the Chinese to thank for introducing them and showing us how to use them, but we have taken to them with such enthusiasm that they are quite as apt to pop up at a fried chicken dinner or a spaghetti supper as they are at an Oriental meal. Chinese peas are tender green young peas that are eaten pod and all. Indeed, the peas within the pods are embryonic, sometimes nonexistent. The pods are usually about 1½ inches long (the smaller the better), and are quite flat, as there's nothing to fill them out. They are prepared by removing the tips and strings, just like string beans, and are then washed but left whole. The trick is in the cooking, and even those who scorn other vegetables cooked in the Chinese manner will admit that these *have* to be done Oriental style. If the peas are to be served as a simple vegetable, like plain garden peas, do them this way: Have ready a pot of boiling water. Put the peas into a wire basket (I use a deep-frying basket) and put directly into the boiling water. Watch them. They will turn bright green almost at once. Boil them for 2 minutes, drain, dress with melted butter, and serve at once.

Now the Chinese don't do them this way. They have a sort of frying-steaming method that they use. The raw peas are put into a couple of tablespoons of oil — usually peanut or sesame oil — cooked a minute, stirring, covered and cooked the required time — another minute or two — and they are done, to be combined with some shining brown pork, or pretty pink shrimps, or almond-covered duck. You'll find the recipes in this book.

Chinese peas are a seasonal affair, and range from 15 cents to $2.00 a pound. But even at top price they are not very expensive when one considers that ½ pound will be vegetable enough for 6 people, and garnish enough for a score of them.

⟨ Chinese Peas with Water Chestnuts

Don't hesitate to serve this delightful combination with an Occidental meal. Roast squab, for instance, and wild rice, with perhaps another Oriental touch in preserved kumquats as a garnish for the meat.

Cook 3 green onions, chopped, in 3 tablespoons of cooking oil for 2 minutes. Add ½ pound of prepared Chinese peas and 8 sliced canned water chestnuts. Stir and cook for 2 minutes, then add a cup of hot chicken stock, ¼ teaspoon of M.S.G., and a tablespoon of cornstarch dissolved in ¼ cup of cold water. Add a little soy sauce, if you wish, and as soon as the sauce is transparent, which will be almost at once, eat them with reverence. SERVES 4 TO 8.

3 green onions	¼ teaspoon M.S.G.
3 tablespoons oil	1 tablespoon cornstarch in
½ pound Chinese peas	¼ cup cold water
8 water chestnuts	Soy sauce (optional)
1 cup chicken stock	Salt if necessary

Vegetables

(Squaw Corn

That's what it's called, and it's good, though I suspect no self-respecting squaw would think so. In the old days, the California Indians wouldn't touch green corn — it had to be dried for them.

Dice 4 slices of bacon and cook it until crisp. Mix with a No. 2 can of cream-style corn, 2 slightly beaten eggs, ¼ cup of cream, ½ teaspoon of salt, some fresh ground pepper, ½ cup of minced green pepper, and ½ cup of crisp toasted croutons. Mix well, cover with buttered crumbs, put the casserole in a pan of water, and bake at 300° until firm. SERVES 4 TO 6.

4 slices bacon	½ teaspoon salt
1 No. 2 can cream-style corn	Pepper
2 eggs	½ cup minced green pepper
¼ cup cream	½ cup toasted croutons
	Bread crumbs

NOTE: Corn is preferred on the cob, with butter, but we're also fond of it in a green corn pudding, Southern style. An old cook book has a recipe for a "Breakfast Luxury" made with grated green corn, mixed with tomatoes, and baked with buttered crumbs. Quite a breakfast!

(Corn in the Open

Corn is a favorite vegetable to serve with patio or barbecue meals. We do it in several ways. One is to strip the husks back, remove the silk, return the husks to their original position, twisting or tying the ends so that they'll stay put. The corn is sometimes soaked in ice water, then is either grilled over the charcoal, or buried under it. Sometimes the stripped corn is brushed with butter, the husks tied back on as above, and the corn grilled right over the coals. Another favorite way is to boil it in a big pot out of doors. The corn is stripped and each piece has a string tied around it. The ends of the strings are gathered together and tied to the handle of the pot, so that all the pieces can be lifted out at once. With corn eaten outdoors, we like to serve butter balls mixed either with chili powder or oregano, or sometimes just with salt and fresh ground pepper — this eliminates extra seasoning. Some prefer to mix the salt and pepper together and have a great big dish of it for everyone to dip into with his fingers. However it's done, there's nothing better than corn eaten in the open.

⟪ Dasheen

Although it is not a very common vegetable as yet, it does grow in California, and so should be mentioned. It is usually cooked as a potato is, baked or boiled, fried or mashed. The flavor is not unlike a chestnut, which means that it's very good indeed. Sliced and fried like potato chips it makes an interesting switch from the usual dunkers. Soak them in ice water, and dry before frying.

⟪ Eggplant Notes

Almost too beautiful to eat, these dark purple beauties, so we often have them lead a double life. First on the table, as the focal spot of a vegetable centerpiece (with bright red peppers, tiny yellow squash, perhaps a silver onion, and some pale green limes), and then to table as a succulent dish. We eat them in many ways. We have a white egg plant, too! It's used in the same way as its colored brother. They are identical under the skin.

Eggplant Luncheon Dish. Egg and crumb the slices and fry them brown, then put two slices together with Monterey Jack cheese between, and slip in the oven just long enough for the cheese to melt. Serve with tomato sauce.

French Fried Eggplant. Cut in ½-inch strips, soak in ice water for an hour, drain, and dry. Dip in batter: 1 cup flour, 1 teaspoon salt, ½ teaspoon sweet basil, pepper, 1 egg, 1 cup milk, 1 tablespoon olive oil. Fry at 370° until nicely brown.

Eggplant, Italian Style. Slice, dip in egg, then flour, and fry in olive oil with a clove of garlic. Serve with tomato sauce and grated Parmesan.

378

Vegetables

◖ Barbecued Eggplant

This recipe has a Syrian air about it. Shish kebab or shasslik being popular for charcoal grilling, it was only natural that we take on other Middle Eastern favorites.

The eggplant is sliced, without peeling, or cut in 8 sections like an orange. A clove of garlic is macerated in a mortar with 2 teaspoons of salt, a pinch of oregano is added, and ¼ cup of olive oil. Some like a tablespoon of red wine vinegar, too. The slices of eggplant are painted with this mix and broiled, slowly, over embers, until brown and tender on both faces. This, still on the Syrian theme, seems best with lamb or mutton steak, and quite naturally a pilaff fits in too, though we can get international and serve a dish of Mexican or Spanish rice. SERVES 6.

1 large eggplant	Pinch of oregano
1 clove garlic	¼ cup olive oil
2 teaspoons salt	1 tablespoon red wine vinegar (optional)

◖ Stuffed Eggplant with Minced Clams

Who first dreamed this up I cannot say, but it has been popular out here for many years.

Cut the top from a large and handsome eggplant, and scoop out the insides, leaving a wall about ¾ of an inch thick. Chop the insides and steam until tender, then add ¼ cup of minced onions cooked in ¼ cup of butter, a 7-ounce can of minced clams, juice and all, 2 tablespoons of minced parsley, ½ teaspoon of minced basil or thyme, an egg, and a cup of soft bread crumbs, or enough to take up the excess moisture. Fill eggplant shell, sprinkle with buttered crumbs, and bake for 30 minutes at 375°. SERVES 6 TO 8.

1 large eggplant	½ teaspoon minced basil or thyme
¼ cup minced onions	
¼ cup butter	1 egg
1 can minced clams (7-ounce)	1 cup soft bread crumbs (more or less)
2 tablespoons minced parsley	Buttered crumbs

379

(Baked Hominy Grits

This makes a particularly good vegetable with roast lamb or fried chicken, or with game of any kind.

Boil a cup of grits in 4 cups of boiling salted water, or according to directions on the box. When thick, stir in a good-sized piece of butter and more salt if necessary. Turn into a well-buttered casserole, dot top with more butter, and bake until it is brown and crusty. Almost anything can be, and is, added to this for variety. Chopped nuts, crisp bacon, onions, and/or green peppers, just to give you a hint. SERVES 6.

(Leeks with Bacon

The craze for Vichyssoise, which hit the West too, seemed to revive our interest in leeks. We now serve them frequently as a vegetable, and a darned good one, too!

Split a bunch of leeks, cut off the tough top part, and wash very thoroughly, being sure to ferret out the sand that will be hiding in the tender heart. Cook 4 slices of bacon until crisp, remove and save, and cook the leeks, cut side down, in the bacon fat until brown. Add 1/4 cup of stock and cover, continuing to cook until tender. Sprinkle the leeks with the crumbled bacon and serve hot, with veal chops and spinach. SERVES 4.

1 bunch leeks   *4 slices bacon*
1/4 cup stock

NOTE: Braised leeks with olives are good, particularly when served with duck. Prepare as above, but use butter instead of bacon fat and substitute green olives, chopped, for the bacon, using 1/2 cup for each bunch.

NOTE: Cold leeks, boiled, then thoroughly drained and gently pressed to remove excess moisture, are delicious when served as a salad with French dressing.

(Mushrooms Corvallis

Clean a pound of large mushrooms and remove stems. Make a slit or two in the top of each mushroom and soak in 1/2 cup of olive oil in which a crushed clove of garlic has been put. After an hour, remove the mushrooms from the oil, sprinkle with salt and pepper, and broil. While the mushrooms are cooking, add ¼ cup each of minced parsley and green onions to the oil (garlic discarded) and heat them for a minute. Put the broiled mushrooms on toast, add the juice of half a lemon to the hot oil mixture, and pour over the mushrooms before serving. SERVES 4.

> 1 pound mushrooms   Salt and pepper
> ½ cup olive oil   ¼ cup minced parsley
> 1 clove garlic   ¼ cup minced green onions
>   Juice of ½ lemon

⟨ Mushroom Pie

This never fails to please when it is served with steak.

The pie may be a large one or individual ones. For 6 servings clean a pound of mushrooms, slice them, stems and all, and cook gently in ¼ cup of butter for about 5 minutes along with 3 tablespoons of minced shallots. Add ¼ cup of flour, cook 2 minutes longer, then pour on a cup of cream and a cup of stock. Season with salt and pepper, and, if you wish, a couple of tablespoons of sherry, and cook until thick and smooth. Pour into a deep pie dish or casserole, or individual dishes, cover with a rich pastry, slash so that the steam will escape, and bake in a hot oven until the crust is a gorgeous brown. SERVES 6.

> 1 pound mushrooms   1 cup cream
> ¼ cup butter   1 cup stock
> 3 tablespoons minced shal-   Salt and pepper
>   lots   2 tablespoons sherry
> ¼ cup flour   (optional)
>   Rich pastry

⟨ Russian River Mushrooms in Sour Cream

I don't doubt that this recipe is like one left by those early Russian settlers who later sold out their holdings to Captain

Sutter, of gold discovery fame. They used wild mushrooms, which were abundant in sections of all three states. Today we use the kind that are cultivated, many of them in Washington state.

Sauté ½ cup of minced onions and a pound of fresh cleaned mushrooms in ¼ cup of butter. The mushrooms may be quartered or sliced if large, left whole if small. (Sheer laziness prompts me to select large mushrooms when the size is unimportant — they take so much less time to clean.) When lightly browned, add a tablespoon of flour, ½ cup of stock, salt and pepper to taste, and ½ teaspoon of crushed dill seeds (optional). Simmer, in the chafing dish if you wish, then add a cup of thick sour cream. Heat and serve with toast, or as a vegetable with roast beef or mutton, or with baked fish. SERVES 4.

½ cup minced onions
1 pound mushrooms
¼ cup butter
1 tablespoon flour
½ cup stock
Salt and pepper
½ teaspoon crushed dill seeds
(optional)
1 cup thick sour cream

⟨ San Joaquin Mushroom Custard

Clean ½ pound of small mushrooms and slice them, stems and all, then cook in 2 tablespoons of butter. Pour off the juice and measure, and add enough hot thin cream to make 2 cups of liquid. Season with salt and pepper, add a tablespoon of sherry, and 2 large or 3 small eggs, slightly beaten. Combine with the mushrooms and bake in buttered custard cups. Place on a rack in a pan of hot water and bake at 350° until set. When a knife inserted in the custard comes out clean, they are done. Unmold, sprinkle with minced parsley, and serve at once with roast chicken. SERVES 5 OR 6.

½ pound small mushrooms
2 tablespoons butter
Thin cream as needed
Salt and pepper
1 tablespoon sherry
2 large eggs
(or 3 small ones)
Minced parsley

382

Vegetables

(Nopal

The nopal cactus, growing in a wild state in most of Southern California, is more often cursed than blessed — this for its spines. Nevertheless, the Franciscan Fathers brought it here, and with good reasons, too. Lots of them. It made a savory vegetable stew, its fruit was delicious, and its joints, when stuck into even the most arid land, would root and make a formidable beastproof barrier. The juice of the cactus was used as a whitewash for adobe walls, and the leaves were split and applied as a poultice. Besides all this usefulness, the nopal has a romantic history. In 1325 (according to their calendar), the Aztecs, who had led the lives of wanderers for many years since they had come into Mexico, saw what they thought was a sign. It was a huge eagle, with a writhing snake in its mouth, resting on a nopal plant, and blocking the path of these nomads. Why this was a divine sign is not clear, but the Aztecs knew that their wanderings were at an end. This was the place where they settled, and they named it "The Place of the Tuna" (cactus), or Tenochtitlan. It is now Mexico City, and the national emblem of Mexico is an eagle with a snake twisting in its beak.

NOTE: Another cactus that was useful to the Indians and early settlers was the barrel cactus. Literally barrel-shaped, it is filled with a liquid that is very thirst-quenching and not unpleasant to the taste, particularly when you are dying for lack of water in the desert. The Indians had a neat trick with this cactus. They cut off the top, scooped out the pulp, squeezed the juice back into the "barrel," and cooked in it by dropping red-hot rocks into the improvised soup pot.

(Nopales

This is the nopal cactus, and the leaves, great fleshy things about the size of the blade of a canoe paddle and an inch or so thick, are what is used. The early Californians used it often, and today our Mexican residents, and those of us who have been initiated into the secret, wait eagerly for the new green

383

leaves and joints to appear on the cactus, which still grows wild in Southern California.

Peel the cactus and cut it either into dice or strips, and boil it in salted water until tender. Drain, and eat just as is with butter and salt and pepper, or do it in the Californian manner: cook a clove of garlic in 2 tablespoons of lard or bacon fat. Add a chopped green chili pepper (peeled, and the seeds removed, page 92, or use the canned variety), ½ cup of chopped onion, a cup of canned tomatoes, and 2 cups of diced parboiled cactus. Add salt, pepper, and oregano to taste, and simmer slowly for 20 minutes. This is served as a vegetable, and a mighty good one it is, too. Canned diced cactus is available in Mexican grocery stores for those of you who don't go in for desert gardening. SERVES 6.

1 *clove garlic*	1 *cup canned tomatoes*
2 *tablespoons lard*	2 *cups diced parboiled*
1 *green chili pepper*	*nopales*
½ *cup chopped onion*	*Salt and pepper*
	Oregano

❨ *Lodi Onions*

This recipe is unusual and very good.

Peel 2 pounds of tiny white boiling onions and cover them with white wine. Add 2 tablespoons of olive oil, a sprig of thyme, a bay leaf, and a tablespoon of sugar. Simmer very slowly until the onions can be easily pierced with a toothpick. Remove the onions, strain and reduce the sauce, and add salt to taste. Pour back on the onions and reheat. Good with fish. SERVES 8 TO 10.

2 *pounds tiny boiling onions*	1 *sprig thyme*
White wine to cover	1 *bay leaf*
2 *tablespoons olive oil*	1 *tablespoon sugar*
	Salt

❨ *Onion Pie with Almonds*

This is very good for a buffet, with baked ham, or to serve with a roast turkey, or saddle of lamb, or roast pork.

Cook 2 cups of sliced onions in ¼ cup of butter until wilted. Add a tablespoon of flour, a cup of cream, 3 eggs, beaten, salt and pepper to taste, and, if to be served with pork, a little sage; with lamb, a little rosemary; with fowl, some marjoram; with ham, any of the three. Pour the mixture into a pie shell, sprinkle the top with chopped almonds, and bake, on the bottom oven shelf, at 400° for 15 minutes, then reduce heat to 325° and finish baking, about 20 minutes longer. SERVES 6.

2 cups sliced onions	3 eggs
¼ cup butter	Salt and pepper
1 tablespoon flour	Sage, rosemary, or
1 cup cream	marjoram
Chopped almonds	

⟨ Shasta Onions with Almonds

Peel medium-sized onions and scrape the roots, and cut the tops straight across about ¼-inch down. Boil until almost tender, drain, and scoop out the insides, leaving 2 outer layers of onion. Chop the insides, and for each cupful add ¼ cup of melted butter, ½ cup of toasted chopped almonds, and ¼ cup of crumbs. Season to taste using salt and pepper and Beau Monde Seasoning Powder. Stuff the onions, arrange in a baking dish, sprinkle crumbs on each, and top with a split blanched almond and a drizzle of butter. Pour a little cream in the baking dish and bake at 375° until the onions are tender.

For each 1 cup chopped onion pulp

¼ cup butter ⎫
½ cup toasted almonds ⎬ and more for top
¼ cup crumbs ⎭
Salt and pepper
Beau Monde Seasoning Powder
Cream

⟨ Onion Notes

Barbecued Onions. Dip thick slices of onion in butter or oil, and grill over charcoal, preferably using a fine mesh toaster, for easy turning.

Ember Roasted Onions. Wrap peeled onions in aluminum foil and bury in the hot embers of a charcoal fire, preferably well at the side. Cook 30 minutes to 1 hour, depending on the size of the onions and the heat of the fire. They may be tested with a fork without unwrapping.

Onions Baked in Cream. Slice onions rather thin and arrange in a deep baking dish with salt and pepper between the layers. Pour on cream to the top, sprinkle with crumbs, and bake at 350° for 30 minutes. The onions will be tender, but still a bit crisp.

Onions with Sour Cream. Boil small onions, drain, and dress with sour cream and salt and pepper.

Onion Shortcake. Hot biscuits, split and buttered, boiled green onions, cut in 1-inch lengths, or chopped onions, mixed with cream sauce made of half onion water, half cream. Serve with baked ham.

⟨ Peas

Peas, or "pease" as some of the early cook books called them, appeared early on our West Coast menus. They were planted in the gardens at Fort Vancouver, and both the missionaries and the voyageurs were said to have carried them, dried, on their travels. In Oregon and Washington they grew so profusely that they were sown, broadcast, and the pigs turned out to fatten on them. Today the state of Washington produces great quantities of dried peas, and ships them all over the world.

Peas Paisano. Two pounds of peas, either fresh or frozen, are cooked with a bunch of green onions sliced into pea-sized pieces, and ¼ cup of butter. Just enough water is added to keep from sticking, and they are cooked, covered, until tender.

Peas with Mushrooms. A favorite, quite naturally. For each 2 pounds of cooked peas, sauté ½ pound of mushrooms in 3 tablespoons of butter. Combine the vegetables and season with salt and pepper.

Vegetables

Peas with Asparagus Tips. Just the tiny tips of the asparagus, cut in pea-sized pieces, are cooked tender-crisp, and combined with cooked peas. Then dressed with a little hot cream or melted butter. Salt and pepper, of course.

Peas with Mint. A favorite, especially in the Northwest, where it is invariably served with lamb or mutton. Simply dress cooked peas with melted butter and chopped mint.

Peas Oakley. Sauté ¼ cup of minced shallots in ¼ cup of butter, with ½ cup of diced cooked ham. Add this to cooked drained peas.

Peas with Herbs. Cook 2 pounds of peas as usual in water, but only until partially tender. Drain, add ½ cup of cream, 2 tablespoons each of chives and parsley, and a teaspoon of thyme, marjoram, or tarragon. (If the peas are to be served with a cheese dish, ½ teaspoon of cumin seed, ground in a mortar, gives an interesting flavor.)

⟨ Peppers

We raise, eat, and ship great quantities of peppers of all kinds. Chili peppers, which no self-respecting Westerner of Mexican extraction would be without, are used in great quantity. This is only natural, particularly in Los Angeles, which has a larger population of Mexican blood than any other city in the world except Mexico City itself. But we also have other peppers, including the tiny hot yellow and red ones, and the sweet, thick-fleshed green or red bell peppers, as well as pimientos. Bell peppers are well liked by the Chinese, who cook them green and crisp and use them for color, flavor, and texture in their dishes, and by Italians, who cook them long and limp and sapid with olive oil and often garlic. Raw green peppers appear often in salads, and in sandwiches, but most often they are used in combination with other vegetables or meats.

Fried Green Peppers. Cut large, thick-fleshed green peppers into 1-inch strips, dip in beaten egg and then in fine seasoned crumbs, and either fry in deep fat or pan fry. Or, if you prefer, simply fry green pepper strips in bacon fat or other shortening until tender. Either is a good vegetable to serve with fish or cheese dishes, or with liver. Fresh pimientos may be prepared in the same ways.

Green Pepper Pie. Not usual but spectacular! Line a pie-pan with pastry. Put layers of green pepper strips, chopped onion, and grated cheese, to the top. Fill with custard: 2 cups of scalded milk, 5 beaten eggs, salt and pepper. Top crust or not — if *not,* end with cheese on top. Bake at 450° for 5 minutes, reduce heat to 300°, bake 45 to 60 minutes more, or until firm.

❲ Potatoes

Potatoes, and potato growing, seem to have had their ups and downs in the early days of our history. Sometimes the pioneers had nothing else but, and grew very weary of them. At other times they had none, and complained bitterly that they had to serve boiled wheat in their place. Henry Spalding, the missionary of Oregon Territory, discovered that they grew gloriously in the rich lands east of the Cascades. That, it is said, was the birth of the Idaho potato industry. The Southern Californians preferred their beloved beans to potatoes, though they did have them in Los Angeles in 1846, we know.

❲ Cattle King Potatoes

This dish was said to have always been served by one of California's early cattle kings, famous for his hospitality. It is one of the best potato dishes I have ever tasted, and is right with *any* meal.

Peel 3 pounds of potatoes and boil them tender with salt and a clove of garlic in the water. Mash them well with ¼ to ⅓ cup of butter, depending on how expansive you feel. Add 2 beaten egg yolks, ½ cup of cream, salt and pepper to taste, ½ pound of sliced sautéed mushrooms, and ¼ cup of minced parsley. Pile in a baking dish and bake until brown. This can be made ahead of time, reheated at the last minute. This is a wonderful solution of what hot dish to serve at a buffet. For instance: lobster mousse; cold sliced tongue; Cattle King potatoes; bacon and avocado salad. Lemon butter tarts for dessert. SERVES 8.

3 pounds potatoes	½ cup cream
1 clove garlic	Salt and pepper
¼–⅓ cup butter	½ pound mushrooms
2 egg yolks	¼ cup minced parsley

(Fried Potatoes Mexican

Though the Mexicans of early California could live without potatoes, those of later California evolved a few ways of their own for cooking them. This is the best.

Cold boiled potatoes are sliced, not too thin, and fried in lard or bacon fat, along with diced prepared or canned green chilies — the proportions depending on how hot you can take it. This is a good dish to serve with hamburgers, or meat that is charcoal grilled. It's also fine with fish, if not prepared with some delicate sauce.

(Hash Browned Potatoes with Almonds

Dice firm boiled potatoes into the tiniest, neatest little squares you can manage, until you have 4 cups of them. Melt ¼ cup of butter in a heavy skillet and add ⅓ cup of finely chopped unblanched almonds and 2 tablespoons of finely minced onion. Cook, stirring, until the almonds are lightly browned, then add the potatoes, salt and pepper, and ¼ cup of heavy cream. Cook, stirring occasionally, until the potatoes are a golden brown. Superb! (Filberts, walnuts, or sesame seeds may replace the almonds, with equally pleasant results.) SERVES 8.

4 cups diced boiled potatoes	2 tablespoons minced onion
¼ cup butter	Salt and pepper
⅓ cup chopped almonds	¼ cup heavy cream

389

⟨ Patio Potatoes

Large potatoes are scrubbed and baked soft, but the skins are *not* rubbed with oil or grease. They want to be crisp. When tender they have the tops cut off about a quarter of the way down, to allow the steam to escape, but they are then allowed to cool and the tops replaced. Come eating time, the insides are cut out carefully, diced, the contents of each large potato mixed with a teaspoon of melted butter, a teaspoon of sesame seeds, and salt and pepper. Do this gently lest the potatoes be mashed. Return to the shells, pour 3 tablespoons of thick cream over each, sprinkle top with more sesame seeds, and bake in the oven until gloriously hot and brown.

For each large potato

1 teaspoon butter	Salt and pepper
1 teaspoon sesame seeds	3 tablespoons thick
(or more)	cream

⟨ Portland Potatoes

Boil potatoes, but not until mushy, having a piece of bay leaf in the water. Cool, cut in cubes, and reheat in the following sauce: For each 2 cups of potato cubes allow 1 cup of sauce made by cooking 2 tablespoons of diced onion and 3 tablespoons of diced green pepper in 3 tablespoons of butter until wilted. Add 2 tablespoons of flour and 1½ cups of rich milk, and salt and pepper to taste. Cook until smooth, then carefully mix in the potatoes. SERVES 6.

For each 2 cups of cubed boiled potatoes

2 tablespoons diced onion	3 tablespoons butter
3 tablespoons diced green	2 tablespoons flour
pepper	1½ cups rich milk
Salt and pepper	

⟨ Potatoes Santa Monica

Bake large potatoes as usual. Scoop out insides, and for each one mix 2 tablespoons of butter, a teaspoon of chopped chives,

390

a teaspoon of chopped tarragon, and a tablespoon of minced ripe olives. Return to shells and reheat. Olive oil is often used instead of the butter, and sometimes the popular garlic shows evidence of its presence.

For each large baked potato

2 tablespoons butter	1 teaspoon chopped tarragon
1 teaspoon chopped chives	1 tablespoon minced ripe olives

⟪ Puffed Potatoes

Three cups of riced potatoes are mixed with 2 tablespoons of grated onion, salt and pepper, ⅓ cup of melted butter, and 2 tablespoons of cream. Three eggs are beaten light and folded into the mixture, and it is piled into a baking dish and topped with chopped walnuts and grated Cheddar cheese. It is reheated in the oven when eating time arrives. SERVES 8 TO 10.

3 cups riced potatoes	2 tablespoons cream
2 tablespoons grated onion	3 eggs
Salt and pepper	Chopped walnuts
⅓ cup butter	Grated Cheddar cheese

⟪ Sheepherder's Potatoes

The Basques, of whom there are many in Eastern Oregon, are quite naturally fine cooks. They use herbs matter-of-factly. . . .

Raw potatoes are sliced and fried slowly in a generous amount of fat. When tender, raw eggs are broken over them — one to a large potato — and they are stirred so that they will run down into the potatoes. They are then sprinkled with salt, pepper, and chopped herbs — usually parsley and chives, and a little thyme. As soon as the eggs are set, the dish is eaten.

❲ Potato Knishes

Our large Jewish population has given us some truly delectable dishes. This one, though perhaps a bit of a chore to make, is worth every second spent on it. It is Mrs. Becky Mauer's recipe.

Make strudel dough or buy ready-made strudel leaves. For the dough sift 2 cups of flour onto a bread board, make a hole in the middle, and add an egg, ½ cup of tepid water, a tablespoon of vegetable oil, and ¼ teaspoon of salt, stirring as the ingredients are mixed. Now mix until pleasantly smooth, then, leaving on the board, cover the dough with a bowl that has been dipped in hot water and dried. Let stand in a warm place for a half hour. Make filling (below). Now cover a large table with a clean tablecloth or sheet and sprinkle with flour. Take half the dough and roll it as thin as possible, then putting your hands under the dough, palms down and fingers curled under, pull and stretch it as thin as possible, transparently thin, so that you can "read a love letter through the dough." Be sure that you've removed your rings, by the way. This paste is more fragile than the sheerest nylons. When all is pulled and stretched so that it looks like a piece of fine parchment, trim off the edges which will be thicker than the rest. Now sprinkle the entire piece with oil. (That's the Jewish way; melted butter is all right if you're not orthodox.) Put a roll of the filling, about 2 inches in diameter, and as long as the pastry is wide, on the edge of the strudel nearest you then lifting the cloth with both hands, let the dough roll up with the potato mixture inside. Divide the roll into slices about 1½ inches wide, using the side of your hand and a sawing motion — this will seal the ends of the rolls, making a tricky little knishe that looks as if it had been gathered with a drawstring. Place the knishes, cut side up, on a greased baking pan, and bake in a hot oven until crispy brown. Serve with pot roast or hasenpfeffer or stew.

The filling: Mash potatoes and season each cupful with a tablespoon of minced onions that have been cooked light gold in 2 tablespoons of chicken fat. Season with salt and pepper, and add more chicken fat if necessary. (Of course, butter may be used.) Four cups of filling for this amount of pastry. MAKES ABOUT 24 KNISHES.

STRUDEL

2 cups flour	1 tablespoon oil
1 egg	¼ teaspoon salt
½ cup tepid water	Oil or butter

FILLING

For each cup mashed potatoes

1 tablespoon minced onions   2 tablespoons chicken fat

Salt and pepper

❬ *Potato Notes*

Potato Cream Roll. Mix 2 cups of chopped cooked potatoes with 2 cups of well-seasoned cream sauce. Press into a large well-buttered skillet, cover, and cook until the sauce is absorbed and the bottom lightly browned. Sprinkle with chopped parsley and, tipping the pan away from you and giving it a nudge with the spatula, roll the potatoes like a jelly roll, then roll onto a hot platter. This is good with fish.

New Potatoes in Crumbs. New potatoes are boiled as usual, their skins rubbed off, and they are then dipped in melted butter and rolled in toasted crumbs or very finely chopped nuts.

Potato Butter. Mix chives and/or parsley with creamed butter, form in a roll, chill, and slice ready to pop into hot potatoes, particularly those that are roasted outdoors. Pepper or chili powder or chopped green onions may be mixed with the butter, or the herbs of your choice.

Potatoes with Croutons. San Francisco, in the '90s, whipped potatoes light with cream and egg yolk, sprinkled them with chopped chervil, and garnished them with tiny fried croutons. Why forget a dish like that?

Fried Potato Balls. Mix 3 cups of hot mashed potatoes with 3 eggs, ½ teaspoon of salt, and a teaspoon of baking powder. Drop by spoonfuls into deep fat (370°), and cook until brown.

Potatoes in Sour Cream. Use either diced or tiny whole potatoes, boiled, and reheat them in sour cream seasoned with salt and pepper. Minced chives or parsley may be added.

Spring Potatoes. Little new potatoes, boiled and dressed with butter flavored with grated lemon rind, lemon juice, and minced chives.

❲ Baked Pumpkin with Ginger

Here pumpkin not only becomes an edible vegetable, it is downright glamorous.

Cut 3 pounds of pumpkin (or Hubbard or banana squash) into individual serving pieces, removing seeds and string portion, but leaving the skin on. Mix ¼ pound of butter, melted, with 3 tablespoons of finely chopped preserved ginger and ¼ cup of brown sugar. Score the inside of the pumpkin deeply, then brush with this mixture, sprinkle with salt, and bake at 350° for 1½ hours, or until tender, basting a few times with the extra melted butter. Serve from the shells with pork or turkey. SERVES 8 TO 10.

> 3 *pounds pumpkin*
> ¼ *pound butter*
> 3 *tablespoons chopped preserved ginger*
> ¼ *cup brown sugar*
>   *Salt*

❲ Colache

This is a really old Californian recipe — one of the few vegetable dishes in which the rancheros indulged. Like all old recipes, there are numerous variations.

Cut a pumpkin or squash into 1-inch squares. (Any squash will do — winter or summer, green or yellow.) Cook 4 cups of these dice in ¼ cup of bacon fat, olive oil, or lard for 5 minutes. Now add a large onion, chopped, a clove of garlic, minced, a chopped green pepper, a chopped chili pepper (or some chili powder), 4 peeled tomatoes, chopped, ½ pound of string beans, cut in ½-inch pieces, and 4 ears of green corn, scraped from the cobs. Add ½ cup of water and salt and pepper to taste, cover, and cook until the vegetables are tender. SERVES 8.

4 cups diced pumpkin or squash	1 green pepper
	1 chili pepper
¼ cup bacon fat, olive oil, or lard	4 tomatoes
	½ pound string beans
1 large onion	4 ears corn
1 clove garlic	½ cup water
Salt and pepper	

NOTE: A dish very much like this, called calabacitos con queso, is made in the same way, with onion, green pepper, squash, and tomato, but it has chopped Monterey Jack cheese added at the last — just long enough to give it time to melt.

⟨ Salsify with Herbs

Scrape 2 bunches of salsify root and drop immediately into acidulated water. (It is well to rub your fingers with lemon juice before and after to prevent and remove black stains.) Boil until tender in the same water, drain, and dress with ½ cup of melted butter that has had a tablespoon each of lemon juice, chopped parsley, and chopped chives added, and a teaspoon of thyme. Salt and pepper to taste. SERVES 8.

2 bunches salsify root	1 tablespoon chopped parsley
½ cup melted butter	1 tablespoon chopped chives
1 tablespoon lemon juice	1 teaspoon thyme
Salt and pepper	

NOTE: *Salsify with Cheddar Sauce* is just that. Boiled, diced, and dressed with a cream sauce in which Cheddar cheese has been melted. A touch of oregano does this no harm.

❨ Chinatown Spinach

Wash 2 pounds of spinach and put in a heavy pot with 2 tablespoons of bland oil. Put over heat and turn so that all the leaves are oil coated, then pour in ¼ cup of whiskey (sherry or ngkapi may be used, or brandy), and add a slice of fermented bean curd if it is available. (If not, a couple of tablespoons of blue cheese may be substituted — it's not the same, but it has a similar sharp flavor.) Stir once more and cover, cooking about 3 minutes in all. Serve without draining or chopping, with spareribs, or fried rice, or fried shrimps. SERVES 6.

> 2 pounds spinach
> 2 tablespoons oil
> ¼ cup whiskey (or sherry, or ngkapi, or brandy)
> 1 slice fermented bean curd or
>   2 tablespoons blue cheese

NOTE: *Ngkapi* is a Chinese whiskey. The word is pronounced as if it were "ing'ka pay" except that the initial *i* is not sounded.

❨ Creamed Spinach, Prime Rib

The Prime Rib, a favorite restaurant of Angeleños, is smart enough to serve but a few dishes, each one perfect. Prime ribs, of course, Yorkshire pudding, baked russet potatoes, horseradish sauce, and this creamed spinach are their specialties.

> 1 pound spinach
> 3–4 strips bacon
> 1 clove garlic, chopped fine
> 1 medium onion
>
> Salt and pepper to taste
> 2 tablespoons butter
> 2 tablespoons flour
> 1 cup milk

"Boil spinach (not too well done). Wash in cold water and squeeze dry. Put through fine food grinder. Grind bacon and sauté, grind onion and add to bacon with garlic, salt and pepper. Sauté until all moisture is gone.

"Make medium cream sauce with butter, flour, and milk.

Add ground spinach, bacon, and onion, and bring to a slow boil. SERVES 4."

(*Spinach Cielita*

And heavenly it is, too, even for those who profess to dislike it.

Wash 2 pounds of spinach and cook, without additional water, until it is limp but still bright green. It will have to be turned 2 or 3 times during the cooking, though it should be covered. This will only take 3 or 4 minutes. Drain very thoroughly, and chop or not as you prefer. Slice ½ pound of mushrooms and cook them for 5 minutes in ¼ cup of butter. Add a cup of sour cream, salt and pepper to taste, and combine with the spinach, and heat. Serve with tongue, ham, or roast beef. SERVES 8.

2 pounds spinach	*¼ cup butter*
½ pound mushrooms	*1 cup sour cream*
Salt and pepper	

(*Spinach Timbales with Ripe Olive Sauce*

Two cups of cooked chopped spinach is mixed with ½ teaspoon of salt that has been ground in a mortar with ½ clove of garlic, a cup of milk, 2 slightly beaten eggs, a teaspoon of lemon juice, 3 tablespoons of melted butter, and a little fresh pepper, with more salt if necessary. This mixture is divided into 6 or 8 buttered custard cups and baked in a pan of water at 325° until firm. The timbales are turned out on very thin rounds of toast, and ripe olive sauce is poured over. These cry for ham. SERVES 6 TO 8.

2 cups cooked chopped	*2 eggs*
spinach	*1 teaspoon lemon juice*
½ teaspoon salt (or more)	*3 tablespoons butter*
½ clove garlic	*Pepper*
1 cup milk	*Ripe olive sauce*

NOTE: For ripe olive sauce add ½ cup of chopped ripe olives to a cup of thin cream sauce, with lemon juice and salt and pepper to taste.

⟪ Spinach with Anchovies

This is an interesting harmony of flavors — one that is marvelous with fish, lamb, or veal.

Cook 2 pounds of washed spinach in the water which clings to its leaves. When completely wilted, drain well, chop or not as you prefer, and dress with 2 tablespoons each of melted butter and hot olive oil, to which 3 tablespoons of minced anchovies have been added. Serve sprinkled with grated Parmesan or with chopped hard-boiled egg. SERVES 8.

2 pounds spinach
2 tablespoons melted
   butter
2 tablespoons olive oil

3 tablespoons minced
   anchovies
Grated Parmesan or
   chopped hard-boiled egg

⟪ Squash

Our squash nomenclature is a bit confusing to cooks from other parts of the country. By "summer squash" we mean the pale green squash known as pattypan, cymlings, or scallops in other places. Our "crookneck squash" is the yellow kind, in other places called "summer squash." Then there is Italian squash, or zucchini, resembling somewhat a dark green cucumber, though smaller. All our "summer squashes" are harvested when very young and tender, though they would grow, no doubt, to gigantic size if left alone.

As for winter squashes, we have Hubbard, a dark and warty green; banana, a rather smooth-skinned yellow affair, and Des Moines or acorn.

⟪ Acorn (Winter) Squash with Rum

"Oh dear, how can I tell it — squash again for breakfast." That's what Dame Shirley wrote from her home in the Gold Country of California. Perhaps if served this way she could have taken it, for she was a woman with a keen appreciation of good food.

398

Vegetables

Split small acorn (Des Moines) squash, and remove seeds and pith. Score deeply, sprinkle each half with salt and pepper, a teaspoon of brown sugar, and pour a tablespoon of melted butter and a teaspoon of Jamaica rum in each hollow. Cover and bake until nearly tender. Uncover, sprinkle with chopped walnuts, almonds, or filberts, baste with a little more butter and rum (¼ cup melted butter to 2 tablespoons of rum), and continue baking until the nuts are brown and the squash tender and glazed.

For each ½ acorn squash

Salt and pepper	*1 teaspoon Jamaica rum*
1 teaspoon brown sugar	*(or more)*
1 tablespoon melted butter	*Chopped walnuts, almonds,*
(or more)	*or filberts*

([Summer Squash in Cream

Tiny yellow crooknecks or green pattypans are used for this dish. Wash and remove ends, then split the crookneck or quarter the others. Peeling is not necessary when the squash is small. For 1 pound, melt ¼ cup of butter, add squash, brown very slightly, sprinkle with salt and fresh ground pepper and a little sweet basil, then put into a casserole. Add ½ cup of heavy cream, press squash down into it, then top with buttered crumbs and bake at 350° until the vegetable is tender and the top brown. SERVES 4 TO 6.

1 pound squash	*Sweet basil*
¼ cup butter	*½ cup heavy cream*
Salt and pepper	*Buttered crumbs*

([Marin County Zucchini

This county, north of San Francisco Bay, has many residents of Italian extraction, and therefore many superb cooks and superb dishes.

399

Wash small zucchini and scrape off the outside fuzz. Split in halves. Now crush a clove of garlic with a teaspoon of salt and rub the cut sides of the zucchini with it, then brown, same side down, in plenty of olive oil. This should be done carefully so that the vegetable won't burn, turning after the cut side is done to do the other. A little fresh ground pepper is sprinkled on before serving, and sometimes it is drizzled with basil vinegar.

Small zucchini	Olive oil
1 clove garlic	Pepper
1 teaspoon salt	Basil vinegar (optional)

❨ Zucchini with Mushrooms and Sour Cream

The squash almost loses its identity in this recipe, but as its new personality is enchanting, we don't mind in the least.

A pound of uniformly sized mushrooms are cleaned and the stems, if long, cut off. They are then sautéed 4 to 6 minutes in ¼ cup of butter. Scrape a pound of small zucchini, cut into 1-inch crosswise slices, and cook them gently in salted water to which a few dill seeds and a clove of garlic have been added. When the zucchini is just tender, drain it well (save liquid), put it on a paper towel or clean cloth, and press out any surplus moisture. To the mushrooms add 2 table-spoons of flour, cook 2 minutes more, then add a cup of sour cream and the cooked squash. Correct seasoning, and add a little of the squash water. As soon as the vegetables are hot again, serve, with beef, or lamb, or tongue. SERVES 4 TO 6.

1 pound mushrooms	Salt
¼ cup butter	1 clove garlic
1 pound zucchini	2 tablespoons flour
Dill seeds	1 cup sour cream
A little of the water in which the squash was cooked	

❨ Zucchini with Green Onions

Cook 1 cup of sliced green onions in ½ cup of olive oil, with a pound of sliced zucchini and a cup of sliced mushrooms.

Cook gently so as not to break, and when all is tender, in about 5 minutes, add 4 tablespoons of very rich stock (reduce canned consommé one half, if no other is available), correct seasonings, and simmer another minute or so. Serve sprinkled with a little lemon juice and minced parsley, and serve with mutton or veal chops. SERVES 4 TO 6.

1 cup sliced green onions	*4 tablespoons rich stock*
½ cup olive oil	*Salt and pepper*
1 pound zucchini	*Lemon juice*
1 cup sliced mushrooms	*Parsley*

❐ Squash Suggestions

These suggestions apply mostly to zucchini, for that is the one for which we are most famous, but they may be used for any summer squash, or for cucumbers, for that matter.

With Cheese. Slice zucchini, fry in olive oil until brown, and serve sprinkled with grated cheese. Salt and pepper, of course, and if you wish, garlic. The cheese may be melted under the broiler.

With Sour Cream. Dress boiled and well-drained zucchini with sour cream and chopped dill. This loves fish.

With Herbs or Nuts. Dress zucchini, or any other squash, with melted butter and toasted almonds, or minced herbs, or cheese sauce flavored with chili powder and oregano.

Zucchini Vinaigrette. Cook zucchini until almost tender, slice or halve, and marinate in vinaigrette sauce for a few hours before serving.

Summer Squash. Parboil, scoop out a bit of the center, fill with a half of a small peeled tomato, top with bacon, or cheese, or both. Bake.

❐ California Candied Sweets

If you would believe all the recipes that are dubbed "Californian," you'd be sure that almost everything we cooked contained honey and oranges and nuts. 'Tain't so, but here's one recipe that does:

Two pounds of sweet potatoes are peeled and sliced and arranged in a baking dish. Over them is poured a cup of orange juice that has been mixed with ¼ cup of honey, ½ cup of melted butter, a little salt, and a tablespoon of orange slivers. (The slivers are made by peeling the zest, or very outside orange, free from the fruit and cutting it into pin-sized pieces.) The dish is covered and the potatoes are baked at 350° until tender, uncovering the last 15 minutes or so, that the top may brown. Basting two or three times during the cooking is important. SERVES 6.

2 pounds sweet potatoes	½ cup melted butter
1 cup orange juice	Salt
¼ cup honey	1 tablespoon orange slivers

❮ Spanish Sweet Potatoes

This is one of the few recipes for sweets or yams where the sweetness is not increased, and a fine idea it is, too.

For each cup of cubed cooked, but not mushy, sweet potatoes, use ¼ cup each of chopped green pepper and onions. Fry all together in ¼ cup of shortening until the potatoes are brown and crisp. Salt and pepper to taste. This is surprisingly good with fish, but it's good with meat, too. SERVES 3.

For each 1 cup cubed cooked sweet potatoes

¼ cup chopped green pepper	¼ cup shortening
¼ cup chopped onions	Salt and pepper

❮ Yam Almond Balls

Yams always seem to end up at a party meal. This way is one of the fanciest, and good too. (But don't let that make you forget the perfection of a baked red yam, split open, and with a huge hunk of butter inserted to melt in its sweet heart.)

Vegetables

Cook yams until tender, peel, and mash. Season to taste with butter, salt and pepper, and if you wish, a little cinnamon or cloves. Add 1 beaten egg for each 2 cups of mashed yams. Cool, roll in balls, then dip in beaten egg and finely chopped almonds (or other nuts). Either arrange on a buttered dish and bake, or fry in deep fat at 390° until brown.

NOTE: Chopped preserved ginger — not too much — may be added to the mashed yams for a little extra touch.

(Tomatoes

Our tomato cookery goes back to Aztec days, for while the rest of the world was debating the "love apple" and its dangers of poisoning, the ancestors of our early Californians were eating it blissfully in Mexico. The Italians fell instantly in love with the tomato, too, for it was so right with their onions and garlic, their pastas, and their cheese. The old recipe for "Purcee de Comate," printed in an early Portland cook book, turns out to be for purée de tomate, copied, I am sure, from some faded manuscript cook book and included to lend class to the ladies' efforts to raise funds for their church.

(Broiled Tomatoes with Green Olives

Select firm ripe tomatoes, remove skins, cut them in halves around their equators, and arrange, cut side up, on a baking dish. Sprinkle with salt, then turn over to drain for a few minutes. Cut ham and green olives into slivers the same size, and mix them together, and pile on top of the tomatoes, about a tablespoon on each one. Sprinkle with a little basil, and drizzle olive oil over all, then broil until the top is brown and the tomatoes thoroughly hot. Wonderful with broiled liver.

NOTE: Stewed tomatoes with stuffed green olives added are good too, especially with fish.

⟨ Ranch Tomatoes

A favorite way is this one, particularly when served with beans and grilled meat.

Slice the tops from 6 uniformly sized, not-too-ripe tomatoes, and arrange in a baking dish. Heap them with a mixture of ½ cup each of chopped green pepper and chopped onion. Sprinkle with salt, pepper, and oregano, and add a good dab of butter. Pour a cup of heavy cream into the dish and bake at 350° until the tomatoes are done, basting once or twice with the cream, which will reduce a bit in the cooking and is served as a sauce. SERVES 6.

6 tomatoes	*Salt and pepper*
½ cup chopped green pepper	*Oregano*
½ cup chopped onion	*Butter*
1 cup heavy cream	

⟨ Water Chestnuts

Fresh water chestnuts are round and flat, rather bulblike in appearance, with a dirty brownish-black skin, but inside they are a beautiful white. They are washed, then peeled, and cut in the desired shapes. Available only in Chinese markets, they are hard to find outside of Chinatown, but the canned variety, all washed and peeled, should be available in gourmet shops throughout the country. The fresh water chestnut has a sweetish flavor, vaguely like that of a fresh cocoanut. The canned kind has not quite so much flavor, but, like its fresh sister, it always retains its wonderful crispness. The texture is the chief charm of the water chestnut.

Wine

THIS IS *a vinous book. Good food is nothing without good wine, and our generous use of it as a beverage and as a necessary part of our cookery has much to do with the pleasure of our table. Jules Harder, first chef of the Palace Hotel, thought it a shame to waste time and talent on "a man who drinks no wine with his dinner, for he never cares much what he eats."*

When I speak of our wines, I mean Californian. The amount produced in Oregon and Washington is negligible. Nevertheless, wine was mentioned as frequently in the early history of Oregon Territory as in that of California. Dr. McLoughlin, famous factor of Fort Vancouver, insisted that he and his officers should live like civilized persons, even though in the "wilderness." This meant full dress and fine wines were both in order at his sumptuous dinners.

That Padre Junipero Serra brought wine with him when he came to California is a fact — a much surer one than that he brought all the other plants and seeds and cuttings with which he has been credited. We know he had wine, for it was part of his business — necessary for the Holy Sacrament. He probably brought grape cuttings with him, too, for authorities credit him with the first planting, at San Diego, in 1769. By 1798 at least five of the Missions were making wine. It was pressed from the grape still called "Mission," brought, apparently, from Spain by way of Mexico. The Mission grape is, like all the fine wine grapes of Europe, of the family Vitis vinifera, *a delicate vine that, in this country, thrives only in California.*

There is still, at Mission San Gabriel, a vine which was said to have been planted by the Franciscan Fathers in 1775. This is a romantic notion, and perhaps a mistaken one. At least there is an affidavit sworn to by one David Hall, saying that he himself planted the vine in 1861. At any rate, it is enormous and beautiful, and is known as the "Trinity Vine." Another famous grape plant has a pretty fable about its origin. One Marcelina Dominguez, when a small child, was riding home to Montecito when she noticed that the switch with which she hastened her horse was sprouting. She planted it, and it grew into a gigantic vine, bearing, at its prime, some four tons of grapes a year. Doña Dominguez became known as "The Old Lady of the Big Grape Vine" (La Vieja de la Parra Grande), a deserved title as she lived to be 105, and the vine covered an arbor of almost 9000 square feet.

The wine of those early days was made by the Indians. According to Bancroft "some well washed Indians, having on only a zapeta, the hair carefully tied up, and the hands covered with cloth to wipe away perspiration, each having a stock to steady himself withal, were put to treading out the grape juice, which was caught in coras, or leathern bags." All this wine making went merrily on until the 1830s, when the secularization of the Missions was ordered. They had become wealthy and powerful, and the state wanted a good thing when they saw it. That was the first big blow suffered by California wine makers. The vineyards went to ruin — some say with a little help from the Padres, who uprooted the vines. By 1837 there was virtually no wine made in California.

The cessation of the wine making at the Missions marked the beginning of the commercial industry. The first American wine grower in California was probably Joseph Chapman, who planted vines at Los Angeles about 1825. The first professional vintner was Jean Louis Vignes, whose name and whose birthplace, Bordeaux, were remarkably apt. He was also the first man to introduce new grape varieties, importing them from Europe. Before long other men saw a future in grape growing; a Kentucky trapper, named Wolfskill, planted vines at Los Angeles, and by 1858 had a tremendous vineyard. Wine growing got its start in Southern California, but it was in the northern part of the state that it got its fame. One of the earliest grape growers there was General Vallejo, who planted vines at Sonoma in 1836. The Russians were at it, too, and Vallejo kept an eagle eye on them. By 1841 they had 2000 vines at Fort Ross. Another famous man, John Augustus Sutter, at whose mill gold was found, also grew grapes until his vineyards were overrun by miners mad for the yellow stuff.

It was the year of the Gold Rush — 1849 — that the "Father of California Viticulture" came first to California. He was a Hungarian nobleman, Colonel Agoston Haraszthy, and his story is long and fascinating — I wish I could go into it. The important thing, from a vinaceous standpoint, is that Colonel Haraszthy saw the possibility of making really fine wines in California, and he did something about it. He tried various locations, finally settling in Sonoma. He traveled through all the important wine districts of Europe, gathering cuttings of their grapes, and brought back 100,000 of them, embracing several hundred different varieties, all carefully described and catalogued. Unfortunately for Haraszthy, politics reared its ugly head, and he never did get paid for his trouble. The vines were scattered and many apparently lost their tags — a fact that has since occasioned considerable confusion. Nevertheless, Haraszthy and his enthusiasm, as well as his vines, did much for California wine. Haraszthy, for one reason and another, left California for Nicaragua, where he was

407

supposedly eaten by an alligator. Three of his sons, Arpad, Attila, and Bela, continued to make wines in California. Two of the boys married daughters of another pioneer wine grower, General Vallejo, and the Haraszthy name continued to be honored by wine lovers.

The California vintners had a lot to learn. The climate which was a blessing was also a drawback until they learned that the grapes ripened faster here than in Europe. The first vintages "were not wines to make glad the heart of man but such as would make his head swim," Husmann wrote. So the wines had to be improved and the public had to be persuaded to drink them. Finally the wine growers learned how to make better wines, and the fact that the French vineyards were hit by the phylloxera didn't do their business any harm. Only trouble was that the pest came to California, too, and by 1879 was widespread in the Sonoma Valley. In four years it had spread to Napa and other counties; in a few years it was a serious problem which was finally overcome. All went well for many years — until, in fact, prohibition came to the wineland. What that "noble experiment" did to the vintners is better forgotten — when it was over most of the vineyards had to be replanted. They were planted with the best grapes, however, and by that time they knew which grape grew best in various locations, and the wine makers had learned new skill. California wines had really come into their own.

Napa and Sonoma Valleys, two of the greatest wine districts in California, were made famous by two different writers. Jack London wrote of Sonoma — The Valley of the Moon *— and Robert Louis Stevenson of Napa —* The Silverado Squatters. *Napa is still one of our best wine districts — particularly for red table wines. Sonoma, too, is still tops as a wine district, and Livermore Valley, Contra Costa, Santa Clara, and the Santa Cruz Mountains all rate high in the growing of table wine grapes. In the warmer* *sections of the state the dessert wines reign supreme.*

What do California wines resemble? Today they stand on their own. There is no need for them to be anything but California wines.

The wine makers of California, although in complete agreement on most oenological questions, still don't see eye to eye on the question of labeling. Should California wines have generic, varietal, or regional names? Some say that in the beginning the wines bore generic names; that early commercial vintners were almost invariably from wine-growing countries, so quite naturally gave their wines the names of the foreign wines they most resembled — claret, Chianti, Burgundy. . . . Well, certainly that was the easiest way, and might do well enough for anyone without knowledge of the French wines. However, it is not accurate enough. The case for varietal, or even regional labeling is stronger. Varietal wines, by California law, have to contain at least 51 per cent of the juice of the grape for which they are named — Pinot noir, Gamay, Folle blanche, and so forth. This means that the wine buyer who knows his grapes gets what he wants. Say he wants a wine made from the same grape used in the fine clarets of France; his best bet is to buy a wine labeled Cabernet Sauvignon. Of course, there is more to it than that. It is not the grape alone that makes the wine, but the region where it is grown. Thus a Cabernet Sauvignon wine from Napa will be superior to one grown in the hotter valleys more suitable to the growing of grapes for dessert wines. So, ideally, California wines should be labeled all three ways: "Napa Cabernet Sauvignon (California Claret)" would tell all. And, it is cheering to note, more and more of this type of labeling is being used, and more and more persons are taking an interest in California wines, because they know, once they have tasted and liked a certain kind, they can enjoy it again. As a slight help to those not familiar with the varietal wines of California, I have compiled a chart which gives their names, their closest European counterpart, and the regions where they are best grown in California. The chart also includes a very brief description — one which may not necessarily be so a few years hence. Our wines are constantly improving. Suggested foods to serve with the wines, and glasses to use are also included on the chart, but may be completely ignored as far as I am concerned. If you like a Pinot noir with sole, go ahead and have it, and if you have naught but jelly glasses in which to pour it, that's all right too — so long as the color of the wine and its bouquet can be enjoyed, as well as the flavor. The wines included in the chart are only the still table wines with varietal names. The sparkling wines, and the dessert and appetizer wines are noted briefly on page 411.

The most important thing is that we have our own wines, and that they are worthy ones. Frona Eunice Waite wrote, in 1889, "It is to California that the American people are to look for wines that will in time make them forget Bordeaux, Rheims, Epernay, Oporto, Madeira, and Tokay." That time has come. Today there are many of us who, knowing the really fine wines that can be produced by California vintners, are well content to forget those of Europe. Forget, not compare them. To compare the wines of California with the wines of any other country is ridiculous. Said André Simon, the foremost living authority on wine, when asked by eager California newsmen how he compared our wines with those of France: "The wines of California are very good indeed, but you can no more compare them with the wines of Bordeaux, for instance, than you can compare the wines of Bordeaux and Burgundy. In each of these districts there are wines that are very good." And so, in California, there are wines that are very good indeed!

410

Wine

([Champagne

Champagne was king in the flush days of San Francisco, but in the early days it was, apparently, always imported. In 1857 Sansevain made what was, so far as is known, the first California champagne, and later General Vallejo and others tried their hands at it. Haraszthy struggled hard to produce a good one, but it was his son, Arpad, who made the first successful California champagne, in 1867. The brand was Eclipse, and for many years it was a favorite. Since the days of Arpad Haraszthy, much has been learned of champagne making — the proper grapes and the old world techniques produce a wine truly comparable with some of France's best.

([Appetizer Wines

The principal appetizer wines are sherry and vermouth. Both are made in California, and well. The preferred sherry for an apéritif is, of course, a dry and comparatively light one. Recent experiments with the Solera system of sherry making, and with "flor" yeasts, have resulted in some really marvelous wines. Of vermouths, we make both the dry, or French type, and the sweet, or Italian type, some of which are truly excellent.

([Dessert Wines

The wine districts that are in the warmer parts of the state — in the south and inland — produce the greatest amounts of the dessert wines, principally sherry, port, angelica, muscatel, tokay, and white port. These wines are useful in cooking, particularly with sweets, and are often served with or as a dessert. They are especially pleasant with cheese or nuts, or with both.

Wine Chart

Name of Wine	Color	Characteristics	Resembles	Serve with	Temperature	Preferred Type of Glass
BARBERA	Red	Robust and full-bodied. Destined to improve	Wines of Piedmont in northern Italy	Italian food, pastas and cheeses; also roasts, stews, and game	Room, or, in hot weather, cellar	4 or 6
CABERNET SAUVIGNON	Red	Fruity, mellow, with a rich bouquet and fine body. One of California's finest	Red Bordeaux (claret)	Meats, turkey, mutton, game, cheese, pork	Room	3
CHARBONNO	Red	Full-flavored, vigorous and pleasant. Not often found under varietal label	A northern Italian wine	Barbecued meats, Italian dishes	Room, or slightly cooler	4 or 6
FOLLE BLANCHE	White	Light, dry, clean, and delicate	Chablis or still champagne	Oysters, fish (especially sole), other sea foods	Cool (not iced)	5
GAMAY	Red	Soft, full-bodied, fragrant, and very pleasant	Lighter Burgundies (Beaujolais)	Mutton, beef, meat entrees, cheese, game, and turkey	Room, or slightly cooler	1 or 3

Wine	Color	Description	Comparable to	Serve with	Temperature	Rating
GAMAY ROSÉ	Pink	A delightfully fragrant pink wine. A perfect summer beverage	Rosé	Cheese, light entrees, sweetbreads, veal, ham	Chilled, not iced	3
GRENACHE ROSÉ	Pink	A charming wine, fragrant and fruity	Tavel rosé	Poultry, lamb, veal, light entrees	Chilled, not iced	3
GREY RIESLING	White	Dry, sprightly, light, not highly flavored. Sometimes sold as "Rhine wine"	Alsatian wine	Fish, oysters, chicken	Chilled	2
GRIGNOLINO	Red	Dry, fine bouquet, good body, very nice	Italian table wine	Heavy entrees, pastas, cheese	Room	4 or 6
JOHANNISBERG RIESLING	White	Brilliant, fruity, medium-bodied, delightful	Riesling	Hors d'oeuvre, chicken, sea food, eggs, pheasant	Chilled	2
MOURESTAL	Red	Undistinguished, but a pleasant, soft wine	Vin du pays	Lamb, hamburg, veal	Room	4
PINOT BLANC	White	Fragrant, dry, and delicate, with real distinction. One of the best	Chablis, white Burgundy	Turkey or other fowl, fish, lobster, quail	Chilled, not iced	5
PINOT CHARDONNAY	White	Distinguished, full-bodied and mellow, with a definite bouquet. The grape also used in champagne	White Burgundy	Sweetbreads, guinea hen, game, especially quail	Chilled, not iced	5

Name of Wine	Color	Characteristics	Resembles	Serve with	Temperature	Preferred Type of Glass
PINOT NOIR	Red	Wonderful bouquet, full and robust, yet velvety soft. One of the finest	Burgundy	Beef, mutton, game, heavy entrees, roast pig	Room	1
SAUVIGNON BLANC	White	Full-bodied, dry and pleasant. A very good wine	Graves or white Hermitage	Crab, creamed dishes, light meats, and poultry	Chilled	5
SEMILLON	White	Soft, delicate, and fragrant, nice bouquet	Sauternes	Chicken, fruit, semi-sweet desserts, omelets, and Newburgs	Chilled	5
DRY SEMILLON	White	Light, dry, clean. Good choice for dry white wine	Graves. Actually much dryer than any sauternes	Sea food, squab, pheasant, chicken, light entrees	Well chilled	5
SYLVANER	White	Delightfully fruity, soft, and slightly tart. A short-lived wine	Alsatian or Rhine wine	Sea food, fowl, veal, light entrees	Well chilled	2
TRAMINER	White	Refreshing, wonderful bouquet, robust. Also short-lived	Alsatian or hock	Chicken, squab, light entrees, fish	Chilled	2
ZINFANDEL	Red	Sturdy, fresh, fragrant, tart, often has great charm	Beaujolais, or light Burgundy	Red meats, pastas, turkey, goose, duck, and game	Room	3 or 4

Index

416

Index

419

Index

Index

Index

433

434

Index

Index